FALLING BEHIND

EDITED BY FRANCIS FUKUYAMA

FALLING BEHIND

Explaining the Development Gap
Between Latin America
and the United States

OXFORD
UNIVERSITY PRESS
2008

OXFORD
UNIVERSITY PRESS

Oxford University Press, Inc., publishes works that further
Oxford University's objective of excellence
in research, scholarship, and education.

Oxford New York
Auckland Cape Town Dar es Salaam Hong Kong Karachi
Kuala Lumpur Madrid Melbourne Mexico City Nairobi
New Delhi Shanghai Taipei Toronto

With offices in
Argentina Austria Brazil Chile Czech Republic France Greece
Guatemala Hungary Italy Japan Poland Portugal Singapore
South Korea Switzerland Thailand Turkey Ukraine Vietnam

Published by Oxford University Press, Inc.
198 Madison Avenue, New York, NY 10016

www.oup.com

Oxford is a registered trademark of Oxford University Press

Library of Congress Cataloging-in-Publication Data
Brecha entre América Latina y Estados Unidos. English
Falling behind : explaining the development gap
between Latin America and the United States / edited by Francis Fukuyama.
p. cm.
Papers presented at an international seminar held in Buenos Aires, November 2005.
Includes bibliographical references and index.
ISBN 978-0-19-536882-6
1. Latin America—Foreign economic relations—United States—Congresses.
2. United States—Foreign economic relations—Latin America—Congresses.
I. Fukuyama, Francis. II. Title.
HF1480.5.Z4U535 2008
338.98—dc22   2007050154

1 3 5 7 9 8 6 4 2
Printed in the United States of America
on acid-free paper

Preface

L ITERATURE TENDS TO precede history and politics, to condense
them, reveal them. Zavalita's phrase in Mario Vargas Llosa's
famous novel, "At what precise moment had Peru fucked itself
up?" has become the painful epigraph of life in Latin America.[1] By asking "when," Vargas Llosa was also asking how much, how, for what purpose, due to whom, and why. The question searched for an explanation
and, secretly, a light, an exit. The character lived in a feeble country,
one that does exist. He lived in a country that took the wrong path,
lost opportunities, lived on dreams, tolerated sharp inequalities, tore its
social fabric, and suffered many times under tyranny. However, he also
lived in a country that held then, and holds now, an invaluable historical, artistic, and cultural treasure: its indigenous roots, those "subter-
ranean rivers" to which José María Arguedas referred, and that miracle
of *mestizo* convergence (communion) between the indigenous and the
Spanish that is the unique essence of "The Inca," Garcilaso de la Vega.

Then came the tumultuous but promising nineteenth century, with
its poorly digested if authentic liberalisms and positivisms, followed by
an inexhaustible flow of *isms* in the twentieth century, some noble (like
those of José Carlos Mariátegui) and some abominable (like Sendero
Luminoso's Maoism). Peru was and is a land emblematic of an unresolved and perhaps insoluble tension between the deep presence of the
past and the urgency of the inevitable future, a mythical paradise yet
also an inferno for the *conquistadores*, a crucible and Babel of ethnicities
and religions.

Zavalita's celebrated phrase reached far and wide, as Vargas Llosa's
mention of Peru referred not only to Peru; his readers in every corner

of the complex and plural subcontinent called Latin America under-stood immediately that, when speaking of Peru, the narrator referred to all of them. When, exactly, had this region—joined together by a shared language, history, set of traditions, and culture, yet separated by political boundaries, countless disputes, geographical barriers, and random events—gone astray in its development path?

Zavalita's lament about Peru and Latin America implied a broader context. At the core of his question lay the shadow of another: why had *this* America (the one that José Martí proudly called "our America") turned out so differently from the *other* America? After all, European presence in Latin America began a century earlier, allowing for the establishment of universities and printing presses, along with the emergence of rich cultural activity, as early as the sixteenth century. Furthermore, Latin America was—and is still today—endowed with seemingly inexhaustible natural resources. A region never lacking in illustrious and patriotic citizens, it achieved independence from Spain and Portugal nearly two centuries ago. Why then did *this* America fall into a premature decline while the *other* America flourished?

This question, which also echoes the issue of destiny, has for more than a century perplexed those interested in the region, and will likely continue to bewilder others for generations to come. Intellectuals from both the Right and the Left have formulated this question through many different lenses, generally expressing the lowest of passions: rancor, resentment, envy. *We* are less fortunate because *they* have made us so: their success is rooted in our failure. *They*—the plunderers, the exploiters, the victimizers—are, in the eyes of many, the United States. And when blame is not squarely placed on the United States, usually a more devious interpretation is offered: rather than outright denial of the development gap, a complete reversal, substituting failure with success, is declared. The latter argument is in line with Rodó, Vasconcelos, and several armed and disarmed prophets of the dogmatic Left who have argued that *they* are not the victors, but rather *we*—the repositories of spiritual truths, which are "superior" to the rude desires that poison the "empire"—are the victors.

But reality speaks for itself. *This* America, Latin America, can be immensely rich culturally, spiritually, and artistically, but it is plagued by economic and social problems. The *other* America, the United States, is the leading world power. Thus, the long-used, irrefutable term that characterizes the condition separating these two Americas, is one simple word: *gap*.

The trajectory that brought the United States to its privileged position in the world in the twenty-first century is well known, yet it is impressive and worth outlining nonetheless. The United States contributes one-fifth of the gross global product, and it generates 25 percent of the world's industrial production. It is the largest food producer, and 5 of the top 12 industrial firms in the world are from the United States. The country's petroleum-refining capacity is about 15 million barrels per day, and its coal reserves are practically inexhaustible. Other factors that help to make the United States the first economic power of the planet include a multitude of large ports, an active railroad network spanning more than 172,000 miles, and a highway network of over 3.7 million miles. Its more than 14,000 commercial banks constitute the world's most extensive and complex financial system. Due to its impressively large internal market, U.S. exports, which represent 7 percent of the country's gross domestic product, are less relevant to its economy than those of other developed countries, such as Japan or Germany, and the United States has maintained a trade deficit of variable magnitude since 1976.

The United States is also home to some of the most influential universities and research centers in the world. With no close rival in science and technology research and development, it is the world's leader in virtually all scientific fields. The United States is also the world's hegemonic military power. Politically, the United States stands out as a federal republic with an effective system of separation of powers and the most overarching and deep-rooted system of civil liberties. In its more than 200 years of history as an independent country, the United States suffered, it is true, a bloody civil war (1861–1865), but from it arose a sustained basic harmony that has allowed the country to avoid any violent change of political regime and institutional framework.

The contrast between the U.S. reality and that of Latin America is painfully palpable. With some exceptions and taking into account that clear differences exist among the different countries, the overall living conditions of most Latin Americans are exceedingly poor. Some parts of the region are stricken by acute poverty, while the subcontinent's levels of economic inequality are among the most extreme in the world. Both unemployment and underemployment are markedly high and chronic. Latin America could effectively compete in the global economy by mobilizing its human resources, but the quality of public education is deficient, and the public and private sectors contribute little to scientific and technological development. Malnutrition is as much a problem as the region's weak public health services. To make matters worse, since the mid-1980s, Latin American countries have witnessed a terrible criminal pandemic led by drug lords and gangsters. The threat to personal safety in Rio de Janeiro, Medellín, San Salvador, and Mexico City drives away investment and discourages social, economic, and political participation. And to top it all, our political institutions, our laws, our civic practices, and our democracies are fragile.

These facts raise several key questions. For example, is Latin America incapable of competing in the current international landscape? Or, why is it that Latin America remains underdeveloped, while countries in other regions that were poor just a few decades ago have managed to emerge from poverty and continue to develop? At the core of these questions lies a deeper one regarding Latin America's place in history: what, really, *is* Latin America? Making reference to Mexico, Octavio Paz answered that question with poetic precision: Latin America is "an eccentric outpost of the West." Latin America *is* the West, but it remains at its margin. There are times when the region appears to wish *not* to be part of the West and to turn its back on the cardinal objectives of Western civilization: individual liberties and material well-being. What, then, are the region's aims? At times, they seem to be elusive utopias, other times bloody revolutions; but they are mostly futile efforts to jump-start history. Meanwhile, the region's eccentricity continues to be a source of confusion. But the facts are there. Both Americas exist and coexist with difficulty: there is no real bridge between them but, instead, a gap.

This volume seeks to explain the development gap between Latin America and the United States, both from a historical viewpoint and from a political/institutional perspective. The implications for Latin America's future are important. Although today most countries in the region embrace liberal democratic values and institutions, a number of past and current leaders have advocated an alternative, less democratic course. What will be the impact on the gap between the two Americas should such leaders prevail? Today's defenders of an alternative course argue that the gap will narrow: high oil and gas prices will better enable them to implement government programs geared toward improving income distribution and social justice. But they are mistaken. Once again, as in the times of Aristotle, the demagogues mislead their people and, while precipitating revolutionary movements, they will quietly kill democracy. Oil, even more so than the ozone layer or the Arctic glaciers, has an expiration date. The West will not sit idle in the face of its own destruction; eventually, new sources of energy will be devised. And what will the oil market–dependent countries do then? The gap will no doubt become an abyss.

The success of an authentically democratic system depends on the support of a virtuous citizenry, which in turn can only exist within the framework of free and transparent law-abiding institutions. At the beginning of the twenty-first century, a majority of the countries in Latin America are firmly set on a democratic course, the true republican course embraced at the time of independence from Europe, not its dictatorial caricature.

The development gap between Latin America and the United States is not a fatal condition. The latter was able to build an admirable political system that runs like clockwork, even if tainted by vestiges of racism and by an often myopic foreign policy. Latin America, on the other hand, inherited an admirable cultural tradition, but proceeded to squander it in a succession of civil wars, military uprisings, atrocious tyrannical episodes, and revolutionary delusions. Fortunately, most of the countries in the region have become aware of their historical failures and of their Western identity. They are no longer frivolous about it, but have instead become serious players who follow clear rules in the most serious of games: building for future generations a social atmosphere in which basic human decency is able to flourish.

Enrique Krauze

Note

1. Mario Vargas Llosa, *Conversation in the Cathedral* (New York: Harper & Row, 1974), p. 3.

Acknowledgments

I OWE THANKS to everyone who played a role in the completion of this volume, especially the Fundación Grupo Mayan, whose generous support made possible its publication. In particular, there are two key individuals who brought this project to fruition: Daniel J. Chávez Morán, founder of the foundation, and Roberto Russell, its president. I would also like to thank the individual authors and everyone who participated in the November 2005 seminar in Buenos Aires—also titled "Explaining the Development Gap between Latin America and the United States"—for their thoughtful contributions. In addition to the authors, the seminar participants included Hernando De Soto, John W. Diamond, Pablo Guidotti, Celso Lafer, Juan Pablo Nicolini, Andrés Reggiani, Fernando Rocchi, Julio María Sanguinetti, Catalina Smulovitz, Ernesto Zedillo, and George Zodrow. Thanks are also due to Valeria Sobrino, who provided key logistical support, and Charles Roberts, who translated into English all of the chapters originally written in Spanish. Finally, special recognition is due to Guadalupe Paz, associate director of the Latin American Studies Program at SAIS, for her help in editing the English version of this volume and her general support of the project as a whole.

Francis Fukuyama

Contents

How and when this gap in economic performance emerged, and why Latin America has not been able to overcome it as many countries in East Asia have, is the subject of this book. The different contributors to this volume—historians, political scientists, and economists— explore the question from a variety of viewpoints, some examining the large historical sweep of trends over five centuries and others looking at narrower issues.

The subject of Latin America's lagging performance is, of course, one that has been addressed at enormous length in the existing academic and popular literature, and there is no lack of theories for why the gap exists and no lack of recommendations for remedies. The present study cannot hope to provide definitive conclusions as to the source of the gap. Latin America is, to begin with, a huge, varied, and complex region; Haiti's problems are of an entirely different order from those of Bolivia or Peru, not to mention Argentina or Uruguay. The sources of the United States' long-term economic performance are, similarly, quite complicated when examined over a centuries-long perspective. Interpretations of the causes of the gap need to take account of the specific history, culture, conditions, and contexts of each society in question.

There is, nonetheless, some virtue in taking a bird's-eye view of the problem. It is clear, for example, that despite Latin America's diversity, there are some overarching patterns in its economic and political development that distinguish the region both from North America and from other parts of the developing world, like East Asia. As pointed out in this volume, there was a tremendous variability in wealth across Latin America by the year 1800, but in the years following, the entire region fell behind—with no exceptions. The debt crisis of the 1980s emerged not just in one country, but in several across the region. Since many analyses and policy prescriptions tend to be shared across regions, it makes sense to look at the broad patterns and toward common policy prescriptions that have applicability beyond individual countries.

The long-term durability of the performance gap between Latin America and the United States suggests that closing it will not be an easy matter. No reader of this volume should expect to find a simple answer to the question of why the gap exists, nor a set of policy prescriptions that will magically raise economic growth rates, solve deeply embedded political conflicts, or provide the key to social problems. On the other hand, Latin America's overall performance relative to that of the United States has dramatically improved in some historical

1

Introduction

FRANCIS FUKUYAMA

I N 1492, ON the eve of the European settlement and colonization of the New World, Bolivia and Peru hosted richer and more complex civilizations than any that existed in North America. After two centuries of colonization, in 1700, per capita income in continental Latin America was $521, and it was a marginally higher $527 in what would become the United States.[1] During the eighteenth century, the sugar-producing island of Cuba was far wealthier than Britain's American colonies. Yet, over the next three centuries, the United States steadily pulled ahead of Latin America in economic growth, such that, by the beginning of the twenty-first century, per capita income in the United States was five times the Latin American average.

It may be that the United States is simply exceptional in its ability to sustain long-term economic growth; if true, any comparison with other parts of the world would be unfair. Yet East Asia has managed to close the gap over a relatively short period of time. For example, per capita income in East Asia was $746 in 1950, or 8 percent of that of the United States; by 1998, it had risen to 16 percent of the U.S. figure.[2] In contrast, Latin America's per capita income in 1950 was 27 percent of that of the United States, and by 1998 it had fallen to only 21 percent. The gap would be even greater if we selected only the high-performing countries of East Asia instead of the region as a whole.

periods, only to fall back again in others. Understanding the reasons for these changes in relative growth rates can help to isolate factors that have been important in keeping the gap alive.

There is another reason to think that centuries-long patterns of growth and divergence may not always persist into the future. In 1492, it is safe to say, there was virtually no contact between North and South America. Since that time, there has been a steady increase in the interchanges between the regions, punctuated by periods of greater isolation (as after the Great Depression). But the phenomenon of globalization has vastly accelerated in the last half century and shows no signs of slowing down.

Globalization is not merely the integration of markets for goods, services, and investments; it also encompasses the flow of people and ideas. In the Western Hemisphere, integration has occurred on the level of populations, with the movement of millions of individuals from Latin America to the United States (and, to a lesser extent, to Canada and Western Europe). This has resulted in a large reverse flow not only of remittances, but also of people and ideas (as in the case of *dependencia* theory). The degree of intellectual interchange and cross-fertilization has been growing far more intensely with the passage of time, and lower communications and travel costs will inevitably serve to continue the trend. Just as there has been a growing Americanization of the cultures of most Latin American countries, so too has there been an increasing Latin Americanization of U.S. culture. Under these circumstances, the prospects for greater convergence seem strong.

Several authors in this volume demonstrate that Latin America has been a constant importer of ideas from North America and Europe. At the time of the wars of independence, the United States was seen as a model of modernity and democracy, whose political institutions (such as presidentialism and federalism) were widely imitated. But even in periods of great American prestige, there was an undercurrent of hurt and resentment, due in part to American disinterest in reciprocating the admiration or focusing properly on the region. When the United States did focus on the region, it was to expand its territory and influence, as in the case of the Mexican-American and Spanish-American wars. The power of the United States has always been more evident to Latin Americans than to others, and its dominance in a variety of realms has led to hostility in a variety of forms, from anti-American versions of Marxism during the Cold War to the contemporary populism of Hugo Chávez.

The Development Gap: Historical Context

Several chapters in this volume deal with the historical origins of the gap in economic growth between Latin America and the United States. The authors agree on the broad outlines of the story. Prior to the arrival of the Europeans in 1492, many parts of Latin America were richer than North America. Colonization, it is widely agreed, had a devastating impact on the welfare of the indigenous pre-Colombian populations in Mexico and the Andean region, as the Spanish set up an empire to extract gold, silver, and other commodities, much in the same way that British and French colonization devastated the smaller numbers of indigenous peoples in North America. But initial conditions were not all that different in the two halves of the New World, in terms either of per capita income or economic structure. Both regions were predominantly agricultural economies and commodity exporters to the more-developed parts of the world. This situation persisted more or less through the end of the eighteenth century and the emergence of an independent United States of America.

The gap that is the subject of this book really emerged in the first two-thirds of the nineteenth century, a period following Latin America's wars of independence from Spain and Portugal during which new states were being formed. The period from 1820 to 1870 was particularly disastrous for Latin America: while U.S. per capita GDP grew at a 1.39 percent annual rate in this period, per capita GDP actually fell by .05 percent per year in Latin America. The struggle for independence was costly both for the new United States and for the countries of Latin America, but it took the latter on average much longer both to win independence and to consolidate new state institutions in their territory. The retreat of the Spanish reduced access to some markets and technology and collapsed the internal customs unions that had existed within their empire, all of which was very costly in terms of growth.

The period from 1870 to 1970 was, in contrast, a period of modest catching up for most of Latin America. In the earlier part of that period, until 1929, per capita GDP growth was actually higher there than in the United States, as it was again in the period from 1950 to 1970. Throughout the region, post-independence regimes slowly consolidated, and there were prolonged periods in which both the internal and external environments were relatively benign. Growth from 1870 to 1970 was, of course, dramatically interrupted by the Great Depression after 1929 and the outbreak of World War II. While these events had important consequences for all countries in the Western

Hemisphere, their impact was arguably less severe in Latin America than in the United States.

The gap widened again in the last three decades of the twentieth century with the spread of authoritarian regimes throughout the region. In addition, many of the large countries in Latin America catastrophically failed to adjust to the rapidly changing external environment, resulting from the two oil shocks of the 1970s. Burgeoning fiscal deficits, attempts to monetize deficits through growth in money supplies, hyperinflation, and overvalued exchange rates in Mexico, Brazil, Argentina, Peru, and other countries set the stage for the debt crisis of the 1980s and the subsequent drop in real growth rates throughout Latin America. The United States, on the other hand, controlled the inflationary spiral set off by the oil crisis relatively quickly in the early 1980s and put into place a series of liberalizing economic policies that laid the groundwork for two decades of almost uninterrupted growth in per capita income. Indeed, growth in total factor productivity, which had been declining through much of the postwar period, began an upward trend in the late 1990s as a series of innovations in information and communications technology began to take root.

The 1990s and early years of the twenty-first century brought to most Latin American countries a return to economic orthodoxy and stable macroeconomic indicators. This set the stage in a number of countries for a return to growth, though not to an appreciable closing of the gap with the United States, due in part to the latter's relatively good economic performance. Moreover, results were noticeably uneven. Mexico and Argentina experienced severe currency and economic crises in 1994 and 2001, respectively. Growth, where it occurred, was steady but not spectacular. While modest progress was made toward reducing the region's levels of economic inequality, in many countries there was little political will to share the gains from growth. This situation brought about the emergence of populist and Left-leaning political leaders in several countries, including Venezuela, Ecuador, Brazil, Uruguay, and Argentina.

Confronting the Gap

The chapters in this volume can only provide the beginnings of an analysis of the development gap between Latin America and the United States. If nothing else, they should demonstrate the complexity of the problem. The gap itself has varied over time, opening up dramatically in some decades and then closing again in others. The causes of the gap are similarly varied. This volume argues that those explanations that focus on geography, natural endowments of resources or other material conditions, culture in a broad sense, or a dependent relationship with the developed world are unlikely to be identifying the true reasons for lagging performance.

There are other factors, however, that the authors agree matter. Latin America must follow sensible economic policies that produce monetary and fiscal stability, while at the same time seeking to open the region's economies to the global trading system. Institutions are critical for formulating, implementing, and supporting good policies. These institutions include property rights and the rule of law, electoral systems, executive branches with appropriate powers, legislatures that are both representative and efficient, political parties that include society's important social actors, court systems that are independent of political authority and effective in implementing the rule of law, and an appropriate distribution of powers to the different levels of government—national, state, and local. Social inequality lies at the root of the region's lack of economic competitiveness, in addition to being a source of political instability. This suggests, then, a need to take a new look at social policy, not by returning to the entitlement politics of the past, but by seeking innovative ways of solving social problems.

It is important not to be excessively pessimistic about Latin America's overall prospects and the likelihood of closing the development gap in the future. For all of the economic turmoil that engulfed the region at the turn of the twenty-first century, there was a remarkable degree of democratic continuity throughout the region, even in its most troubled countries. Conflicts that in previous decades had been addressed through military coups or violence tended to be resolved through elections or judicial proceedings. There has been institutional and policy learning, as traumatic experiences like currency crises and hyperinflation created political incentives for reform. And the process of institutional growth and state building has proceeded, not as rapidly or evenly as one would hope, but steadily nonetheless. There is reason to hope, therefore, that the history of the gap over the next generation will be written differently than that of the past.

Notes

1. All currency figures are in U.S. dollars unless otherwise noted.
2. These figures include Japan and exclude India. Source: OECD.

PART I

THE HISTORICAL
CONTEXT

2

Two Centuries of South American Reflections on the Development Gap between the United States and Latin America

TULIO HALPERIN DONGHI

THE ABYSS THAT separates history from other, younger academic disciplines is readily discernible when experience in the former field spans enough decades. However, historians with such experience should not be expected to accomplish the impossible feat of bridging this abyss across two millennia, but rather should remind practitioners of those sciences born yesterday that a problem's scope of analysis can always be viewed through a wider lens. It can be argued that a historian's most useful contribution is to remind those studying a problem that said problem has a history. That is precisely what this chapter will do, by providing a historical framework to analyze the development gap between Latin America and the United States.[1]

This gap can be traced back almost 200 years, to the period in which the United States began to coexist alongside those other states that sought to fill the vacuum created by the dissolution of the Spanish empire in the Western Hemisphere.[2] From the outset of that coexistence, there was no shortage of anticipation in neo-British America and in neo-Spanish America that relations among the countries in the hemisphere would be plagued by difficulties. Thinkers on both ends of the Americas coincided in the analysis that the anticipated difficulties were attributable to the more general ones that Ibero-America faced in successfully joining the complex process of profound economic, social, and political change centered in the North Atlantic. This situation is what eventually led to significantly different approaches to what would later be labeled the "development gap."

In the United States, it was evident that the presence of this gap would make it more difficult for the new republics of Ibero-America to resist interventions from the Old World, which, following the catastrophic revolutionary cycle that began in 1789, proclaimed itself engaged in the process of restoring the Old World order. The difficulty faced by the newly formed states in Latin America derived not from any resistance to reshaping their institutions in a new mold, but rather from an unfortunate legacy in which Catholicism and absolutism were ingrained in the culture, making those societies radically incapable of successfully embodying the republican institutional ideal. It soon became clear, however, that the support granted by the Old World for the restorationist enterprise was less unanimous than might have been apparent in 1815. By 1823, when President James Monroe warned the restored monarchies of Europe that the United States was determined to keep them from extending their legitimist crusade to the American hemisphere, he was aware that these monarchies already faced a much more serious obstacle: opposition from Britain, the power that, for a quarter century, had kept alive the fight against revolutionary and imperial France and that, after its victory, was more than ever the queen of the seas.

Since then, because it was clear that the development gap with Latin America was simply a fact rather than a problem, nothing impeded the United States from focusing its attention elsewhere until new critical junctures brought the gap back to the forefront. In the mid-nineteenth century, following the territorial expansion of the United States that incorporated an immense stretch of land previously owned by Mexico, the development gap once again became a subject of debate, albeit fleetingly, as the changing landscape in the north inspired a new, if still ambiguous, vision of the role that the United States would play vis-à-vis its southern neighbors.[3] Although the United States felt called upon to guide along the path of republican virtue (by example and perhaps not only by example) those new states that were proving less and less capable of discovering on their own how to bridge the north-south gap, it is also understandable that it sometimes felt tempted to profit from the weakness of those sad caricatures of republics with which it shared the New World.

From a Latin American perspective, the problems posed by coexisting in a single continental mass with a neighbor endowed with a fearsome expansive capacity were perceived early on. So were those problems that stemmed from the persistent delays that Latin America faced while seeking to advance toward the goals centered in Atlantic Europe. The absence of such a delay in the former British America was invoked primarily as additional evidence that the key to explaining the gap lay in certain specific features of the region's Hispanic heritage, just as it suggested—perhaps even more convincingly—that an analogous gap separated the former imperial metropolis from its Old World neighbors.

In order to proceed with the analysis that the problem originated from a specific gap that separated Latin America from the United States, the latter must not be viewed as a more prosperous disciple of the European model than its neighbors to the south, nor as an ever more successful promoter of the British model in the Americas. That was not to happen until the twentieth century, when the United States became much more than that. It should be noted, however, that although the problems surrounding the development gap between the two sections of the New World were already present in the earlier stages of Latin America's development, they were not yet as clearly defined as they are today.

Bolívar and the United States: Views and Distance

In 1815, Simón Bolívar discussed in his "Letter from Jamaica" the difficulties that Spanish America faced in moving forward along the path forged by its independence movement, and he delved more deeply into the issue in his 1819 inaugural speech at the Congress of Angostura. However, it would take another century before the concept of economic development took hold. Perhaps more important, the problems that the notion of economic development evoked occupied a marginal place compared to those that were exclusively political and dominated the era of revolutions, a context in which Bolívar had anticipated playing a leading role.

The challenges faced at that time by Spanish America appeared to be aggravated in Bolívar's eyes because, he argued, the region was not experiencing a revolution like those in the United States and France, but rather a historical catastrophe even more profound than that suffered by the Romans after the fall of the empire. In Bolívar's own words:

> Each part of Rome adopted a political system conforming to its interest and situation or was led by the individual ambitions of certain chiefs, dynasties, or associations.... [In effect, while] those dispersed parts later reestablished their ancient nations, subject to the changes imposed by circumstances or events...we scarcely retain a vestige of what once was; we are, moreover, neither Indian nor European, but a species midway between the legitimate proprietors of this country and the Spanish usurpers. In short, though Americans by birth, we derive our rights from Europe, and we have to assert these rights against the rights of the natives, and at the same time we must defend ourselves against the invaders.[4]

In hindsight, it is difficult to understand why the collective subject of the Spanish American revolution would not be composed of the "legitimate proprietors" of the countries in question, but instead of those who proclaimed themselves the heirs of certain rights whose legitimacy they were the first to denounce. Bolívar shied away from posing that question for two reasons. The first is the obvious fact that he himself belonged to that "species midway." And, second, all who knew something about Spanish America would have agreed that the three centuries of colonial rule had not been in vain, and, as had been proven three decades earlier by the successful suppression of the vast indigenous rebellion that shook the ancient Incan empire to its core, the other kind of revolution was already an impossible feat.

As a direct descendant of Creole aristocracy, Bolívar could no doubt refrain from lamenting that such an alternative was unavailable, but his heritage did not keep him from envisioning, through the successful marginalization of the "legitimate proprietors" of the land, the legacy of a historical experience that was tainted from the very start. In novelesque fashion, he sought to make of the Spanish conquest a second original sin on a hemispheric scale that forever marked the lineage arising from it, which he would describe, writing to Santander, as the "abominable offspring of those raging beasts that came to America to waste her blood and to breed with their victims before sacrificing them."[5]

In the context of a yet unfinished struggle, that powerful image merely came to express the hopelessness that the course of the revolution inspired in those who felt responsible for bringing it to a successful conclusion.[6] It is not surprising, therefore, that Bolívar disregarded that cursed legacy when he sought to overcome the paralyzing pessimism he confronted in his mission to ensure that emancipation did not reduce itself to proving that Spanish America was completely inept at self-government. His speech in Angostura attempted to convey that message, first by evoking his "Letter from Jamaica" but later setting it aside to invoke, instead, the "humiliating maxim...[that]...it is harder to maintain the balance of liberty than to endure the weight of tyranny."[7]

Bolívar argued that the problems faced by Spanish America were not unique to the region, but shared with all humankind. In order to resolve them, he claimed, all societies should turn to "the teachings of experience" offered by "the schools of Greece, Rome, France, England, and North America instruct us in the difficult science of creating and preserving nations through laws that are proper, just, legitimate, and, above all, useful."[8] From the moment he included the political model offered by the United States among those that Spanish America should take into account, Bolívar necessarily had to include in his analysis those that would later become part of the literature dedicated to exploring the gap between neo-British America and neo-Ibero-America. However, his judgment was affected by the climate of ideas that was dominant at the time and, even more so, by the nearly obsessive concern with which he contemplated the future of the political experiment on which the region's destiny depended.

The most immediate reason that Bolívar could not exclude British America in his analysis was that its federal institutions had already served as a model for Venezuela and New Granada. In both cases, such a course of action contributed decisively to bringing to a disastrous denouement their early revolutionary experiences. He dwelled so much on that example because it appeared to refute the lessons of the hitherto universal experience that had confirmed, time and again, that "from absolute liberty one always descends to absolute power."[9]

Bolívar had no choice but to admit that the United States had enjoyed absolute liberty for a third of a century. Although he fully understood "what political virtues can accomplish and the relative unimportance of institutions," he did not cease to celebrate that, even in a "people who constitute an outstanding model of political virtue and moral rectitude...so weak and complicated a government as the federal system has managed to govern them in the difficult and trying circumstances of their past."[10] Yet celebrating that as a remarkable feat is a way of denying that it could offer a valid example for its neighbors, since nothing would be more dangerous than seeing in that inexplicably successful challenge to all of the laws of political science something more than the exception that confirms the rule.

Nonetheless, the political efforts in the Old World to attain such an enlightened ideal were able to offer the lessons, both positive and negative, needed by Spanish America to find its way.[11] Beyond offering Bolívar a revolutionary model that had gone even further than he was willing to go in his effort to maintain continuity with the prerevolutionary past, England also provided a doctrinal justification for his proposal to ensure the future of the Spanish American revolution by placing it under British protection.[12] Even after Ayacucho, by which time "there [was] nothing to fear and everything to hope for from Europe," Bolívar continued to believe that "if we join England [through an offensive and defensive alliance] we can exist—if we do not, we shall inevitably be doomed." Clearly, Bolívar no longer expected from Great Britain protection from an external danger that had seemingly dissipated, but rather sought protection against an internal demon that Spanish America needed to exorcise forever. In Bolívar's own words, "if we remain in our present state of pernicious isolation, we shall destroy ourselves through our own efforts to pursue an illusive freedom."[13]

Bolívar's preference for Great Britain was justified by its unchallenged role as arbiter between the Old World and the New World, coupled with its naval superiority and the greater relevance of its political formula for Spanish America, reasons which also led Bolívar to distance himself from the United States. During the struggle for independence, the implicit British veto of any active support by the continental powers for the royalist cause had contributed more than any other factor to the triumph of the insurgency. At the same time, the scrupulous neutrality adopted by the United States almost until the eve of the region's independence victory suggested an absence of solidarity with the republics that arose after the fall of the Spanish empire, a fact that did not auger well for the future of U.S.–Latin American relations.[14]

In this manner, Bolívar laid the foundation for his proposal, which was aimed at establishing a regime of order and liberty in Spanish America, while avoiding in the discussion the issues that he himself recognized are more unique to the history of Spanish America, and thus avoiding attention to the issue of guilt of origin. When forced to consider that the incorporation of Spanish America into a liberal world posed problems that were specific to the region, Bolívar argued that the main impediments originated from the immaturity of a New World that, three centuries after its conquest, still presented characteristics of "mankind...in its infancy, steeped in uncertainty, ignorance, and error," as all humankind had been at the dawn of its historical trajectory.[15] He concluded that it would be too risky to make any prognosis for the region's future.

By eliminating from the list of problems a key factor such as the brutal historical origin of Spanish America, Bolívar was renouncing a confrontation of the global challenges posed by the internal boundaries of that legacy, which continued to divide the heirs of the conquerors and the conquered. In so doing, he took a decisive initial step in the debate about the development gap that would ultimately define the gap itself. Only if one recognizes the foundational nature of the conquest does it become clear that, for most successor states of the Spanish empire—on which that legacy has weighed with full force—the ability to assert themselves as nation-states has by no means been easy to achieve. It follows that, to gauge Spanish America's success or failure in its post-independence development, the region must be measured with a different yardstick than that employed to measure the success of the United States.

To what extent did the differences between Bolívar's proposals and those that would soon follow originate from diverging visions of the Spanish American question? Were these differences due to Bolívar's strongly personal relationship with a revolution to which he devoted his life and through which he hoped that the New World would provide the solution for the "great problem of man in liberty"? This question had never before been addressed by "the civilization that blew in from the East," a civilization in which "every manner of grandeur has had its type, all miseries their cradle."[16] It is that complete dedication to the revolutionary project that caused Bolívar to experience with tragic depth—the kind later sought in vain by his successors—the discovery that a solution to the Spanish American question had proven unattainable.[17]

Bolívar's conclusions that led him to make such a bitter discovery nevertheless closely resembled those that dominated the neo-Spanish South American discourse in the two decades that followed his death. As of 1830, many opportunities had arisen to rediscover the fact that, as he had proclaimed, drawing on Rousseau's authority, "liberty...is a succulent morsel, but one difficult to digest," and "our weak fellow-citizens will have to strengthen their spirit greatly before they can digest the wholesome nutriment of freedom."[18]

Great Britain as an Example: A Middle Ground between Reaction and Revolution

In the decades following the Spanish American independence wars, a new generation of leaders came to accept more moderate variations of Bolívar's views. That the revolutionary movements had left as a legacy more calamities than blessings was not a late discovery for them. Although the nascent liberalism of the early 1820s proclaimed that the revolutionary efforts ended prematurely, it is also true that entire societies were shaken to their foundations by the torments of their struggles, and there was a risk of destroying with continued violence the last ties that kept them precariously united, ultimately risking a plunge into extreme anarchy. At this juncture, the region faced the prospect of a protracted limbo originating from the irreversible collapse of the old order and the absence of a viable alternative.

In the midst of this period of great uncertainty, one thing became clear: the emerging Spanish America was a satellite in an international system centered in London. This became evident with the political and ideological impact of the 1825 financial crisis, which drew to a catastrophic close the flow of British investment to the region and put an end to the optimism that had engendered the first wave of Spanish American liberalism. Not only had Great Britain been the arbiter of the destinies of these new countries, but its example also proved the feasibility of a middle way between reaction and revolution, especially for those who aspired to promote a conservative orientation in states whose very existence was considered subversive by the dominant powers in continental Europe. The use of Great Britain as the political point of reference par excellence would eventually become a natural occurrence rather than a deliberate selection of that model over others.

During the two decades following the independence wars, the most successful political experiments to unfold in South America—Diego Portales' Chile, which became the model republic of that period, together with New Granada and Venezuela—owed their success largely to the choice made to advance "slowly on the former Spanish structures while considering first what to do," which had been the approach taken by Bolívar.[19] This approach was clearly emerging as the most appropriate for the postrevolutionary era, not only because of the extreme fragility of the region, but also because no incentives or threats existed to incite them to accelerate the pace of political consolidation.

The mid-nineteenth century brought with it radical change. One important change was that the place occupied by the United States on the Spanish American horizon expanded considerably as it began to be perceived as the source of new or renewed threats in the region. While the territorial expansion of the United States into the heart of the North American continent had already begun to inspire mounting alarm, particularly following the Louisiana Purchase, the clear-cut victory of the United States over Mexico in 1848 gave an ominous sense of truth to Bolívar's somber forecasts. After that, there was no shortage of fear that the formidable expansionist potential of the neo-English republic of North America might put at risk the very survival of the fragile neo-Spanish nations.

The United States also played a significant role in a transformation of much greater reach: the discovery of gold in California, which integrated the Pacific basin into a network of commercial activity. The resulting economic bustle contributed decisively to a new phase of expansion in the United States characterized by a dizzying transformation of its transportation and communication systems. The danger that U.S. expansionism represented to the region, a danger that not even the most alarmist countries believed had equal weight across Latin America, was a significantly different kind of threat than the ambiguous impact of the rapidly evolving global economic landscape. While new economic opportunities were emerging worldwide, both the pace and the ever more encompassing consequences of the economic transformations under way led to fear that Latin American nations would prove incapable of keeping up, thus putting at risk their future and perhaps even their very existence.

The Gap in Sarmiento's View

Domingo Faustino Sarmiento's writings describing the United States admirably reflect the resoluteness of that moment in which the great Anglo-Saxon neighbor came to occupy a key role in the mindset of the Spanish American nations. Sarmiento, one of many Argentines who had found political refuge in Chile, became known as a great political ideologue during the postrevolutionary consolidation of the Spanish American states; by 1847, he had already established his reputation as a conflictive promoter of ideological and cultural innovations.

During a mission to study elementary education institutions abroad, carried out between 1847 and 1849, Sarmiento chronicled his travel experiences in his book *Viajes por Europa, África y América* (published in 1849), including his impressions of the United States.[20] Alexis de Tocqueville had already perceived, and later verified in situ, that nowhere could he explore better than in the United States the issues raised by the inexorable advance of democracy. It is not surprising that Sarmiento, who aspired with his first volume, *Facundo*, to do for Spanish America what Tocqueville did for Anglo-Saxon America, would rely on *La démocratie en Amérique* as his principal guide for the exploration of the immense democratic experiment unfolding in the United States.[21]

Yet, whereas in *Viajes* Sarmiento identified as the central problem in the United States that posed by the eruption of democracy, he had to address the issue in entirely different terms than those preferred by Tocqueville. For Tocqueville, a regime that seeks both to attain the equality previously fostered by monarchical absolutism and to extend the reach of freedoms to all of society far beyond the levels enjoyed and defended by the privileged sectors under monarchical rule—a regime like the one that arises from a democratic revolution—embodies a contradiction that he considered impossible to fully resolve.[22] In his analysis, Sarmiento clearly diverged from Tocqueville's perspective when he classified the U.S. experience as superior, arguing that it had surpassed Europe's attempts to achieve full equality without compromising liberty.

This divergence did not preclude Sarmiento from learning from Tocqueville to view the United States as much more than just the result of the experience of colonization by a great European power. The U.S. case, when compared to the colonizing of Spanish and Portuguese America by the Iberian monarchies, may, indeed, cast new light on the circumstances under which the new Latin American republics emerged. But, for Sarmiento, the U.S. experience pointed to a new and better road toward full democracy compared to that ushered in by the French Revolution. The sections of *Viajes* dedicated to France illustrate that the significance of the questions posed by Tocqueville clearly had an impact on Sarmiento and helped him to conclude that, in France and the rest of Europe, an outbreak of social conflicts even more violent than those known during the previous revolutionary cycle was imminent.

We should note an addition to Sarmiento's conclusion, which was clearly influenced by Tocqueville's work: an earlier discovery that the material and intellectual progress that had so impressed those who observed them from overseas had only taken root in isolated locations in an ocean of rustic primitivism. The first lesson that this new perspective taught Sarmiento was that, when comparing Europe's gains with those of that "new animal produced by political creation" that was the United States, Europe shared more than one essential aspect of a backwardness he had imagined was only present in Spanish America. What made the United States unique was that, while the "French or Chilean village stands out as a negation of France or Chile, respectively, and no one would claim that its local customs, traditional dress or ideas represented the national identity," in the United States the village "is a complete State, with its own civilian government, press, school system, banking system, municipality, census, spirit and appearance."[23]

This distinction, like most others made by Sarmiento during his short six-week visit to the United States, had been previously highlighted by Tocqueville in his portrait of the U.S. political system and by other travelers whose writings also left their unmistakable mark on Sarmiento's work.[24] Yet, even if the image was essentially the same, what Sarmiento valued most about the United States differed from Tocqueville's reasons to consider that country a model for Europe's future political development. Sarmiento warned his readers that those who seek in the United States "our republic, liberty, strength, intelligence, beauty, the republic of our dreams" are condemned to suffer a harsh disappointment, since "although North America has put an end to the worst ulcers of the human race, scars remain even among some European societies, which here would become cancerous."[25]

Even if the ideal republic was not to be found in the United States, the existence of democracy was enough to propel that improvised North American nation further along the path of progress than the most illustrious nations of Europe. As Sarmiento concluded, "[T]hese democrats are the ones who today are furthest along in finding the answers that the Christian peoples seek in the darkness, stumbling on monarchical systems as in Europe, or tied down by brutal despotism as in our poor fatherland."[26] But that was not all. While observers pondered these questions, the United States was already growing at a pace unthinkable in Europe, and Sarmiento believed he knew why.

Whereas Europe dedicated a disproportionate part of its resources to ensuring the stability of a hierarchical and sharply unequal society, the United States was the seat of a people "free as air, with no army or Bastille," a nation able to be thus because it was "without kings, nobles, privileged classes, men born to rule or human machines born to obey."[27] The end result was a land where "well-being is more generally distributed than in any other country... and the population grows under laws that are yet unknown in other nations [and] production increases at a remarkable rate."[28] As William Katra rightly points out, what Sarmiento offered his readers was, strictly speaking, a utopia built on an image of the U.S. experience in which its exceptionality was presented in much sharper relief than what was depicted by Cooper, Chevalier, or Tocqueville.[29] Katra argues that Sarmiento had a tendency "to generalize based on his observations" and that his limited contact with the United States had, in this case, particularly problematic consequences.[30]

Beyond the accuracy of the image of U.S. society presented by Sarmiento in 1849, what is of particular interest here is the absence in his text of that other exceptionality of opposite and strongly negative nature, which, beginning with Bolívar, so many Spanish Americans believed to be specific to their corner of the world. For Sarmiento, when France and Chile are compared with that country in which the future is already the present, they do not appear to be separated by an abyss. That difference is very clearly illustrated in the last conclusion that Sarmiento drew from his U.S. experience. While his predecessors tended to summarize the issue in a question which was simultaneously a lamentation—why can't Spanish America be more like the United States?—Sarmiento offered as a corollary a persistent invitation to become another United States.

This view was not, however, the only reason that he adhered to the optimism displayed in that wild ambition. He was also influenced by an awareness that the glasshouse in which the colonial monopoly had enclosed Spanish America was nearing its complete collapse, and, although this colonial environment had impeded any progress in the Spanish Indies, it had at least opened the door to the alternative of stagnation. With this alternative no longer an option, the Spanish American nations gambled their future and perhaps their very survival on a struggle in which inevitably, as stated by Sarmiento, they were to be actors and also run the risk of becoming victims.[31]

In reference to Chile during his exile, but equally applicable to his native Argentina, Sarmiento argued in one of his last works that, for countries with temperate climates, the rapid consolidation of a genuine world market made imperative their entry into the market "for the surplus production of their goods, in competition with Europe and the United States" or "with the whole of civilization covering every period and every country."[32] In that text, titled "The Influence of Primary Instruction on Industry and the General Development of the Nation's Prosperity," Sarmiento offered for the first time an explicit definition of the terms that would later be used to explain the development gap. It is true that, long before 1855, it was common to compare the achievements of neo-English America and neo-Iberian America, but these accounts invariably examined gains in the civic, cultural, and social spheres primarily, as they were considered intrinsically valuable. Sarmiento had done this in the U.S. section of his 1851 edition of *Viajes*, though he underscored more forcefully than earlier travelers the important impact that those gains were having on the U.S. economy. Later, in contrast, he placed great value on the gains that he proclaimed to be urgent and necessary in all spheres in order to attain what had become indispensable for the very survival of the fragile nations of Spanish America that sought to consolidate themselves.

The subject of the development gap between the United States and Latin America invaded the Spanish American discourse upon the discovery that, with greater integration into the world economy, becoming economically competitive among the nations that constituted that market was quickly becoming for them—in the most literal sense—a matter of life and death. It should not be surprising, therefore, that in the following eight decades—during which that troublesome discovery became credible only at certain critical junctures that were fortunately exceptional—the development gap reemerged with a new perspective less focused on its economic dimension.

Thus, Sarmiento's negative assessment in 1883 of Argentina's progress recognized that, what in 1852 had still been an almost desert-like plain, 30 years later was "countryside covered with golden grains throughout entire provinces."[33] He also acknowledged that Argentina's gains in wealth and population had reached "the point of not knowing in Buenos Aires whether one is in Europe or in America."[34] In Sarmiento's view, however, those gains did not suffice to celebrate that stage as successful, when the "republic of our dreams" remained more distant than ever. He argued that Argentina's reality increasingly resembled that of Venezuela, where the senate had just approved a new equestrian statue of the "illustrious American" who had governed it for more than a decade, adding yet another to the "several that already infest[ed] all its public squares."[35]

Contrasting Models and the Lineage Clash

The diminished interest in the economic dimension of the development gap coincided with a period when the economic performance of the Spanish American countries was falling noticeably behind that of the United States. In sum, it was a period when the economic gap widened considerably.[36] The most obvious reason for this lack of concern over the gap was that it did not prevent the majority of countries in Spanish America from finding a secure place in an ever more clearly structured world economic order, in particular as providers of foodstuffs and raw materials for their North Atlantic partners. That, too, is why the issues that inspired such dark conclusions by Bolívar did not this time around lead to equally somber conclusions.

The most conspicuous legacy of the conquest, which was the presence throughout most of Spanish America of an entire sector of the population whose lineage derived from the conquered peoples, did not weigh any more as the legacy of a second original sin destined to forever pull them down. That characteristic was more closely associated with the subjects of the enlightened monarchy, who saw it reflected in a set of unmet needs and shortcomings that would prove difficult but not impossible to overcome.

Not even the growing influence of positivism succeeded in reintroducing the fatalistic views that, in Bolívar's most desperate moments, had dominated his discourse.[37] As Nancy Stepan has rightly pointed out, even if they declared themselves to be followers of Darwin, Latin Americans were inclined, in practice, toward Lamarck's version of the theory of evolution, which admitted that one could transmit acquired characteristics to one's offspring.[38] The corollary of that spontaneous transference can be seen once again in Sarmiento, who had read somewhere that a study of bony remains in Parisian cemeteries had made it possible to verify that the cranial capacity of the French had been steadily growing since the end of the Middle Ages. If in the Hispanic world nothing similar had been discovered, and, to the contrary, cranial capacity was no greater than that attained centuries earlier in France, it should be attributed to the negative influence of the Inquisition. And since that obstacle had been eliminated, nothing would stand in the way of Spanish Americans being able to rival the cranial capacity of the French—and therefore their intellectual endowment—within a few centuries. As is apparent, the preference for Lamarck's views over Darwin's did not derive from any critical comparison of the two; instead, it is likely that most of those in Spanish America who proclaimed themselves to be followers of Darwin were unaware of his opposition to the notion that acquired characteristics could be transmitted. Thus, the apparent preference for Lamarck's view seemed to originate from a faith in the capacity to transform social realities, which preceded any theoretical justification.

Those nations that were better poised to surmount the growing challenges stemming from the advances in the world market were considerably less pessimistic. The vanity that was characteristic of this stage in Argentina found expression in Carlos Octavio Bunge's 1903 book, *Nuestra América*, which offered a close-minded assessment of the biological and psychological heritage that Latin Americans in general, and Argentineans in particular, have received from their indigenous, Iberian, and African ancestors. In the prologue, Bunge asserted that, once the deficiencies he listed in the book were eliminated, Argentineans would not only catch up to, but surpass, the level attained by Europe and the United States. Around the same time, in neighboring Uruguay, this greater confidence in the future found less strident but perhaps more ambitious expression in *Ariel*, an essay in which José Enrique Rodó contrasted the grossly materialistic model flourishing in the United States with the much more harmoniously balanced one of classical Greece, which, according to him, had seen a resurgence in France. Rodó no doubt found it easier to put forth such a challenge from the modest platform offered by such a small country as Uruguay because, in terms of the material progress that he openly criticized, it was, together with most of Spanish America, finally advancing at a pace comparable to that of the United States.[39]

This is just one of the reasons that the previously pessimistic comparison between Spanish America and the United States, which usually focused on their political/institutional progress, now tended to be more optimistic. Adding to this new perspective was the enthusiastic way in which, in 1884, the first president of a unified Argentina—General Bartolomé Mitre—celebrated the democratic republic as "the last rational form and the last word of human logic, which answers to the reality and to the ideal of free government," but which, with each passing day, appeared to be losing steam.[40] Also at work was the French defeat of 1871, which confirmed the military supremacy of the German empire that arose from it, together with the naval supremacy of the British empire, and signaled that all of neo-Spanish America was being threatened by a creeping decadence.[41] Seen from that perspective, the issue considered to pertain specifically to Spanish America—which Bolívar thought he had found in the trauma of the conquest, while his positivist followers thought they had found in the biological and cultural heritage of the races that it had brought into contact with one another—found a new key explanation in the rivalry among the ancestors that fought to dominate in the Old World, such as the invasion of the barbarians, and spread overseas to the conquered lands.

These circumstances provided the backdrop for two books published in Paris by Peruvian writer Francisco García Calderón. In *La creación de un continente*, he stylized the Spanish conquest as the titanic opus of a few heroes whose feats, like those of the supermen announced by Nietzsche, placed them beyond good and evil.[42] In *Les démocraties latines d'Amérique*, García Calderón offered the French public a no less enthusiastic analysis of the constructive progress that the nations of the subcontinent were making under the guidance of caudillos and aristocracies who were just as much heirs to the superhuman virtues of those illustrious ancestors.[43] This progress translated into democratic experiences that, thanks to their Latin roots, were not limited by the institutional recipes of the modern representative regimes, which were characterized by the pedantic literality inherent in all regimes of Anglo-Saxon origin.

In a prologue to García Calderón's text, Raymond Poincaré—the future president during the victory with which France would cleanse itself of the humiliation suffered in 1871—shared with its author the hope that an ascending Latin America would prove capable of reestablishing in the New World a less biased equilibrium among the races that disputed their dominance in the Old World. He lamented the fact that the Latin nations were inexorably falling behind the Germanic ones in terms of economic and technological advances and behind the Slavic nations in terms of demographic advances.

This vision of the role reserved for Spanish America in the lineage clash that both the author and the prologue writer guessed was imminent—a clash among those who for more than a millennium had disputed primacy first in Europe and then in the Atlantic world—was sketched in a historical narrative in which the issue of the gap could not retain the centrality that Bolívar and Sarmiento had given it. This centrality could not be retained in the economic dimension either, and this was so for two reasons. On the one hand, in the new century, the economies of Spanish America had grown at a pace comparable to that of the United States. On the other hand, the anticipated decisive clash in which primacy between the two rival lineages was to be decided would not have as its theater the economy, but rather the more traditional military battlefields.

Furthermore, in the framework of that vision of the past and of the future, it was not possible for the political/institutional question that had drawn Bolívar's attention to retain a central role when explaining the question of the gap. The imminent issue was to continue those conflicts whose protagonists had been military heroes, from Charles

Martel to Napoleon. The Duke of Wellington had a place in these conflicts, because, along with Blücher, he had consolidated the primacy of the Germanic lineage at Waterloo, before becoming the hero of extreme conservatism in the Parliament of Westminster, which had drawn the attention of Portales. That vision of the past and the future made it possible to gauge to what extent there had been, on the eve of the war that was to deal them the death blow, a weakening of the political/ideological consensus on which the examination of the issues related to the development gap depended.

The Legacy of World War I

The immensity of the conflict that Europe had blindly fallen into in 1914 cast doubt on the validity of what the region had been preaching to the rest of the world regarding science and the art of government. The other legacy of the war—the installation through revolution of a political regime in Russia devoted to imposing an alternative to the liberal and capitalist model of social and political organization—proved, against what hitherto had been the prevailing belief, that a socialist experiment was not inherently condemned to collapse under its own weight within a matter of weeks. The end of the military conflict instilled even more doubts about the capacity of liberal constitutionalism to succeed in taking over the legitimacy monopoly, which had seemed an attainable goal in the quarter century prior to the outbreak of World War I.[44]

In 1923, it became clear that the failures of the movements that, in the convulsed social climate of the early postwar period, had sought inspiration in the triumphant Russian Revolution were already irreversible. At the same time, the reaction brought about by those initiatives allowed in Italy the victory of a movement that, even though presented as an alternative to the Russian model, also aspired to fill the vacuum created by the end of a historical period marked by the widespread installation of representative democratic regimes. And, thus, the Old World seemed to be on a path toward a secularized war of religions that threatened to reach apocalyptic dimensions.

On the other side of the Atlantic, a very different mood characterized the New World's first postwar experience. After Europe's hegemony suffered a fatal blow, the United States—which had gained all of the ground lost by Europe in the economic arena—refused to play the role in world affairs that its enhanced power seemed to warrant.

Though for a fleeting moment the United States appeared poised to embark on the project of shaping the world based on the principles that had guided its development from its revolutionary origins, as President Woodrow Wilson had proposed in 1917 to the nation and to the world, in the end, the formula "the business of America is business"—offered as an implicit alternative by President Calvin Coolidge—would find a longer-lasting echo among Americans.

The collective resolute mood that dominated in Latin America during the decade that separated the end of World War I from the outset of the devastating 1929 economic crisis also inspired an inward-looking regional orientation. However, this inward reorientation had little in common with the one taking place in the United States. A less negative view of the Latin American past, which had been put forth in 1912 in *La creación de un continente*, was now more widespread, yet the past it evoked had little in common with the one which, in García Calderón's account, had assigned a leading role to the conquerors and their heirs.

The new image of Latin America's past implied new collective actors in the present. As the postwar period dawned on the world, the process of incorporating the popular masses into public life had already peacefully taken place in Argentina and Uruguay. Yet, it was not in these two countries that the surviving indigenous groups, small in numbers and limited in terms of genetic contribution to an overwhelmingly Hispanicized population, had been decisively marginalized as a consequence of the massive transatlantic immigration waves. It was in Mexico that the revolutionary movement brought with it a state ideology that celebrated the arrival of the hitherto erratic indigenous population to its promised land as the starting point of the country's national history. In Mexico, the incorporation of the popular masses was taking place through a cycle of war and revolution even more intense than the one that had culminated in independence. This new image of its past and present was less a nativist rejection of all transatlantic heritage and more an expression of a growing confidence in Mexico's place in the world on behalf of a state that, for the first time, seriously aspired to lay its foundation on the political expression of the nation as a whole.

Mexico more decisively than ever embraced as the moment of its origin the legendary encounter of the eagle with the serpent and also took pride in having, by its own initiative, chosen to head down the path upon which Europe would later attempt to embark during the turbulent and hopeful early postwar years. In fact, solid arguments in favor of such a notion could be readily invoked. For example, Mexico's constitution, proclaimed in Querétaro in 1917—two years before the

Weimar Constitution was written—offered the first example of a new constitutionalism that placed social rights alongside individual rights. Yet, the recognition of the so-called social problem was not exclusive to the Mexican case, but rather had found expression throughout Latin America as early as the 1890s—not merely as an element that could lead to violent disturbances of the social and political order, but as an item to include on the political agenda.

Moreover, this view relied on the less pessimistic assessment of the Latin American historical experience and on a decidedly optimistic assessment of the potential opportunities opened by the postwar historical moment, an optimism that in Latin America would outlive that of Europe. What is most significant is that officials in the government actively sought to advance along the path of the social reformism set forth by the new Mexican regime. This view was also expressed in the writings of Peruvian José Carlos Mariátegui, by far the most noteworthy of the interpreters of the Latin American reality, for whom the example offered by the Russian Revolution had led to an embrace of the Leninist version of Marxism adopted by its leaders.

In Mariátegui's rich, complex, and also ambiguous message—which celebrated the Leninist experience as the most significant fruit to arise from the same postwar climate under fascism during his years in Italy—was a testimony to a new way of conceiving Latin America's historical experience within the context of all humankind.[45] His work *Siete ensayos de interpretación de la realidad peruana* underscored the experience of his native Peru, according to which the Spanish conquest brought down an economic system that had developed in Peru and "sprang spontaneously and freely from the Peruvian soil and people," which was characterized by "collective work and common effort...employed fruitfully for social purposes."[46]

Mariátegui was painfully aware that his Peru, which was on the verge of a radical transformation along with the rest of the world, had been extremely ill prepared for it. The Spanish conquest had reorganized Peru's society along feudal lines, which persist to this day, barely hidden under the individualistic, liberal political and legal apparatus that emerged after independence. Yet, for Mariátegui, a follower of the communism of Marx and Georges Sorel (no doubt more so of the latter than the former), Peru's past also signaled a valid path to the future, one embodied in that indigenous and *campesino* Sierra where the "habits of cooperation and solidarity" that had survived the blows suffered under the colony and the republic attested to the persistent "vitality of indigenous communism."[47]

The memory of that original communism, alive in the minds of the rural masses throughout the majority of the twentieth century in Peru, was ready to feed a myth with the capacity to mobilize and orient the revolutionary potential of the masses whom Sorel had taught to appreciate more positively. In Peru, this myth aligned itself behind a revolutionary project as radical in its ambitions as that which in Russia sought to apply Lenin's teachings. Accordingly, the role of political protagonist that the peasant masses played through their revolutionary mobilization made it possible for a country like Peru to be at the vanguard, despite having yet to come out of a period in which advancing at the pace of ascendant capitalism had not been possible.

It was not Mariátegui's political proposal, which he only articulated on the eve of his premature death in 1930, that, as Richard Morse pointed out and rightly so, assured him such a central place in the intellectual history of Latin America as Bello and Sarmiento had occupied in the nineteenth century.[48] Nor was his proposal echoed in the then incipient Soviet-line parties or in those reformist parties that were to win a mass base in subsequent decades. Winning that place rewarded, rather, his capacity to integrate into a persuasive overall vision of the historical experience of Latin America the disjointed proposals that were emerging at each step of the way, in that time of febrile exploration of constantly renewing issues and perspectives in which he lived. Shifting the focus to Latin America was clearly Mariátegui's central contribution. Answering the already declining role of Europe in the transition from an authentically universal history that was nearing completion, Mariátegui's message echoed widely among his contemporaries, no doubt because they perceived with the same clarity what the decline of Europe as the key point of reference meant.

In that new context, it was impossible to examine Latin America's experience from the starting point of the development gap. The region underwent a temporary eclipse, an inevitable consequence when Europe, which had offered until then the point of comparison vis-à-vis Latin America, was itself performing increasingly poorly. Such an eclipse did not necessarily presuppose a more positive assessment of the current situation and future prospects for Latin America, but during the 10 years that separated the end of the war from the beginning of the crisis, a decidedly optimistic view prevailed. Mariátegui drew on his conviction that the rise of a socialist revolution in an area marginal to Atlantic Europe would open the way to a finally universal history, one in which peoples and continents would have an opportunity to overcome their marginal roles by offering their support to the revolutionary process that began in 1917. At the same time, Latin American sociopolitical elites found encouraging the return of an export boom which, after the pause imposed by the war, surpassed in more than one area what had been attained before 1914.

The Rise of the United States and a Changing World Order

The new focus on Latin America's problems, which centered on the region itself, undercut the reasons that those who examined those problems considered the United States to be a benchmark for gauging accomplishments and failures. However, no approach could ignore the consequences of the rise of the United States for the region. On the one hand, there was a genuine preoccupation over the implications of the accelerated global economic and financial emergence of the United States during the interwar period. On the other hand, Latin America had reason to be concerned about certain episodes taking place in Central America and the Caribbean, namely, the U.S. military occupation of Nicaragua, the Dominican Republic, and Haiti for prolonged periods.

For the smallest countries in the Western Hemisphere, the fear of suffering a similar fate as these regional neighbors quickly broke the optimism that had characterized the interwar period. For the rest of the region, these occupations confirmed the collective notion that their proximity to the United States was far from a blessing. While the famous quote attributed to Mexico's Porfirio Díaz—"poor Mexico, so far from God and so close to the United States"—could be heard ever more frequently in Latin America, it also became increasingly common to base the problematic relationship with the United States on an anti-imperialist argument. Anti-imperialism would continue to have resonance through the influence of Rodó and Lenin on a platform that would be as unstable as it was enduring.

The optimism that characterized the interwar period ended abruptly in 1929, when the most serious economic crisis in the entire history of capitalism erupted. The period that came to be known as the Great Depression had devastating effects comparable to those of a natural disaster on the entire planet.[49] Latin America's optimism was shattered not by the region's own economic performance, but rather by that of the countries that had, until then, been considered their unattainable models. However, the question of the development gap did not reemerge after 1933, when an end to the seemingly indefinite free fall of the world economy was finally visible. This was because the experience of those years had clearly demonstrated that the crisis had been less devastating for the larger Latin American countries than for the industrialized countries they had hitherto sought to emulate. Thus, while the Brazilian economy regained its 1929 level in 1935, and the Argentinean and Chilean economies did so in 1937 and 1938, respectively, the United States only recovered from over 10 years of crisis with the enormous economic mobilization triggered by World War II.

The Post–World War II Era and the Reemergence of the Development Gap

The post–World War II era presented an even more decisive turning point than the 1929 crisis with respect to how the question of the development gap was addressed. This was the moment when the concerns that had existed in Latin America from its early origins found their expression in a comparison between neo-British America and neo-Iberian America. This was so for two reasons. First, the combined effects of the enormous expansion of the U.S. economy and the negative impact of years of conflict on continental Europe and Japan ultimately made the United States the only logical benchmark when assessing Latin America's economic performance. Second, a strong consensus emerged that the incipient period of international reconstruction presented a unique opportunity for Latin America to prove its ability to overcome the economic backwardness that had characterized the countries in the region from the very moment they joined the concert of nations.

Although the belief that nothing less than Latin America's emergence from backwardness was at stake made the challenge a serious one, the basic premise upon which it was based was nonetheless an optimistic one: it was finally possible to overcome the development gap. That optimism coincided with a period of ambiguous contrast in which it would flourish, as much in what would soon be called the First World as in what was already known as the socialist world. It became increasingly clear that the postwar reconstruction period, which advanced more vigorously than the one following World War I, would give way to an ascendant world economy that would surpass in duration and intensity every previous experience.

The sudden popularity of the subject of development economics in Latin America and the First World suggests that the optimism that reigned in those areas was based on shared assumptions about the requirements that national economies must meet in order to perform successfully. Perhaps the most significant of those shared assumptions was the premise postulated by Rostow in his stages of growth model, which stated that, in order to attain lasting success, an economy must advance following a valid path of growth through the five stages spelled out in his model.[50] Undoubtedly, the parallelism of those advances was better perceived when contemplated from enough distance to blur the details, and Alexander Gerschenkron knew what he was talking about when he alluded to the delightful *pressappochismo* that characterized Rostow's manifesto.[51] Rostow's description of the stages of growth, although generic and approximation-based, did not reflect any incapacity on his part to attain greater precision, as proven by his noteworthy studies of Britain's economy in the nineteenth century. What Rostow offered the reader in *The Stages of Economic Growth* was closer to what a century and a half earlier was generally offered under the heading of philosophy of history than to a historical reconstruction of the stage ushered in by the industrial revolution.

Thus, when Rostow projected a future in which all humankind would enjoy indefinitely the increasingly abundant fruits of the industrial revolution, he merely translated to a philosophy of history terminology the conviction that it was the industrial revolution that already offered the central theme of present history. The wide echo provoked by that prophetic vision reflected a general agreement with this conclusion by those who set out from Spanish America to explore the question of development. Nonetheless, this did not keep them from considering the process ushered in by the industrial revolution, which appeared destined to continue until it conquered the entire planet, from a perspective that differed in essential aspects from that held by those studying the issue from a North Atlantic viewpoint. And one can understand why. Those who lived through the second postwar period from that perspective, having left behind an era of devastating turbulences, were preparing to let themselves flow with the current, and they allowed themselves to look at the present and future with undiluted optimism. On the other hand, those who lived through that same period in a region that lacked comparable progress found that the center's progress toward prosperity placed on the immediate agenda the inveterate problem of their regional backwardness, for which the thematic study of development came to offer new instruments.

Although nothing justified concluding that all Latin American nations had hitherto followed parallel paths based on their common

backwardness, those who were concerned about the region's development gap took more interest in their persistent inability to overcome
it than in what had differentiated their histories. This was clearly the
central issue that aligned the region behind Raúl Prebisch's argument,
even if his analysis was based on an experience as inapt for generaliza-
tion as the Argentine case.

Prebisch: The Pinnacle and Decline of the Development Challenge

Between 1930 and 1943, Raúl Prebisch played a leading role in a
profoundly innovative stage of Argentina's economic development
through policymaking aimed at improvising answers to the immense
challenges posed by the international crisis. When that stage ended
abruptly with the military coup that overthrew the existing political regime—itself of dubious constitutional legitimacy—a new stage
began for Prebisch. From 1950 to 1962, he served as secretary general of the United Nations' Economic Commission for Latin America
and the Caribbean (ECLAC), and, beginning in 1965, he served at the
UN Conference on Trade and Development (UNCTAD). From those
international forums, Prebisch became the spokesperson for the Latin
American periphery of the capitalist world. The region was plagued
with difficulties in reducing its distance to the center, as Prebisch had
already learned through his experience in Argentina, an experience
that he was poised to project on a stage that was quickly expanding to
the point of reaching worldwide dimensions.

It is useful to underscore here one of Prebisch's characteristics
that, as Joseph Hodara rightly indicated, places him among Latin
America's cultural authority figures of the caliber of Sarmiento and
Mariátegui.[52] Like some of his well-known predecessors, Prebisch
put forth a theoretical conundrum that served as the basis to devise
practical initiatives that would be part of a transformation project for
Latin America. The prescribed policies, however, could only reach
the desired effectiveness if the implementer(s) held an adequate position of power or influence to carry them through. Having satisfied
that prerequisite until 1943 under the title of *grand commis d'État*
in his own country, Prebisch then sought to fulfill it as a prophet of
humanity's marginalized majority.

One consequence of Prebisch's practical background was the biased
relationship that he later maintained with economics as a theoretical
discipline. Whereas initially his attention was focused more on the

here and now as he pursued ad hoc solutions to specific problems, after 1943 he became increasingly prophetic and focused on a utopian vision that would later come to characterize his interventions. It should be noted that Prebisch, like his intellectual predecessors, had a tendency toward eclecticism of ideas and doctrines; in his case, however, it was more noticeable because the prophet was also an international official who needed to temper his message to avoid alarming anyone across the various sectors of his diversified audience.

Inspired by his earlier experience as a policymaker, Prebisch's preference to assign the state the leading role in introducing the reforms he considered imperative was a widely supported view in Latin America and beyond during the boom of development economics. Such an environment clearly gave him the confidence—which retrospectively seems hardly justifiable—to argue that the establishment of a world monetary and financial order even more solid than the one in place prior to 1929 ought not to diminish the central role of the state, which had been augmented earlier precisely in response to the economic collapse.

Despite the contrasting views on the present and the future that, from the periphery, Prebisch advocated and, from the center of the First World, Rostow proposed, the optimism that prevailed made both sides consider the advances of the present to be a continuation of the past, however different the present was from the previous era of crisis. Likewise, the advances of the present were perceived as a preliminary indication of what was to come for an indefinite time into the future. That perceived dual extension of a period of prosperity, which made the development question a central one was, in fact, a period that lasted but a fleeting moment. The brevity of this period is underscored by the fact that, no more than 20 years after Rostow's *Non-Communist Manifesto* was published, Albert Hirschman—who had done so much to introduce the question of development economics—was already casting an unmistakably retrospective gaze on the episode.[53] However, it was preserved in the public memory, as the title of this volume can attest.

There is one common characteristic in the various theories of development that may explain the rapid decline of development economics: because each of them hid below the surface a historical philosophy that inevitably presupposed a gamble regarding the future, it was difficult for them to survive the refutation of that future once it became the present. That occurred in the First World when the expansionary wave that began in 1945 was prolonged against any reasonable expectation for 30 years, but then gave way to a stagnation that only avoided becoming a recession by repeatedly turning to a dangerous inflationary remedy in ever less prudent doses. Around 1980, when such measures became unsustainable as inflation threatened to spiral out of control, it became clear that the current situation was not the final apotheosis of industrial civilization predicted 20 years earlier by Rostow, but rather the beginning of a new era that would come to be known as the post-industrial period.

Whereas in the First World the question of development economics easily faded into the background after advancing with little opposition during almost three decades of an exceptional economic bonanza, its Latin American trajectory was more tumultuous from the outset. Perhaps one key element of this divergence is explained by the notion that, having crossed the economic development threshold, development would continue automatically, safeguarded from calamities to which no economy was invulnerable, as recent experience appeared to prove. This feature, as Hirschman highlighted and quite rightly so, seemed notable when the experience of several major countries that had attained a high degree of development and had later fallen victim to the most calamitous "historical derailings" was still so recent.[54] It was precisely the shared conviction that, after crossing a certain threshold, the process of development became a causa sui that generated divergent reactions among those who observed its advances from the center and from the periphery. That vision of the development process created a corollary that Rostow had sought to explain when he gave the "take-off" concept its decisive moment: once economic development had crossed that threshold, the economy would continue advancing indefinitely.

Pursuing a development course thus became a one-time, all-or-nothing gamble, which was addressed quite differently by those who were sure they had already confronted it successfully and those who, as was the case in Latin America, believed Prebisch's notion that any delay in facing that challenge diminished the chances of overcoming it. The awareness that the time had come to follow such a course led to negative readings of economic performances that were less unsatisfactory than what is generally remembered. During those years, for example, Argentina was the epitome of Latin American failure, even though its rate of growth after 1945 was higher than that of the United States. Even Brazil's economy, which in the late 1950s had the highest growth rate of all nonsocialist countries, was not recognized as totally successful because its progress was seen as insufficient to firmly embark on a path of sustained development.

The 1960s: A Decade Defined by Choice

One key feature of the 1960s, which further differentiated the center's views on development from those of the Latin American periphery, was the latter's perception of choice in what course to follow. The center, after years of contemplating its rapid economic advances in spite of the political/ideological conflicts that, on more than one occasion, threatened to sink the planet into a catastrophe of apocalyptic proportions, began to view the confrontation with socialism as a peaceful rivalry of two competitors in the development race. The Third World, on the other hand, viewed the development landscape through a very different lens, as it still confronted internal conflicts that had long been overcome in the rest of the world. The periphery offered a space in which contrasting views that were clearly too dangerous to confront at the global level could still be considered, even if on a decidedly lower scale. Therefore, when contemplating the issue of development from the Third World perspective, it was difficult to do so from the Olympic heights that allowed analysts like Rostow to integrate in a single process the development progress made by imperial Russia and by the USSR. The Third World view, instead, considered the capitalist and socialist routes as two different options and a choice still to be made.

Even before the Cuban Revolution raised that option to a level of potential impact never before imagined in Latin America, the region's own perspective on the development gap was best articulated by Brazil's Celso Furtado and Chile's Aníbal Pinto.[55] In their works published in 1959, Furtado and Pinto offered views inspired by Prebisch, which were later adopted by ECLAC in its review of Latin America's historical experience. This perspective underscored the importance of developing a mature industrial economic base if the region aspired to escape the increasingly dire consequences of the growing gap between the agricultural and mining countries of the periphery and the fully industrialized economies of the center.

Despite significant differences in approach, which undoubtedly stemmed from the very different historical experiences of Brazil and Chile, Furtado and Pinto shared something more than the common goal of promoting strong industrial economies. Their views shared an implicit optimism about the prospects for progress toward that goal. It would be a mistake to interpret that optimism as excessive after it was adopted as the preferred strategy by ECLAC, when, in fact, it reflected a Latin American zeitgeist at a time when worldwide economic progress appeared poised to break all barriers. That collective positive mood outlived the era in which Latin America entered the Cold War combat zone, and contributed to the widespread view that the Cuban Revolution was proof that what had hitherto been deemed impossible, even in the economic realm, had mysteriously ceased to be seen as such. Furthermore, the triumph of the Cuban Revolution suggested that the path of insurrection was perhaps a more viable option than was previously believed by political leaders of partially Marxist tendency—such as those in Peru and Venezuela who had adopted an ever-cautious reform path and were firmly aligned with the United States—and those of Soviet-style communist inclination.

As is well known, the introduction of choice in Latin America's political landscape further heightened tensions that, along with the economic and social transformations under way, were already deeply intensifying, to the point of reaching unbearable levels in the following decade. Cuba's failed attempt in 1970 to harvest 10 million tons of sugar, which the Cuban Revolution sought to make the touchstone to validate the socialist option, could be seen as a sign that the impossible was, once again, becoming impossible (or perhaps had never ceased to be so).

This is how the decade of choice in Latin America came to a close. Even if that choice never became a reality in most countries, the fact that the decade ended on a failed note suggested in which direction the region was headed in the next stage of the struggle. Throughout the 1960s, it appeared that Latin America had reached the international protagonism that Mariátegui had predicted in the 1920s. One sign of this was that the vicissitudes that it experienced were followed from the so-called First World more closely than ever before, to the point that it was two observers/participants from the First World who offered interpretations of that stage whose conclusions would have enormous influence in Latin America itself.

Cardoso: Dependency Theory

Although for profoundly different reasons, the vicissitudes that cut across Latin America in the convulsions of the 1960s also made the reformist option seem less attractive. At the onset of the decade, this option had enjoyed a universally favorable consensus, as was evident by the echo elicited by Fidel Castro's proposal—put forth in the name of the victorious Cuban Revolution—that the United States earmark $30 billion for programs geared toward technological progress and social reform in Latin America. Taken up immediately by Brazilian president Juscelino Kubitschek under the heading of Operation Pan America, this concept finally came to fruition in the Alliance for Progress, sponsored by the United States at the initiative of President John F. Kennedy. ECLAC's proposals could be clearly recognized in the alliance's views on the economic and social issues facing Latin America. Two examples stood out: agrarian and fiscal reform, the latter aimed at putting an end to tax systems that were designed to lighten the burden on the landed classes and, in effect, condemned national treasuries to perpetual shortages.

As was to be expected, U.S. support did not facilitate the adhesion of the progressive sectors in Latin America to the alliance's program. On the one hand, the role assigned to the alliance in the Cold War strategy had the effect of driving certain sectors away. On the other, it was resented that, in terms of U.S. participation in this program, the initiatives planned and financed by the state were relegated to a very remote secondary role. The total cost of the project was $20 billion—the figure to which Kubitschek had reduced what Castro originally suggested—of which half would come from those countries in which the alliance programs were to be implemented, while the other half would come from the United States. However, 90 percent of the U.S. contribution was private direct investment. It should come as no surprise that, for those who shared progressive views, this was sufficient reason to reject the proposal. Even if it incorporated some of their most deeply rooted beliefs, they were convinced that the proposed implementation process, far from opening access to independent development, would ensure the perpetuation of dependency and, therefore, of underdevelopment.

The 1960s introduced enough changes to render partially outdated, by the decade's conclusion, the diagnoses and prognoses shared earlier by the reformist consensus. At that time, Brazilian Fernando Henrique Cardoso offered an assessment of what those changes had contributed and what their consequences were likely to be.[56] Cardoso argued that, when examining the transformations that had taken place during the 1960s, while the situation of dependency had not diminished, it was clear that it was not incompatible with the continuation of a process that could only be called development, even though it was headed in a different direction than the one endorsed by ECLAC. In that process, which Cardoso characterized as associated-dependent development, industrialization—almost exclusively entrusted to multinational firms—reoriented its focus to the production of durable consumer goods only accessible to the highest-income sectors. That is the reason that the economy could continue developing while social inequality grew, disappointing those who expected that the negative income effect suffered by the mobilized popular masses and the resulting contraction in the consumption of industrial goods would lead to chronic economic stagnation that would, in turn, eventually force the government to combat inequality.[57]

Two aspects of Cardoso's argument are particularly significant when studying the development gap between the United States and Latin America. One is the tendency to perpetuate the characteristics that had come to define Latin American intellectual thought. The most important of these is the systematic effort to ensure that the theoretical basis of the argument remained flexible enough to take into account a constantly changing sociopolitical reality. The other aspect that should be underscored is Cardoso's interpretation of those changes. Even though he judged them all in a negative light, he placed them in a very different context than the one preferred by those who continued to view the 1960s as the decisive decade. For him, that decade was merely an inflection point in the course of a long-term historical process in which the power relations among the classes had already experienced ups and downs and would no doubt continue to do so in the future.

Cardoso's refusal to embrace any desperate conclusion was clearly influenced by the fact that his native Brazil played a central role. Although the triumphant counterrevolutionary forces in Brazil had replaced in 1964 the constitutional regime with a semi-military one—a regime that by 1968 reached the zenith of its repressive tendencies—it became ever more dubious in the next decade that the turn to dictatorship had taken the country down a path of no return. Beginning in 1968, the Brazilian economy resumed its progress along the path of associated-dependent development at an even quicker pace than in the most successful years of the period prior to the change in regime (in which, it should be noted, it had progressed considerably along that same path, though in a political framework of representative democracy).

The course followed by Brazil in the years since Cardoso offered his diagnosis and prognosis confirmed up to the point he had been able to do justice to the characteristics that distinguished his country's development process in the Latin American context. None of the other Latin American economies came close to the success experienced by Brazil in those years. Unfortunately, the increasingly acute political crises that continued to debilitate many of the region's countries culminated in some cases, particularly in the Southern Cone, in the rise of state terrorism, which reached levels that no one had hitherto thought possible in Argentina, Chile, and Uruguay.

It is thus understandable that those who viewed that period from the perspective of these state terrorism–stricken nations were less inclined to attribute the development gap problem solely to its economic dimension. Chile's Claudio Véliz, for example, focused on the key sources of Latin America's extreme political degradation, when at the outset of the twentieth century the region seemed poised to regain its place in the vanguard of institutional development.[58] Véliz claimed that Latin America was endowed with a genetic code that had indelibly engraved on the region a tendency toward centralism. Precisely because the Southern Cone countries had advanced more in adopting institutional frameworks that were as alien to them as to all of the other countries in the region, they found themselves once again in the vanguard of a movement arising from the legacy of a frustrated decade defined by choice. Unfortunately, this movement led to an unequivocal relapse into barbarism. While that experience indisputably proved that, in Latin America, it is impossible to build anything stable if it is not based on the centralist option, Mexico offered a most convincing example of how it was possible to build on such a foundation a political order endowed with enviable stability and with a great deal more tolerance.

Yet, decidedly, the future would never seem benevolent in a framework that, like Véliz's, sought out constants in a world and a region undergoing dramatic change. It didn't take long for such views to be disputed, especially once history took an unexpected turn toward the irrefutable supremacy of representative democracy based on the principle of popular sovereignty. By the end of the twentieth century, after representative democracy had been restored in the Southern Cone and a very slow transition in Mexico had reached its conclusion, it was not difficult to deduce that Véliz had squandered his knowledge and ingenuity in an effort to provide a solution to a problem that had, in the end, worked itself out.

The End of the Cold War: New Parameters to Interpret the Development Gap

In the post–Cold War era, the economic dimension of the development gap once again took the lead over the political component. However, as the economic dimension regained its predominance, it quickly became evident that the radical transformations that had rendered Véliz's propositions obsolete had also undermined the assumptions on which the issue of the development gap had been based both explicitly and implicitly. When the 1989–1991 collapse of the socialist world ushered in a new historical era, the uncertain path of the events that followed intensified the skepticism that had already begun to inspire the great historical narratives seeking to offer a unified interpretive analysis. The emerging situation inspired new doubts regarding the age-old ambition of finding an explanation based on Latin America's historical experience that was capable of clarifying the enigmas posed by the region's recurrent failure to emulate the success of neo-British America.

The question of the development gap did not come out unscathed from the rise of a new climate of ideas and perceptions characteristic of a radical historical change. In the framework of modernity, the stage in which the development process unfolded had not ceased to expand, from the time that Sarmiento identified as its protagonists two rival colonization ventures in the New World until, a long century later, Prebisch expanded that stage to span the entire globe. From beginning to end, the central argument that dominated that ever-growing stage was based on the confrontation between one collective subject (the United States or the First World), which had discovered the secret to successful economic development, and another (first Ibero-America and then the Third World), which desperately sought to share it. For a fleeting moment, it appeared that the 1989–1991 transition had reinforced the relevance of that perspective on the development gap. Such a conclusion was easily reached, based on the unexpected collapse of the revolutionary movement that, since 1949, had come to dominate one-third of the planet and that, in the name of socialism, had sought to open the way to a future different from the one Sarmiento, after Tocqueville, had seen embodied in the United States. A few years sufficed, however, for the then logical conclusion that following in the footsteps of the Cold War victor would lead to a golden future, to give way to a more tempered prognosis.

When that decisive historical turning point came about, Latin America was undergoing one of the most disappointing moments in its long history of searching for the secret to economic development. That was sufficient motivation for the problems evoked in the discussions of the development gap to create a renewed sense of urgency. At the same time, the characteristics of that turning point appeared to dissipate any doubt as to the validity of the model of development that had just received the most clamorous favorable verdict in world history. This helps to explain the enthusiasm with which most Latin American countries decided to resolve, once and for all, the age-old problem of endorsing the principles of the so-called Washington Consensus.

As is well known, the neoliberal model prescribed by the Washington Consensus came significantly short of fulfilling its initial promises, but that did not preclude the later posing of the question of Latin America's development gap in its original terms. More influential on this point was the fact that, once the Cold War was over and, with it, the contrast between capitalist development and the alternative proposed by socialism, the specific characteristics of different experiences within the framework of capitalism came to dominate the debate. Such an analysis began to receive growing attention even before the United States emerged victorious from the Cold War; for example, in the 1980s, there was ample discussion about the likelihood that the greatest challenge to U.S. economic primacy came not from competition with the Soviet bloc, which was increasingly mired in stagnation, but from Japan.

From the perspective of the leading political, military, and economic power of the world, the discovery of the existence of more than one path within the capitalist framework had the effect of intensifying doubts about the future. From Latin America's perspective, that same discovery awakened concerns that were no less unsettling, though different from those of the United States. The corollary of that discovery, which seems most relevant from a Latin American perspective, was that the experiences of the second half of the twentieth century demonstrated that the boundary separating the periphery from the center of the capitalist world is surmountable.

A new landscape that illustrated the development gap thus began to emerge, one in which attention was no longer focused on what Latin America had in common with the rest of the so-called Third World, but rather on the characteristics that distinguished it from the rest of that group. First among those characteristics was an income distribution more unequal than even that of sub-Saharan Africa. It should also be noted that South Korea and Taiwan began to replace the United States as the development benchmark and object of emulation for Latin America. Yet, it is not certain that the new landscape that is framing the debates about the failure of the Washington Consensus is destined to reach maturity, especially at a time when the economic vicissitudes of the so-called Asian tigers weigh much less than the vast frenetic advances of the Chinese economy since the 1980s.[59]

These circumstances beg the question: what lessons can Latin America draw from the successes of a colossal experiment that, without repudiating its original goal of building a socialist order, made the ancient empire of the center the most dynamic nucleus of the capitalist economic order? It would be premature to try to formulate a solid prognosis which would confirm that the 1989–1991 juncture was a turning point in world history that affected not only the destiny of the socialist experiment. Accordingly, with terms of reference that, for more than a century, framed the question of the development gap but have now vanished without a replacement, the reflections on the fall of empires offered, among others, by Paul Kennedy in 1987[60] may well offer the best analysis for the time being to understand today's world and Latin America's place in it.

Notes

1. I would venture to say that, for too many decades, I played the role of historian. In the early years of my career, the "non-communist" manifesto of W. W. Rostow, entitled *The Stages of Economic Growth* (Cambridge: Cambridge University Press, 1960), was still the cause of great furor.
2. The dialogue established in 1814 between the United States, which had just emerged from its second war of independence, and the Spanish American insurgents, who were still far from attaining their goal of independence, was not to be joined by Portuguese Brazil for another seven decades, the time it took for that country to transition from the old colonial monarchy to the new republican regime.
3. These reactions were ambiguous because, while it was regrettable that the gap prevented the Western Hemisphere from becoming a monolithic republican fortress, it certainly offered Anglo-Saxon America the opportunity to look at itself in a mirror that reflected a most gratifying image of superiority.
4. "Contestación de un americano meridional a un caballero de esta isla" (Carta de Jamaica), in Simón Bolívar, *Doctrina del Libertador* (Caracas: Biblioteca Ayacucho, 1976), p. 62. English translation: F 2235.3 B535, Columbus Memorial Library, Organization of American States (OAS), Washington, DC.
5. Letter from Bolívar to Santander, July 8, 1826, in *Obras completas de Simón Bolívar*, edited by Vicente Lecuna (Havana: Lex, 1947), vol. 1, p. 1390. English translation: *Selected Writings of Bolívar*, compiled by Vicente Lecuna, edited by Harold A. Bierck, Jr., and translated by Lewis Bertrand (New York: Colonial Press, 1951), p. 624.
6. This image would remain indelibly engraved in the Spanish American historical memory, and in the following century it would inspire some of the most insightful pages in Ezequiel Martínez Estrada's *Radiografía de la Pampa* and Octavio Paz's *The Labyrinth of Solitude*.
7. Bolívar, "Discurso de Angostura," in *Doctrina del Libertador*, p. 106. For English translation, see *Selected Writings of Bolívar*, compiled by Vicente Lecuna, edited by Harold A. Bierck Jr., and translated by Lewis Bertrand (New York: Colonial Press, 1951), p. 178.
8. Ibid., *Doctrina del Libertador*, p. 113; ibid, *Selected Writings of Bolívar*, p. 184.
9. Ibid., *Doctrina del Libertador*, p. 120 (editor's translation).

10. Ibid., *Doctrina del Libertador*, pp. 108 and 113; ibid., *Selected Writings of Bolívar*, pp. 179 and 184.

11. Bolívar had already defined the objectives of this ideal in the oath of Rome as "emancipation of the spirit, the elimination of cares, the exaltation of man, and the final perfectibility of reason," and he continued to hold them as inviolate. Simón Bolívar, *El Libertador: Writings of Simón Bolívar*, translated by Frederick H. Fornoff (New York: Oxford University Press, 2003), p. 113.

12. At the time, there was a reverence for England as the nation destined to guide all humankind in the age of revolutions, an age initiated by England itself one century prior to the outbreak of the much more boisterous French Revolution.

13. Letter from Bolívar to Santander, Cuzco, July 28, 1825, in *Doctrina del Libertador*, p. 197, and *Selected Writings of Bolívar*, p. 513.

14. Letter from Bolívar to José Rafael Revenga, May 25, 1820, in *Doctrina del Libertador*, pp. 147–149 ("never has conduct been more dreadful than that of the Americans toward us"); to Colonel Patricio Campbell, Chargé d'Affairs of His British Majesty, August 5, 1829, ibid., p. 295 ("the United States seems destined by Providence to plague the Americas with miseries in the name of freedom").

15. Bolívar, "Discurso de Angostura," in *Doctrina del Libertador*, pp. 60–61; in *Selected Writings of Bolívar*, p. 110.

16. The text of the "Juramento de Roma," as transmitted in 1850 by Simón Rodríguez, before whom Bolívar had pronounced it in 1805, is in *Doctrina del Libertador*, pp. 3–4; and *El Libertador: Writings of Simón Bolívar*, p. 113.

17. Thus, he wrote on April 12, 1828, in a letter to José Antonio Páez:
   > It would be necessary for us to alter our very natures in order to be able to live under an absolutely free government. We would have to change our habits and customs, become austere, and free ourselves of our baser passions, or else forego [*sic*] the chimera that forms our plans. I was the most deluded of all, and it has taken forty years of disillusionment for me to arrive at this pessimistic and despairing conclusion. (*Doctrina del Libertador*, p. 266; and *Selected Writings of Bolívar*, p. 689)

18. Bolívar, *Doctrina del Libertador*, pp. 108 and 105; and *Selected Writings of Bolívar*, p. 177.

19. Letter from Bolívar to Andrés de Santa Cruz, October 14, 1826, in *Obras*, 1:1444n3.

20. Domingo Faustino Sarmiento, *Viajes por Europa, África y América* (Mexico City: Fondo de Cultura Económica and UNESCO, 1993).

21. Domingo Faustino Sarmiento, *Facundo*, edited by Roberto Yahni (Madrid: Cátedra, 1990), pp. 40–41.

22. This liberal aristocrat, convinced that the movement toward equality could not be stopped, considered it hardly relevant to pass judgment on the intrinsic validity of the egalitarian ideal. He was content to find a way in which its inevitable triumph would not bring about a despotism closer to that of imperial Rome than to the much less extreme one of the ancien régime.

23. Sarmiento, *Viajes*, p. 297.

24. In this respect, Sarmiento appears to owe more to *Lettres sur les États Unis* by Michel Chevalier (Paris: Gosselin, 1837), although he does not cite it explicitly in his text, than to *Notions of the Americans Picked Up by a Travelling Bachelor*, by James Fenimore Cooper (Albany: State University of New York Press, 1991 [1828]), which he does mention.

25. Sarmiento, *Viajes*, p. 291n21.

26. Ibid.

27. As stated by Sarmiento, "France has a King, 400,000 soldiers, fortifications of Paris that have cost two billion francs, and a starving people." Ibid.

28. Ibid., p. 313n17.

29. William H. Katra, "Sarmiento en los Estados Unidos," *Todo es historia* 22, no. 253 (1988): 8–45.

30. Ibid.

31. Sarmiento, *Viajes*, p. 313.

32. Sarmiento, "Influencia de la instrucción primaria en la industria y en el desarrollo general de la prosperidad nacional," in *Proyecto y construcción de una nación, 1846–1880*, edited by Tulio Halperin Donghi (Buenos Aires: Ariel, 1995), pp. 258 and 262.

33. Sarmiento, "Carta-prólogo a 'Conflicto y armonías de las razas en América' a Mrs. Horace Mann (1883)," in *Proyecto y construcción*, n. 23, pp. 588–660.

34. Ibid.

35. Ibid.

36. According to an estimate by John Coatsworth and Alan Taylor, the per capita gross domestic product of the six largest Latin American economies dropped between 1850 and 1900 from 51 percent to 27 percent of that of the United States. See John H. Coatsworth and Alan M. Taylor (eds.), *Latin America and the World Economy since 1800* (Cambridge, MA: Harvard University Press, 1998), p. 26.

37. Among other things, positivism called for transposing to a language of biologically based racism the enlightened denunciation of the adherence by the heirs of the conquered ethnicity to their ancestral views, which were a serious obstacle to making progress with the necessary reforms.

38. Nancy Stepan, *The Hour of Eugenics: Race, Gender and Nation in Latin America* (Ithaca, NY: Cornell University Press, 1991).

39. This was suggested by Victor Bulmer-Thomas in *The Economic History of Latin America since Independence* (Cambridge: Cambridge University Press, 1994), pp. 63–64.

40. Bartolomé Mitre, *Historia de San Martín y de la emancipación sudamericana* (Buenos Aires: Anaconda, 1950 [1884]), p. 53.

41. This was made evident by Rodó's proposal, which offered as an alternative to the U.S. model the one that France had inherited from ancient Greece.

42. Francisco García Calderón, *La creación de un continente* (Paris: Ollendorf, 1912).

43. Francisco García Calderón, *Les démocraties latines d'Amérique* (Paris: Flammarion, 1912).

44. It was the European liberal constitutional model that Spanish America sought to emulate after the fall of the Iberian empires.

45. The text was first published in 1925 and was included by Mariátegui in the volume that he prepared for publication on the eve of his death in 1929, which would not become available until 1950: "La emoción de nuestro tiempo," in José Carlos Mariátegui, *El alma matinal y otras estaciones del hombre de hoy*, 2nd ed. (Lima: Amauta, 1959), pp. 13–23.

46. José Carlos Mariátegui, *Siete ensayos de interpretación de la realidad peruana* (Lima: Editorial Librería Peruana, 1934 [1928]), p. 7; translated as *Seven Interpretive Essays on Peruvian Reality* (Austin: University of Texas Press, 1971).

47. Mariátegui, *Siete ensayos*, p. 68n32.

48. Richard M. Morse, "La cultura política iberoamericana, de Sarmiento a Mariátegui," in *De historia e historiadores: Homenaje a José Luis Romero* (Mexico City: Siglo XXI, 1982), pp. 225–257.

49. It is no surprise that in 1933 a former treasury minister under an ultraconservative Argentine military dictator could openly discuss, without generating alarm, whether the capitalist system could survive the Depression. See Enrique Uriburu, "La crisis económica del mundo," *Revista de Economía Argentina*, no. 181 (July 1933). One must add that, following Keynes, Uriburu concluded that the fact that it had not already succumbed signaled that it would survive the crisis, but only if it were realized soon enough that change was inevitable.

50. The five stages of growth postulated by the Rostovian take-off model are (1) traditional society; (2) preconditions for take-off; (3) take-off; (4) drive to maturity; and (5) age of high mass consumption. Walt Whitman Rostow, *The Stages of Economic Growth: A Non-Communist Manifesto* (Cambridge: Cambridge University Press, 1960).

51. Alexander Gerschenkron, "The Early Phases of Industrialization in Russia—Afterthoughts and Counterthoughts," in *The Economics of Take-Off into Sustained Growth*, edited by W. W. Rostow (New York: Macmillan/St. Martin's, 1965), p. 166.

52. Joseph Hodara, *Prebisch y la CEPAL: Sustancia, trayectoria y contexto institucional* (Mexico City: El Colegio de México, 1987), p. 12.

53. Albert Hirschman, "The Rise and Decline of Development Economics," in Albert Hirschman, *Essays in Trespassing: Economics to Politics and Beyond* (Cambridge: Cambridge University Press, 1981).

54. Ibid., p. 23.

55. Celso Furtado, *Formação economica do Brasil* (Rio de Janeiro: Fundo de Cultura Economica, 1959); and Aníbal Pinto Santa Cruz, *Chile, un caso de desarrollo frustrado* (Santiago, Chile: Editorial Universitaria, 1959).

56. Fernando Henrique Cardoso wrote a set of essays published from 1972 to 1979, which he pulled together in 1980 in the book *As Idéias e Seu Lugar: Ensaios sobre as Teorias do Desenvolvimento* (Petrópolis, Brazil: Vozes, 1980). The book was also published in French as *Les Idées à Leur Place* (Paris: Métaillé/Maison des Sciences de l'Homme, 1984).

57. Fernando Henrique Cardoso, "L'originalité de la copie: La CEPAL et l'idée de développement," in *Les Idées à Leur Place*, pp. 19–69.

58. See Claudio Véliz, *The Centralist Tradition of Latin America* (Princeton, NJ: Princeton University Press, 1980).

59. For more on this issue, see John Coatsworth, "Structures, Endowments, and Institutions in the Economic History of Latin America," *Latin American Research Review* 40, no. 3 (2005): 126–144.

60. Paul Kennedy, *The Rise and Fall of the Great Powers: Economic Change and Military Conflict from 1500 to 2000* (New York: Random House, 1987).

3

Looking at *Them*

A Mexican Perspective on the Gap with the United States

ENRIQUE KRAUZE

I<small>N NO OTHER</small> country is the gap with the United States more palpable than in Mexico. This is because the gap is much deeper and wider than just the economic disparities between the two countries. It is a moral gap, one that has grown over two centuries of incomprehension and contempt on the part of the United States and ignorance and resentment on the part of Mexico. There is no single explanation for this mutual estrangement, of course, but the two countries find themselves, border to border, in a paradoxical situation.

One of today's realities in the region is that a part of Mexico, as well as Latin America as a whole, has moved—literally—to the United States. At the risk of failing to recognize itself, Mexico's northern neighbor cannot afford to disregard the Mexican and Hispanic population that now resides in its cities and rural areas, from Texas to Alaska and from New York to California. By the same token, Mexicans and other Latin Americans cannot succumb to simplistic and Manichaean visions of history, nor cling to the notion that the United States is the source of all of the region's ills. Therefore, it is important to study the gap between the United States and its southern neighbors not only as an economic, social, and political phenomenon, but also as the evolution of a complex collective sentiment that the United States holds toward Mexico and the rest of Latin America, and vice versa.

Bridging a Wider Gap: Historical and Cultural Roots of the Chasm between Mexico and the United States

It is not surprising that a history of U.S. perceptions of Mexico has yet to be written. In geopolitical terms, Mexico ceased to be a priority for the United States a long time ago. Yet the history of Mexico's perceptions of the United States has not been the subject of extensive and rigorous historical analysis either, although for Mexico, living alongside the richest and most powerful country of the twentieth century always has carried great importance. It is thus worthwhile to examine a panoramic view of the gap, understood as a collective stance over time.

Mexico's development of its stance toward the United States has a unique history, different from the histories of other countries in the Caribbean, Central America, and South America. It is worth noting, however, that the solidarity displayed by other Latin American countries at various points in time decisively shaped the spirit of Mexicans with respect to their admired and feared neighbor to the north. To better understand Mexico's views—and in particular those of the country's elites—regarding the United States, it is necessary to review how the nation's collective stance has oscillated from admiration to disdain, from praise to criticism, from estrangement to collaboration. This overview is a brief, schematic, and partial examination whose center of gravity is Mexico, but it may well illustrate, by reflection or refraction, attitudes common to others in Latin America who have also been, to a larger or lesser degree, affected by the actions and reach of the U.S. government, economy, and culture. It is also worth exploring specific proposals—however modest they may be— to reduce the moral gap that separates Mexico from the United States, which, most analysts would agree, is nothing but detrimental. Today, this gap is already being bridged by the arduous efforts of those Mexicans who are working, as José Martí famously put it, "in the belly of the beast."

From Admiration to Rejection

In a phrase that summarizes entire history tomes, Octavio Paz stated that Mexico was born with its back turned to its indigenous past, to Spanish tradition, and to the Catholic church. Although quite correct, one could also add to this phrase that Mexico was born looking at *them*, the United States. The great insurgent caudillos and their successors, the liberals of the nineteenth century, viewed the United States in the same way that twentieth-century Marxists looked at the Soviet Union: as a land of progress and future promise. It is well known that Miguel Hidalgo, the priest who initiated Mexico's War of Independence, sought refuge in the United States when he fled with his decimated forces to the north, and that José María Morelos—another great insurgent caudillo and also a priest—sent his son Juan Nepomuceno to pursue his studies in New Orleans.

When Mexican independence was achieved and ties with Spain were broken, the United States recognized the new nation and designated its first ambassador, Joel R. Poinsett. Poinsett's assignment explicitly focused on modifying the border treaty with Spain (and, therefore, with New Spain, i.e., Mexico) through the purchase—or eventual annexation—of bordering territories. His appointment also coincided with the declaration of the Monroe Doctrine (1823) prohibiting any European meddling in the Americas. In those enthusiastic early days of the Mexican republic, few foresaw that a defensive doctrine would transform itself, within a few years, into the aggressive and expansionist concept of "Manifest Destiny" (1839), according to which the historical plan of the United States was to expand its frontiers and its civilization all the way to Patagonia.

In 1824, Mexico adopted a federal constitution inspired to some extent by the U.S. Constitution. Lorenzo de Zavala, a brilliant journalist, politician, and historian of the southern state of Yucatán, was a leading figure during this historical period. His admiration for the United States—which he considered more remarkable than Greece and Rome—and his interest in shaping nascent Mexico in its image is brilliantly presented in his memoirs, *Journey to the United States of North America* (1830), which appeared around the same time as Alexis de Tocqueville's *La démocratie en Amérique*. In his prologue, Zavala presented a relentless comparison of the two neighboring cultures:

> [The United States has] a people that is hard working, active, reflective, circumspect, religious in the midst of a multiplicity of sects, tolerant, thrifty, free, proud and persevering. The Mexican is easy going, lazy, intolerant, generous almost to prodigality, vain, belligerent, superstitious, ignorant and an enemy of all restraint. The North American works, the Mexican has a good time; the first spends less than he has, the second even that which he does not have; the former carries out the

most arduous enterprises to their conclusion, the latter abandons them in the early stages; the one lives in his house, decorates it, furnishes it, preserves it against the inclement weather; the other spends his time in the street, flees from his home, and in a land where there are no seasons he worries little about a place to rest. In the United States all men are property owners and tend to increase their fortune; in Mexico the few who have anything are careless with it and fritter it away.[1]

The comparison was itself a tacit suggestion regarding the only way to diminish the gap, yet Zavala preferred to be explicit and preach the remedy to his compatriots—be like them:

[M]end your ways. Get rid of those eighty-seven holidays during the year that you dedicate to play, drunkenness and pleasure. Save up capital for the decent support of yourselves and your families in order to give guarantees of your concern for the preservation of the social order. Tolerate the opinions of other people; be indulgent with those who do not think as you do; allow the people of your country to exercise freely their trade, whatever it may be, and to worship the supreme Author of the Universe in accordance with their own consciences. Repair your roads; raise up houses in order to live like rational beings; dress your children and your wives with decency; don't incite riots in order to take what belongs to somebody else. And finally, live on the fruit of your labors, and then you will be worthy of liberty and of the praises of sensible and impartial men.[2]

Years later, with the Texas war of separation from Mexico, Zavala took his rejection of authoritarian centralism and his federalist and liberal convictions to the extreme by becoming, at the end of his days in 1836, a founder of the republic of Texas and its first vice president.

The centralist faction, equally obsessed with the United States, had a better sense of reality than its liberal counterpart. It understood not only the economic weaknesses of the new Mexican nation, but also that the *ad litteram* application of federalism could lead to the country's disintegration or could break it into ungovernable and disjointed units. The centralist faction also weighed the territorial risks of Mexico's very large northern region—rich yet defenseless and almost unpopulated— in addition to feeling a religiously rooted distrust, a remote echo perhaps of the Protestant Reformation in Europe.

Lucas Alamán, the founder of Mexico's Conservative Party and a renowned historian, stated in 1846 that the country would be lost if Europe did not come to its aid, and he was soon proven right when it became evident that Mexico's salvation lay in defending itself from the United States. In August 1847, while observing through a spyglass from the roof of his house the sad denouement of the battle of Padierna, when Mexican troops capitulated before the U.S. invader, Alamán saw the foreign flag hoisted among clouds of smoke. He recalled the fall of the ancient pre-Hispanic civilizations and feared that war, unjust by any measure, would mean the end of the Mexican nation. Although the outcome was not that severe, Mexico did lose more than half its territory: 2 million square kilometers, including the gold deposits of upper California, which were among the richest anywhere.

For many moderate liberals in Mexico, the war represented the collapse of their faith in the neighboring country and its institutions. Yet, significantly, the "pure" liberals, the radicals, enamored of the doctrines of progress and remaining fierce enemies of the viceroyal and Catholic orders, continued believing in the virtue of the ideas and institutions on which the United States had been founded. Some recalled that the war was a decision of the administration of James K. Polk, which faced opposition from intellectuals such as William Prescott and Henry David Thoreau and from politicians like Abraham Lincoln.

The liberal Justo Sierra O'Reilly, a Yucatán native like Zavala and also a fervent federalist, saw the need to travel to the United States to offer the annexation of his state, which, it should be recalled, at that time encompassed the entire southeastern peninsula of Mexico. In exchange, Sierra O'Reilly sought protection and military support from the United States during the atrocious racial war that, around 1847, the Mayan Indians were waging against the white population of that remote state of the fragile Mexican republic. In his view, it was no longer a question of having to be *like* them; there was no choice but to *be* them. Yet the U.S. Senate never considered the proposal.

From 1858 to 1861, Mexico lived through the so-called War of the Reform, a civil conflict among the political elites that was little rooted in the masses. The civil war was nonetheless waged with merciless military conscription, with ill-gained funding, contributions of ever more questionable origin—provided largely by the high-level clergy—and strong ideological connotations. What was at stake for the liberals (in all their different shades) was the opportunity to finally break the church's stronghold on national affairs and the consequent possibility of definitively establishing a republican order based on the rule of law, civil liberties, and individual guarantees. These values were enshrined in the Constitution of 1857, which was expressly condemned by Pope Pius IX, who was among the first to fan the flames of the War of the

Reform. With the help of various European nations (France, Spain, and even England at times), the conservatives sought to preserve the monarchical and centralist tradition tied to the church, which was itself suffering in Europe the onslaught of secular ideologies, not only liberalism, but also anarchism, socialism, and a nascent materialist communism.

The liberals, who often conspired from New Orleans or New York, turned once again to the United States to garner support from *them* even if the costs were high. For the liberal faction, the economic and military support of the United States in crucial episodes of the cruel and costly war was a key factor in their triumph (1861). Under pressure to secure funding for their cause, two of the great liberal figures of Mexican history—Melchor Ocampo and Benito Juárez—opened negotiations for the 1859 McLane-Ocampo Treaty with the United States, which, although never ratified, would have granted the perpetual right of transit to U.S. military and commercial interests through several key ports in Mexico in exchange for a sum of money. Had the treaty been approved by the U.S. Congress, Mexico's relationship with its northern neighbor would have forever been transformed into one of a protectorate. As has often been the case in Mexican history, good fortune was on Mexico's side, and the civil war that broke out in the United States interrupted any such prospects. Misfortune, however, more common still in the Mexican experience, soon reared its ugly head, as Napoleon III seized the opportunity of a U.S. retreat into civil war to attempt a European reconquest of Mexico.

With the nearly parallel triumphs of the Union in the United States and the republicans in Mexico (1867), Mexican liberals were finally in a position to set in motion the representative, democratic, and federal republic that since 1824 had been little more than a dream. However, the U.S. government and a number of public opinion organizations showed scant interest in Mexico's democratic initiative. For their part, Mexico's liberals began to resent U.S. disdain; distrust of the *yanqui* struck a deep chord in Mexico and surfaced in the lyrics of the national anthem, which had been commissioned and premiered by General Santa Anna and his conservative faction in 1854. The Americans were, and would always be, the "strange enemy" who dared to "profane with his footstep" the national ground. Perhaps that is why liberal president Sebastián Lerdo de Tejada (1872–1876) phrased his judgment in the following terms: "between strength and weakness, the desert," the corollary being that it was necessary for Mexico to distance itself from the United States. It should be noted that when Lerdo was overthrown in an 1876 coup d'état by General Porfirio Díaz, he lived the rest of his days (until his death in 1889) as a refugee in New York.

Reality, however, put forth a different postulate from Lerdo's: "between strength and weakness, the railroad." On completing, at Mexico's expense, its first cycle of territorial expansion and having put down secession with the Union victory in the Civil War, the United States began a new stage. In 1883, Secretary of State James Blaine, in his learned manner, characterized this new period as one of "peaceful penetration" by showering "deposits of national vitality on other countries," which, in practical terms, implied immediate concessions in the matter of railroads and, sometime later, came to include oil, land, and mines.

Porfirio Díaz, who received recognition from the United States in 1878, two years after his coup d'état, did not hesitate to open Mexico's doors to foreign investment. He believed that only with foreign investment and within a framework of order and peace could the country hook its wagon onto the train of progress that the West had been riding for at least a century. Mexico had no other way to grow and modernize. Nonetheless, despite what legend claims, Díaz effectively protected Mexican interests through diplomatic and commercial diversification that looked to both oceans: his strategy invariably accorded priority to Europe (in particular to England, Germany, and France) but even reached out to Japan. The new stance under Díaz was: work with *them*, but with caution and at a distance.

In 1897, the most outstanding Mexican intellectual of the day, historian, orator, journalist, jurist, and educator Justo Sierra Méndez, like Zavala and his father, Sierra O'Reilly, before him, traveled to the United States. As a young man, he had heard President Benito Juárez argue, in keeping with pure liberal beliefs, that Mexico would benefit a great deal from Protestant immigration, so the people could learn habits of frugality and education and develop a positive work ethic. Yet Sierra Méndez had been gradually abandoning purely liberal doctrine, not only in order to embrace the evolutionist concept, but also because of his distrust (based in an embryonic nationalism, which brought him closer to the conservative position) of the U.S. cultural presence. Indeed, he considered himself a "conservative liberal."

In his travel diary, "En tierra yanquee," Sierra Méndez examined turn-of-the-century liberal thought regarding that Janus-like country, both imperial and democratic. In a meeting with some liberals of the Cuban exile community in New York, he discussed the Cuban situation, how the island was embroiled in a fruitless and extremely bloody war of independence and found itself torn between a desire to be free from Spain and the fear—so often anticipated by José Martí—of falling into the hands of the United States:

> What we have here is formidable greed; what we face here is the same cynical appetite that led the American Congress to annex Texas....the truth is that Cuba is a great business....the preparation will be complete during the course of 98; then the friendly reprimand to Spain will turn into harsh intimidation, and the colossus will raise its formidable voice to formulate an ultimatum....a war for Cuba that would begin to make of Cuba itself an antichresis, would be enormously popular here.[3]

Sierra Méndez's prophecy materialized in the exact time frame he had predicted. Later, standing in front of the U.S. Capitol, he suffered a sort of transfiguration:

> I belong to a weak people, who can forgive but should not forget the terrible injustice committed against it half a century ago; and, like my country, I would like to hold before the United States—an extraordinary product of nature and chance—the proud and quiet resignation that has allowed us to become dignified owners of our destinies. I do not deny my admiration, but I seek to explain it to myself, my head bows down but does not remain in that position; it then becomes erect, to see better.[4]

The ambivalence of this liberal figure was extreme: on the one hand, Sierra Méndez expressed clear distrust of that machine blinded by ambition and force; on the other hand, he expressed admiration for the "unrivalled task of the Capitol...saturated in constitutional law to the last corner....how can we not bow before her, we, poor nameless atoms, if history bows?"[5]

As in Sierra Méndez's consciousness, everything changed in Spanish America with Spain's defeat in 1898—that "splendid little war," as Secretary of State John Hay, one of the first great theoreticians of U.S. imperialism, called it. Mexican and Spanish American liberals like Justo Sierra Méndez stopped "bowing down." That was the breaking point in the history of Spanish American thinking: it became imperative to build a historical alternative and be radically different from *them*. The Latin Americans could not accept a freedom imposed by arms nor an independence converted into a protectorate. Cuba's situation had shed light on the significance of several episodes that took place in the nineteenth century: it was the latest chapter in a long history that included the annexation of Texas, the Mexican-American War, the filibuster tactics in Central America, and even certain explicit designs (for example, of Henry Cabot Lodge) to have the stars and stripes flying from the Rio Grande to Tierra del Fuego. After that collective awakening, it is only natural that liberal admiration of U.S. democracy receded into the background; what now prevailed was condemnation and fear of the next blow of the "big stick" in each corner of the Caribbean and the mainland. It was then that liberals in Latin America began to converge with the long-standing apprehensions of the conservatives with respect to the United States and a new region-wide nationalism, a Spanish Americanism formulated in explicitly anti-U.S. terms.

In the Path of Ariel

With the dawn of the twentieth century and in the aftermath of Spain's 1898 defeat, Uruguayan writer José Enrique Rodó published a seminal essay titled *Ariel*. In the context of the history of ideas in Spanish America (see chapter 2 by Tulio Halperin Donghi for an exquisite history of South American thinkers), Rodó's celebrated essay should be considered—along with prescient texts by Martí and Rubén Darío's poem "To Roosevelt"—as Latin America's complement to Spain's historical crisis of 1898. The very homeland of democracy and liberty, the world of progress and future promise, had knocked down the Spanish tree trunk and threatened its American branches. As a creative response, Rodó proposed that Spanish America construct a spiritual and aesthetic culture opposed to the "crude and savage" materialism of Caliban, which in *Ariel* represented the United States. Excel over *them*, he argued. His message struck a chord in the countries of Latin America, to the point of laying the groundwork for a movement called Arielismo, without which it is impossible to understand the region's twentieth-century intellectual history.

Spanish America's youth awoke to the twentieth century by reading *Ariel*. "In its luminous pages," wrote the Dominican Pedro Henríquez Ureña in 1904, "began, with glorious foresight, the vision of the Americas."[6] Sometime later, in the thriving state of Nuevo León, Governor Bernardo Reyes commissioned the first Mexican edition of Rodó's book, and similar editions appeared throughout Latin America. The work of José Vasconcelos in the 1920s, in particular *La raza cósmica*—a prophecy of Latin America as a melting pot of races and cultures—can be considered a variation on Rodó's theme. All of these writers recognized the Bolivarian echo in Arielismo, the ideal of a nation of nations united by "lofty values of the spirit." In sum, the Arielismo they preached was the first alternative ideology developed in Latin America in response to (i.e., against) classical liberalism and its direct substitutes (positivism and evolutionism). Over time, it became an antecedent or a complement (near or remote, tacit or open) of the great and impassioned *isms* of the twentieth century in Latin America: anarchism, socialism, indigenism, nationalism, *iberoamericanismo*, Hispanicism, populism, fascism, communism.

And while those ideological ferments ripened their explosive reactionary or revolutionary content, the United States appeared indifferent or blind to the effect of its international conduct on the countries of the Americas. Although, to be fair, just as in 1847, the dawn of the twentieth century did witness the rise of internal voices, among them Andrew Carnegie and Mark Twain, who cautioned against the moral cost of such policies. In any event, that moment in history witnessed the birth of a regional common voice: against the United States.

Porfirio Díaz handled the U.S.–Mexico relationship with great care, knowing that a serious disagreement could easily lead to a new invasion. But the last president who was justified in fearing a war with the United States was Plutarco Elías Calles in 1927. Yet, in the face of the imperial escalation of President Theodore Roosevelt (1901–1908), alarm spread rapidly, as revealed by an entry in the diary of Mexican writer Federico Gamboa, at the time an official at the Mexican embassy in Washington. It was made on June 17, 1904, when Gamboa received a copy of a circular instructing the embassies, legations, and consulates of the United States to use the term "America" as a synonym for "United States": "[t]he beginning of the end! Now it is the plundering of a name that belongs to all of us equally. Tomorrow it will be the plundering of the earth!"[7] This continent-wide insult was compounded with each island-hopping war undertaken by the U.S. Marines in the first two decades of the twentieth century. That was perhaps when Porfirio Díaz pronounced the famous expression attributed to him: "poor Mexico, so far from God and so close to the United States."

In exile in Paris, where the revolution that broke out against him in 1910 had confined him, Díaz lived to confirm his fears. A distant but decisive event—tragically set in motion by the United States—hammered home Mexico's resentment toward its northern neighbor: the 1913 coup d'état against the legitimate president, Francisco I. Madero, perhaps the purest liberal democrat in Latin American history, known in his time as "the apostle of democracy." Henry Lane Wilson, then

U.S. ambassador to Mexico, had plotted President Madero's assassination. Though scarcely remembered by his own country, Mexican textbook writers will not forget Wilson's role in this episode of Mexico's history.

One week after Ambassador Wilson ushered General Victoriano Huerta to power, Woodrow Wilson entered the White House. Appalled by Madero's murder, President Wilson declared that he would not recognize a "government of butchers," but his good intentions did not go very far. It should be noted, however, that President Wilson proved to be patient and prudent in his dealings with Mexico. Had he listened to the oil companies, which were threatened by the new nationalist legislation, he would have invaded Mexico. He refused to do so, except during two brief episodes, when the U.S. Marines landed in Veracruz (1914) and during the "punitive expedition" against Pancho Villa commanded by John J. Pershing (1916–1917).

Convinced that a naval blockade would precipitate the fall of the "butcher" and would improve the position of the United States as guardian in the process of democratizing the country, Wilson ordered the temporary occupation of Veracruz. The maneuver, which included the capture of a German weapons shipment to Huerta's federal army, lasted just over five months and precipitated the fall of Huerta, but in historical terms it was a disaster. It provoked the generalized ire not only of the local population (which put up a tenacious defense) but of the entire country, including the constitutionalist forces, who were purportedly supported by the U.S. president. By that point, Mexicans could no longer distinguish between Wilson the good guy and Wilson the bad guy. Emiliano Zapata, the prototype of a revolutionary leader, detested Venustiano Carranza, but when it came to the *gringos*, they all agreed: "it doesn't matter whether they send millions of soldiers," said Eufemio, Zapata's brother, "we will fight one against two hundred.... We don't have weapons or ammunition, but we have chests to receive bullets." With those antecedents, it is understandable that the 1917 Constitution (still in force) adopted nationalism as the state's ideology, as its secular faith.

The liberal democratic alternative had been blocked for Mexico. Like a comet, it would take another 90 years to present itself anew. Now, nationalism reigned, in the form of legislation reclaiming lands, industries, and natural resources. The legislation nearly caused President Coolidge to declare war on "Soviet Mexico" in 1927, and President Calles threatened to blow up the oil wells. That year, the famous liberal journalist Walter Lippmann wrote that what ignorant people called

"Bolshevism" in the Latin American countries was simply nationalism and that nothing would endanger North American security more than "the realization in Latin America that the United States had adopted a policy, conceived in the spirit of Metternich, which would attempt to guarantee vested rights against social progress as the Latin peoples conceive it."[8]

Heeding Lippmann's advice, the United States attempted a new diplomacy in Mexico based on prudence, collaboration, and understanding. Also in 1927, the United States sent Ambassador Dwight D. Morrow, who worked to put Mexican public finances in order, became a friend and protector of the great Mexican muralists, among them Diego Rivera, and went so far as to purchase a home in Cuernavaca. His successor, Josephus Daniels, had been secretary of the navy during the occupation of Veracruz (the assistant secretary at that time was Franklin D. Roosevelt), and perhaps that is why he understood Mexican sensibilities. Immersed like Morrow in the Mexican culture—to the extreme of dressing like a *charro*—the "ambassador in shirtsleeves" implemented the Good Neighbor policy, which withstood difficult tests such as the expropriation of oil interests in 1938. Thanks to this new diplomacy (and in opposition to a broad sector of the Mexican middle class that clearly had sympathies with Adolf Hitler), the Mexican government declared war on the Axis in 1942. In fact, the entire region (except Argentina) experienced an interlude of pan-American solidarity marked by economic growth and creative cultural output (the Mexican film industry, for example, had its golden age). It was a fleeting moment together with *them*.

Yet, with the arrival of the Cold War, the Latin American governments (including Mexico's) again came to feel—as Lippmann had warned—that the United States was subordinating its diplomacy to the commercial interests of big business. And although these governments aligned themselves diplomatically with the United States, a new and more radical wave of anti-Yankeeism—clothed now in extreme revolutionary doctrine (of Marxist or Maoist inspiration)—began to rear its head in the region.

On a Theme by Darío

There is enough history to allow for sufficient perspective on events in the region. On the whole, it seems clear that the United States made at least three mistakes with respect to Latin America that were unpardonable. The first was to ignore (in the sense of disregarding, neglecting, disdaining) the history, traditions, languages, art, religion—in short, the identity—of Spanish America. At its core, the U.S. attitude was characterized by an irresponsible indifference (not without some racism) regarding the humiliation provoked by its physical, economic, political, and especially military presence in these lands. In the words of José Martí, "The disdain of our formidable neighbor, who does not know it, is the greatest danger to Our America."[9] Significantly, Theodore Roosevelt (who gained notoriety with the Spanish-American War in Cuba) never mentioned Martí in his voluminous writings, which is analogous to not mentioning George Washington when referring to the independence of the United States. Did Roosevelt ever read the poem that Rubén Darío dedicated to him in 1904? He should have, for it encapsulated how Latin America perceived the United States as an insensitive and blind power, as the "future invader of the naive America that has Indian blood, that still prays to Jesus Christ, and still speaks Spanish."[10] That ignorance was—and, unfortunately, continues to be—a key aspect of the anti-U.S. sentiment in these countries. In one of his last stanzas, Darío prophesied: "Be careful. Long live Spanish America! A thousand cubs of the Spanish lion are roaming free."[11] Years after the poem was written, those "cubs" came to life, grew up, and were called Augusto César Sandino, Che Guevara, Fidel Castro.

The second mistake was almost a sin: in the eyes of its Latin American democratic sympathizers, the United States forgot and even betrayed its own democratic principles during its first imperial incursions, or "splendid little wars" as Secretary of State John Hay called them. In his poem to Roosevelt, Darío characterized the United States as "one part Washington, four parts Nimrod."[12] The image would very soon be played out in Mexico, with the assassination of Madero. This was a cruel paradox: the greatest democracy of the Americas overthrew the first democratic leader of Mexico. It would not be the only case, but it was the first one. The U.S. government not only tossed away its democratic ideals, it supported several dictators. Franklin Roosevelt purportedly remarked in reference to Nicaraguan dictator Anastasio Somoza that he "may be a son of a bitch, but he is our son of a bitch." Another common practice was to view Latin American liberals with contempt. The Cuban patriots, who thought they enjoyed U.S. support for their country's independence, were displaced from the outset and then forced to accept protectorate status for their nation. Latin American liberals, like many Marxists in 1989, were ultimately orphaned. A few solitary ones continued to inhabit a very narrow liberal ground, but the majority embraced a series of ideologies whose common denominator was their aversion for liberal democracy, which the United States itself had discredited: chauvinism, fascism, statism, populism, militarism, Marxism.

Darío also wrote about the United States, "A wealthy country, joining the cult of Mammon to the cult of Hercules."[13] In the United States, the subordination of diplomacy to big business (the oil and sugar sectors, for example) was seen as normal, but to many countries and cultures it was, understandably, interpreted as repugnant greed. The presence of the Marines as strike breakers in the Caribbean became engraved in the public's mind as a mythological affront. In Gabriel García Márquez's imaginary Macondo, the repression of the strike against the United Fruit Company in 1928 took on the dimension, not entirely off-base, of a biblical plague. Indeed, Franklin D. Roosevelt's "Good Neighbor" team included cabinet secretaries with sugar interests in Cuba.

The net result was tragically negative, even for loyal friends of the United States. A disenchanted Mexican liberal, Daniel Cosío Villegas, foretold what would happen in the second half of the twentieth century, first in Cuba and later throughout the region:

> Latin America will boil with discontent and dare all. Carried away by absolute despair and blazing hatred, its nations, seemingly abject in their submission, will be capable of anything: of sheltering and encouraging the adversaries of the United States, of themselves becoming the fiercest enemies imaginable. And then there will be no way to subdue them, or even frighten them.[14]

This passage anticipated the arrival of Fidel Castro and Hugo Chávez in the war against *them*.

In 1959, nearly six decades after the first edition of *Ariel* was published, a language and literature teacher by the name of Rosario María Gutiérrez Eskildsen preached to her middle-school students in Mexico City two virtually religious commandments. First, they must read Darío's poem "To Roosevelt" and, second, read Rodó's *Ariel*. She famously characterized them as "gospel" of "Our America." That same year, Fidel Castro took power. Soon thereafter, in a reversal of the war of 1898, Cuba aligned itself with the Soviet Union and adopted the communist system. Yet, in the mind of his companion in arms, Ernesto "Che" Guevara, and increasingly in Castro's own, resonated an issue more decisive than dialectical materialism: the Latin American idealism of *Ariel*. That collective nationalism—so gracefully expressed in Darío's poem—bore its best fruits in the areas of literature and art, but in the spheres of politics and economics, it would be defined by an almost ontological rejection, purely negative, paralyzing, and sterile, of Nimrod, of Mammon, of the Caliban of the north.

Distant Reconciliation: Toward a New Era as Neighbors and Partners

Beginning in 1959, Mexico and the United States embarked on a protracted period of distant reconciliation. In a subtle diplomatic role, Mexico served for several decades as a communications bridge (and security and buffer zone) between Cuba and the United States. Thanks to that delicate and difficult diplomacy, not always understood by the U.S. or Mexican right wings, Mexico was able to make it through the Cold War, from beginning to end, without suffering the continental plagues of guerrillas financed and trained by the Cubans. Given that the United States put years of concern and billions of dollars into fighting the guerrilla movements in Central America, one can imagine the alarm that similar movements in Mexico would have caused.

However, despite such judicious mediation, the United States maintained a distant relationship with Mexico, skillfully depicted in a book by journalist Alan Riding entitled, precisely, *Distant Neighbors*.[15] Despite being united by geography, migratory flows, and significant trade, the two neighbors lived at a distance from one another, separated by an immense development gap and an even greater divide of a mutual lack of understanding. Although, in the 1980s, Mexico suddenly and timidly began to change its economic policies, reducing its tariffs and partially opening up to international trade, signs of real change did not arrive until the fall of the Berlin Wall. It was this historical opportunity that both countries were able to read: Mexico and the United States could, for mutual benefit, become closer trading partners.

The Mexican administration of Carlos Salinas de Gortari (1988–1994) demonstrated courage and audacity by proposing to Mexican society a pact with the United States. It is true that ill will toward the United States was always less evident in Mexico than in the Caribbean and the former "banana republics," where the U.S. presence had been more permanent and its political and military dominion much more direct. Cosío Villegas is known to have heard a Cuban journalist say in the 1920s that hatred of the *yankee* was to be the religion of the Cubans, and the expression always resonated in the conscience of that historian and prophet, who was intrigued by the gap between the United States and Latin America.

Yet Cosío Villegas himself noted that the Mexican case was different. Perhaps because more time had passed since the invasion of 1847. Or because, after all, that ill-fated war—as Cosío Villegas called it—had reduced Mexico's historical effort to consolidate as a nation to manageable limits. Perhaps because Mexico (a larger, more established, better endowed nation than the Central American countries) was able to better defend itself from the United States in the diplomatic arena. Or perhaps because sharing such a long and porous border has in fact created a binational culture. For these and other reasons, average Mexicans, according to Cosío Villegas, did not feel any particular animosity toward the *gringos*, even if it cannot be said that they liked them. That may be why, combined with the leadership displayed by the Salinas administration, the North American Free Trade Agreement (NAFTA) was officially approved and accepted by society at large.

As the twentieth century drew to a close, Mexicans were engaged in heated debate about the advantages and disadvantages of the NAFTA. But the consensus tended to be favorable, not only because of the agreement's tangible modernization benefits in industry and agriculture, but also because of its unexpected political effects. By relieving the state of many of its long-standing, inefficient, and onerous responsibilities in managing the economy, the NAFTA has contributed decisively to the process of political liberalization. The advent of democracy was just a question of time, but making that transition possible required from President Ernesto Zedillo (1994–2000) even greater courage than his predecessor needed to push the NAFTA through. In a matter of months, Zedillo consolidated the Federal Electoral Institute, which finally achieved complete autonomy and freed itself from meddling by the regime in power. Zedillo also gave full independence and autonomy to the judiciary; put in place the conditions for a true separation of powers; welcomed an opposition Congress after the midterm elections; and, in July 2000, crowned a surprisingly peaceful, orderly, and clean democratic transition with the triumph of opposition presidential candidate Vicente Fox. Mexico entered the new century under the most auspicious circumstances and, for the first time in its history, constituted an open society, both economically and politically, a liberal democracy, a U.S. neighbor of equal standing.

It was no accident that President George W. Bush invited President Fox to the White House on September 6, 2001. During the impressive state visit that week (applauded almost unanimously in Congress and the press), Bush proclaimed that the top issue on his agenda was to definitively consolidate the relationship with Mexico, the best friend of the United States. Unfortunately for Mexico, the United States, and the world, history had—as is often the case—unimaginable surprises on the horizon. Five days after fireworks were set off over the Potomac to honor Mexico, terrorists set fire to the Twin Towers, the Pentagon, and the twenty-first century.

Framing the Relationship

In an unpardonable omission—as New York, Washington, and the entire United States debated how to confront the September 11, 2001, tragedy—the Fox administration made no gesture of sympathy toward its "best friend." Yet it is doubtful that any gesture would have modified the new priorities of the United States. Sometime later, disagreement over the Iraq war chilled diplomatic ties even further. Today, however, those wounds appear to have healed. Mexico and the United States are active partners, if somewhat distant again; but, as always, real forces—economic, demographic—work against distance. Bilateral ties have never been closer nor as interconnected as they are today. In the midst of uncertainty regarding the new world order, one thing remains clear: so long as a meteorite doesn't come down on the Rio Grande, the United States will continue to be the most powerful country on the planet, and Mexico will continue to be its expectant and anxious neighbor. For that dual reason, Mexico must continue to think about how to frame its relationship with the United States.

This last statement is worth examining carefully. First and foremost, it is a matter of "thinking," a challenging endeavor when emotions are overflowing. At stake, among many other things, is not a problem of academic interest, but the fate of 24 million Mexicans who live "on the other side" (9 million of them born in Mexico) and of 5 million households that depend on their multimillion-dollar remittances. Almost every one of the 2,443 municipalities and counties that make up Mexico has a record of individuals who have emigrated. One of every three persons from the state of Zacatecas and one of every six from the state of Jalisco live in the United States today. It is one of the most impressive waves of migration in history. In the economic sphere, the basic figures describing the bilateral ties are well known: 90 percent of Mexico's trade, 90 percent of tourism, and 70 percent of foreign investment comes from the United States. But, in Mexico, these numbers are quickly glossed over, erasing the fact that they represent, once again, the activities of millions of persons whose lives depend on the consolidation and expansion of that relationship, on a more cordial and fluid interaction—or something close to that.

Although it is customary to speak of *a* relationship, it would be more appropriate to speak of relationships, because the bilateral ties between the two countries form a highly complex structure that requires sophisticated analysis. There are political and diplomatic relations, economic and business relations, social and demographic relations, and more. Each category, in turn, has any number of subdivisions. The greatest mistake is to identify the United States with the specific administration occupying the White House—i.e., that Bush is today what Reagan or Nixon were yesterday, and all of them are a diabolical Hegelian embodiment called "the United States" or, more colloquially, the *gringos*. This is not only a gross oversimplification, but also a falsehood. The Mexican projects onto them the internalized conception of Mexico's old political system, a realm where all things human and all things divine began and ended on the desk of *el señor presidente*. Mexico then, as now, was much more than a mere biography of power, yet the bad habit of transferring that collective subordination to the international arena has remained, with disastrous results, because in the United States things do not work that way. The United States, as should be obvious, is not a historical pipe dream or a homogeneous aggregate: it is a democracy. And it has been a democracy for more than two centuries.

But the United States is also an empire. In the words of Octavio Paz:

> Standing bewildered in the face of its dual historical nature, the United States does not know which way to turn today. The dilemma is a fateful one. If it chooses an imperial destiny, it will cease to be a democracy and will thereby lose its reason for being as a nation. But how to renounce power without being immediately destroyed by its rival, the Russian Empire?[16]

Paz wrote these lines in 1984, without suspecting that, just a few years later, the Soviet Union would, in an unexpected implosion of modern times, resolve the dilemma on its own. But with that historical surprise came another, perhaps greater one: the militant return of Islam. With the war in Iraq, the United States appears to have made a choice regarding the crossroads noted by Paz when it chose an imperial destiny in the Middle East, which could well lead it to "lose its reason for being as a nation."

On the other hand, the same arguments about empire are applicable, at least potentially, to Islamic fundamentalism, an implacable and unprecedented international power whose differences with the United States (and the West as a whole) are not only geopolitical and ideological, but religious and, therefore, perhaps irreconcilable. And to further complicate the horizon, to make it even more uncertain, history has put forward yet another novelty: the modern rise of the very ancient Chinese dragon. At this juncture, several questions surface. Will the United States ultimately fail in its aim of democratizing the Middle East by force? What, at the end of the day, will the U.S. position be if China continues its irresistible commercial advance and eventually turns into an overwhelming military force?

While history or chance discover the answers to these serious issues, what should Mexico's policy be? One thing is clear: Mexico will continue to coexist with the United States, with all of its contradictions. Therefore, Mexico must ask not only what its relationship with the United States is like, but also how it would like it to be in the future. One example: in the two most sensitive areas of the relationship—immigration and trade—what can or should become of that itinerant part of Mexico that has established itself in the United States? What will its influence be in domestic politics, both in Mexico and in the United States? And if the benefits of the NAFTA are diminished as other countries establish similar agreements or better apply their comparative advantages—the huge difference in labor costs in the case of China, for example—will Mexico persist down the road opened up by the NAFTA? Will Mexico finally modernize its labor legislation and its infrastructure and truly strengthen the rule of law and its political institutions? Or will it succumb to its old defensive and autarchic instincts?

The border between Mexico and the United States is a demarcation line; it should not be a wall: in history there have always been other neighboring countries with more conflictive relationships. Yet, it is true that the U.S.–Mexico boundary is not characterized by harmony. It is a fluid neighborhood, a bridge crossed like no other on the planet, a bridge where goods and services are traded and offered, where values, frustrations, hopes, and, especially, people travel across and are transformed, day in and day out. Historical affronts aside, today that famous expression attributed to Porfirio Díaz seems more out of place than ever. Mexico's poverty, as vast as it is, is not due to its proximity with the United States. The opposite seems true: Mexico's poverty is mitigated in large part thanks to, and not in spite of, its proximity to the United States. In any event, few issues are more urgent for Mexico than deciding, once and for all, and without hesitation, what kind of long-term relationship it wishes, it should, and it can establish with the United States.

A Cultural Proposal

In Mexico, past is present. The injuries and affronts are real, and their memory still weighs heavily on daily life. It is what Hindus call karma. Yet it is an ideological weight delimited to the political and intellectual middle classes, and it has to do, above all, with only half of the story. The other half of the story, which many professional anti-Americans disregard, is in Mexico's own responsibility for its dreadful problems and in the country's undeniable historical errors; its authoritarian, demagogic, and corrupt politicians; its inefficient economy; its costly and bureaucratized educational system; its self-complacent and fanaticized universities. Blaming the big bad wolf—the United States—for Mexico's ills is casting a smokescreen over reality. And there is still another part of the story—which, out of small-mindness, is rarely mentioned—which entails weighing the real economic benefits (investments, industries, credits, imports, technology, information, equipment, jobs) that Mexico has obtained and continues to obtain as a result of its proximity to the United States.

"Our hatred toward the United States may be sickness too. After all, I'm a Mexican for something," says a character in Carlos Fuentes' book *Where the Air Is Clear*.[17] Fuentes should have delimited his assertion, referring not to all Mexicans, but to that sector of the middle class (particularly its politicians, ideologues, and intellectuals) for whom the conviction that nothing good can be expected of Mexico's northern neighbor became, some time ago, a truism. For that very reason, the character is correct when he speaks of sickness—that sickness is called schizophrenia. Only a schizophrenic who is not in touch with reality can remain stuck on the affronts of the past and make up the notion that the border between Mexico and the United States has been the most conflictive in history. It suffices to review the maps of Europe, the Middle East, or Asia to note how untrue that is.

It is true that the Rio Grande separates the two countries with what may be an unprecedented asymmetry, but to truly understand its nature, this asymmetry must be approached from different perspectives. The Mexican who emigrates does not see the border as a scar, but rather as an opportunity for a better life which, unfortunately, he cannot hope to pursue in his own country. That Mexican is not guided by the traumas, justified or not, provoked by history, and in his day-to-day life he has no use or time for myths. Many Mexicans who are not ideologically influenced think the same way: the avocado exporter, the elderly *campesino* who awaits the remittances from his children, the woman who fears that if the *maquiladoras* are shut down she will lose her job, the globalized entrepreneurs. None of them agree with the persistent anti-U.S. sentiment embraced by the intellectual and political middle class, which rants and raves against the *gringos* at every opportunity, but then goes to the universities, cities, and malls of *gringolandia*. Interestingly, the guru of that sector in Mexico is none other than Noam Chomsky, an irascible *gringo*.

What, then, should Mexico do? Overcome the schizophrenia and get a grip on the complex reality of U.S.–Mexico relations. Move forward on the project of smart convergence. Not *be* them, but be *with* them while being ourselves. Learn to lobby the U.S. government at the state and federal levels. Use the growing Hispanic influence in the press and the media. Having made the transition to democracy, Mexico is obligated to reformulate its nationalism in positive terms, like many exporters and globalized companies do.

One example of negative nationalism will suffice: despite having vast natural gas deposits to satisfy its domestic demand and export needs, Mexico imports gas at the rate of $2 billion annually. The reason: "to defend ourselves from foreign investors, to shore up our nationalism." Duly regulated by a modern fiscal regime, those investors would not properly be owners but concessionaires, and their investments, projects, and technology would be an incentive to the national economy. Yet the sector remains closed to foreign investment. In the name of sacrosanct nationalism, natural gas is sleeping in the subsoil, like the white-elephant steel plants sleep in Moscow. Or it is lost in the burners. In the meantime, who pays those millions? It is time to recognize that nationalism, even if it has given the country political cohesion, has turned out to be very expensive.

What should the United States do? In the political and diplomatic realm, the U.S.–Mexico relationship has been bumpy. In the economic arena, convergence continues to move forward. But there is one aspect of the relationship in which Americans have been particularly sensitive, attentive, and generous, without realizing it: culture. In the twentieth century, hundreds of films using Mexican themes were produced in the United States. Although many relied on stereotyping, others demonstrated a genuine effort to understand the social reality and history of

Mexico; some of them were true works of art. Many travelers drawn by the Mexican Revolution, in which they often saw reflected their own anarchistic or socialist ideals, visited Mexico and sometimes became genuinely involved in Mexican life, with all of its glories and miseries. For many decades, traveling through its rural areas and cities, and often settling in them, travelers have left behind rich testimonies through their stories, novels, news articles, essays, photographs, oil paintings, poems, local histories, anthropological essays, archaeological studies, and musical works.

The list of U.S. authors who have written serious works on Mexico is impressive, including John Reed, Hart Crane, Jack London, Katherine Ann Porter, John Dos Passos, Bruno Traven, Wallace Stevens, John Steinbeck, Tennessee Williams, Kenneth Rexroth, William Carlos Williams, Robert Lowell, Allen Ginsberg, Jack Kerouac, and many, many more. From William Prescott on, each period of Mexican history has had a prominent historian in the United States. In literary genealogy, the work of women has been especially sensitive, nuanced, and tender, as displayed some decades back by the novel *Stones for Ibarra* by Harriet Doerr. The U.S. film industry has also produced a treasure of hundreds of works on Mexico—through the work of actors, directors, photographers, scriptwriters—that deserve to be rediscovered and recirculated. Many of those works—films, novels, poems, travel diaries, epistolaries, history books—have been forgotten in the United States and in Mexico.

It would be of extraordinary benefit to explore the possibility of promoting documentary and publishing projects geared toward recovering the great history of cultural warmth between the United States and its Latin American neighbors, as it no doubt echoes throughout the region, especially in Cuba with Ernest Hemingway. The reading public and refined television audience in the United States would be surprised by that enormous cultural wealth. There are many U.S. works and authors that have been marked by Mexico, just as many U.S. works and authors have left their mark on Mexico. And to complete the project as a reciprocal effort, it would be worthwhile to republish the works and testimonies, no less rich, of the Mexican and Latin American artists and writers who, over two centuries, lived temporarily or permanently in the United States. They would offer the U.S. public a remarkable mirror image.

We should get to know one another before we condemn one another. Anglo Americans have made some progress in this terrain (the serious press covers Latin America better than 10 or 20 years ago), but the average American's ignorance of our countries continues to be abysmal. As for Latin America, Daniel Cosío Villegas' thoughts in 1968, referring to the Mexican, continue to apply, but to the whole region:

> One of the disconcerting traits of the Mexican . . . is his Olympic disdain for the United States: the country fills him with insults, he blames all his ills on it, he is overjoyed by its failures, and he yearns for its disappearance from this earth; but, sure enough, he has never attempted to study the country or to understand it. The Mexican has prejudices but no judgment, that is, opinions based on research and reflection.[18]

It was Cosío Villegas himself who first noted that the solution was to work toward mutual understanding: "[r]esearching current issues or the history of the other country is perhaps the best path toward greater mutual understanding."[19] He was right then, as now: there is an urgent need for projects that foster mutual understanding. The academic, literary, and intellectual bibliography concerning relations between the two countries is vast indeed, but it is not incorporated into the live debate. Introducing it to the public at large would benefit the bilateral relationship more than all of the presidential summit meetings or the arduous interparliamentary meetings put together. The national craze for surveys, as well as press and media coverage, should encourage such inquiry. To cite just one example: we need to know (by strata, regions, professions, ages, sex) what Mexicans think of Americans, and vice versa, regarding their respective histories, cultures, political positions, and values.

Mutual understanding through culture would be a natural complement to the integration that is de facto taking place, due to the presence of 35 million "Hispanics" throughout the United States. It may seem utopian, but it is not. It can be done with creativity and a practical sense: *they*, the United States, could be looking at *us*, Mexico. Though it seems utopian, for Mexico—and by extension for the rest of Latin America—it would be a lesson and the best antidote to anti-American sentiment. For the United States, it would be a revelation: the evidence that Americans can, if they set out to do so, understand the world and contribute enormously to making it more inhabitable.

Notes

1. Lorenzo de Zavala, *Journey to the United States of North America*, translated by Wallace Woolsey, edited by John-Michael Rivera (Houston, TX: Arte Público Press, 2005), pp. 2–3.

2. Ibid., p. 3.
3. Justo Sierra Méndez, "En tierra yanquee," in *Obras completas del maestro Justo Sierra*, vol. 6, edited by José Luis Martínez (Mexico City: Universidad Nacional Autónoma de México, 1948), p. 107. Editor's translation.
4. Ibid., p. 119. Editor's translation.
5. Ibid., p. 120. Editor's translation.
6. Pedro Henríquez Ureña, *Selección de Ensayos*, edited by José Rodríguez Feo (Havana: Casa de las Américas, 1965), p. 22.
7. Federico Gamboa, *Diario de Federico Gamboa (1892–1939)*, edited by José Emilio Pacheco (Mexico City: Siglo XXI, 1977), p. 117.
8. Ronald Steel, *Walter Lippmann and the American Century* (Boston: Little, Brown, 1980), p. 238.
9. José Martí, "Nuestra América," essay published in the *New York Illustrated Magazine* (January 10, 1891) and in the Mexican newspaper *El Partido Liberal* (January 30, 1891).
10. Rubén Darío, "To Roosevelt," in Darío, *Cantos de vida y esperanza: Los cisnes y otros poemas* (Madrid: Tipografía de la Revista de Archivos, Bibliotecas y Museos, 1905), p. 640.
11. Ibid.
12. Ibid. Nimrod is the legendary hunter of Genesis, the pagan king who dared to kill, before God, his creatures. Genesis 10:8–10.
13. Darío, "To Roosevelt."
14. Daniel Cosío Villegas, *Problemas de América: Rusia, Estados Unidos y la América Latina* (Mexico City: El Colegio Nacional, 1997), p. 77.
15. Alan Riding, *Distant Neighbors: A Portrait of the Mexicans* (New York: Knopf, 1985).
16. Octavio Paz, *One Earth, Four or Five Worlds: Reflections on Contemporary History*, translated by Helen R. Lane (New York: Harcourt Brace Jovanovich, 1985), p. 34.
17. Carlos Fuentes, *Where the Air Is Clear* (Champaign, IL: Dalkey Archive Press, 2004), p. 218.
18. Cosío Villegas, *Problemas de América*, p. 365. Editor's translation.
19. Ibid. Editor's translation.

4

Explaining Latin America's Lagging Development in the Second Half of the Twentieth Century

Growth Strategies, Inequality, and Economic Crises

JORGE I. DOMÍNGUEZ

W HAT A SHAME that the Latin American twentieth century was so short! The gap in the pace of economic growth between Latin America and the United States in terms of per capita gross domestic product (GDP) began in the seventeenth century, widened in the eighteenth century, and became extreme in the nineteenth century. In particular, the half century following independence in Latin America was, in these terms, disastrous for Mexico and bad for Central and South America. The "more-or-less twentieth century" that I evoke began with the consolidation of the Latin American states around 1870 and lasted approximately until the 1970s. From 1870 to 1950, growth of per capita GDP in Latin America was similar to or just a bit less than in the United States. From 1950 until the 1970s, the rate of growth of per capita GDP in Latin America was slightly greater than that of the

United States, but it has dropped off sharply once again since then.[1] The period between 1870 and 1970 was the only time when economic growth in Latin America was good—albeit still insufficient.

That short-lived similarity in the rate of per capita growth between the United States and Latin America implies that the relative difference between them was more or less constant over that time. According to John Coatsworth and Alan Taylor, since 1900, per capita GDP in Latin America has almost invariably been, and is to this day, just over one-fourth that of the United States.[2] As of 1950, the gap between the United States and the largest countries of Latin America, as one would expect from Coatsworth's observation, also experienced little change. There was generalized growth of per capita GDP of the Latin American countries from 1950 to 2000, but at a pace that was not sufficient to close the gap with the United States. As the information in table 4.1 indicates, Brazil has closed the gap to some extent, Colombia and Chile have fallen back a bit, and Mexico remains almost unchanged in terms of its gap with the United States. One notable exception is Argentina, which suffered a comparative collapse from 1950 to 2000 (see table 4.1). There are two other exceptions (not included in table 4.1) where per capita GDP declined not only in relative terms, but also in absolute terms, compared to the United States: Nicaragua and Haiti. Nicaragua's per capita GDP as compared to the United States fell from 17 percent to 6 percent during those years, while Haiti's dropped from 11 percent to 3 percent.

The difficulty facing Latin American economic growth is more striking when one takes note of the experiences of some countries from outside the region. As is also indicated in table 4.1, South Korea and Taiwan

TABLE 4.1 Per Capita Gross Domestic Product (GDP) of Some Countries as a Proportion of per Capita GDP of the United States

	1950	2000
Argentina	52	30
Brazil	17	20
Chile	40	35
Colombia	23	18
Mexico	25	26
South Korea	8	51
Taiwan	10	59

Source: Calculations used data from Angus Maddison, *The World Economy: Historical Statistics* (London: Development Centre, OECD, 2003), tables 2c, 4c, and 5c.

closed a good part of their welfare gap with the United States while they opened up a new gap with Latin America. In 1950, South Korea's per capita GDP was one-third of Mexico's, while in 2000 it was two times that of Mexico's. In 1950, Taiwan's per capita GDP was less than one-fifth of Argentina's, while in 2000 it was twice that of Argentina.

There is, nonetheless, a second gap between the United States and Latin America, and between countries of the Americas and some East Asian countries. The Latin American countries are characterized by inequalities in income distribution that are much more extreme than in the United States. Table 4.2 presents information on the magnitude of this second gap, i.e., an indicator of income inequality of several countries as a proportion of the indicator of income inequality in the United States. Table 4.2 indicates the very high inequality in the major Latin American countries and the much lesser inequality that prevails in Japan and South Korea, in both cases also as compared to the United States.

Just as the gap in economic growth between Latin America and the United States has been relatively constant over time, so too has income inequality in Latin America as compared to the United States. For example, in 1956–1957, income inequality in Mexico was 136 percent that of the United States, almost identical to what it would be more than 40 years later. In addition, the lack of variation in income distribution can also be observed by comparing each country with its own history. For example, Mexico's inequality index (Gini coefficient) was 54.0 in the mid-1950s and 54.6 in 2000.[3] According to Werner Baer, the inequality index in Brazil in 1981—the last year of its economic "miracle"—was 57.9; then, as a result of the economic crisis that erupted in 1982–1983, it rose to 59.7, only slightly dropping down to 59.1 in 1998.[4] In other words, income distribution, both within countries over time and as compared to the United States, has been relatively steady despite economic crises, changes in macroeconomic models, and the resulting adjustments in economic policy.

TABLE 4.2   Income Inequality in Some Countries as a Percentage of Income Inequality in the United States, c. 2000

Argentina	Brazil	Chile	Colombia	Japan	Mexico	South Korea
128	145	140	141	61	134	77

Notes: Measurement by the indicator of income inequality known as the Gini coefficient. United States = 100.
Source: Calculations based on data from World Bank, *World Development Indicators 2004* (Washington, DC: World Bank, 2004), table 2.7.

Both gaps with the United States originated before the period covered in this chapter, i.e., they appeared long before 1950. They arose from factors particular to the colonial period and especially in the half century after the wars of independence. Other chapters in this volume address the origins of these gaps and discuss possible explanations. The combination of both gaps, however, implies that a large part of the Latin American population has suffered and continues to suffer the dual blow of insufficient economic growth and major limitations on personal income. In short, many Latin Americans remain in poverty while the countries in which they live are not growing fast enough to generate prosperity for all of society.

This chapter analyzes two distinct and more recent moments in Latin American economic history: growth during the 1950s and 1960s, and crises since then, with reminders of the major variations among countries during this half century. It underscores the importance of the policies that several Latin American governments adopted, compared to others they could have adopted or that were adopted in other countries. All of the arguments set forth coincide on one important factor: the events that transpired could have been avoided. There is no genetic or cultural ill that impedes Latin American economic development. There are no structural factors that always and inevitably resist and impede fundamental changes in development policy.

In particular, this chapter emphasizes the following international comparative aspects:

- the general relationship between the domestic economy and the international economy
- specific policies with respect to international trade and the exchange rate
- neglect of economic inequality and poverty
- insufficient investment in human resources
- institutional instability and lack of juridical security

The general arguments made are the following:

1. The domestic economies that were able to insert themselves into the international economy have experienced swifter economic growth, both during the great international expansion of the half century preceding World War I and in recent decades, as exemplified by the countries of East Asia.
2. Those countries that adopted trade and monetary policies designed to stimulate trade with the international economy have grown more.

3. Those countries that stimulated the growth of their domestic market by reducing poverty linked to economic growth have grown more.
4. Those countries that supported and promoted the training and health of their citizens, thereby contributing to greater productivity and efficiency as well as to a better standard of living, have grown more.
5. Those countries that provided guarantees for savings and investment and kept in place reliable mechanisms for resolving litigation and political conflicts have grown more.

Latin America has performed poorly when examined under the scope of these five arguments. At critical junctures, the region has attempted to cut itself off from the international economy, often adopting policies adverse to international trade (sometimes even repressing exports). Some political leaders have confused populist rhetoric with a very limited reduction in poverty and made insufficient efforts to train their people. At key moments of the region's history, repeated military interventions have led to ruptures of the institutional order and dismantling of judicial systems.

At times, the five arguments mentioned above are presented in academic debates as contradictory, or at least as fundamentally different. This chapter recognizes that it is useful to specify whether the explanation of economic results in Latin America is due mainly to institutional factors, weak investment in human resources, or economic inequality. This is an intellectually crucial, active, and attractive debate. For the purpose of this chapter, however, it suffices to propose that these arguments actually converge. Latin America has invested insufficiently in human resources, is characterized by marked and unchanging inequality, and has suffered from an institutional framework adverse to economic growth. The accumulation and convergence of these factors explains the gap between Latin America and the United States and between Latin America and the fast-developing countries in Asia as of the end of the twentieth century.

The Worldwide and Latin American Economic Boom of the 1950s and 1960s

One important factor explaining Latin America's economic growth in the 1950s and 1960s was the benevolent context of the world economy. Japan's extraordinarily fast growth and the notable growth of the

Western European economies shaped the international economic landscape in those years. Japan's growth in per capita GDP was more than three times that of the United States, and Germany and Italy grew at double the pace of the United States. In South Korea and Taiwan, per capita growth in GDP, while less than in Japan, was faster than growth in Germany, the United States, and all of the Latin American countries. The rate of growth in the United States, however, was not insignificant: GDP per capita grew faster than at practically any other time in its history.[5] In those years, the economies of the already-industrialized world, therefore, had the best moment in their shared economic history, with their international trade growing at almost twice the rate of growth of GDP.

In Latin America, three groups encompassing different types of economic development can be distinguished within a generalized framework of economic growth. The first includes the small Central American and some Caribbean countries. Despite difficulties during the second half of the 1950s, these countries were able to tie in to world economic growth to accelerate their own economic development and begin to diversify their productive base, especially in the 1960s. From the end of World War II until the outbreak of the world economic crisis in the early 1970s, the pace of growth of GDP in Central America was consistently greater than 5 percent annually.[6] For these small countries with limited domestic markets, the boom in the world economy was the fundamental explanation for their economic dynamism during that period. Within this group, the champion of growth in per capita GDP was a small exporting country, the only one in the region whose rate of increased prosperity exceeded Hong Kong's and came close to that of South Korea. That country was Puerto Rico, which had free access to the U.S. market and which, in terms of income distribution and growth, outperformed both Argentina and Mexico in the 1950s.[7]

A second group of countries dominated the overall statistical results for Latin America because of the disproportionate size of their economies and, in those years, their solid economic growth patterns: Brazil and Mexico. In both countries, sustained GDP growth at more than 6 percent annually for the better part of a quarter century exceeded that of Germany and Italy during the same period, was much faster than that of the United States, and brought about major transformations in their internal economic structures.[8] However, both Brazil and Mexico were less successful in generating prosperity than their European and East Asian counterparts, though more successful vis-à-vis the

United States, given the higher population growth rates in Brazil and Mexico.

A third group of countries—Argentina and Chile—remained below the Latin American average, with lower growth rates than those of the first two groups as well as Colombia and Peru. Nonetheless, the members of this third group did yield some growth results. The experiences of Argentina and Chile dominated much of Latin America's economic intellectual debate, thanks in large part to the renowned Argentine economist Raúl Prebisch, the key public intellectual on economic thinking for the entire region and long-time leader of the Santiago-based Economic Commission for Latin America and the Caribbean (ECLAC).

Brazil and Mexico from 1950 to the 1970s

Brazil and Mexico merit special attention for the period from 1950 to the 1970s for two reasons: their ability to grow more quickly during those decades and the fact that they account for a solid majority of Latin America's population. Brazil and Mexico stand out in many ways when compared to their Central American neighbors; however, their rate of economic growth is not a distinguishing factor. From 1950 to 1970, both the Central American economies and the economies of Brazil and Mexico grew more quickly than the U.S. economy, but they accomplished this in different ways. Central America retained a model of economic growth tied to the world economy. In contrast, Brazil and Mexico developed a model based on import substitution industrialization (ISI) and on fostering domestic production, especially in the industrial sector.

The industrialization process in Brazil and Mexico began in the late nineteenth century, when both economies were open to international trade. This process deepened and consolidated in response to the great world economic depression of the 1930s, reaching their high point in Brazil and Mexico, as well as in other South American countries, in the quarter century after World War II. Growth rates were noticeably high even when compared to the fastest-growing economies. For example, from 1950 to 1960, per capita GDP in South Korea increased by a factor of 1.44, in Brazil by 1.40, and in Mexico by 1.33. (In Argentina, by way of contrast, the increase was only by 1.11.)[9] The differences between South Korea, on the one hand, and Brazil and Mexico, on the other, were considerable only in subsequent decades.

The annual growth of industrial production was the fundamental factor in this strategy of economic development. According to Ricardo Ffrench-Davis, Oscar Muñoz, and José Gabriel Palma, annual industrial growth in Brazil was greater than 9 percent in the 1950s and 8.5 percent from 1960 to 1973. In Mexico, it was more than 6 percent in the 1950s and 8.8 percent from 1960 to 1973.[10] This notably positive experience also motivated the small Central American countries to attempt industrialization by import substitution through the formation of the Central American Common Market, a process whose success, however, was limited to the 1960s.

The import substitution strategy, it should be recalled, was not invented by Brazil or Mexico for large economies, nor did it date back only to the mid-twentieth century. At the beginning of World War I, the United States imposed a tariff on its industrial imports similar to that of Mexico, somewhat less than Brazil's, and far greater than Argentina's. In the 1950s and 1960s, as Dani Rodrik notes, there was little liberalization of imports in South Korea or Taiwan.[11] The Latin American innovation after 1950 was the imposition of very high barriers that hindered international trade. In Brazil, for example, as Werner Baer reminds us, the combination of tariff and nontariff barriers resulted in a level of protection in the 1950s equivalent to a tax of 250 percent on imports of manufactured goods, at the same time as exports were neglected. In the 1960s, the effective rate of protection vis-à-vis the imports of durable consumer goods was greater than 100 percent in Argentina, Chile, and Mexico, and it was 200 percent in Brazil.[12] That exaggeration of the model, in the long run, resulted in the creation of inefficient Latin American firms, poor-quality products, and worse service for consumers, who were increasingly dependent on direct and indirect government subsidies.

Neglecting exports was not an exclusively Latin American problem, though there should be no doubt that it was a problem. From 1950 to 1960, South Korea, which also followed the import substitution model at that time, increased its exports at a pace slower than that of Brazil (2.1 percent) and Mexico (3.1 percent). From 1960 to 1965, exports as a share of GDP were practically the same for Brazil, Mexico, and South Korea, which were only slightly below the figure for Taiwan. At that time, none of these were export economies.

The role of the state in setting the direction for the economy was another fundamental feature of the experience that became generalized in Latin America beginning in the 1930s. This was especially the case in Brazil and Mexico, although the state's role as the central promoter of economic development and industrialization in "lagging" countries was not a Latin American innovation either. It had already been a major component of European industrial development in the late nineteenth century, as Alexander Gerschenkron pointed out some time ago.[13] The Japanese experience also underscores the role of the state as a coordinator and source of capital and even as a promoter and accelerator of exports—a task carried out after World War II by Japan's Ministry of International Trade and Industry.[14] One difference that over time would take on greater importance is the fact that the role of the state in Latin America was in many cases improvised, poorly coordinated, and incompetent. In short, the ineffective action and incapacity of the Latin American state was more important than its total size in relation to the economy.

Another important element of the Brazilian and Mexican experiences was the creation of state-owned enterprises. In so doing, they merely emulated the experiences of many European countries (South Korea and Taiwan also established many state-owned enterprises in the 1950s and 1960s). By the late 1970s, according to studies sponsored by the International Monetary Fund, state-owned enterprises accounted for 25–32 percent of total domestic investment in South Korea and Taiwan, comparable to 23 percent and 29 percent in Brazil and Mexico, respectively. The contribution of these state enterprises to the deficit as a percentage of GDP was greater in South Korea and Taiwan than in Brazil and Mexico. In all four countries, it should be noted, state-owned enterprises were established in those years often in response to ad hoc situations, not as part of coherent development strategies.[15] In general, state-owned enterprises running a deficit gave rise to problems in quite different countries, with the peculiarity in Latin America that these were not addressed until it was too late.

It is true that the role of the state distinguishes the economies of the United States, Brazil, and Mexico—and other countries in Latin America and Asia—but it is false that a major role for the state, in itself, impedes fast-paced economic growth. It has been a normal historical experience in several countries for the state to have a fundamental economic role, and it has been so more recently in the experiences of the countries of East Asia. From 1950 to the 1970s, the state in Brazil and Mexico—as in East Asia—facilitated the mobilization of public and private resources. The objective was, simply put, to grow, at any cost, as quickly as possible, and against every obstacle. Another difference between the role of the state in Latin America and in East Asia, beyond those already indicated, is that the first, compared to the second, neglected both economic inequality among its citizens and investment in human resources, as we will see.

Contemporary Roots of the Latin American Lag

As already indicated, the origins of the development gap between the United States and Latin America go back much further than recent decades. Nonetheless, it is still important to analyze the shortcomings in Latin America's economic performance in the contemporary period, once again with particular attention to the larger countries of Brazil and Mexico.

When the quarter-century boom that followed World War II came to an end, four problems loomed that were also part of the experience of the 1950s and 1960s but whose harmful results would only be apparent sometime later: lack of exports, overvaluation of the exchange rate, neglect of the economic inequality problem, and a scandalously inadequate investment in human capital. The great divergence between the economic strategies of East Asia and Latin America, as Alice Amsden argues, originated from the role of exports as a motor of development.[16] Brazil and Mexico exported little and, in contrast to the countries of East Asia, did not change their strategies over time to adjust to the changes in the global economy. As of 1980, for example, exports already represented 34 percent of GDP for South Korea, 53 percent for Taiwan, and 24 percent for Thailand—a notable turnabout in their performances compared to the data cited above from the 1950s. Yet, in Brazil, this figure was only 9 percent. Comparing two oil-exporting countries that also exported other goods, both with large populations and extensive territories, exports accounted for 33 percent of GDP in Indonesia in 1980 but only 11 percent in Mexico.

In an insightful comparison of the experiences of the large Latin American and East Asian countries, Jeffrey Sachs notes that the East Asian countries persistently prevented overvaluation of their exchange rates and, therefore, did not punish their export sector.[17] The Latin American countries, however, had a much more volatile experience, in some cases allowing an extraordinary overvaluation of their exchange rates, which required, from time to time, drastic devaluations of their currencies. In several Latin American countries, overvaluation of the exchange rate indirectly subsidized middle-class consumption.

These two shortcomings of economic policy in Brazil and Mexico were not impossible to rectify. In the 1950s, South Korea's economic profile was hostile to exports. Academics outside and inside Korea were concerned that Korean cultural values might prove to be an insurmountable obstacle that would impede economic growth. But South Korea, like Taiwan, was able to modify its economic strategy after the 1950s, just as the United States had done after World War II by establishing an international system for the liberalization of trade. While some countries carried out the necessary structural reforms for trade liberalization, Latin American countries opted not to do so.

There were, however, two other major areas in which Latin America and East Asia diverged: agrarian reform and human capital development. At the end of World War II, the United States imposed drastic agrarian reform on Japan and its former colony, South Korea; the Nationalist Party government in Taiwan also carried out major agrarian reform. In those three countries of East Asia, the rupture of the old property rights system imposed from abroad fostered equality and served as a vaccine for the future; the inequality issue was removed from the national political agenda. As table 4.2 indicates, income inequality today in South Korea and Japan is far less than in the United States and Latin America.

In comparison, Stanley Engerman and Kenneth Sokoloff indicate that, around 1900, three-fourths of the families in the United States and an even higher proportion in Canada owned their land in rural areas. At that time, the proportion of families who owned land in the Argentine pampas was less than 10 percent and in rural Mexico less than 3 percent.[18] While in the United States a process of generalized acquisition of rural property was implemented, this was not the case in Latin America. In most Latin American countries, agrarian reform did not take place, and where it did, the process was partially delinked from a market economy framework (in contrast to the countries of East Asia). The Mexican agrarian reform, for example, hindered the full participation of the *ejido* system in the market economy, condemning the *ejidatarios* to poverty. In Brazil and Mexico, as in other Latin American countries, the demand for land redistribution in violation of property rights persisted.

Neglect in addressing economic inequality has another component: racial or ethnic discrimination. Countries as different as Cuba, the United States, India, and South Africa have shown that official policy can change inequality among racial or ethnic groups, but of course, it is necessary to develop an effective policy. In general, Latin American governments, until very recently, paid little attention to this issue and, in many cases, even denied the existence of a problem. Research at the World Bank, however, indicates that—controlling statistically for individual factors such as education, occupation, and income—racial or ethnic discrimination may explain one-fourth of the differences in income between indigenous and nonindigenous persons in Bolivia; half in Guatemala, Mexico, and Peru; and half in Brazil between whites and nonwhites.

Finally, Latin American countries in general, not just Brazil and Mexico, have invested much less in the development of human resources than have the countries of East Asia. In Latin America, compared to other countries, enrollment rates of students in primary and secondary schools have remained low, and the quality of the educational system has generally been inferior. Table 4.3 summarizes the information on secondary school enrollment. The enrollments in Mexico are approximately half of those recorded in South Korea, Spain, and the United States. Brazil's results are especially poor: enrollment of the appropriate age group in secondary education is one-fourth what one finds in Korea, Spain, and the United States.

In addition, as indicated in table 4.3, teachers with 15 years of experience in primary schools in Brazil receive salaries that are less than half

TABLE 4.3   Enrollment in Secondary Education and Public Primary School Teacher Salaries, 1995–1998

	% Net Enrollment in Secondary Education, 1995	Public Primary School Teacher Salary ($), 1998
South Korea	96	39,921
Spain	94	29,590
United States	89	33,973
OECD	nd	28,441
Thailand	nd	15,759
Argentina	59	9,442
Chile	55	15,233
Malaysia	nd	10,876
Colombia	50	nd
Mexico	46	12,450
Brazil	19	6,451

Notes: nd = no data available
The salary is for a teacher with 15 years experience, in U.S. dollars, expressed as per the purchasing power parity (better known by its acronym in English, PPP).
The enrollment figure shows enrollment as a percentage of the secondary school–age population.
OECD = Organisation for Economic Co-operation and Development.
Source: Partnership for Educational Revitalization in the Americas, *Lagging Behind: A Report Card on Education in Latin America, 2001* (Washington, DC: Inter-American Dialogue, 2001), pp. 29, 42, based on UNESCO and OECD data.

of what their peers in Thailand are paid. The salaries of primary school teachers in Mexico do not even reach half the average of the member countries of the Organisation for Economic Co-operation and Development (OECD), of which Mexico is a member. It should not surprise us, therefore, that the quality of education imparted is deficient. Take Chile as an example. It leads Latin America in terms of pay for schoolteachers and ranks second in secondary school enrollment. Yet Chile performs poorly in the quality of its education according to international comparisons. Table 4.4 presents calculations derived from an international test done in 1999 in dozens of countries on eighth-grade students' knowledge of mathematics. The results in the United States are just above the world average. South Korea's results are better than those of the United States in both tables 4.3 and 4.4. Chile, the best performer in education in Latin America, is far behind in relation to the rest of the world: its performance is surpassed by Thailand in both tables 4.3 and 4.4 and in academic performance even by Malaysia, where teachers' salaries are below those of Chile. If Chile's quality of investment for human development lags behind internationally, it follows that the overall weakness of Latin America's competitiveness should not be surprising.

The low investment in and poor quality of human resources in Latin America hinder the development of alternative mechanisms of social mobility, greater prosperity, and the total elimination of poverty. The region's growth from the end of World War II until the 1970s owed more to population increase, which fed the labor market, and the injection of capital (largely foreign), and not to productivity gains. It is not surprising that annual growth of productivity in Latin America, according to World Bank and Inter-American Development Bank studies, has been less than the annual increase in productivity in the countries of East Asia in the three decades since 1970 and, in the two decades beginning in 1980, even less than the annual productivity gains in the countries of South Asia.

TABLE 4.4   Academic Performance in Mathematics of Eighth-Grade Students as a Percentage of Performance in the United States, 1999

South Korea	Malaysia	United States	International Average	Thailand	Chile
117	103	100	97	93	78

Source: Calculations based on data from Partnership for Educational Revitalization in the Americas, *Lagging Behind: A Report Card on Education in Latin America, 2001* (Washington, DC: Inter-American Dialogue, 2001), p. 32.

Poverty impedes full participation in the economy and society. As the twentieth century drew to a close, the proportion of the population with incomes lower than $2 per day was 22 percent in Brazil and 26 percent in Mexico, but less than 2 percent in South Korea and 9 percent in Malaysia, according to World Bank figures.[19]

The Basket of Institutions

One purpose for developing political economy institutions is to reduce uncertainty so as to facilitate investment, innovation, and efficiency. For Douglass North, among others, democratic political regimes and decentralized market economies, with clear and well-protected guarantees for property rights, are the preferred institutions for generating an institutional framework with an effective capacity to adapt.[20]

The most developed economies in the world are in countries with democratic regimes. Yet economic growth has occurred in both dictatorships and democracies. In the years covered by this chapter, for example, there was impressive economic growth in the European democracies and Japan as well as in China, South Korea, and Taiwan, the last two ruled by dictatorships until the early 1990s. In addition, there was economic growth a hundred years ago in both the United States and czarist Russia.

The Latin American countries that grew the most from 1950 to the early 1970s were Brazil, Costa Rica, and Mexico. During those years, there was a high rate of growth in per capita GDP in both democratic Costa Rica and Nicaragua under the Somoza family dictatorship—greater in Costa Rica in the 1950s and greater in Nicaragua in the 1960s.[21] Mexico maintained an authoritarian political regime, and Brazil had a democratic regime (with major shortcomings) until 1964 and an authoritarian one from 1964 on. From the world crisis of 1973 to the end of the twentieth century, the best growth in per capita GDP occurred in Colombia (democratic) and Paraguay (authoritarian until the end of the 1980s).[22]

It is useful to think in terms of a basket of rules, or institutions, which in different combinations generate economic growth, despite other differences between countries and political regimes. This concept of a basket of institutions also helps to account for what appear to be anomalous cases. For example, one institution particularly favored by Douglass North and many others is the guarantee of property rights, which is fundamental for reducing uncertainty as it guarantees the future for many economic actors. However, when the United States gained its independence in 1783, there was a dramatic redistribution of property—uncompensated expropriations—through emigration, in many cases forced, to British North America (today, Canada) of many of those who were loyal to the colonial regime. There was a second major violation of property rights in the United States in the wake of the Civil War in the 1860s. The agrarian reforms in South Korea, Japan, and Taiwan shortly after World War II have been previously mentioned. In the case of South Korea, the dictatorship that began in 1961 instituted, among its initial measures, the imprisonment of large entrepreneurs in addition to confiscating their property. It is clear, then, that economic growth is achievable in countries where property rights have been violated. One possible response is that property rights may be violated just once, but the examples above show two violations in the United States and two in South Korea during the same decade. In these various examples, property rights violations occurred in connection with war or similar major events. In Western Europe, North America, and East Asia, property rights have ordinarily been protected in peacetime, and this is a key difference with Latin America.

A distinctive feature in Latin America has been the systematic and enduring persistence of violations of property rights, even in the absence of international wars or prolonged civil wars. That persistence, in several cases still a pressing issue to this day, brings about conditions of permanent insecurity for savings and investment and stimulates capital flight in search of the rule of law. Accordingly, most of the Latin American countries lack institutions capable of creating trust in the existence of a rule of law that protects long-term investments, which in turn would bring about sustained economic growth.

Democracy is also an institution that guarantees future stability, since it regulates the rotation of the president or prime minister depending on the constitutional arrangements. The replacement of one head of government by another, even if by a politician from an opposition party, is a normal procedure under established and known rules in a democratic regime. That rotation does not pose a danger to stability; to the contrary, it consolidates it.

This analysis suggests a way of distinguishing dictatorships capable of making commitments that affect the future from those that do not have that capability. For example, the old absolute monarchies had a mechanism to guarantee commitments into the future: dynastic succession. Some of the dictatorships with better economic results have also been dynastic, as in the case of Taiwan. Nicaragua's economic growth accelerated after the assassination of Anastasio Somoza García because there was a successful transition from unipersonal to dynastic power, in sequence, to his two sons. Dynastic succession, of course, does not replace the need to adopt effective economic measures, and such a system is vulnerable depending on the quality of the heirs. Spain's economic experience in the seventeenth century, Haiti's under the Duvalier family from the 1950s to the 1980s, and North Korea's since the 1980s are examples of dynastic systems that have encountered such problems. Dynastic succession is, thus, not a reliable solution nor is it to be recommended.

More effective have been the institutions of authoritarian regimes that adopted orderly mechanisms of succession, in many cases written into the constitution. Mario Vargas Llosa characterized the old Mexican political system as a "perfect dictatorship" for various reasons, but one was its capacity to assure a peaceful transfer of power from one president to another, on schedule, every six years.[23] The military regime that came to power in Brazil in 1964 also adopted, over time, Mexican-style procedures for succession. Both Brazil and Mexico, as already noted, had excellent results in terms of economic growth from the end of World War II until the early 1970s.

Communist China did not yield significant economic growth results during its period of authoritarian rule by one person, whose caprices brought about spectacular human and economic disasters. China's subsequent economic growth occurred for several reasons, but one of them is a major change in its political system: it ceased to be a one-person dictatorship. Relatively stable mechanisms for political succession were put in place, allowing the government to make commitments into the future and in the name of the party and state institutions.

The institutions of the political regime alone do not generate economic growth. Adequate economic policies are required to achieve growth, but the political institutional frameworks offer reasonable guarantees that the policies established will endure, thereby encouraging economic actors—in both democracies and in authoritarian regimes with mechanisms of succession under a constitutional regime—to commit to invest more and to innovate in a more predictably stable future.

The relationship between the rotation of the head of state or government and the ability to guarantee property rights is crucial. In a political regime without institutionalized procedures for presidential rotation, a president and his or her minister of finance can only make a commitment to the fundamental rules that guarantee property rights and frame the conduct of the economy up to the time of their deaths or removal from office. A political regime with institutionalized procedures for the rotation of the head of state, whether authoritarian or democratic, has the means to guarantee fundamental economic rights in the long term. Compliance with those economic rules does not depend on a single person but on the constitution of the regime.

In Latin America, therefore, the excellent economic performance from 1950 to 1973 of Brazil, Costa Rica, and Mexico has one main factor in common: the three very different political regimes had institutions that governed the peaceful and constitutional transfer of the presidency (the main exception being the military coup in Brazil in 1964). The solid economic growth of the Central American countries in the 1950s and 1960s mentioned above was also accompanied by relatively stable mechanisms for the rotation of the presidency through selections internal to the armed forces. Among the larger economies of Latin America, the one that avoided a major economic setback from 1981 to 1983 was Colombia, which had effective constitutional mechanisms for managing its macroeconomic policy despite suffering terrible problems of public violence.

The worst result, as table 4.1 indicates, was in Argentina, the only Latin American country with triumphant military coups in the 1950s, 1960s, and 1970s and repeated military uprisings or attempted coups during the 1980s and up to 1990. The Argentine military regimes, moreover, suffered from another shortcoming: they generated their own instability, since the country suffered military coups under each of the military regimes established in 1962, 1966, and 1976.[24]

Argentina's exception in terms of its poor economic performance has another institutional characteristic that has been identified in Gretchen Helmke's research: the creation of juridical insecurity through the systematic destruction of the capacity for autonomous action in the Supreme Court.[25] One crucial function of the Supreme Court is to provide a collective and institutional guarantee of the established rules, including the guarantee of property rights, which is necessary for economic growth. That guarantee of the rule of law must necessarily be independent of the political affiliations of the members of the Supreme Court. It should be a guarantee of the state, not of the individuals who perform public functions.

One moment of transition on the road to juridical insecurity in Argentina was the removal of three of the five members of the Supreme Court and the forced resignation of the fourth one in 1947. That decision had enduring repercussions. As of the military coup in 1955, most of the members of the Supreme Court were replaced with each change in political regime until 1983. Under the military government, they were removed by decree; under democratic governments, by forced resignation. The result was a notable politicization of the Supreme Court, which, in different ways, persists to this day because something similar happened in the transition from the presidency of Raúl Alfonsín to the presidencies of Carlos Menem and Néstor Kirchner. The Supreme Court in the Argentine republic can only guarantee those rights of interest to the incumbent president, whoever he or she may be. That guarantee is only useful so long as that president is president; in other words, it is not truly a guarantee of the state. It is thus understandable that crises have interrupted the moments of economic growth.

A Bad Start to the Twenty-First Century in Latin America

The world economic crisis of the early 1970s—which combined a devaluation of the dollar, an abrupt increase in oil prices, an increase in inflation in both the developed countries and the less developed ones, and a world economic recession that characterized a good part of that decade—left Latin America poorly positioned to start the twenty-first century. The old patterns of stability in the international economy suddenly broke down, requiring countries to become more agile in their capacity to maneuver. It is not difficult to understand why Latin America faced economic difficulties after the 1970s, as did the rest of the world. However, by the 1980s, North America, Western Europe, and in particular East Asia were emerging from those difficulties; Latin America was not.

The key question is: what happened in Latin America during the 1970s when North America, Western Europe, and East Asia were reorganizing their economies? In several Central American countries—Guatemala, El Salvador, and Nicaragua—cruel internal and international wars broke out, indirectly affecting Honduras and Costa Rica. The constitutional governments were overthrown in Argentina, Ecuador, Chile, and Uruguay, the latter two having stood out for decades for their institutional stability. The military governments of the Southern Cone, in the name of protecting "Western civilization," assassinated thousands of their fellow citizens without the least respect for legality and human rights. In addition, the institutional instability of authoritarian military regimes, already noted in the extreme case of Argentina, was also observed in the military regimes of Bolivia and Peru, i.e., military coups were launched even against military governments. In such cases, the "forces of order" were the worst generators of disorder. By the mid-1970s, authoritarian regimes, almost all of them military, prevailed in Latin America except for Costa Rica, Colombia, and Venezuela.

It was these authoritarian governments that made the decision to go into debt rather than adjusting Latin America's economic structures to address the world economic crisis. They were the ones that retained, and around the late 1970s exaggerated, the overvaluation of the exchange rate. They were the ones (except for Chile) that ignored the need to fundamentally modify the anti-export orientation of a large part of the national economy. One may also recall that they invested little in human resources and neglected the issues of inequality and poverty. By postponing the adjustment, as in any case of deferred maintenance, they necessarily increased the later cost of that adjustment, which came the next decade.

The fatal governmental decision to fall into debt instead of adjusting—to borrow money for the state's consumption rather than using those resources to stimulate production and promote exports—was particularly evident on the eve of the Latin American economic catastrophe known as the debt crisis, as summarized in table 4.5. Abruptly increasing interest payments to service the debt in a context of insufficient exports was irresponsible, and it was impossible to use the vast new financial resources efficiently and productively in such a brief period. While the most worrisome financial behavior was on the part of the Argentine military government, the conduct of the government of General Augusto Pinochet in Chile does not merit any praise either.

TABLE 4.5   Ratio of Total Interest Paid to Exports of Goods and Services (%)

	1978	1982
Argentina	9.6	54.6
Brazil	24.5	57.1
Chile	17.0	49.5
Mexico	24.0	39.9

Source: United Nations Economic Commission for Latin America and the Caribbean, *Balance preliminar de la economía latinoamericana durante 1984*, LC/G.1336 (Santiago, Chile, 1984), table 14.

After the economic crisis of 1982–1983 erupted, Latin America did not grow for the remainder of the 1980s. The region's collective per capita GDP that decade fell more than 7 percent, while only three Latin American countries achieved positive GDP growth: Colombia, Chile, and Paraguay, in that order. Paraguay's growth was insignificant, and none of these three countries came even close to 2 percent growth.[26] It should be emphasized that the rate of economic growth in Chile under the government of General Pinochet in the 1980s was not at all miraculous: the miracle was in a public relations success that consisted of convincing so many of Chile's purported economic growth.

From 1973 until 2000, per capita GDP for the world economy grew at a pace of 1.3 percent per annum. The U.S. economy, based on this measure, grew almost 2 percent, compared to Latin America's growth of almost 1 percent.[27] During this period, the gap between the United States and Latin America increased once again, and, when compared to its own history, the rate of growth in Latin America was the poorest since the 1870s. The growth of several countries in East Asia, despite the financial crisis of 1997 (and of other lesser financial crises in the preceding quarter century), was excellent. Growth of per capita GDP in those years was more than double that of the United States in China, Malaysia, Singapore, South Korea, Taiwan, and Thailand. The annual rate of growth also picked up in India and Sri Lanka, where it exceeded the growth rate of the U.S. economy.

How is this interruption in the growth of Latin American GDP explained? Latin America was able to grow during previous decades of growth of the world economy—the 1950s and 1960s—with various economic models, albeit suffering the problems of institutional, economic, and social design already mentioned. When the generalized growth of the world economy was interrupted in the 1970s, that previous benevolent international framework was also interrupted. The burden placed on economic growth by the bad decisions adopted in Latin America and by the possible good decisions that were deferred, as already summarized, was at long last clearly apparent.

With a delayed adjustment thanks to external indebtedness in the 1970s, impressive and persistent hindrances to international trade, the overvaluation of the exchange rate, mediocre investment in human resources, a limited domestic market punished by inequality and poverty, and, finally, an institutional rupture of the magnitude noted in the 1970s, the economic model of the 1950s and 1960s finally broke down in the 1980s.

As of the 1970s, Latin America faced a world economy that demanded greater participation in international trade in order to grow. With start dates that ranged from the 1980s to the 1990s, the countries of Latin America liberalized their foreign trade, but with major lags compared to the experiences of the already developed countries or the quickly developing countries of East Asia. The Latin American governments adopted reforms to their banking systems and modified their fiscal policies and exchange rates, but with the obvious inexperience of beginners.

In the 1980s, governments as diverse as those of Argentina, Brazil, Venezuela, and Peru adopted fiscal and exchange rate measures of such ineptitude that they guaranteed disastrous results. These countries' efforts at monetary stabilization without appropriate reduction of the fiscal deficit in so-called heterodox economic programs led to failures to abide by the governments' set economic policies, booms in the informal sectors of the economy, replacement of the ministers in charge of economic policy, and, especially in Argentina, Brazil, and Peru, extraordinary rates of inflation. In these countries, by 1989–1990, inflation exceeded 1,000 percent annually, which in turn fostered deep disillusionment with the government instead of citizens' jubilation over democratic progress.[28]

The last two decades of the twentieth century were marked by repeated financial crises in Latin America. After the debt crisis of 1982, at least one other major financial debacle took place in Argentina, Brazil, Bolivia, the Dominican Republic, Ecuador, Mexico, Peru, and Uruguay, in addition to the continuation of the Central American wars until the early 1990s.

The cost of Latin America's procrastination in adjusting and implementing structural economic reforms delayed the region's potential to reap the benefits of the global economic boom sparked by the growth experienced in North America, Western Europe, and East Asia in the 1980s and 1990s. Under the tutelage of the International Monetary Fund, the process of adjustment and structural reform in Latin America during these two decades had, in general, a recessive bias in the region that weakened the recovery of its economic growth. Latin America was perhaps on the verge of its own economic take-off in the mid-1990s, but it was shaken once again when the economy of the already-developed countries and, more broadly, the international economy suffered another setback. The economic crisis of the East Asian countries in 1997, the stagnation of the Japanese economy in the 1990s, the slowdown of economic growth in Western Europe in the late 1990s, and the recession in North America in the early 2000s drastically reduced external financing in Latin America. European investment was directed to the former communist countries of Central and Eastern Europe, and international investment from Japan and the United States dropped off. As a result of the new international economic pressures, a financial crisis erupted in Brazil in 1999, and the economy collapsed in Argentina at the turn of the twenty-first century. Bolivia, Ecuador, and to a lesser extent Uruguay suffered equally serious problems, including grave social and political crises in Bolivia and Ecuador.

Despite the varied reform programs that have been implemented in Latin America, much remains to be done. Consider, for example, a simple institutional indicator: the number of days required to start up a new business. As indicated in table 4.6, starting up a new firm is relatively simple in countries such as Australia, the United States, and Puerto Rico. Chile has amended its regulations so as to compete with the countries of East Asia. It is interesting and ironic that it is easier to open a new business in the People's Republic of China than in Mexico or Argentina, and three times easier in communist China than in Brazil. It should come as no surprise that the countries that facilitate the creation of new businesses, which generate employment and income, grow more.

There are, however, some positive cases in Latin America. Mexico's trade liberalization program, which allowed its subsequent entry to the North American Free Trade Agreement (NAFTA), generated quick growth in the sectors linked to the international economy. Despite

TABLE 4.6   Number of Days Required to Start Up a New Firm, 2003

Australia	2
United States	4
Puerto Rico	6
Chile	28
Japan	31
South Korea	33
Thailand	42
People's Republic of China	46
Mexico	51
Argentina	68
Brazil	152

Source: *World Development Indicators 2004*
(Washington, DC: World Bank, 2004).

retaining a counterproductive exchange rate regime and other problems, Mexico's revolution in international trade in the 1990s rescued the country from its financial panic of 1994–1995, allowed it to grow at a fast pace during the second half of the 1990s for the first time in two decades and enabled it to survive the economic recession in the United States in the first years of the twenty-first century.

That very experience in Mexico, however, highlighted the legacies of the decisions that Latin America had put off earlier. Mexico and the rest of Latin America today can compete with the up-and-coming Chinese economy by reducing workers' wages, which already are not high, or by investing in human resources to bring about increased productivity. No one wants to pursue the first option, and the second one takes years to bear fruit. Argentina—a country long accustomed to a high level of consumption—is also facing that dilemma. Latin America could grow more if its domestic market were larger and if its citizens could contribute more to its economic growth. Yet income inequality (always neglected) and poverty (whose reduction has only received attention in recent years and only in some countries) reduce the real size of each domestic economy, and weak institutional frameworks hinder the coordination of efforts to foster economic growth.

Conclusion

The origins of the gap between the United States and Latin America date back centuries. Latin America's economic performance improved, however, during the period from 1870 to the early 1970s. Even during that century of better per capita GDP growth in Latin America, however, the region neglected to invest in human resources and to reduce inequality and poverty when compared to the gains made in the United States and in other countries that have successfully developed their economies. As the twentieth century advanced, there was a marked preference in Latin America for autarchic economic strategies, which were taken to extremes never seen in the countries of the North Atlantic or East Asia, and which experienced faster economic development. In addition, weak institutions in Latin America—a persistent problem—worsened even more in the 1970s. A terrible decade for the region, the 1970s witnessed unproductive, fleeting, and irresponsible sovereign indebtedness by governments, as well as the killing of thousands of citizens, instead of a reorganization of economic structures that would allow for a more felicitous shared prosperity.

The combination of pervasive neglect of necessary investment in human resources, dysfunctional institutions, and poorly designed and implemented economic measures, concomitant with the suicidal conduct of many of the region's governments in the 1970s, explains the interruption in the rate of growth of Latin America's per capita GDP and the severity of its economic depression in the 1980s. The much-delayed process of adjustment and structural reform—still incomplete, as illustrated in table 4.6—precluded Latin America from fully benefiting from the growth of the world economy in the 1980s and 1990s. The region's growth was further delayed by the international crises that unfolded at the turn of the twenty-first century.

There is no magic wand that will close the development gap between the United States and Latin America. The instruments for closing the gap are not new. No genetic injections or culturalist experiments are needed. Moreover, the military governments that presided earlier already proved their colossal ineptitude, which brought Latin America to the brink of the precipice in the 1970s and 1980s.

Looking to the future, there is a clear need in Latin America to increase investment in human resources. With a stronger population capable of building its own future, reliable institutions under a democratic political framework that can guarantee the rule of law are also needed. Promoting human development through sensible economic policies in a market economy framework makes the most sense. It is time for Latin America to stop ignoring the obvious next steps to take.

Notes

1. Sources for these and other statistics are Angus Maddison, *The World Economy: Historical Statistics* (London: Development Centre, OECD, 2003); and Angus Maddison, *The World Economy: A Millennial Perspective* (London: Development Centre, OECD, 2001).
2. John H. Coatsworth and Alan M. Taylor, *Latin America and the World Economy since 1800* (Cambridge, MA: Harvard University, David Rockefeller Center for Latin American Studies, 1998).
3. World Bank, *World Development Indicators 2004* (Washington, DC: World Bank, 2004), p. 61.
4. Werner Baer, *The Brazilian Economy: Growth and Development*, 5th ed. (Westport, CT: Praeger, 2001).
5. Calculations based on Maddison, *The World Economy: Historical Statistics*, tables 4b, 4c, 5b, 8c.
6. Sources on Central America are Victor Bulmer-Thomas, *The Political Economy of Central America since 1920* (Cambridge: Cambridge University Press, 1987); and Marc Lindenberg, "World Economic Cycles and Central American Political Instability," *World Politics* 42 (1990): 397–421.

7. Richard Weisskoff, "Income Distribution and Economic Growth in Puerto Rico, Argentina, and Mexico," *Review of Income and Wealth* 16, no. 4 (1970): 303–332.
8. Ricardo Ffrench-Davis, Oscar Muñoz, and José Gabriel Palma, "The Latin American Economies, 1950–1990," in *The Cambridge History of Latin America: 1930 to the Present*, vol. 6, part 1 (Cambridge: Cambridge University Press, 1994), table 4.3.
9. Calculations based on Maddison, *The World Economy: Historical Statistics*, tables 4c, 5c.
10. Ffrench-Davis, Muñoz, and Palma, "The Latin American Economies," table 4.6.
11. Dani Rodrik, "Understanding Economic Policy Reform," *Journal of Economic Perspectives* 34 (March 1996): 9–41.
12. Baer, *The Brazilian Economy*; and Alan M. Taylor, "On the Costs of Inward Looking Development: Price Distortions, Divergence, and Growth in Latin America," *Journal of Economic History* 58 (March 1998): 1–28.
13. Alexander Gerschenkron, *Economic Backwardness in Historical Perspective* (Cambridge, MA: Harvard University Press, 1962).
14. Chalmers A. Johnson, *MITI and the Japanese Miracle: The Growth of Industrial Policy, 1925–1975* (Stanford, CA: Stanford University Press, 1982).
15. Robert Floyd, Clive Gray, and R. P. Short, *Public Enterprise in Mixed Economies* (Washington, DC: International Monetary Fund, 1984).
16. Alice H. Amsden, *The Rise of "the Rest": Challenges to the West from Late Industrializing Economies* (Oxford: Oxford University Press, 2001).
17. Jeffrey D. Sachs, "External Debt and Macroeconomic Performance in Latin America and East Asia," *Brookings Papers on Economic Activity* 2 (1985): 523–573.
18. Stanley L. Engerman and Kenneth L. Sokoloff, *Factor Endowments, Inequality, and Paths of Development among New World Economies*, Working Paper 9259 (Cambridge, MA: National Bureau of Economic Research, 2002).
19. All currency amounts are in U.S. dollars unless otherwise noted. World Bank, *World Development Indicators 2004*, p. 54.
20. Douglass C. North, *Institutions, Institutional Change, and Economic Performance* (Cambridge: Cambridge University Press, 1990).
21. Calculations based on Bulmer-Thomas, *The Political Economy of Central America since 1920*, table A.3.
22. Maddison, *The World Economy: Historical Statistics*.
23. Cited by Jorge Chabat, "Mexico's Foreign Policy in 1990: Electoral Sovereignty and Integration with the United States," *Journal of Interamerican Studies and World Affairs* 33, no. 4 (1991): 12.
24. Argentina's exceptional status is evident in an international comparison on democracy and development. See Adam Przeworski, Michael Alvarez, José Antonio Cheibub, and Fernando Limongi, *Democracy and Development: Political Institutions and Well-Being in the World, 1950–1990* (Cambridge: Cambridge University Press, 2000).
25. Gretchen Helmke, *Courts under Constraints: Judges, Generals, and Presidents in Argentina* (Cambridge: Cambridge University Press, 2005).
26. United Nations, Economic Commission for Latin America and the Caribbean (ECLAC), *Preliminary Overview of the Economy of Latin America and the Caribbean, 1990*, LC/G.1646 (Washington, DC: ECLAC, 1990), table 3.
27. Maddison, *The World Economy: Historical Statistics*, table 8b.
28. ECLAC, *Preliminary Overview of the Economy 1990*, table 5.

PART II

THE POLITICS OF UNDERDEVELOPMENT IN LATIN AMERICA

5

Does Politics Explain the Economic Gap between the United States and Latin America?

ADAM PRZEWORSKI WITH CAROLINA CURVALE

THIS CHAPTER EXAMINES whether and in what ways political institutions and events were responsible for the existing economic gap between the United States and Latin America.[1] In the process of writing, it became evident that this effort was more pioneering than anticipated. While dependency theory correctly emphasized the importance of political conflicts and the potential role of the state, in the end it found the key to economic retardation in the initial insertion of particular countries into the world economy. Yet, as Stephan Haggard argued, dependency is not a condition but a strategy.[2] Because of the incorrect view of economic openness, dependency theory failed to elucidate the political factors that may explain why Latin American countries stayed behind while the East Asian countries overtook them.

New institutionalism, in turn, is a mirror image of dependency theory where institutions are the key to development.[3] The central claim of new institutionalism is that institutions are the primary driver of economic development, more so than features of the natural environment, geography, the supply of factors, and the technologies for their use.[4] Studies point to the importance of the *quality* of institutions, yet even if the use of the term "quality" is in vogue, it remains enormously vague. The institutions that matter likely include not only those that protect property rights, but also those that mobilize savings and coordinated investments and those that subject those in government to the approval of the governed.[5] Yet institutionalist answers to why Latin America fell behind are often drowned in ritualistic invocations of the institutionalist approach.[6] In Stephen Haber's most recent collection, for example, the culprit is Latin American "crony capitalism," as if capitalism in the United States could be categorized differently.[7]

While recent works resulting from a revived interest in Latin America's lagging development provide several insightful case studies,[8] this chapter's analysis is conducted at the cross-national level. Moreover, to the extent to which data limitations allow, this study closely adheres to the facts. The caveats should be obvious: reconstructing historical data is a hazardous undertaking, and the data are replete with errors and omissions.

Latin America's delay in reaching independence when compared against the United States, as well as the political turmoil that followed independence, are two factors that had significant economic repercussions in the region. While the magnitude of their effects can be estimated, it is not clear why late independence retarded development. The long period of post-independence political turmoil in Latin America resulted from the breakdown of colonial institutions, which left the region without institutions to manage conflicts. The rebuilding of institutions thus depended on the military victory of a viable political force or on agreements between armed elites. Neither could be accomplished overnight.

Once founded, political institutions tended to be highly exclusionary and oligarchical. Yet, as long as the elites peacefully resolved their conflicts—typically over centralization, tariffs, or the role of religion (conservatives versus liberals)[9]—Latin American economies developed. While political inequality coexisted with economic inequality, inequality in general recurrently undermined institutional stability. Economic inequality meant that the political incorporation of the poor, urban workers, agricultural laborers, and tenant farmers could not be achieved peacefully, and political instability is economically costly. Even today, Latin American democracies are riddled with political and social conflicts, making Latin America's economies exceptionally volatile.[10]

This chapter argues that economies grow when political power protects economic power—what is known as the "security of property"—as long as political institutions manage conflicts within a legal framework.[11] However, unequal political institutions perpetuated economic inequality and generated conflicts—over land (or wages of agricultural workers) and over wages and conditions of work in industry—which were politically destabilizing and economically costly. Hence, while political inequality may be statically efficient, it is dynamically inefficient.

Based on historical evidence, this chapter begins by illustrating the origins of the economic gap between the United States and Latin America. The next section focuses on the timing of independence and its aftermath, analyzing why the economic gap was already visible in 1820 and had markedly deepened by 1870. The analysis then turns to the post-independence period, when Latin American countries had achieved some political stability, focusing on political institutions and their impact on development. The chapter then examines the hypothesis that Latin America fell behind economically because it failed to extend political rights to a majority of its citizens.[12] A final section focuses on political pluralism, political instability, and the economic consequences of political weakness.

The Origins and Timing of the Economic Gap

The obvious first question is whether there is an economic gap that warrants analysis. When considering that, in the year 2000, average per capita income in the United States was $28,129 compared with an average per capita income in Latin America's 19 countries of only $5,844, there is no doubt that a significant gap exists.[13] But the issue is whether this gap is the result of something that happened in the independent lives of these countries or rather of inherited conditions from the time of colonization or from independence. Abhijit Banerjee and Lakshmi Iyer juxtapose these two possibilities:

> In the new institutionalist view, history matters because history shapes institutions and institutions shape the economy. By contrast, in what one might call the "increasing returns" view, historical accidents put one country ahead in terms of aggregate wealth or human capital...and this turns into bigger and bigger differences over time because of the increasing returns.[14]

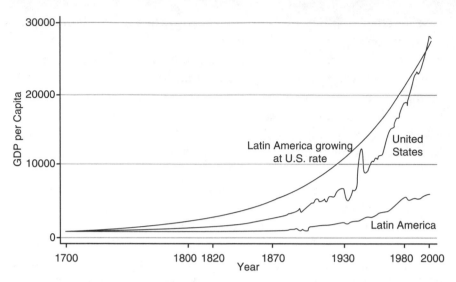

FIGURE 5.1 Per Capita Income Gap between the United States and Latin America, 1700–2000. *Source*: Angus Maddison, *The World Economy: Historical Statistics* (Paris: OECD, 2003).

If the gap were just the result of countries growing at the same rate from different initial conditions, then politics could not have played a role in generating the gap.

A look at the raw data would be useful at this juncture. The irregular lines in figure 5.1 illustrate per capita income in the United States and in Latin America between 1700 and 2000. The smooth line indicates what *would have been* the income in Latin America had it grown at the same rate as that of the United States from the initial conditions in 1700. According to Angus Maddison, in 1700 the average per capita income in continental Latin America was $521 and in the United States it was $527.[15] If all incomes had grown at the rate of the United States, the gap in 2000 would have been only $364. Hence, the gap in 2000 is almost entirely due to the slower growth of Latin America, rather than to conditions as of 1700.

Another interesting approach is a comparison between the 2000 per capita income of Latin American countries with that of the United States over time. As shown in figure 5.2, the dates in which the United States reached the equivalent to the 2000 per capita income of selected countries are about 1950 for Chile, about 1900 for Colombia, and about 1880 for Paraguay.

This picture raises a methodological problem, which will be evident throughout this analysis. By 2000, the most developed Latin American

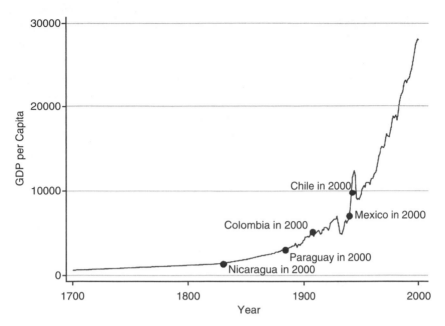

FIGURE 5.2 Per Capita Income Gap between the United States and Latin America: Comparisons with Nicaragua, Paraguay, Colombia, Mexico, Chile. *Source*: Angus Maddison, *The World Economy: Historical Statistics* (Paris: OECD, 2003).

country, Chile, lagged 50 years behind the United States. This means that it is possible to group all of Latin America together when asking why the region fell behind the United States. Yet such a formulation provides two observations: the United States (or North America, if we include Canada) and Latin America; and with only two observations no causes can be identified. We can learn more by observing that, when compared against each other, Latin American countries have had different characteristics. However common it is to generalize regionwide, the individual countries of Latin America have always exhibited a wide range of economic, cultural, and political characteristics that distinguish them from one another. For example, Coatsworth observed that "the variation in the productivity of Latin American colonial economies in 1800 was almost as great as for the entire world."[16] More recently, it can be noted that Chile's per capita income in 2000 was six times that of Nicaragua.

However, considering the variations among Latin American countries does not suffice: the entire region did, after all, fall behind. Yet Latin America is not alone; the rest of the world, including Western Europe, also fell behind the United States.[17] Thus, perhaps the question should be framed differently: why did the United States develop faster than any other country in the world? Why some countries developed and others did not is the key question, but, even when considering all of the data available for the world as a whole, the causes specific to Latin America are not always identifiable. As Leandro Prados de la Escosura points out, it is therefore important to examine what the feasible counterfactuals are.[18] All we can say now is that we will return to this problem each time it is relevant.

In addition to the origins of the economic gap between the United States and Latin America, one must address the issue of timing. As stated earlier, in 1820 the gap was already noticeable, and by 1870 it was enormous (see table 5.1). Remarkably, between 1871 (the date after which continuous time series are available) and 1930, per capita income grew slightly faster in Latin America than in the United States; but by then it was too late—compounded at the same rate, incomes diverged even more. After 1930, growth of per capita income slowed down markedly in Latin America, while it accelerated in the United States. Hence, by 2000, the average income in the latter was 4.8 times higher than in the countries south of the Rio Grande.

Before proceeding, it would be pertinent to examine the evolution of per capita income by looking at the growth of total gross domestic product (GDP) and of population (see table 5.2). Note that the period 1820–1870 was disastrous for Latin America.[19] On the other hand, between 1871 and 1980, total GDP growth in Latin America was slightly higher than in the United States.[20] The faster GDP growth in the United States between 1700 and 1870 was accompanied by a much faster increase in population, in large part due to immigration.[21] From 1930, population growth was higher in Latin America, but growth of

TABLE 5.1   Per Capita Incomes, 1700–2000

	1700	1820	1870	1930	2000
Brazil	459	646	713	1048	5556
Mexico	568	759	674	1618	7218
Latin America*	521	701	756	1873	5844
United States	527	1257	2445	6123	28129
Latin America: United States	0.99	0.56	0.31	0.31	0.21

*Population weighted averages for countries for which data are available: 17 countries in 1700 and 1820 (excluding Cuba and Dominican Republic); Brazil, Mexico, Argentina, Uruguay, and Venezuela in 1870; 13 countries in 1930; 18 in 2000.
Source: Angus Maddison, *The World Economy: Historical Statistics* (Paris: OECD, 2003), p. 114 and data set.

TABLE 5.2 Rates of Growth of Total GDP, Population, and per Capita GDP, by Period (1700–2000)

	GDP Latin America	GDP United States	Population Latin America	Population United States	GDP per Capita Latin America	GDP per Capita United States
1700–1870	0.84	3.12	0.68	2.20	0.14	0.92
1700–1820	0.77	2.67	0.55	1.94	0.22	0.73
1820–1870	1.02	4.21	1.07	2.83	−0.05	1.38
1871–2000	3.76	3.52	2.22	1.51	1.54	2.02
1871–1929	3.91	3.77	1.89	1.90	2.02	1.87
1930–2000	3.73	3.32	2.31	1.18	1.42	2.14
1930–1980	4.34	3.43	2.45	1.23	1.89	2.20
1981–2000	2.34	3.06	1.99	1.07	0.36	1.98

Note: Until 1870, exponential rates of growth of population weighted averages. After 1870, unweighted averages of country growth rates.
Source: Angus Maddison, *The World Economy: Historical Statistics* (Paris: OECD, 2003), p. 114 and data set.

per capita income was slower than in the United States, indicating that productivity per worker in Latin America must have remained low.[22]

To summarize these patterns, it is useful to think in terms of three periods: 1700–1820, 1820–1870, and 1870–2000. Already by 1820, the difference between the United States and Latin America was sufficiently large that, even if the region had grown at the same rate since then, the gap in 2000 would have been large. Between 1820 and 1870, the gap increased further because total output grew very slowly in Latin America. After 1870, the total output in Latin America grew somewhat faster than in the United States, but so did the population. Finally, the growth of total output slowed down sharply after 1980, but we will not delve into this period.

In figure 5.3, the smooth lines represent the counterfactual per capita incomes of Latin America, the counterfactual being that the region would have grown at the same rate as the United States from the initial conditions in the different periods.[23] The upper irregular line is the actual income path of the United States, while the lower is the average per capita income in Latin America.[24] When looking vertically in 2000, the last year represented, the distance between the actual income of Latin America and the smooth lines originating in 1700, 1820, and 1870 can be interpreted as the income gap due exclusively to growth rates falling behind those of the United States after these dates. As

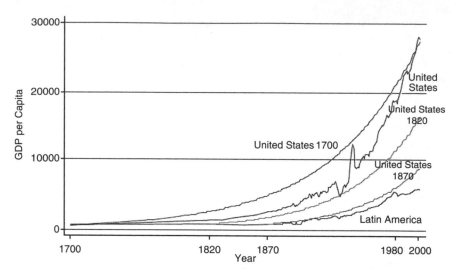

FIGURE 5.3 Decomposing the Income Gap by Period. *Source*: Angus Maddison, *The World Economy: Historical Statistics* (Paris: OECD, 2003).

can be noted, the gap in relation to 1700 is very large: the difference between the income that Latin America would have had if it had grown at the same rate as the United States since 1700 and the actual income it had in 2000 is $23,123. The 2000 gap relative to the initial conditions in 1820—$10,040—though smaller, is still very large. In turn, the gap relative to the conditions in 1870 is relatively small: $2,780. Indeed, the post-1870 gap is due almost exclusively to the slowdown of growth in Latin America after 1980.[25] Hence, while Latin America fell further and further behind in each period, it is clear that the current gap is due mainly to the period before 1870, and particularly before 1820, with a downward trend after 1980.

Independence and Its Aftermath

There are very few systematic data for the early period, and this paucity makes it difficult to date the origin of the gap with more precision. According to Maddison, as seen in table 5.1 above, the income of the United States in 1700 was only slightly higher than the Latin American average, with the income of Mexico higher and that of Brazil lower than the income of the United States.[26] Coatsworth gives the income of Mexico in 1700 as 89 percent of that of the United States; he does not have data for Brazil, but shows Cuba to have been much wealthier than the United States.[27] In a more recent paper, Coatsworth concludes that "the areas of Latin America under effective Spanish and Portuguese control probably enjoyed per capita incomes on a par with Western Europe and at least equal to the British colonies that became the United States well into the eighteenth century."[28]

The question we cannot answer is whether the gap opened up during the eighteenth century or only during the Latin American wars of independence. Victor Bulmer-Thomas cites estimates according to which the per capita income of Latin America was at least as high as that of the United States still in 1800.[29] Coatsworth, however, finds these Latin American estimates exaggerated, giving the ratio of the unweighted average of Latin American countries to the income of the United States as 66 percent in 1800.[30] If incomes were identical in 1700, this ratio would imply that the United States grew at the rate of 0.4 percent, while Latin America stagnated throughout the century. In fact, standard estimates of the growth of per capita income in the United States during the eighteenth century range from 0.3 to 0.6 percent. However, Peter Mancall and Thomas Weiss estimate that, between 1700 and 1800, the incomes of the colonists and their slaves grew at the rate of only 0.04 percent, so that the growth of average income in the United States was due to the fact that Native Americans, who had lower incomes, were becoming a smaller part of the total population.[31] In turn, Bulmer-Thomas claims that the Bourbon reforms generated growth in Latin America in the second half of the eighteenth century.[32] Hence, it is not apparent why incomes would have diverged during the eighteenth century.

It is clear, however, that the wars of independence and their aftermath were costly in terms of growth. Per capita income in the United States fell by about 7 percent between 1775 and 1800, mainly because of the decline of agricultural exports.[33] In turn, Bulmer-Thomas concluded, "The economic difficulties encountered in the first two decades of the nineteenth century can safely be assumed to have reduced real income per head in Latin America considerably," again due to the disruption of trade but also to the decline of mining.[34] Prados de la Escosura, in turn, observed that "independence was followed by a marked decline in economic activity: per capita income did not return to colonial levels until the mid-nineteenth century."[35]

It is useful to examine how the timing of independence and the duration of the subsequent turmoil affected the gap of incomes in 2000. As the date of independence, we take the year when the last metropolitan soldier left a territory. In turn, we measure the duration of the subsequent political turmoil as the length of the period between independence and the first completion of a constitutionally specified term by a chief executive. When the date of independence is combined with the duration of political turmoil, both reduce the 2000 incomes: each year of delay in independence cost $165 (t = –3.05; p = 0.007) in 2000 and each year of turmoil an additional $70 (t = –1.89; p = 0.076).[36] Given these numbers, one can calculate that waiting for independence for one additional year had an opportunity cost of $4.50, while waiting for political conflicts to settle had a cost of $6.61.[37] As these costs became compounded, Bolivia, independent in 1825 and waiting 59 years before the completion of the first term, suffered a loss of $11,225 in relation to the United States, which was effectively independent in 1782 with the first term completed by 1793. The impact of these dates on the 2000 incomes is shown in table 5.3.

TABLE 5.3   Costs of Delaying Independence and of Subsequent Turmoil

Country	Year of Independence[a]	Turmoil[b]	Cost[c]	Gap in 2000[d]	Ratio[e]
Argentina	1816	44	8,690	19,585	0.4437
Bolivia	1825	59	11,225	25,554	0.4393
Brazil	1822	80	12,200	22,573	0.5405
Chile	1818	18	7,200	18,288	0.3937
Colombia	1819	18	7,365	23,033	0.3198
Costa Rica	1821	8	6,995	21,955	0.3186
Cuba	1898	8	19,700	25,715	0.7661
Dom. Rep.	1821	32	8,675	24,466	0.3546
Ecuador	1822	12	7,440	25,028	0.2973
El Salvador	1821	29	8,465	25,413	0.3331
Guatemala	1821	14	7,415	24,733	0.2998
Honduras	1821	23	8,045	26,172	0.3074
Mexico	1821	8	6,995	20,911	0.3345
Nicaragua	1821	96	13,155	26,571	0.4951
Panama	1821	87	12,525	22,347	0.5605
Paraguay	1811	75	10,035	25,115	0.3396
Peru	1824	52	10,570	24,443	0.4324
United States	1782	11	770	0	0
Uruguay	1815	20	6,845	20,270	0.3377
Venezuela	1821	14	7,415	19,714	0.3761

[a]Year of Independence = year of effective independence of colonial power.
[b]Turmoil = number of years between the year of effective independence and the first completion of a previously specified constitutional term.
[c]Cost = cost in 2000 of postponing independence and of the turmoil.
[d]Gap in 2000 = difference between the per capita income of each country and that of the United States in 2000.
[e]Ratio = Cost/Gap in 2000.

Given the limited information available, it is not possible to determine why postponing independence has been so costly. One possibility is that colonial control retarded growth, mainly by restrictions on trade. The alternative hypothesis entails the timing of independence. The United States reached independence exactly in time to reap the fruit of the technological revolution that shook England after 1750, while continental Latin American countries became independent some 35 to 50 years later.[38] Hence, the gap that emerged by 1820 could be due to the fact that the United States was quietly growing at the rate of 0.3 percent between 1800 and 1820, while Latin Americans fought for independence. Perhaps, if the wars of independence had occurred in Latin America 40 years earlier, there would have been no gap by 1820. According to Maddison, Canada, which remained a British colony, had per capita income of $430 in 1700 and $904 in 1820, thus surpassing Mexico.[39] In turn, as noted by Coatsworth, Cuba, which remained a Spanish colony, had income higher than that of the United States until 1830.[40]

Unfortunately, this is as far as we can go in analyzing the impact of the early period. Moreover, the timing of independence may be endogenous with regard to the possibilities of development[41] or it may have been related to some unobserved country characteristics that also influenced development. Hence, although these findings are quite impressive, one should treat them with a grain of salt. It is clear that the gap was present by the time the wars of independence ended on the continent. Compounded over about 180 years, the differences at the time of independence explain a large part of the gap in 2000.

Why did the effects of independence differ so drastically between the United States and Latin America? One answer may be the effect of independence on intraregional trade. Although there was little trade between the South and the North in the United States, independence removed all barriers to internal trade. In contrast, in Latin America, independence destroyed what was de facto a customs union during the colonial period.[42]

From the political point of view, the startling difference is the length of time it took Latin American countries to settle their boundaries and to establish state institutions. The period after independence was not completely peaceful in the United States, and the election of 1800 brought the country to the edge of violence.[43] As we have seen, per capita income declined during this period. But the political unrest in the United States pales in comparison to most Latin American countries, where the wars of independence were, to a large extent, protracted civil wars that continued well after independence had been achieved. Although a wealth of explanations exists,[44] there are few systematic tests.[45]

One story is that conflicts were more acute in Latin America, either because inequality generated more pressure toward redistribution or because of the contest between *peninsulares* and creoles for the rents accruing to political power.[46] Note, however, that the question over whether and to what extent the wars of independence resulted in social transformations is also quite familiar to students of the United States (Charles A. Beard versus J. Franklin Jameson).[47] But even if both economic and political conflicts were equally intense, there was a crucial institutional difference. The fact that the British North American colonies had self-governing institutions is crucial, since it permitted the United States to gain independence without a break of institutional continuity. Colonies became states of the Union, with the same boundaries,[48] and the newly founded federal institutions emanated from self-governing institutions established under the British rule. In contrast, the Spanish colonial administration was much more direct and much more centralized, leaving little space for self-government. No one born in the colonies—creoles—could hold high posts in the Spanish colonial administration. The only institution that entailed some modicum of self-government in Spanish America—the *cabildo*—was an estate body, with offices that could be purchased and kept in perpetuity after 1556, and there were a few elective posts under highly restricted suffrage and subject to confirmation by the Crown. The fiscal powers of the *cabildo* were minimal. This institution functioned so badly that, in 1789, *intendentes* appointed by the Crown took over most of its functions. Summarizing its evolution, Haring concluded that "the cabildo had virtually disappeared at the end of the colonial era."[49]

Hence, when the Spanish colonial administration disintegrated—and it collapsed not because of any pressure for independence in the Americas, but because of events in Europe—the ensuing conflicts, whether between territorial units or between landowners and peasants over land or between creoles and *peninsulares* over political power or just among different militias over nothing, could not be resolved within a preexisting institutional framework. Until one of the forces established its military domination or the opposing forces agreed to process conflicts according to some rules, conflicts could only take violent forms. And it took time before any kind of stable institutions were established.

Post-Consolidation Period

Once countries became independent, they could and eventually did develop political institutions. We examine first the arguments that unequal political institutions, those that restrict political rights and limit political participation, retard development and perpetuate economic inequality. We do not find support for either of these hypotheses in Latin America but observe that, through mechanisms that remain opaque to us, inequality was highly persistent, and we believe that persistent inequality generated recurrent political instability, which was costly to growth. In contrast, we find that political pluralism—situations in which those who enjoyed political rights processed their conflicts peacefully following certain rules, even if highly biased—was conducive to growth.

Political Rights, Development, and Inequality

Many argue that political rights in the form of suffrage promote development, either by protecting property rights and thus inducing investment or by stimulating the demand for public goods, including public productive goods.[50] Yet the effect of political rights on economic development is subject to sharply divergent beliefs. In a view dominant during the first half of the nineteenth century and represented in contemporary economics by the median voter model, extensions of suffrage, by lowering the relative income of the decisive voter, should lead to increased demand for redistribution, higher taxes, and lower growth.[51] Kenneth Sokoloff entertains both possibilities:

> Where an economic elite wields highly disproportionate political power..., a broadening of political influence through an extension of the franchise might diminish the returns to members of the elite and dampen their rates of investment. On the other hand, there could well be advantages for growth to having a more equal distribution of political influence. Many would expect, for example, more substantial support of infrastructure and other public goods and services..., a reduction in the levels of corruption, and perhaps more competition throughout the economy.[52]

Since both views may be correct, we may be observing only net effects, and they can be positive or negative.

Suffrage restrictions were prevalent in both the United States and Latin America. The formal restrictions for free males were gradually removed in the United States around 1830, and former male slaves were legally enfranchised as of 1869, but since the regulation of elections was the prerogative of state governments and since U.S. law always required voluntary registration, de facto restrictions were present throughout. Women, in turn, obtained the right to vote in 1919. In Latin America, male suffrage was typically restricted first by property or income requirements and subsequently by literacy requirements, which were aimed specifically to exclude agricultural workers and tenant farmers. Female suffrage came relatively late. The proportion of the total population that had the right to vote is shown in figure 5.4.[53]

The general trends can be seen more clearly in figure 5.5, in which the Latin American data are averaged and the series are smoothed. Note, however, that the U.S. eligible series is for the proportion of the population qualified to vote, given only requirements based on sex, age, and slavery, not the proportion that was registered to vote.[54] The latter series is available only after 1960, and during this period it tracks closely the Latin American series, which mixes eligibles and registered (it is not always possible to tell what the numbers refer to). Hence, the gap may have been much smaller than the U.S. eligible series indicates. Having the right to vote, moreover, is not the same as actually voting. Since electoral turnout in the United States has tended to be low, particularly in the years without presidential elections, the gap in

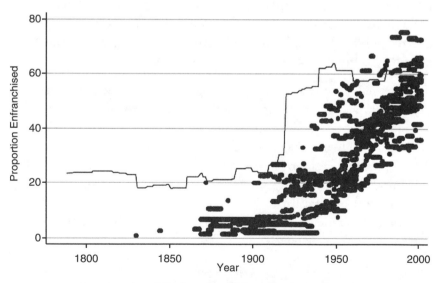

FIGURE 5.4 Proportion of Enfranchised Population in the Americas, I. *Note*: Line for the United States, scatter for Latin America. Only if legislature is elected and opposition is allowed. *Source*: Author's data.

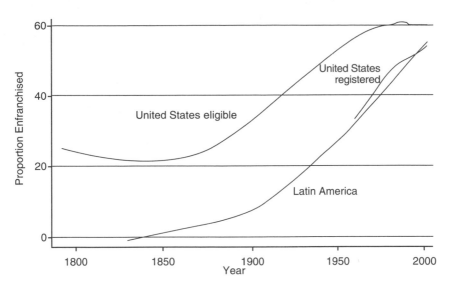

FIGURE 5.5 Proportion of Enfranchised Population in the Americas, II.
Note: Lowess smooth. *Source*: Author's data.

electoral participation is smaller than in eligibility. But during most of the nineteenth century, there was a gap.

With these descriptive preliminaries, we can approach the analytical question: is the income gap explained by the gap in suffrage or in electoral participation? Here, we face the methodological problem we announced earlier. In the OECD (Organisation for Economic Co-operation and Development) countries, more extensive suffrage and broader participation in legislative elections accelerated growth. Yet this was not true in Latin America, where broader suffrage and more extensive participation had almost no effect on growth (see figures 5.6 and 5.7).[55]

Without delving further, one can only conclude that, while in the currently developed countries the positive effects of suffrage dominated the negative ones, in Latin America, either they canceled each other out or the extent of suffrage was simply irrelevant. Tulio Halperin Donghi has argued, "The weakness of the vote made its nature irrelevant: since the voters were called upon above all to legitimize a preexisting situation and had already learned that it was expedient to do so, in the last resort it made no difference what part of the population held this dubious privilege."[56] Why this would be so, whether this is a matter of timing or a matter of the incomes at which suffrage was extended to particular groups, or something else, are fascinating questions that we must unfortunately leave aside. It is not obvious what

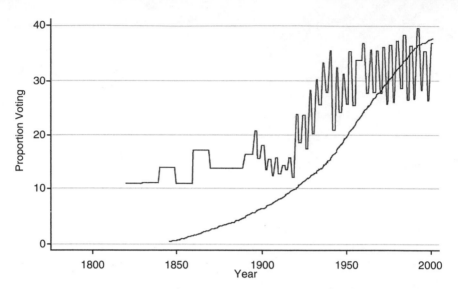

FIGURE 5.6 Proportion of the Population Voting in Legislative Elections in the Americas. *Note*: Line for the United States, lowess smooth for Latin America. *Source*: Author's data.

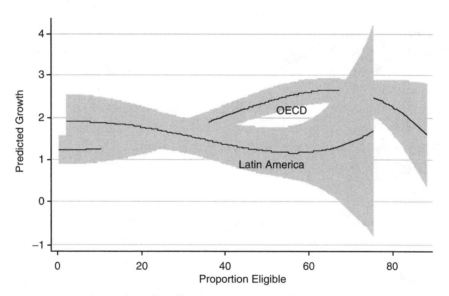

FIGURE 5.7 Growth and Suffrage in Latin American and OECD Countries. Shaded areas: 95% confidence interval. *Note*: fpsmooth. The shaded area is the 95% confidence interval. *Source*: Author's data and Angus Maddison, *The World Economy: Historical Statistics* (Paris: OECD, 2003).

the appropriate counterfactual is: should we be asking what would have happened had Latin America extended suffrage earlier in time, at higher income levels, at lower levels of inequality, or to different groups? All we know is that, in Latin America, the extent of suffrage and electoral participation did not affect growth. Did restricted political rights perpetuate economic inequality? In a series of papers, Stanley Engerman and Kenneth Sokoloff proposed the following explanation of Latin American underdevelopment:

1. The natural endowments found by European colonizers in Latin America could be operated only with unfree labor and, in turn, the legal inequality left a legacy of economic inequality even after it was abolished. According to Sokoloff, "Extreme inequality arose in the colonies of the Caribbean and in Brazil because their soils and climates gave them comparative advantage in growing sugar and other lucrative crops that were produced at lowest cost on large slave plantations.... Extreme inequality in wealth and human capital came to characterize much of Spanish America as well."[57]

2. Political institutions reproduced economic inequality: "Not only were certain fundamental characteristics of the New World economies and their factor endowments difficult to change, but government policies and other institutions tended to reproduce the conditions that gave rise to them."[58] Among the instruments by which inequality was maintained was restricted suffrage.

3. Inequality was adverse to development, because the poor did not have access to productive resources: "the greater inequality in wealth contributed to the evolution of institutions that commonly protected the privileges [of elites] and restricted opportunities for the mass of the population to participate fully in the commercial economy even after the abolition of slavery."[59] In turn, Engerman and Sokoloff, with the United States in mind, maintain that "greater equality provides support, if not impetus, to self-sustaining processes whereby expanding markets induce, and in turn are induced by, more effective or intensified use of resources, the realization of scale economies, higher rates of inventive activity and other forms of human capital accumulation, as well as increased specialization by factors of production."[60] In sum, political inequality led to the establishment of institutions that retarded

development by perpetuating economic inequality and restricting productive opportunities for the large mass of the population.

Coatsworth finds this story "plausible [but] almost certainly wrong."[61] He maintains that "land ownership (and wealth more generally) was not more concentrated in Latin America than in the thirteen British colonies (or the industrializing Britain itself)," pointing out that (1) most of the Spanish colonies were not slave economies; (2) throughout Mesoamerica and the Andes, the indigenous populations occupied most of the arable land; and (3) even where large estates existed, land was abundant and its value contributed little to concentrating wealth. Both Coatsworth and Prados de la Escosura maintain that inequality increased in Latin America only during the second part of the nineteenth century, when improved transport and expansion of trade made land more valuable.[62] Jeffrey Williamson demonstrates that, if in 1913 the proportion between real wages and land value was 1.0, in Argentina it decreased from 6.9 in 1880–1884 to 0.7 in 1930, and in Uruguay from 11.1 in 1870–1874 to 1.1 in 1930.[63]

In the end, it is not clear whether inequality was an original sin of Latin America or whether it was generated only when the continent embraced an export-oriented development strategy during the second half of the nineteenth century. Three main lessons about inequality can be drawn from the available data, which include the proportion of family farms between 1850 and 1970[64] and scattered information about household income distribution for the post–World War II period:

1. In light of Vanhanen's numbers, as of 1850 the difference in land ownership between North America and Latin America was startling: the average proportion of family farms in Latin America was 7.2 percent, with a minimum of 1 percent and a maximum of 25 percent.[65] At the same time, in the United States, 60 percent of farms were in family hands and, in Canada, 17 years later, 63 percent. It is not clear, however, whether land distribution was an important ingredient of total wealth distribution as of 1850 (see figures 5.8 and 5.9).

2. The proportion of family farms in 1970 did reflect the conditions as of 1850, but land distribution became more equal in all Latin American countries. Between 1850 and 1970, the proportion of family farms increased by 16.5 percent in an average Latin American country, with a range of 2–40 percent.

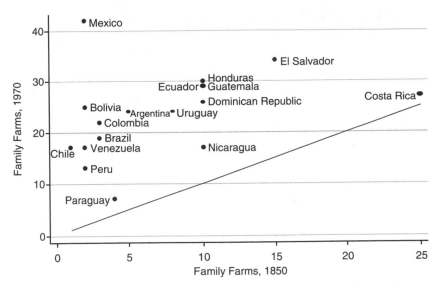

FIGURE 5.8 Proportion of Family Farms in 1850 and 1970. *Source*: Tatu Vanhanen, *Prospects of Democracy: A Study of 172 Countries* (London: Routledge, 1997).

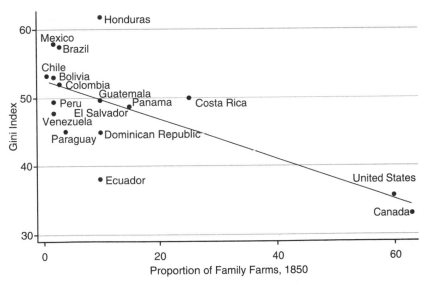

FIGURE 5.9 Gini at Last Date before 1982 as a Function of Family Farms in 1850. *Note*: Straight line is linear regression. *Source*: Tatu Vanhanen, *Prospects of Democracy: A Study of 172 Countries* (London: Routledge, 1997); and Klaus Deininger and Lyn Squire, "A New Data Set Measuring Income Inequality," *The World Bank Economic Review* 10, no. 3 (1996): 565–591.

3. Household income distribution during the 1960s and 1970s bears the traces of land distribution going as far back as 1850. Since the share of agriculture in national incomes was already low by the 1960s, what we see is the reproduction of inequality after 1850, rather than a contribution of land ownership to the current inequality of household incomes. Hence, it appears that inequality persisted even when the assets that gave rise to it changed. Since the post-1930 Latin American growth was labor intensive and it entailed little improvement in labor productivity, this may be the reason why inequality persisted.

Most important, to the extent that land redistribution did occur in Latin America, it was not because the poor acquired political rights and used them by voting: we find no relation between suffrage or participation and land redistribution. In turn, those Latin American countries which had more family farms in 1850 tended to redistribute more land.[66] Hence, the mechanisms by which the inequality was perpetuated remain obscure to us.

In conclusion, the inequality of political rights—the extent of suffrage and of voting participation—did not directly affect growth in Latin America. Moreover, there are grounds to doubt that restricted suffrage was the mechanism that perpetuated inequality, at least land inequality.

Political Pluralism, Political Instability, and Development

Is inequality the culprit for the slow development of Latin America? The relation between inequality and growth is notoriously difficult to disentangle. Having asked the question "Inequality and Growth: What Can the Data Say?" Banerjee and Duflo could only respond "not much."[67] The crux of the question concerns the mechanisms through which inequality affects development. Engerman and Sokoloff repeatedly argue that these mechanisms were institutional.[68] Others have emphasized the role of conflicts induced by inequality.

To put the contrast sharply, we have two rival political hypotheses.[69] The neo-institutionalist proposition says that Latin America had "bad" institutions, that is, institutions that protected the power of the already powerful by not educating the masses, limiting political rights, preventing the masses from availing themselves of economic opportunities, keeping internal markets small, and, as a consequence, retarding growth as well as perpetuating inequality. The conflict theory maintains that inequality intensifies conflicts over distribution, which result in diverting resources from production to fighting and impeding collective actions oriented toward providing public goods.[70] Moreover, prospects of future redistribution dampen current investment.

We have seen that unequal political institutions did not prevent development. What mattered, as will be shown below, is whether conflicts were processed according to rules, without violence, even if the institutions that processed them were not egalitarian and the rules were highly biased. The intra-elite conflicts in nineteenth-century Latin America concerned the organization of the state, the role of religion or, more broadly, conservatism versus liberalism, tariffs, and the location of state-financed infrastructure. As long as political institutions could absorb these conflicts and process them in relative peace, economies developed. Yet inequality persisted, and so did political instability. Instability, in turn, was costly in terms of development.

Regular elections, every four years for the president and every two for the lower house of the legislature, began in the United States in 1788 and have taken place regularly ever since. In Latin America, the occurrence of elections was frequent but much less regular, and, for varying periods after independence, countries were ruled without elected chief executives or legislatures.[71] Unfortunately, systematic data about the occurrence of elections are not yet available and difficult to compile.[72] We can, however, judge whether politics were pluralistic once we observe the first completed constitutional term in a country.

By pluralistic politics, we mean something very weak: only that a legislature is elected and that there is some electoral opposition.[73] Many elections that we consider pluralistic were manipulated, vote buying (*cohecho*) was widespread, and the results were frequently fraudulent.[74] Indeed, to our best knowledge, in the entire history of Latin America, only two incumbent presidents who presented themselves for reelection ever lost: Hipólito Mejía, of the Dominican Republic, in 2004, and Daniel Ortega of Nicaragua, in 1990.[75] As Halperin Donghi observed, "Among the many ways of overthrowing the government practiced in post-revolutionary Spanish America, defeat at the polls was conspicuously absent."[76] Yet we do not exclude manipulation or fraud in our definition of pluralism, because we think that they are prima facie evidence of political competition. Even when harassed, opposition was legally tolerated and allowed to win some seats in the legislature, and sometimes even a share of power. And these incentives were sufficient for the opposition to participate. Hence, intra-elite conflicts were processed according to some rules and, even if not without sporadic rebellions, were peacefully resolved.

Following Chile after 1831, several Latin American countries established stable systems of political competition in which the incumbent president, faithfully obeying term limits, chose his successor and through various devices assured his victory at the polls.[77] The stability of such systems of oligarchical competition—Chile between 1831 and 1891 and then again until 1924, Brazil between 1894 and 1930, Argentina between 1864 and 1892, and then again until 1916, Mexico between 1934 and 2000—was remarkable. Indeed, the last of such systems died in Mexico only in 2000.

As figure 5.10 shows, when elections were instituted during the nineteenth century, they tended to be pluralistic. Yet, in the twentieth century, rulers learned that they could hold rituals called "elections" without allowing any opposition. Later, when the military stepped into politics as an institution, most decided they did not need legislatures and elections at all. Only the post-1980 wave of democratization restored competitive elections in Latin America.

Thus defined, pluralism of the political process had a positive effect on growth. Within Latin America, the average growth rate during the 1,219 years when politics were pluralistic was 1.67 percent, while during the 267 years when there were no legislatures or no opposition,

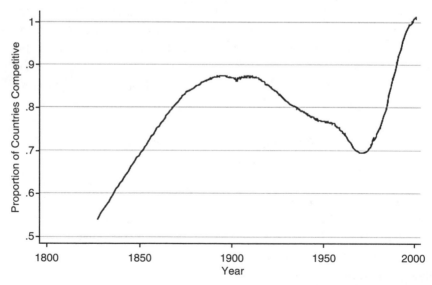

FIGURE 5.10 Competitive Politics in Latin America Once First Term Has Been Completed. *Note*: Lowess smooth. *Source*: Author's data.

this rate was 0.52 percent. Regression analyses lead us to believe that political pluralism had a positive effect on growth.[78]

The peaceful processing of conflicts according to some rules, however, is possible only if the resulting distribution of incomes (or the assets that generate them) is acceptable to all of the political forces that have the military prowess to engage in conflicts aimed at establishing their political monopoly.[79] Whenever the degree of redistribution that results from processing conflicts according to rules is excessive to some or insufficient to others, they may attempt to establish their monopoly of power. The result is political instability.

There are many ways to think about political instability. One is whether the chief executive completed a previously specified constitutional term, as distinct from periods when there was no effective constitution or the chief executive was deposed unconstitutionally or employed an *autogolpe* strategy to extend his term. Another way to think about instability is to count the number of chief executives during a particular year or a moving average of this number over some number of years (in this chapter, we take five).[80] Yet another way to think of instability is to focus on the frequency of coups or irregular transfers of power. Perhaps the best way to summarize these measures is to compute the number of consecutive years during which chief executives completed their terms. Given that in Latin America there were 157 cases in which the head executive changed at the time the term of the predecessor expired, over a total of 708 years (of the 1,527 for which we have data) in which the alternation of power occurred within the framework of constitutional norms, this measure indicates constitutional stability regardless of who occupied the government posts. In this sense, the number of consecutive years during which chief executives completed their terms is an indicator of the rule of law, even if the law was often manipulated in favor of the governing oligarchy.

As figures 5.11, 5.12, and 5.13 show, the political dust of independence settled around 1870, and by the eve of World War I stability reigned. A new wave of destabilization, however, occurred after 1924, when several countries experienced the first military coups in their histories.[81] Only after 1980 was political stability restored again, even if turnover of the chief executives accelerated again in the most recent years.[82]

While the above characterizes the general pattern for all of Latin America, particular countries have experienced highly divergent trajectories. For example, executive turnover peaked during different periods and at different levels in Brazil, Chile, and Mexico.[83] And

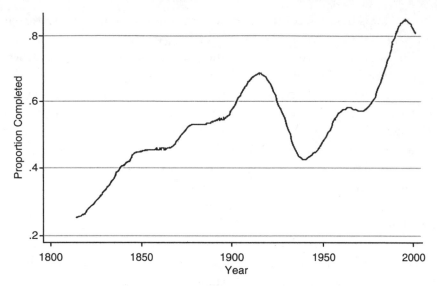

FIGURE 5.11 Proportion of Countries with Completed Terms.
Note: Lowess smooth. *Source*: Author's data.

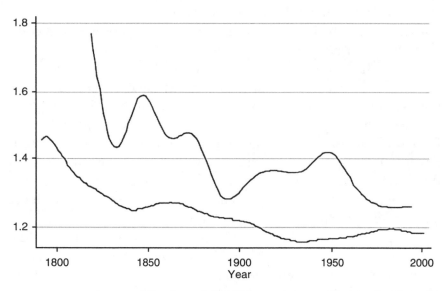

FIGURE 5.12 Average Number of Chief Executives per Year in the United
States and Latin America. *Note*: lowess smooth for the United States,
mspline for Latin America. *Source*: Author's data.

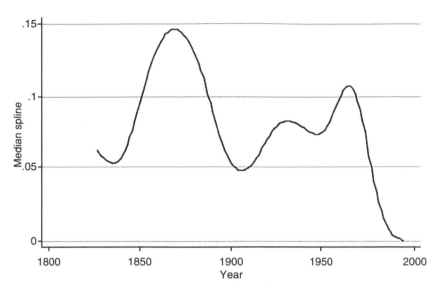

FIGURE 5.13 Average Number of Coups per Country in Latin America.
Note: mspline smooth. *Source*: Author's data.

again, the frequency of coups differed importantly among countries: by 2000, Uruguay had experienced 8, while Bolivia had 36.

None of these analytical approaches captures fully the importance of instability, since what probably matters more for development are expectations of future conflicts, rather than current disorders.[84] Yet, current disorders divert resources from producing to fighting and impede collective actions designed to produce public goods. Hence, one should expect that current political instability retards growth. The numbers support this prima facie assertion. During 997 years of completed terms, incomes grew at the average rate of 1.93, while during 631 years of interrupted terms, they grew at the rate of 0.94.[85] The average rate of growth during 1,412 years when there was just one chief executive was 1.88; during 366 years when there were two, it was 1.01; and during 96 years with more than two chief executives, it was –0.55. The average rate of growth during 1,468 years without coups was 1.59, while during 95 years when at least one coup occurred, it was 0.78. Our measure of the number of consecutive years of completed terms shows, once again, that thus defined political stability had positive effects on growth.[86]

Completed terms were more frequent at higher levels of suffrage, while executive turnovers and coups were more frequent at lower levels: political inequality thus seems to have a direct impact on

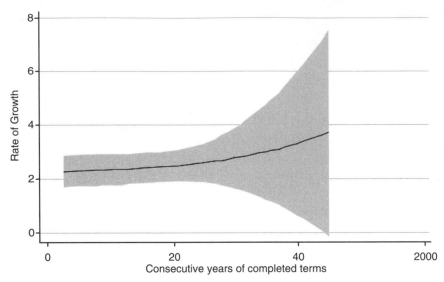

FIGURE 5.14 Rate of Growth of per Capita Income as a Function of Consecutive Years of Completed Terms. *Note*: fpsmooth. Shaded area is 95 percent confidence interval. Pre-1979 only. *Source*: Angus Maddison, *The World Economy: Historical Statistics* (Paris: OECD, 2003), and Authors' data.

political instability. However, we cannot show statistically that political instability was caused by economic inequality.[87] The reason is perhaps that the only measure of inequality we have is the proportion of family farms, and this measure changes significance as assets other than land become important for income distribution. But there is ample historical evidence that destabilizing conflicts were distributional.

The development of Latin America during the second half of the nineteenth century led to the emergence of two major distributional conflicts: over land or wages in agriculture and over wages and working conditions in industry.[88] Land distribution was a perennial issue in Latin America and continued to be so in the second half of the twentieth century, when 12 Latin American countries instituted 27 reforms that entailed some land redistribution.[89] In several countries, military regimes followed a breakdown of what was once called the *pacto urbano*: the tacit consent of the urban bourgeoisie and industrial unions to the exploitation of tenant farmers and agricultural workers by landowners. In turn, the rise of working-class movements—industrial union militancy and the accompanying specter of communism—was a major factor in destabilizing political regimes. As Collier and Collier report, "the incorporation [of the working-class] experience produced a strong political reaction and in most countries this reaction culminated in the breakdown of the national political regime under which the incorporation policies had been implemented."[90] Indeed, we believe that extensions of political rights were threatening not because they could have generated redistribution via fiscal mechanisms (taxes and transfers), but because of the rights to organize and strike.

In sum, whenever political institutions absorbed conflicts and processed them according to rules, economies developed, even though unequal political institutions promoted political instability. Moreover, since income inequality persisted, distributional conflicts were destabilizing, and political instability recurrently interrupted development.

Conclusion

This chapter has highlighted institutional dynamics in Latin America and its consequences for development. Latin American economies developed whenever conflicts were processed according to some rules that allowed political pluralism, even when suffrage was extremely narrow. What mattered was not whether institutions were broad or narrow, egalitarian or not, but whether they could structure and absorb conflicts as they arose. The well-entrenched oligarchical republics, in which the masses were barred from participating in politics but the elites found some modus vivendi, were not inimical to development.

Economies grew when political power protected economic power.[91] Hence, we agree with Coatsworth that "[w]hat Engerman and Sokoloff saw as obstacles to economic growth—elite power and economic inequality—actually facilitated the region's transition to sustained, if unstable, economic growth."[92] Yet, since development reproduced or perhaps even increased economic inequality, the prospects of political incorporation, particularly the right of workers and peasants to organize, threatened property. This threat was not that the newly enfranchised voters would demand redistribution through the fiscal system,[93] but that they would use their political rights to organize, strike, and thus redistribute private incomes or even productive assets. As a result, a new wave of violent conflicts ensued.

Political inequality, therefore, appears to be statically efficient. But since it perpetuates economic inequality, it renders foreboding the prospect of redistribution that may result from political incorporation of the masses. And since the expectation of political instability is economically costly—probably more costly than the occurrence of instability itself—political inequality is dynamically inefficient.

Notes

1. This work was supported in part by a grant from the National Science Foundation. For comments on earlier drafts, we thank John Coatsworth, Bill Easterly, John Ferejohn, Raquel Fernandez, Russell Hardin, Stephen Holmes, Fernando Limongi, Norman Loayaza, Bernard Manin, Pasquale Pasquino, and the participants in the seminars held at the Universidad de San Andrés and the Universidad Torcuato Di Tella.

2. See Stephan Haggard, *Pathways from Periphery: The Politics of Growth in the Newly Industrializing Countries* (Ithaca, NY: Cornell University Press, 1990). See also *Encuentros y desencuentros de dos primos lejanos: Un ensayo de historia económica comparada de Argentina y Australia*, Working Paper 006 (Buenos Aires: Fundación Pent, 2005), in which Pablo Gerchunoff and Pablo Fajgelbaum offer a clear analysis on how two countries with similar factor endowments—Argentina and Australia—differed in their economic strategies.

3. Adam Przeworski, "The Last Instance: Are Institutions a Deeper Cause of Economic Development?" *European Archives of Sociology* 45, no. 2 (2004): 165–188.

4. The theoretical program has been laid out by North: "To make sense out of historical and contemporary evidence, we must rethink the whole process of economic growth.... The *primary source* of economic growth is the institutional/organizational structure of a political economy." See Douglass C. North, "Some Fundamental Puzzles in Economic History/Development," in *The Economy as an Evolving Complex System*, edited by W. Brian Arthur, Steven N. Durlauf, and David A. Lane (Reading, MA: Addison-Wesley, 1997), vol. 2, p. 224. Specifically, "Third World countries are poor because the institutional constraints define a set of payoffs to political/economic activity that do not encourage productive activity." See North, *Institutions, Institutional Change, and Economic Performance* (Cambridge: Cambridge University Press, 1990), p. 110.

5. On the importance of judicial systems, see Rafael La Porta, Florencio López de Silanes, Andrei Shleifer, and Robert M. Vishny, "Law and Finance," *Journal of Political Economy* 106 (1998): 1113–1155. John H. Coatsworth and Gabriel Tortella Casares analyze the effect of the Spanish judicial system on the development of Spain and Mexico in their initial periods; see John H. Coatsworth and Gabriel Tortella Casares, *Institutions and Long-Run Economic Performance in Mexico and Spain, 1800–2000*, Working Paper 02/03-1 (Cambridge, MA: David Rockefeller Center for Latin American Studies, Harvard University, 2003). See also Pranab Bardhan, "History, Institutions and Underdevelopment," unpublished manuscript, Department of Economics, University of California, Berkeley, 2004; Michael D. Bordo and Roberto Cortés Conde, "Introduction," in *Transferring Wealth and Power from the Old to the New World*, edited by M. D. Bordo and R. Cortés Conde (Cambridge: Cambridge University Press, 2001); and Philip Keefer, "From Settler Mortality to Patrimonialism: Weaving the Dynamics of Political Competition into the Political Economy of Development," *Political Economist* 12, no. 3 (2005), pp. 1, 5, 8, 10, and 13.

6. See, for example, Stephen Haber, ed., *How Latin America Fell Behind: Essays on the Economic Histories of Brazil and Mexico, 1800–1914* (Stanford, CA: Stanford University Press, 1997); and Stephen Haber, ed., *Political Institutions and Economic Growth in Latin America* (Stanford, CA: Hoover Institution Press, 2000).

7. According to Haber, crony capitalism "is usually thought of as a system in which those close to the political authorities who make and enforce policies receive favors that have large economic value." He could have in mind the restrictions on sugar imports, or the Halliburton Iraq contracts, or the $14 billion subsidy to

the oil industry. But none of these are possible, because in the United States the government is "limited." Stephen Haber, *Crony Capitalism and Economic Growth in Latin America: Theory and Evidence* (Stanford, CA: Hoover Institution Press, 2002), pp. 12, 13.

8. See, for example, Leandro Prados de La Escosura and Samuel Amaral, eds., *La independencia americana: Consecuencias económicas* (Madrid: Alianza, 1993); John H. Coatsworth and Alan M. Taylor, *Latin America and the World Economy since 1800* (Cambridge, MA: Harvard University Press, 1998); and Haber, *How Latin America Fell Behind, Political Institutions and Economic Growth*, and *Crony Capitalism*.

9. See Roberto Gargarella, *Los fundamentos legales de la desigualdad: El constitucionalismo en América (1776–1860)* (Madrid: Siglo XXI, 2005).

10. José Luis Machinea and Cecilia Vera, "Comercio, inversión directa y políticas productivas," paper presented at the seminar "Una nueva agenda de desarrollo para América Latina," Salamanca, October 7–8, 2005.

11. This is contrary to what some scholars have argued. See, for example, Stanley L. Engerman and Kenneth L. Sokoloff, "Inequality, Institutions, and Differential Paths of Growth among New World Economies," paper presented at the meeting of the MacArthur Research Network on Inequality and Economic Performance, Boston, 2001. See also Daron Acemoglu, Simon Johnson, and James A. Robinson, "The Colonial Origins of Comparative Development," *American Economic Review* 91 (2001): 1369–1401. This is not the place for theoretical discussions, but note that "security of property rights" is a notoriously fuzzy concept. For one, in a Schumpeterian world of creative destruction, property would be secure only if it were defended by barriers to entry (see Daron Acemoglu, "The Form of Property Rights: Oligarchic vs. Democratic Societies," Working Paper, Department of Economics [Cambridge: Massachusetts Institute of Technology, 2005]). Secondly, property can be made secure not by right but by might: in Latin America, land was often protected by private militias (see Fernando López-Alves, *State Formation and Democracy in Latin America, 1810–1900* [Durham: Duke University Press, 2000]). Most importantly, however, property rights mean something different for those who possess it and for those who do not. In the presence of barriers to entry and credit constraints—both prevalent in Latin America—property rights are exclusionary.

12. See Elisa Mariscal and Kenneth L. Sokoloff, "Schooling, Suffrage, and the Persistence of Inequality in the Americas, 1800–1945," in *Political Institutions and Economic Growth in Latin America*, edited by Stephen Haber (Stanford: Hoover Institution Press, 2000), pp. 159–218; Kenneth L. Sokoloff, "The Evolution of Suffrage Institutions in the New World: A Preliminary Look," in *Crony Capitalism and Economic Growth in Latin America: Theory and Evidence*, edited by Stephen Haber (Stanford: Hoover Institution Press, 2002), pp. 75–107.

13. Angus Maddison, *The World Economy: Historical Statistics* (Paris: OECD, 2003). Unless otherwise noted, all figures are in U.S. dollars and are Geary-Khamis (G-K) index 1990 purchasing power parity dollars. While this is the most comprehensive income series available, Maddison's figures are not universally accepted by historians. Indeed, at times they constitute only rough guesses.

14. Abhijit Banerjee and Lakshmi Iyer, "History, Institutions, and Economic Performance: The Legacy of Colonial Land Tenure Systems in India," unpublished manuscript, Department of Economics, Massachusetts Institute of Technology, Cambridge, 2002, p. 1.

15. When, in 1969, Kuznets posed the question of whether Europe was wealthier than the rest of the world in 1750, his estimate was that the ratio of the lowest to the highest per capita income in the world was 1:2, perhaps even 1:2.5. Newer

estimates reduce this difference. Bairoch claims that contemporary less developed countries were not poorer than Europe (Paul Bairoch, *Economics and World History: Myths and Paradoxes* [Chicago: University of Chicago Press, 1993]), as does Pomeranz (Kenneth Pomeranz, *The Great Divergence: China, Europe, and the Making of the Modern World Economy* [Princeton, NJ: Princeton University Press, 2000]). Maddison believes the ratio was about 1 to 1.5 (see Maddison, *The World Economy*, p. 114).

16. John H. Coatsworth, "Economic and Institutional Trajectories in Nineteenth-Century Latin America," in Coatsworth and Taylor, *Latin America and the World Economy*, p. 26.

17. One can ask the same question with regard to every region of the world and find some idiosyncratic reasons why it fell behind. See, for example, Pomeranz, *The Great Divergence*, on China; and on the Middle East, see Timur Kuran, "Why the Middle East Is Economically Underdeveloped: Historical Mechanisms of Institutional Stagnation," *Journal of Economic Perspectives* 18 (2004): 71–90.

18. Leandro Prados de la Escosura, *Assessing the Economic Effects of Latin American Independence*, Working Paper 03-12 (Madrid: Universidad Carlos III, 2003), p. 11.

19. Coatsworth refers to this period as "the catastrophic second quarter of the nineteenth century." John H. Coatsworth, "Structures, Endowments, and Institutions in the Economic History of Latin America," *Latin American Research Review* 40 (2005): 137.

20. Coatsworth argues that "all of the significant obstacles to economic growth in nearly all of the countries of Latin America had disappeared by the late nineteenth century." John H. Coatsworth, "Notes on the Comparative Economic History of Latin America and the United States," in *Development and Underdevelopment in America: Contrasts of Economic Growth in North and Latin America in Historical Perspective*, edited by Walther L. Bernecker and Hans Werner Tobler (Berlin: de Gruyter, 1993), p. 10.

21. According to Cortés Conde, growth in the United States between 1774 and 1905 was due mainly to an increase in productive factors rather than in productivity. Roberto Cortés Conde, *Historia económica mundial* (Buenos Aires: Ariel, 2003), p. 143.

22. Cole, Ohanian, and Schmitz also attribute Latin America's economic lag after 1950 to stagnant labor productivity. See Harold L. Cole, Lee E. Ohanian, and James A. Schmitz, Jr., *Latin America in the Rearview Mirror*, Working Paper 11008 (Cambridge, MA: National Bureau of Economic Research, 2004).

23. There is nothing special about using the same rate of growth as a yardstick. Indeed, in the light of convergence theories (see, for example, Robert Lucas, "Some Macroeconomics for the 21st Century," *Journal of Economic Perspectives* 14 [2000]: 159–168), one would expect countries that lag behind the technological leader to grow faster. We use the same rate of growth merely as an accounting device.

24. Remember that this is not quite accurate, since data for different countries are only available for certain dates.

25. In 1980, this gap was $528; by 2000, it was $2,858.

26. Maddison, *The World Economy*, p. 114.

27. John H. Coatsworth, "Economic and Institutional Trajectories in Nineteenth-Century Latin America," in Coatsworth and Taylor, *Latin America and the World Economy*.

28. Coatsworth, "Structures, Endowments, and Institutions," p. 128.

29. Victor Bulmer-Thomas, *The Economic History of Latin America since Independence*, 2nd ed. (Cambridge: Cambridge University Press, 2003), p. 27.

30. Coatsworth provides ratios of per capita incomes of some Latin American countries to that of the United States. Assuming the income in the United States to have been $1,000 (extrapolation from Maddison's numbers for 1820–1830) and using these ratios, the income of Argentina in 1800 would have been $1,020; of Brazil $360 (Maddison's figure for 1820 is $646); Chile $460; Cuba $1,120; Mexico $500 (Maddison's 1820 figure is $759); and Peru $410. See Maddison, *The World Economy*; and Coatsworth, "Structures, Endowments, and Institutions."

31. See Peter C. Mancall and Thomas Weiss, "Was Economic Growth Likely in Colonial British North America?" *Journal of Economic History* 56 (1999): 17–40.

32. Bulmer-Thomas, *The Economic History of Latin America*, p. 27.

33. See Mancall and Weiss, "Was Economic Growth Likely in Colonial British North America?" p. 26, Table 2.

34. Ibid.

35. Prados de la Escosura, *Assessing the Economic Effects of Latin American Independence*, p. 4.

36. These results are based on a regression that includes the 19 Latin American countries and the United States. If we drop the United States, both numbers become smaller, but the estimates are still statistically significant. Hence, these relations hold within Latin America.

37. Here is how we reason. The regression shows that the 2000 cost of postponing independence one year is $165. Hence, it must be true that $y_t(1+r)^{2000-t} - y_{t+1}$ $(1+r)^{2000-(t+1)} = 165$. Solving yields $y_{t+1} - y_t = ry_t - 165(1+r)^{-(2000-(t+1))}$. Letting $t = 1820$, using the U.S. growth rate for r, and assuming $y_{1820} = 700$ yields the numbers in the text. Analogously for turmoil.

38. On the costs of waiting for independence, see Coatsworth, who estimates that had Mexico gained independence in 1800 instead of 1821, its GDP at the time of his writing would have been 7.2 percent higher. Coatsworth, "Notes on the Comparative Economic History," p. 16.

39. Maddison, *The World Economy*, p.76.

40. John H. Coatsworth, "Economic and Institutional Trajectories in Nineteenth-Century Latin America," in Coatsworth and Taylor, *Latin America and the World Economy*, p. 25.

41. Amaral, for example, argues that Argentine independence resulted from local pressures on institutions that could not satisfy the needs of trade and production. See Samuel Amaral, "Del mercantilismo a la libertad: Las consecuencias económicas de la independencia argentina," in Prados de La Escosura and Amaral, *La independencia americana*, pp. 202–203.

42. See Bulmer-Thomas, *The Economic History of Latin America*.

43. See Susan Dunn, *Jefferson's Second Revolution: The Election Crisis of 1800 and the Triumph of Republicanism* (Boston: Houghton Mifflin, 2005); and Bernard A. Weisberger, *America Afire: Jefferson, Adams, and the First Contested Election* (New York: Perennial, 2001).

44. See, for example, Fernando López-Alves, *State Formation and Democracy in Latin America, 1810–1900*.

45. For an explanation of the difficulties in reaching national unity in Argentina, particularly in contrast to the United States, see Julio Saguir, "Entre el Conflicto y la Organización Institucional: Los Procesos Constituyentes de Estados Unidos (1776–1787) y Argentina (1810–1860)," *Agora*, no. 8 (1998): 123–144.

46. On the controversies over whether and to what extent the Latin American wars of independence were social revolutions, see the essays in Lewis Hanke, ed., *History of Latin American Civilization: Sources and Interpretations*, vol. 2: *The Modern Era* (Boston: Little, Brown, 1967), pp. 1–59.

47. See J. Franklin Jameson, *The American Revolution Considered as a Social Movement* (Princeton, NJ: Princeton University Press, 1973), originally published in 1926; and Charles A. Beard, *An Economic Interpretation of the Constitution of the United States* (New York: Houghton Mifflin, 1913).

48. Territorial consolidation in Latin America entailed some national failed attempts (Cundinamarca, Gran Colombia, Central American Republic) and the failed attempts of some provinces to become independent on their own. Interstate wars, however, were rare in Latin America.

49. Clarence Henry Haring, *The Spanish Empire in America* (New York: Harcourt, Brace, 1947), p. 165.

50. See Douglass C. North and Barry Weingast, "The Evolution of Institutions Governing Public Choice in 17th Century England," *Journal of Economic History* 49 (1989): 803–832; Acemoglu, Johnson, and Robinson, "The Colonial Origins of Comparative Development," pp. 1369–1401; and Alessandro Lizzeri and Nicola Persico, "Why Did the Elites Extend the Suffrage? Democracy and the Scope of Government, with an Application to Britain's 'Age of Reform,'" *Quarterly Journal of Economics* 119 (2004): 707–765.

51. See Allan Meltzer and Scott F. Richards, "A Rational Theory of the Size of Government," *Journal of Political Economy* 89, no. 5 (1981): 914–927.

52. Kenneth L. Sokoloff, "The Evolution of Suffrage Institutions in the New World: A Preliminary Look," in Haber, *Crony Capitalism*, p. 76.

53. Note that the ratio of eligibles to the total population is sensitive to the age composition. Some of the upward trend of the data is due to the aging of the populations, and the difference between the United States and Latin America in the recent period is due only to the age structure.

54. See Jerrold G. Rusk, *A Statistical History of the American Electorate* (Washington, DC: CQ Press, 2001).

55. The results about the positive effect of suffrage on growth in the world and the lack of effect in Latin America are robust to different estimators (2SLS with fixed effects, 3SLS, SURE) and different specifications of control variables. Results are almost identical for electoral participation.

56. According to Halperin Donghi, indirect elections favored the appointment of local dignitaries, so even when suffrage was extensive, the result was the same as if only the very rich could vote. Tulio Halperin Donghi, *The Aftermath of Revolution in Latin America* (New York: Harper & Row, 1973), p. 116.

57. Kenneth L. Sokoloff, "Institutions, Factor Endowments, and Paths of Development in the New World," Villa Borsig Workshop Series 2000, on The Institutional Foundations of a Market Economy, pp. 78, 79 [summary version available online at http://www.inwent.org/ef-texte/instn/sokoloff.htm]. Terry Karl echoes the prevailing view: "In Latin America from the very beginning, mineral and agricultural riches were a mixed blessing; in the context of a specific form of colonial rule they produced concentrated rents that centralized economic and political power and established the region's patterns of inequality." Terry L. Karl, *The Vicious Circle of Inequality in Latin America*, Working Paper 2002/177 (Madrid: Centro de Estudios Avanzados en Ciencias Sociales, Instituto Juan March, 2002), pp. 7, 8.

58. Sokoloff, "The Institutional Foundations of a Market Economy," p. 5.

59. Ibid., p. 4.

60. Engerman and Sokoloff, "Inequality, Institutions, and Differential Paths of Growth," p. 35.

61. Coatsworth, "Structures, Endowments, and Institutions," pp. 139–140.

62. See John H. Coatsworth, "Economic and Institutional Trajectories in Nineteenth-Century Latin America," in Coatsworth and Taylor, *Latin America and the*

World Economy, p. 39; Coatsworth, "Structures, Endowments, and Institutions," p. 30; and Prados de la Escosura, *Assessing the Economic Effects of Latin American Independence.*

63. Jeffrey G. Williamson, "Real Wages, Inequality and Globalization in Latin America before 1940," *Revista de Historia Económica* 17 (2004): 101–142, table 7.

64. Note that this variable is a highly imperfect indicator of income inequality since it does not take into account the changing relative value of land. In addition, we are not clear how Vanhanen treated communal lands.

65. See Tatu Vanhanen, *Prospects of Democracy: A Study of 172 Countries* (London: Routledge, 1997).

66. Fixed-effects regression with first-order autocorrelation and with the current proportion of family farms as control shows a negative effect of eligibility both in Latin America and the rest of the world. The persistence coefficient (on the current proportion) is, in turn, positive and high. Note, however, that these results are very sensitive to the choice of estimator.

67. See Abhijit V. Banerjee and Esther Duflo "Inequality and Growth: What Can the Data Say?" *Journal of Economic Growth* 8 (2003): 267–299.

68. Engerman and Sokoloff, "Inequality, Institutions, and Differential Paths of Growth."

69. There is also a third theory that relies on market imperfections and credit constraints. See Abhijit V. Banerjee and Andrew F. Newman, "Poverty, Incentives, and Development," *American Economic Review* 84 (1994): 211–215.

70. See Banerjee and Iyer, "History, Institutions, and Economic Performance"; and Pranab Bardhan, *Scarcity, Conflicts, and Cooperation* (Cambridge, MA: MIT Press, 2005), chapter 10.

71. As Jonathan Hartlyn and Arturo Valenzuela point out, "liberal principles found a tenuous hold in Latin America before they took root in much of Europe." Hartlyn and Valenzuela, "Democracy in Latin America since 1930," in *The Cambridge History of Latin America*, vol. 6, part 2, edited by Leslie Bethell (Cambridge: Cambridge University Press, 1994), p. 108. Antonio Annino points out that, in many Latin American countries, local elections took place long before they did in Europe. Between 1809 and 1814, a period of intense electioneering erupted. According to Eduardo Posada-Carbó, "most provinces lived through cycles of political agitation motivated by successive elections, including those for the juntas, the Spanish Cortes, for municipal offices and bodies, and provincial *diputaciones*." Posada-Carbó, "Electoral Juggling: A Comparative History of the Corruption of Suffrage in Latin America, 1830–1930," *Journal of Latin American Studies* 32 (2000): 621. It should be noted, however, that most of these elections were local, granting local governments legitimacy not enjoyed by national ones and thus strengthening centrifugal tendencies. See Antonio Annino, *Historia de las elecciones en Iberoamérica, siglo XXI* (Mexico City: Fondo de Cultura Económica, 1995), p. 10.

72. We do know when some elections took place but cannot be certain that there were no elections during periods about which we have no information.

73. Specifically, politics is considered pluralistic if there exists an elected legislature and some, even minimal, legal opposition. Nonpluralistic years, therefore, are those without an elected legislature or those with only one party or those in which a party (or presidential candidate) runs unopposed.

74. Electoral fraud is notoriously difficult to define. On the ambiguity of this concept in nineteenth-century Latin America, see Annino, *Historia de las elecciones en Iberoamérica*, pp. 15–18.

75. One other exception is the Costa Rican Braulio Carrillo, who was first elected in 1835 to complete the term of an incumbent who was forced to resign. Braulio

Carrillo lost reelection in 1837, but one year later he overthrew the electoral winner and enacted a constitution that declared him president for life. He was deposed in 1843.

76. Halperin Donghi, *The Aftermath of Revolution*, p. 116.

77. See Samuel J. Valenzuela, *The Origins and Transformation of the Chilean Party System*, Working Paper 215 (Notre Dame, IN: Helen Kellogg Institute for International Studies, University of Notre Dame, 1995). For a summary of devices by which governments control electoral results, see Posada-Carbó, "Electoral Juggling."

78. We explain competitiveness by lagged per capita income, lagged military expenditures, proportion of family farms, and lagged unrest. The growth equation has only competitiveness, rate of growth of population, and the average rate of growth of GDP per capita in the world in a particular year. The estimators we used include different forms of matching, Heckit, 2SLS with fixed effects, and fixed effects with AR1. Whenever the coefficient on competitiveness is significant, it hovers slightly above 1. The results do not depend on including the United States.

79. Note that we do not argue that conflicts were peacefully resolved when institutions managed to impose order, but rather when politically relevant groups had incentives to follow the institutional process. In other words, we consider institutions to be endogenous. See Jess Benhabib and Adam Przeworski, "The Political Economy of Redistribution under Democracy," *Journal of Economic Theory* 29, no. 2 (2005): 271–290; and Adam Przeworski, "Democracy as an Equilibrium," *Public Choice* 123 (2005): 253–273.

80. Note that if the constitutional term of the chief executive is for a nonrenewable four years and if this norm is always observed, then we would expect the five-year moving average to be 1.25 heads per year, while with a six-year term the five-year moving average would be 1.1666. Protracted dictatorships or repeated reelections would generate lower numbers, while coups and other contests for power would be seen as more frequent turnovers. During the post–World War II period, the terms in Latin America ranged from four to six years, with an average of 4.64. We do not have systematic data for the earlier period, but there were some two-year terms. Term limits were ubiquitous and, surprisingly, whenever in place were almost always observed.

81. The first in a series of coups occurred in Chile in 1924. According to Alain Rouquié:

> Between February and December of 1930, the military were involved in the overthrow of governments in no fewer than six, widely differing Latin American nations—Argentina, Brazil, the Dominican Republic, Bolivia, Peru, and Guatemala. The same year also saw four unsuccessful attempts to seize power by force in other Latin American countries. Over the following years, Ecuador and el [*sic*] Salvador in 1931, and Chile in 1932, joined the list of countries in which military-provoked political shifts and unscheduled changes of the executive had taken place.

Alain Rouquié, "The Military in Latin American Politics since 1930," in Bethell, *Cambridge History of Latin America*, vol. 6, part 2, p. 223.

82. Over 10 Latin American presidents have left office precipitously since the mid-1990s. It is notable, however, that contrary to the past, in most cases succession occurred with strict observance of constitutional rules.

83. Coatsworth and Tortella Casares, *Institutions and Long-Run Economic Performance* (2003), p. 18, report, for example, that Mexico changed presidents 48 times between 1825 and 1855.

84. Adam Przeworski, Michael E. Alvarez, Jose Antonio Cheibub, and Fernando Limongi, *Democracy and Development. Political Institutions and Well-Being in the World, 1950–1990* (New York: Cambridge University Press, 2000), pp. 187–215.

85. The positive effect of completed terms on growth defends itself in a fixed-effects regression with controls for growth rates as well as instrumental variables fixed-effects estimation with the history of past coups and a moving average of past executive turnovers as instruments.

86. Regression analysis (with country fixed effects) with several controls and a dummy variable for the post-1978 period shows that this effect is sizable and statistically significant. The same holds true when we instrument years of completed terms.

87. While signs of family farms in regressions that take as the dependent variable the three indicators of instability are always correct, the coefficients are rarely significant.

88. According to the data collected by Julio Godio, the reasons for strikes in Argentina became increasingly heterogeneous with time. See Godio, *Historia del movimiento obrero argentino: Inmigrantes, asalariados y lucha de clases, 1880–1910* (Buenos Aires: Tiempo Contemporáneo, 1972).

89. Based on data kindly provided by Anjali Thomas.

90. Ruth Berins Collier and David Collier, *Shaping the Political Arena* (Princeton, NJ: Princeton University Press, 1995), p. 8.

91. Roland Bénabou presents a formal argument to that effect. See Bénabou, "Inequality and Growth," in *NBER Macro-Economics Annual*, edited by Ben Bernanke and Julio Rotemberg, (Cambridge, MA: National Bureau of Economic Research, 1996), pp. 11–74.

92. Coatsworth, "Structures, Endowments, and Institutions," p. 140.

93. See Daron Acemoglu and James Robinson, "Why Did the West Extend the Franchise? Democracy, Inequality, and Growth in Historical Perspective," *Quarterly Journal of Economics* (2000): 1167–1199; and Acemoglu, Johnson, and Robinson, "The Colonial Origins of Comparative Development."

6

The Role of High-Stakes Politics in Latin America's Development Gap

RIORDAN ROETT AND FRANCISCO E. GONZÁLEZ

THE TWENTIETH CENTURY was a period of unpredictable institutional turbulence for Latin America: failed economic development models, elite-mass conflict, a natural resource "curse" (the reliance on traditional mineral and commodity exports and the inability to add value to exports and replicate the industrial development model of the countries of Southeast Asia, the so-called Asian Tigers), regime breakdowns, severe social inequality and appalling poverty, and the emergence, at the end of the century and into the early twenty-first century, of new forms of populism. Overall, Latin America's growth record has been characterized by progress, poverty, and exclusion,[1] and, as many observers agree, there has been relatively little progress and too much poverty and exclusion. What explains, first, the failure to address social inequality and economic models that have been found wanting in terms of employment, income, and status? And, second, what explains the lack of learning to understand, on the part of the region's political leaders and elites, that political instability is directly related to their inability and/or unwillingness to address economic underdevelopment and social distress?

The failure to develop, when compared to the United States, is obvious.[2] As telling, though, is the sharp contrast between Latin America and the Asian Tigers. In the early 1960s, the Tigers and Latin America were at a comparable stage of economic and social development. Quickly, almost inexorably, Asian regimes negotiated a social contract with their populations, which emphasized quality primary and secondary education, public health programs, and housing. This provided a trained and competitive workforce for the industrial model adopted in the region, and it led to decreasing poverty and social exclusion within a period of 25 years.

The Tigers developed a "smart state" as they began their journey to higher levels of growth and development. The social contract was the backbone of that state, but good outcomes resulted from intelligent public policy decisions. This became increasingly the case as the twentieth century peaked because of the challenge of competitiveness in the international marketplace. Asia competed and Latin America followed, but very slowly and with growing resistance toward the end of the century to the so-called liberal economic models embodied in the Washington Consensus.[3] By the end of the 1990s, fierce resistance to the reform agenda had developed in many countries, leaving the Washington Consensus in tatters. The challenge in the twenty-first century is to undo or neutralize the errors and lapses in judgment of the old century. To do so will require a major reassessment of both the resources and the leadership required to close the gap with the United States and with developing Asia.

In this chapter, we will address four issues that we believe help to explain the development gap between Latin America and the United States. The first addresses what some authors have called high-stakes politics—when the fight for shares escalates, and there is a standoff, even sharp polarization, between different social groups in a society. The second is the emergence of a process of ruling elite understandings, or "pacts," in some countries. These political arrangements or understandings have been able to produce relative social peace and a certain political stability, but they have failed to address the poverty and inequality questions. Third, we look at the challenge for the region to develop a smart state in the twenty-first century. Finally, we address the challenge of negotiating a social contract between government and the governed, which has eluded Latin America but must be addressed if poverty and inequality are to be alleviated and if a modicum of political stability is to be institutionalized.

The Distributive Conflict in Latin America and the United States

There is no sharper contrast between the United States and Latin America than in the manner in which the fight for shares of the economic pie has been addressed. One way of considering this aspect of development in the two Americas is through the concept of "high-stakes politics."[4] Simply put, those who hold or wield power are extremely reluctant to share it and often very unwilling to use state power to distribute or redistribute economic resources and, therefore, power. For both groups—the haves and the have-nots—the stakes are very high indeed. In fact, it is often seen as a fight for survival. Those who have power work to assure that they continue to divide and rule and prosper; those below seek strategies to restructure the old order in their favor, peacefully or not, as the polarization deepens.

The Great Depression and World War II were two critical junctures that catapulted the state to center stage in the process of economic development in both the United States and Latin America. A key feature of these two world events was the rise of a distributive conflict between capital and labor—the haves versus the have-nots. As Collier and Collier have argued, the way in which the conflict was institutionalized in both the United States and Latin America had enduring consequences for the extent and the intensity of political and economic conflict.[5] The two areas experienced different forms of political institutionalization of the fight for shares. That, in turn, resulted in higher or lower political stakes for both groups. The outcome of that process either nurtured or defused political and economic conflict.

The Colliers have a useful approach to looking at this process in Latin America. They argue, persuasively, that Latin American elites addressed the issue of labor movements, which had become increasingly demanding of inclusion around the time of the First World War, in two different ways. The first was through a government-led process of tying urban labor to the state through an elaborate set of institutional mechanisms. Basically, this ended the autonomy of labor as a coherent political actor for decades. The best examples in Latin America were Chile (1920–1931) and Brazil (1930–1945).

In other countries, a second strategy was followed: elites chose to use a political party as the mechanism for capturing and attempting to neutralize and control labor. Traditional political parties in Uruguay (1903–1916) and Colombia (1930–1945) succeeded in linking labor and ruling economic elites. This process of incorporation resulted in limited political mobilization, usually for electoral purposes only. Some countries in the region experienced a process of radical populism, or a broad and deep mobilization of both labor and other social actors, such as the peasantry and the emerging middle class. Venezuela (1935–1948) and Mexico (1917–1940) are classic examples in Latin America of that approach. Finally, Argentina (1943–1955) and Peru (1939–1945) are good examples of labor populism in which the organizing political party, the Peronists in Argentina and the Apristas in Peru, developed as a fiercely anti-oligarchic movement. This resulted in the politicization of labor and the monopolization of organized labor representation through the two parties.

These two strategies in Latin America contrast sharply with the U.S. experience. The two dominant parties—Democrats and Republicans—tend to be characterized by ideological pragmatism, internal dissent, and relatively open recruitment of new members.[6] These characteristics (along with the single-member congressional district and the simple plurality system) diminish the potential for third parties, from the Left or the Right. It is true that organized labor in the United States has often sought to provide electoral alternatives for the working class, including the Progressive movement (1880s–1910s), the People's Party (1880s–1890s), and the Socialist and Communist parties in the early years of the twentieth century. But one of the two traditional parties—the Democrats—successfully absorbed or neutralized or bought off splinter-party efforts through pro-labor legislation and patronage. The classic example was Franklin Delano Roosevelt (1930–1945) who captured and incorporated labor into the Democratic "big tent." Labor leadership concluded by the end of the Roosevelt period that, while they were not happy with everything the Democrats did for labor, it was far preferable to Republican administrations, which were seen as closely tied to the private sector.

The American model most resembles that adopted in Uruguay and Colombia. Labor peace resulted in electoral support and reasonable annual real gross domestic product (GDP) per capita growth in the second half of the twentieth century. This was not the case where incorporation was through populist parties or radical populism (see figure 6.1).

The outcome was fairly straightforward. In those countries in which the distributive conflict was settled by incorporation through traditional two-party systems, the result was lower-stakes politics. The traditional parties in Uruguay (Colorados) and in Colombia (Liberals) were multiclass, multisectoral organizations. In both countries, there

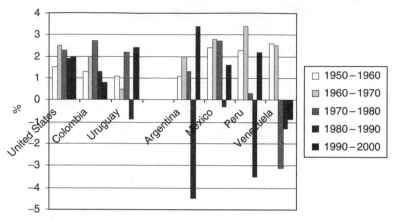

FIGURE 6.1 Sustained versus Boom and Bust Economic Growth in Latin America and the United States. *Source*: Data elaborated from the Penn World Table, http://pwt.econ.upenn.edu/php_site/pwt_index.php.

was alternation in power between two parties, which ensured that actors of different political persuasions participated in a positive-sum game. No single group was able to impose all of its policy preferences on the rest of society. One important outcome in both countries was less social polarization and a lesser chance of regime breakdown.

In sharp contrast, the political stakes were higher and sharper in the countries in which organized labor was a pillar of the incorporating party or movement: Argentina (PJ), Mexico (PRI), Peru (APRA), and Venezuela (AD). Such high stakes were fueled by each of these parties in their effort to become the dominant political force. Actors not identified with, or uncomfortable with, the pro-labor party felt excluded and came to see politics as a zero-sum game: they win, we lose.

How did the fight for shares impact policy? If we consider inflation as a proxy for the intensity of the distributive conflict, countries that saw labor incorporated through populist parties (Argentina and Peru) suffered the highest rates. Countries with radical populist parties (Mexico, Venezuela, and those countries with traditional two-party systems, although not Uruguay) had the lowest inflation rates (see figure 6.2).

High-stakes politics—an all-or-nothing approach—in Argentina and Peru resulted in uncompromising conflict between anti-oligarchic parties and the social and economic elites or in very high-intensity distributional conflicts. The most dramatic case, perhaps, was Argentina. Juan Domingo Perón came to power democratically in 1946 and ruled increasingly undemocratically until he was overthrown in 1955.

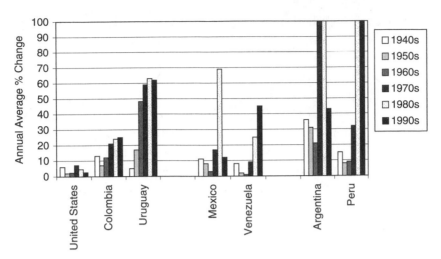

FIGURE 6.2 Inflation Rates in Traditional and Populist Labor
Incorporation. Annual inflation rates over 100 percent are plotted as
100 percent. *Note*: 1990s covers 1990–1995. *Sources*: U.S. Department
of Labor, Bureau of Labor Statistics, http://www.bls.gov/cpi/home.
htm#overview; Rosemary Thorp, *Progress, Poverty and Exclusion: An
Economic History of Latin America in the 20th Century* (Washington, DC:
Inter-American Development Bank, 1998), appendix V, p. 332.

The period witnessed uncompromising strife between labor and capital, with labor always on the winning side. Following his departure,
all of the efforts to lower the stakes in politics for either group failed,
and frequent military intervention (1955–1983) was used as a way
of attempting to neutralize the bitterness in public life between the
two groups. The return to democracy in 1983 did little to resolve the
impasse, and a final round of hyperinflation led to a hasty government
change via democratic elections (1989), which finally began to address
the high political stakes of the preceding decades.

In contrast, the conservative governments in Peru—both military
and civilian—from 1939 to 1968, implemented orthodox macroeconomic policies. A reformist military regime ruled from 1968 to 1980,
and two subsequent civilian regimes executed expansionist policies
that also resulted in high inflation and a hyperinflationary episode. In
both countries, the real GDP per capita in 2000 was still slightly lower
than in 1980.

In the countries that experienced radical populist labor incorporation—Mexico and Venezuela—the fight for shares or the distributive
conflict was less divisive, and both sought the mobilization and incorporation of all social actors. This gave the political leadership more

leverage over the influence of any single sector or interest group in the economy. In Mexico, the PRI relied on strong vertical control of the various sectors' demands. In Venezuela, the distributive conflict was structured by a broad elite settlement that led to strong control over access to the policy process.

The slow demise of the PRI in Mexico and the collapse of the AD/COPEI elite pact system in Venezuela started in earnest as a consequence of the 1982 debt crisis. Both processes can be viewed as a function of the raising of the political stakes. Resources were increasingly scarce, and the fight for shares escalated. New actors emerged—the private sector in Mexico and the armed forces in Venezuela—and demanded a different model.

But even in the two countries in which traditional political parties had done the heavy lifting of labor incorporation, polarization still occurred. The impasse in Uruguay led to a collapse of democracy in 1973 and to a conservative coup in Colombia in 1953. Thus, labor incorporation by a traditional party cut both ways in Latin America. It ameliorated the impact of the distributive conflict on the state, but at the same time it became more prone to escaping the control of the traditional parties, which resulted in serious regime crises.

In sum, in traditional multiclass, multisector parties in both the United States and some of the bigger Latin American economies, there was a lower variation in real GDP per capita growth and lower inflation in the second half of the twentieth century. Although there were exceptions (Mexico and Uruguay), institutions similar to those in the United States proved unable to curb high-stakes politics. The historical legacy in Latin America had produced high levels of income and wealth inequality, as well as social conflict. In such circumstances, one group's advantage tended to be another's loss. As the next section illustrates, zero-sum political conflict resulted in regime breakdown time and again in Latin America. But some regimes were able to lower the political stakes in the political process and, in so doing, established the foundations for relatively long periods of institutional stability.

Lowering the Political Stakes: Elite Pacts and Regime Change in Latin America

Political instability and regime change in Latin America are another illustration of how high-stakes politics have hindered the political and economic development of the region. While the U.S. institutional architecture, although subject to constant revision, managed to remain the same throughout the second half of the twentieth century, many Latin American countries fell victim to political instability and institutional breakdowns. This, in turn, undermined the prospects for economic growth amid rising uncertainty and investment risk.[7]

Similar contrasts with the United States are evident when Latin America is compared with the Asian Tigers. For example, in a study focusing on Latin America and Southeast Asia between the mid-1940s and the early 1980s, Dani Rodrik noted that the most striking difference between the regions in that period was the distribution of income and wealth. By 1960, Rodrik stated, both measures were "exceptionally equal by cross-country standards" in Southeast Asia, which led to three important conditions that furthered sound economic goals in this region. First, governments did not have to contend with powerful industrial and landed interest groups that might have felt threatened by progressive reforms. Second, in the absence of massive inequality, governments were in no hurry to undertake large-scale redistributive policies. And finally, given the absence of such political pressures, policymakers in these countries were able to focus on economic goals through close supervision of their bureaucracies.[8]

In contrast, Latin America's deep income and wealth inequality had the opposite effect: economic elites usually felt threatened by promises of progressive political reforms; political leaders were under stronger pressure from popular constituencies to implement bold redistributive measures in the short term; and political leaders had to operate in an environment characterized by the permanent politicization of the economy. These constant strains led to a permanent state of high-stakes politics in many Latin American countries. The corollary to this situation was a weakening of economic growth prospects in those countries where high-stakes politics led to recurrent instability and regime breakdowns. As figure 6.3 indicates, Latin America accounted for 45 percent of total worldwide regime changes between 1950 and 1990. There was not a single Latin American country that did not experience at least one regime change during this period. The average number of regime changes per country was six, making it the most unstable region in the world (if regime change is taken as a proxy for political instability).

Why is it that some Latin American countries suffered more regime changes than others during this period? Przeworski and colleagues have observed a strong negative association between per capita income levels and numbers of regime changes worldwide between 1950 and

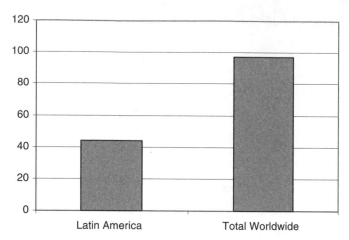

FIGURE 6.3 Total Regime Changes in Latin America and the Rest of the World, 1950–1990. *Source*: Adam Przeworski et al., *Democracy and Development: Political Institutions and Well-Being in the World* (Cambridge: Cambridge University Press, 2000), p. 48.

1990.[9] Most Latin American countries experienced the demise of democratic as well as nondemocratic regimes after World War II. We can illustrate the extent to which per capita income levels and numbers of regime changes were correlated throughout Latin America in the second half of the twentieth century (figures 6.4 and 6.5).

The correlation between per capita income and regime change levels varied considerably between 1940 and 1970 and between 1970 and 2000. The most important contrast between both subperiods is the transition of nearly every country from the upper left portion in figure 6.4 to the lower right portion in figure 6.5. This means that, between 1940 and 2000, almost all Latin American countries experienced at least moderate per capita income gains and a decrease in the number of regime changes. This is consistent with the argument offered by Przeworski et al.: as per capita income grew in the second half of the twentieth century, there were fewer regime breakdowns in Latin America. This is especially true for democracies, as evidence for exogenous factors in the process of democratization suggests: when a transition to democracy occurs in a given country, its chances of survival in the short and medium term are heavily dependent on that country's per capita income level.

Figures 6.4 and 6.5 also illustrate some exceptions to the Przeworski et al. argument. Countries in the upper right portion—that is, countries

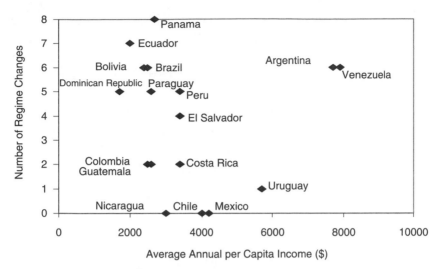

FIGURE 6.4 Per Capita Income and Regime Change in Latin America, 1940–1970. *Note*: Income per capita expressed in 1996 purchasing power parity dollars. *Sources*: Data elaborated from the Penn World Table, http://pwt.econ.upenn.edu/php_site/pwt_index.php; and the Third World Government Stability database, http://colfa.utsa.edu/govstability.

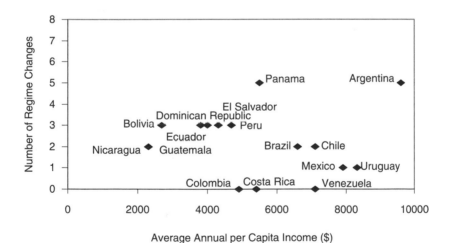

FIGURE 6.5 Per Capita Income and Regime Change in Latin America, 1970–2000. *Note*: Income per capita expressed in 1996 purchasing power parity dollars. *Sources*: Data elaborated from the Penn World Table, http://pwt.econ.upenn.edu/php_site/pwt_index.php; and the Third World Government Stability database, http://colfa.utsa.edu/govstability.

with relatively high per capita income levels and high numbers of regime changes, such as Argentina (for both subperiods) and Venezuela (for the first subperiod)—should have experienced fewer instances of regime change. Likewise, following the hypothesis that poor democracies are considerably more fragile,[10] poor electoral democracies are more likely to fall into the upper left rather than lower left portion, with their regimes having broken down time and again. Nonetheless, Colombia (first subperiod) and Nicaragua (second subperiod) defied expectations based on this model and retained electoral arrangements despite high levels of poverty and social conflict.

Elite pacts (Colombia and Venezuela in 1958; Nicaragua in 1989–1990) and, in some cases, their absence (Argentina) might help to explain these exceptions. As some scholars have shown in studies about Latin America and Southern Europe,[11] elite pacts offer their participants mutual assurances about the entry, duration, and composition of governments. They are usually not all-inclusive, as they tend to exclude relevant political forces from the original power-sharing agreement (such as with the left-wing parties in Colombia and Venezuela after 1958). This type of agreement gives mutual assurance to the participant groups that they will all be included in the government and policy processes. The alternative to power sharing usually results in high-cost conflict between elites who are more or less evenly matched opponents.

There are two downsides to elite pacts. The first is that, as evidenced in some Latin American countries like Colombia and Venezuela, the legal exclusion of important, legitimate political groups sometimes provides their leaders with incentives to organize, fight, and try to overturn the political system that legally excludes them. The second is that maintaining an elite pact incurs enforcement costs. As Weingast has argued, pacts only work if "elites and their followers [are] willing to punish those who seek unilateral defections from the pact."[12] This means that, unless elite pacts can become self-enforcing, there is no guarantee that they can become permanent. Nonetheless, they can be important short- and medium-term mechanisms that lead to better management of political conflict and distributive struggles.

In Latin American countries where political conflict remained beyond the elites' capacity to mediate it, the military intervened time and again, assuming power either as a temporary solution to defuse civilian conflict or as more permanent military regimes. Some examples include the bureaucratic authoritarian regimes in Brazil (1964), Argentina (1966), Chile (1973), and Uruguay (1973), which attempted to implement political and economic reforms. In cases of acute political conflict and recurrent regime breakdowns, economic growth prospects remained subject to high uncertainty; Argentina is one such example. Some stable, nondemocratic regimes achieved good economic performance through state-led growth in the 1960s and 1970s, such as Brazil under the military and Mexico under the civilian hegemony of the PRI. However, in most instances, economic growth in authoritarian contexts was fueled by massive external borrowing, as was the case in Chile under General Augusto Pinochet, where the economy collapsed in 1982 along with the economies of neighboring countries.

In contrast, Latin American countries that were able to control political uncertainty through elite pacts, such as Colombia, were, not surprisingly, the ones that sustained good economic performance under civilian electoral arrangements throughout the 1960s and 1970s. Costa Rica also reached an elite pact after the country's short-lived civil war of 1948–1949. This is not to say that elite pacts were either a necessary or a sufficient condition to create the basis for strong economic performance. Venezuela was a case of successful elite compromise that resulted in political stability and regime continuity, yet the country's economic growth record, measured in real GDP per capita growth, was among the worst in the largest Latin American economies between the 1970s and 2000 (see figure 6.1). Countries that forged elite pacts benefited primarily from temporary institutional continuity, without which laying the foundations for sustained economic growth was more difficult.

In hindsight, it is clear that the 1982 regional economic debacle led to a redefinition of political stakes in Latin America. However, as the following section explains, rolling back the state and bringing macroeconomic fundamentals back on track did not guarantee sustained improvement in economic growth throughout the region.

Neoliberal Restructuring and the Challenge of Creating a Smart State

Since the mid-1990s, there has been an increased concern for state capacity in Latin America. In a series of reports published in 1997, the World Bank advocated "refocusing on the effectiveness of the state" and proposed a reform agenda for the region for the next decade.[13] A year later, the bank published a seminal report titled *Beyond the Washington Consensus: Institutions Matter*,[14] and the growing priority given to modernizing the state in Latin America crystallized in a more recent volume that calls for "restarting growth and reform in Latin America" and creating a "smart state."[15] As explained by Laurence Wolff and Claudio de Moura Castro, the reforms undertaken in the 1990s focused primarily on trimming down the "bloated" role the state had assumed.[16] The result of such restructuring is a smarter state, which they define as one that requires a more competent, though perhaps smaller, bureaucracy that is far more understanding of the challenges presented by "competition, transparency, value added, and equity."[17]

The bloated, outmoded state was a legacy of the post–World War II drive to consolidate the import substitution industrialization (ISI) model of economic development. The ISI strategy led to an unsustainable situation in which the government became the main provider of certain goods and services that the private sector could supply more efficiently, while simultaneously becoming an excessively centralized and oppressive regulator of the economic sector.[18] The so-called lost decade of the 1980s' debt crisis ultimately spelled the death knell for the ISI model. In the words of Pedro-Pablo Kuczynski, when "growth ground to a halt…because the population continued to grow, the result was an erosion of living standards and a reversal of the downward trend in poverty of the preceding decades."[19] As the lost decade unfolded, specialists attempted to lay out a new, alternative agenda for Latin America.[20]

The possibility of renewal was informed by two important events: the success of the Chilean state in renewing growth, albeit under a brutal dictatorship, and the policies of openness and macroeconomic discipline of the Asian Tigers, which also had produced an economic miracle.[21] A key component of the Chilean "miracle" was the redesign of the state. In East Asia, success was tied to the institutional design of reform that provided the critical framework for the concept of shared growth. As José Edgardo Campos and Hilton Root noted, the leaders in high-performing economies appreciated the importance of public expectations and of the wide distribution of benefits gained through growth policies, while confidence in the success of the institutional reforms (i.e., that individuals and firms were likely to share the growth dividend) was rooted in the high cost of reversing those reforms.[22]

The Washington Consensus

The debate quickened at the end of the 1980s about an appropriate reform agenda for the region. There was a sense that a critical juncture had been reached, and the moment was opportune to address the challenge of economic reform and growth. The Brady Plan had reduced the burden of foreign debt, with Mexico securing the first debt reconstruction in 1989, followed by the sale of the controlling interest of the state in Teléfonos de México (TELMEX) to a private consortium. The democratic transitions were nearing completion, with the last in Chile (1990) about to take place.

At a conference at the Institute for International Economics in 1989, a group of economists identified 10 key reforms that were essential to restore economic growth.[23] The now well-known shopping list dubbed the Washington Consensus included fiscal discipline, trade liberalization, tax reform, a competitive exchange rate regime, privatization, liberalization of foreign direct investment inflows, market-determined interest rates, and deregulation. And there were two additional priorities: one focused on reducing subsidies and redirecting government spending toward education, health, and infrastructure development; the second was the enforcement of property rights. The argument was simple: weak laws and poor judicial systems reduce incentives to save and accumulate wealth.

As the decade of the 1990s progressed, most governments addressed the first set of challenges, some with success, some less so. What became clear was that the last two priorities—the purview of the state—had been overlooked or deliberately forgotten in response to vested interests that were able to mobilize political power to influence negatively the intentions of the states in these areas. Not directly included in the Washington Consensus was the role and responsibility of the state. That issue began to be addressed in the latter years of the decade.

The State in a Changing World

The early discussions about rethinking the role of the state focused on a two-part strategy. The first component was to match the state's role to its capability, and the second was to raise state capability by reinvigorating public institutions. As the World Bank's 1997 report stated, capability, as applied to states, is the ability to undertake and promote collective actions efficiently, such as law and order, public health, and basic infrastructure. Effectiveness, on the other hand, is a result of using that capability to meet society's demand for those goods. Therefore, a state may be capable but not very effective if its capability is not used in society's interests.[24] The World Bank report pointed out that a new model of government was emerging in Latin America, but that greater emphasis was needed on reform of the legal system, the civil service, and social policies.[25]

In the World Bank report *The Long March*, the need to consolidate the stabilization gains that had been achieved was addressed. Emphasis was given to fiscal policy, international trade openness, labor market liberalization, and efficient financial markets. Short sections were devoted to human development (health and education), poverty reduction, and improving the legal and regulatory environment.[26]

By 1998, it was clear that the initial enthusiasm for the Washington Consensus was fading quickly, as state capacity was found wanting. In an effort to address this issue, the World Bank issued another report that year that starkly argued: institutions matter.[27] Clearly, it was time to move beyond the first generation of reforms embodied in the Washington Consensus, whose policy prescriptions (with the exception of property rights) overlooked the potential role that reformed institutions could play in accelerating the economic and social development of the region. Referring to Latin America, the World Bank stated that institutional reforms were "greatly needed to enhance the competitiveness of the private sector, to reap the potential benefits of the economic reforms undertaken in the last decade, and to reduce the LAC region's financial vulnerability."[28] The report also noted that most Latin American and Caribbean (LAC) countries were lagging in institutional development compared with other countries—the Asian Tigers in particular—with which they have to compete in international markets.

After the Washington Consensus

The formulators of the Washington Consensus gathered again in a series of meetings in 2000–2002 to try and understand what had gone wrong. The conclusion was that Latin Americans wanted a new agenda that would correct the failures of the previous one.[29] So, as we look to the future, what are the new priorities in addition to completing the first-generation list of reforms? They include legal and political reform, regulatory institutions, anticorruption measures, labor market flexibility, financial codes and standards, social safety nets, and poverty reduction policies, among others. In discussing the new agenda, John Williamson poses the question: what steps need to be followed to modernize the state?[30] Kuczynski is right in his statement that "a major political debate is beginning in the region on the role of the state."[31] However, although this is simply said, it is not simply done.

It is clear that political leaders need to formulate coalitions that understand the need for state reform. Vested interests need to be confronted. As Dani Rodrik has phrased it: "the question before policymakers...is no longer do institutions matter, but which institutions matter and how does one acquire them?"[32] Rodrik sets out a cogent agenda for state reform, and he states that institutions must facilitate the development and consolidation of

> a clearly designated system of property rights, a regulatory apparatus curbing the worst forms of fraud, anti-competitive behavior and moral hazard, a moderately cohesive society exhibiting trust and social cooperation, social and political institutions that mitigate risks and manage social conflicts, the rule of law and clean government.[33]

The challenge is enormous. But Latin American leaders need to assume the responsibility of creating smart states or run the risk of continued discontent and resentment by their citizens at their failure to produce growth and improve equity. From this perspective, and as we explained in the previous section, even though there has been dramatic institutional change in Latin America since 1982, characterized by transitions from authoritarian to democratic rule and from relatively closed, state-led economies to open, market-driven economies, weak states whose jurisdiction and enforcement capacities have remained weak and open to traditional capacity-draining activities, such as rent seeking and moral hazard, have helped to reproduce the conditions that allow the survival and growth of high-stakes politics. To this element, we have to add others, namely, the persistence of dramatic socioeconomic inequality and widespread poverty, which have nurtured the zero-sum conditions that allow high-stakes politics to thrive and dominate in Latin America at the beginning of the twenty-first century.

The Need to Have a Social Contract: Addressing Poverty and Inequality in Latin America

The theme is constant in the literature on Latin America. Terry Karl has stated it succinctly: "Latin America is the region in the world with the greatest inequities."[34] Karl attributes the poor development results in the region since the mid-1980s to inequality, pointing out that more than one-third of the population lives in poverty, and nearly 80 million live in extreme poverty (earning less than one U.S. dollar a day).[35] Rosemary Thorp, in summarizing the economic history of

Latin America in the twentieth century, comments that "poverty and exclusion remained extensive and deeply rooted, and inequality persisted" while "effective relations between the public and private sectors and a well-trained bureaucracy...has in a number of respects and places deteriorated rather than improved."[36] In setting the stage for restarting growth and reform in Latin America, Pedro-Pablo Kuczynski starkly commented that the region has not shown progress in alleviating its "long-standing and endemic maldistribution of wealth" and that "indeed, the region may have retrogressed in what were already among the most highly skewed distributions in the world."[37]

Does it matter? Poverty and inequality are so deeply ingrained in Latin American societies that the expectation of change remains relatively low. But it does matter for a number of reasons. The quality of democracy is severely limited by persistent and pervasive inequality.[38] As we have argued, the high-stakes politics derived from the growing distance between the haves and the have-nots in Latin America are incompatible with the compromises and give-and-take accommodations that are necessary to establish firm foundations in young democracies. The possibilities for rapid growth and development are compromised because citizens do not have the skill sets to participate and compete in open economies. And for the region, competitiveness is key to improving living standards, attracting foreign investment, and escaping the natural resource curse of continued dependence on highly volatile commodity and mineral exports.

According to Karl, the "commodity lottery" remains the fundamental basis for the vicious cycle of unequal development in the region, and mitigating inequality remains the central task that policymakers must address.[39] She states that "this winner-loser setup is a self-reinforcing economic and political dynamic based on the concentration of both assets and power, the institutionalized bias this creates in political structures, and the permanent exclusion of large segments of the population."[40] Until this challenge is met, high-stakes politics will continue to dominate the scene.

Social Inequality and Civil Society

Philip Oxhorn has made the argument that a direct correlation between inequality levels and resistance to equity-enhancing measures may exist in Latin America, arguing that "extremes in socioeconomic inequality can raise the stakes of the politics of (re)distribution, making substantial reforms least likely in precisely those countries where they are most needed for maintaining democratic stability."[41] It is clear that we need to be concerned with the quality of democratic life in the region. Since the 1990s, we have witnessed frequent crises of leadership, impeachments, constitutional breakdowns, and unresolved conflicts between legislatures and presidents. While military coups d'état appear to be a thing of the past, social inequalities have created powerful forces lobbying for structural and institutional reforms that, from the viewpoint of the poor, have been deliberately blocked by powerful elites.

The endemic fragility of political life remains a key to understanding the persistence of poverty and inequality. The institutionalized bias in the region's political structures, mentioned above, often precludes the implementation of policies that favor the poor. Perceived instability or political risk from the viewpoint of the investor limits the flow of capital that is desperately needed to compensate for factors such as low savings rates and high levels of debt servicing.

Competitiveness as the Key to Economic Growth

It is generally accepted today that competitiveness is the key to resolving the economic and social challenges in Latin America. The region needs to break the deadlock of slow growth, commodity and mineral dependence, and high levels of indebtedness. Higher levels of growth may allow political leaders to develop policies that address issues of distribution and social inequality, which, in turn, will reduce poverty and lead to greater support for democracy. Given the dependence of the region on foreign capital flows—foreign direct and portfolio investment—to achieve these goals, two questions are fundamental. First, how does the investment community view Latin America and its potential? And, second, what needs to be done specifically to move the region into a virtuous cycle of growth and development?

One useful index as to how the region is perceived by investors is *The Global Competitiveness Report*, published annually by the World Economic Forum (WEF) in Switzerland.[42] The report's global competitiveness index (GCI) is composed of twelve pillars: (1) institutions; (2) infrastructure; (3) macroeconomic stability; (4) health and primary education; (5) higher education and training; (6) good market efficiency; (7) labor market efficiency; (8) financial market sophistication; (9) technological readiness; (10) market size; (11) business sophistication; and (12) innovation. For 2007–2008, the WEF ranked 131 countries. Latin America fared poorly when compared to the Asian Tigers, with the clear exception of Chile, which ranked 26th (see figure 6.6).

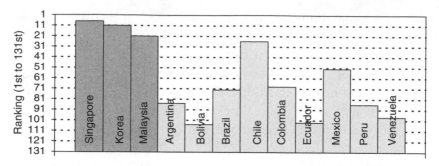

FIGURE 6.6 Growth Competitiveness Index Rankings, 2007–2008.
Source: World Economic Forum, *The Global Competitiveness Report,
2007–2008* (New York: Palgrave Macmillan, 2005), p. 10.

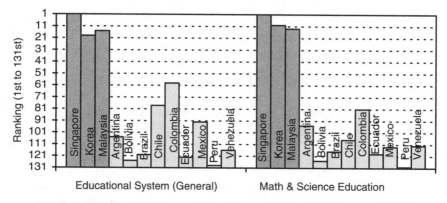

Educational System (General)   Math & Science Education

FIGURE 6.7 Quality of Education Rankings, 2007–2008. *Source*: World
Economic Forum, *The Global Competitiveness Report, 2007–2008* (New
York: Palgrave Macmillan, 2007), pp. 428–429.

In examining specific areas linked to enhancing efficiency and competitiveness, the region also scored poorly. When respondents were
asked about the quality of the educational system in the 131 countries,
12 countries, including Argentina, Bolivia, Brazil, Ecuador, Peru, and
Venezuela, ranked below 100th. When asked about the quality of math
and science education, the results were no better, with Brazil ranking
117th and Peru 130th (see figure 6.7).

On the subject of institutions—which are vital to the creation of a
smart state, the vitality of civil society and democracy, and the ability
of the region to attract investment—the rankings were disappointing.
In three key areas—judicial independence, property rights, and waste-
fulness of government spending—Singapore, Korea, and Malaysia
scored well above Latin American countries (see figure 6.8). Especially

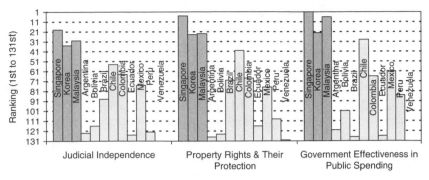

FIGURE 6.8. Ranking of Institutions in Latin America, 2007–2008.
Source: World Economic Forum, *The Global Competitiveness Report,*
2007–2008 (New York: Palgrave Macmillan, 2007), pp. 376, 380, 382.

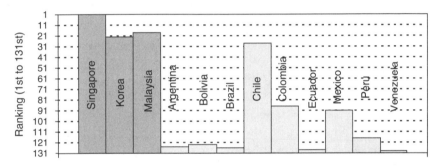

FIGURE 6.9. Ranking of Public Trust of Politicians, 2007–2008.
Source: World Economic Forum, *The Global Competitiveness Report,*
2007–2008 (New York: Palgrave Macmillan, 2007), p. 379.

disappointing were Argentina, Bolivia, Ecuador, Peru, and Venezuela,
each of which ranked below 100th in most of the three areas mentioned above. Chile remains the exception to the rule, ranking not too
far below Korea on all three areas.

Finally, critical to democratic governance and a perceived capacity
to mitigate asset and income inequities, respondents were asked about
the public trust in the financial honesty of politicians. Once again,
Latin America lagged significantly behind its Asian Tiger counterparts,
with the exception of Chile (see figure 6.9). Argentina, Bolivia, Brazil,
Ecuador, Peru, and Venezuela all ranked below 115th, with Argentina
ranked 125th, Bolivia 123rd, Brazil 126th, Ecuador 128th, Peru 117th,
and Venezuela 129th.

The question of why the Asian countries consistently outrank
Latin America remains an important one. As argued earlier, a likely

explanation is that Asian political leaders were able to legitimate the policy of shared growth. The rise of industrial Asia suggests that the key to uninterrupted growth was, as Campos and Root argue, the states' success in convincing their constituents that a sacrifice in the present would yield gains in the future; in their own words: "Making the promise of shared growth credible allowed East Asian leaders to alter the risk-reward calculations that motivate economic behavior, so that the compensation for taking smaller benefits in the present was greater gains over time."[43] To establish this partnership between civil society and the regime required trust. It also needed sustained public sector policies to reduce asset inequality through carefully planned investments in health, education, and public housing. As Campos and Root note, "Wealth sharing insured broad social support, thereby reducing the threat that the regime would fall to destructive rent seeking or insurgency. It encouraged the belief that the government was acting on behalf of citizens' interests."[44]

All too often, it is the "destructive rent seeking" among Latin America's economic and political elites that preclude confidence-building strategies and set citizens against political authority. Creating a consensus about growth and development requires mutual trust and shared goals. These are in short supply in most of the countries of Latin America and the Caribbean.

How to Address Poverty, Inequality, and Social Policy Challenges

The most recent effort to offer a plan of attack argues that Latin America suffers from a vicious circle in which low growth contributes to the persistence of poverty, particularly given high inequality, and that "Latin America's high inequality of assets poses a deep structural barrier to raising the productivity and incomes of poor people."[45] Critical to achieving the goal of equitable social policy is increased public spending on health and education programs.

Constructive social policy should also make explicit efforts to ensure the access of the poor to land and financial markets. Not only is increased access to credit for poor people very important, but so are raising the participation of women in the market, which will require subsidized child care services; the socializing of maternity benefits; labor legislation that allows more flexibility in contracting conditions; and a labor framework that encourages collective bargaining while enforcing the accountability of labor union leaders. A clear attack on ethnic and racial discrimination needs to be given high priority.

These and other commonsense policies are essential to increasing competitiveness, reducing inequality and poverty, and giving citizens a stake in their democratic political systems. This is the only way in which high-stakes politics can give way to a more level playing field for all citizens in the subcontinent's young democracies. The suggestions made above will require determined political leadership to replace exclusionary policies with policies that seek to enhance the assets of the poor. A commitment to greater social equality through poverty reduction makes good sense from the perspective of productivity and growth. It also addresses the core question of the need to strengthen democratic institutions as part of the social development of Latin America.

Conclusion

The prevalence of high-stakes politics in many Latin American countries throughout the second half of the twentieth century was a key difference, among others, that permitted the development gap between this region and the United States to continue growing. Not all Latin American countries operated similarly. As the first two sections of this chapter explained, institutional arrangements such as labor incorporation into traditional two-party systems and the establishment of elite pacts contributed to lowering the political stakes in some countries that might otherwise have experienced higher political conflict and worse economic prospects. In sections three and four, key deficiencies in the current development model followed by Latin America—namely, the absence of smart states and the prevalence of growing socioeconomic inequality and poverty—have led to the continued operation of high-stakes politics in many countries in the region.

As recently indicated in *Latinobarómetro*, public opinion data show that, in Latin America, "all things have changed to remain the same. There is no improvement in the topics essential to democratic political culture: distrust has increased or remained the same, there have been no changes in civic culture, perceptions about the rule of law have not improved, and expectations keep growing."[46] People have increasingly taken to the streets to bring down governments that were perceived as not carrying out their electoral mandate. The recent cases of Argentina, Bolivia, and Ecuador represent the tip of the iceberg in a context centered not on the breakdown of democracy nor on the return of military regimes, but rather on "reasserting respect for citizens' demands within the [democratic] system, but [increasingly] on its edge."[47]

Given this polarized context, in addition to the need to create and nurture political institutions that help to bring down the stakes of politics in Latin America, the region is also in need of what Juan Linz identified in one of his classic early works as a key ingredient to recalibrate democratic systems: the availability of responsible political leadership capable of dealing with a loss of efficacy and legitimacy.[48] Credible political institutions and responsible political leadership are preconditions to address the main regional challenge. As Terry Lynn Karl points out, the economy and the polity go hand in hand in Latin America, and she adds, "to the extent that both are reformed to benefit those in society who are worst off, Latin America's vicious cycle can be stopped... [and] the alternative is not pretty."[49]

Notes

1. As depicted in Rosemary Thorp's book, *Progress, Poverty and Exclusion: An Economic History of Latin America in the 20th Century* (Washington, DC: Inter-American Development Bank, 1998).
2. See John Coatsworth, "Notes on the Comparative Economic History of Latin America and the United States," in *Development and Underdevelopment in America: Contrasts of Economic Growth in North and Latin America in Historical Perspective*, edited by Walther L. Bernecker and Hans Werner Tobler (New York: de Gruyter, 1993), pp. 10–30.
3. For more on the structural reforms proposed for Latin America under the so-called Washington Consensus, see John Williamson, ed., *Latin American Adjustment: How Much Has Happened?* (Washington, DC: Institute for International Economics, 1990).
4. Adam Przeworski, *Democracy and the Market: Political and Economic Reforms in Eastern Europe and Latin America* (Cambridge: Cambridge University Press, 1991), pp. 79–99; Barry Weingast, "The Political Foundations of Democracy and the Rule of Law," *American Political Science Review* 91, no. 2 (June 1997): 245–263.
5. Ruth Berins Collier and David Collier, *Shaping the Political Arena: Critical Junctures, the Labor Movement, and Regime Dynamics in Latin America* (Princeton, NJ: Princeton University Press, 1991).
6. J. F. Bibby, *Politics, Parties, and Elections in America*, 4th ed. (Belmont, CA: Wadsworth, 2000); J. H. Aldrich, *Why Parties: The Origins and Transformation of Party Politics in America* (Chicago: Chicago University Press, 1995); D. R. Mayhew, *Placing Parties in American Politics: Organization, Electoral Settings, and Government Activity in the Twentieth Century* (Princeton, NJ: Princeton University Press, 1986).
7. Douglass C. North, William Summerhill, and Barry R. Weingast, "Order, Disorder, and Economic Change: Latin America versus North America," in *Governing for Prosperity*, edited by Bruce Bueno de Mesquita and Hilton L. Root (New Haven, CT: Yale University Press, 2000), pp. 17–58.
8. Dani Rodrik, "Understanding Economic Policy Reform," *Journal of Economic Literature* 34, no. 1 (March 1996): 9–41.
9. Adam Przeworski et al., *Democracy and Development: Political Institutions and Well-Being in the World* (Cambridge: Cambridge University Press, 2000), p. 93, table 2.3.

10. Ibid., p. 111.
11. See, for example, John Higley and Richard Gunther, eds., *Elites and Democratic Consolidation in Latin America and Southern Europe* (Cambridge: Cambridge University Press, 1992).
12. Weingast, "The Political Foundations of Democracy and the Rule of Law," p. 258.
13. *World Development Report 1997: The State in a Changing World* (New York: Oxford University Press, 1997); Shahid Javed Burki and Guillermo E. Perry, *The Long March: A Reform Agenda for Latin America and the Caribbean in the Next Decade* (Washington, DC: World Bank, 1997).
14. Shahid Javed Burki and Guillermo E. Perry, *Beyond the Washington Consensus: Institutions Matter* (Washington, DC: World Bank, 1998).
15. Pedro-Pablo Kuczynski and John Williamson, eds., *After the Washington Consensus: Restarting Growth and Reform in Latin America* (Washington, DC: Institute for International Economics, 2003).
16. Ibid., p. 198.
17. Ibid.
18. Ibid.
19. Ibid., p. 22.
20. For one of the first efforts to "bury" the ISI model, see Bela Balassa, Gerardo M. Bueno, Pedro-Pablo Kuczynski, and Mario Henrique Simonsen, *Toward Renewed Economic Growth in Latin America* (Washington, DC: Institute for International Economics, 1986).
21. See José Edgardo Campos and Hilton L. Root, *The Key to the Asian Miracle: Making Shared Growth Credible* (Washington, DC: Brookings Institution, 1996).
22. Ibid., p. 2.
23. John Williamson, ed., *Latin American Adjustment: How Much Has Happened?* (Washington, DC: Institute for International Economics, 1990).
24. *World Development Report 1997*, pp. 2–3.
25. Ibid., p. 14.
26. Burki and Perry, *The Long March*.
27. Burki and Perry, *Beyond the Washington Consensus*.
28. Ibid., p. 5.
29. Kuczynski and Williamson, *After the Washington Consensus*, p. 2.
30. Ibid., p. 308.
31. Ibid., p. 34.
32. Dani Rodrik, "After Neoliberalism, What?" remarks at the Banco Nacional de Desenvolvimento Econômico e Social (BNDES) seminar on New Paths of Development, Rio de Janeiro, September 2003, quoted in Patricio Navia and Andres Velasco, "The Politics of Second-Generation Reforms," in Kuczynski and Williamson, *After the Washington Consensus*, p. 269.
33. Ibid.
34. Terry Lynn Karl, "The Vicious Cycle of Inequality in Latin America," in *What Justice? Whose Justice? Fighting for Fairness in Latin America*, edited by Susan Eva Eckstein and Timothy P. Wickham-Crowley (Berkeley: University of California Press, 2003), p. 133.
35. Ibid.
36. Thorp, *Progress, Poverty and Exclusion*, p. 281.
37. Pedro-Pablo Kuczynski, "Setting the Stage," in Kuczynski and Williamson, *After the Washington Consensus*, p. 27.
38. Philip Oxhorn, "Social Inequality, Civil Society, and the Limits of Citizenship in Latin America," in Eckstein and Wickham-Crowley, *What Justice? Whose Justice?* p. 35.

39. Karl, "The Vicious Cycle of Inequality in Latin America," pp. 150–151.
40. Ibid.
41. Oxhorn, "Social Inequality," p. 35.
42. For example, World Economic Forum, *The Global Competitiveness Report, 2007–2008* (New York: Palgrave Macmillan, 2007).
43. Campos and Root, *The Key to the Asian Miracle*, p. 6.
44. Ibid., p. 176.
45. Nancy Birdsall and Miguel Székely, "Bootstraps, Not Band-Aids: Poverty, Equity and Social Policy," in Kuczynski and Williamson, *After the Washington Consensus*, pp. 51, 66.
46. *Latinobarómetro*, 2005, available at: http://64.233.161.104/search?q=cache:v-puWQG8W68J:www.-latinobarometro.org/uploads/media/LB_2005.pdf+Latinobarometro+2005&hl=es, p. 5.
47. Ibid.
48. Juan J. Linz, *The Breakdown of Democratic Regimes: Crisis, Breakdown, and Reequilibration* (Baltimore, MD: Johns Hopkins University Press, 1978), p. 87.
49. Karl, "The Vicious Cycle of Inequality in Latin America," p. 153.

PART III

INSTITUTIONAL FACTORS IN LATIN AMERICA'S DEVELOPMENT

7

The Latin American Equilibrium

JAMES A. ROBINSON

ONE OF THE enduring puzzles of Latin American history is its comparative economic performance.[1] At the time of conquest and settlement, though Latin American countries were relatively poor and economically backward compared to their colonists from Spain and Portugal, the gap was small in relation to what it is today. For example, in 1500, Spain's income per capita was probably about 50 percent greater than the Latin American average. Today, average income in Spain is about 300 percent greater.[2] Even more puzzling, at the time of conquest, the most prosperous parts of the Americas were not those which are today the richest. In 1492, it was not Canada, the United States, or the Southern Cone of Latin America that were the most economically advanced; it was Mexico, Peru, and Bolivia with their complex centralized societies.[3] Though the technology of the Mexicas or Tawantinsuyu may not have been very advanced by modern standards, they had developed extraordinary abilities to provide public goods, irrigation works, and infrastructure, and they had systems of taxation and resource mobilization that would be the envy of many modern developing countries.

One might have thought that the processes unleashed by the conquest would have leveled rather than exacerbated differences. Economists generally believe that the increased global integration of nations is a powerful force for economic convergence. Indeed, Diamond has posited that the backwardness of Peru relative to Spain in 1532 was due to environmental and geographical factors that limited agricultural productivity in the Americas relative to Europe.[4] The arrival of previously absent European technologies, such as writing, money, or the production of steel, and the sudden availability of Eurasian crops (wheat) and animal species (horses, cows, and pigs) ought to have led the Peruvians to converge toward European levels of prosperity. In fact, the arrival of the Europeans with their basket of technologies was subsequently followed by massive economic divergence.

It is perhaps not hard to explain why Latin American countries did not prosper in the three centuries after 1492. Though they suddenly had access to European technologies, they were also placed under the yoke of European colonization. The impact of this colonization is revealed by figures 7.1 and 7.2. Figure 7.1, from W. George Lovell and Christopher Lutz, shows the evolution of the population of Guatemala since the conquest.[5] From an estimated 2 million in 1520, the population collapsed to 6 percent of this number a century later. The total population of Guatemala only recovered to the 1520 level in the 1920s, and the Mayan population only in the 1960s. Figure 7.2, from Barry Bogin and Ryan Keep, presents data on the evolution of height in Guatemala before and after the conquest.[6] Data on heights are one of the few sources we have to judge living standards and welfare in the premodern period.[7] Though the evidence is imperfect, and there are concerns about the nature of the sample, figure 7.2 shows that heights fell monotonically after the conquest, bottoming out in the 1940s. These data are consistent with a view that the conquest had a highly adverse effect on the welfare and nutrition of the indigenous population. As a final and telling piece of evidence, information about nominal wages and prices in central Mexico from Charles Gibson suggests that, in the century after the conquest, while the indigenous population collapsed, real wages were at best unchanged and probably fell.[8] This fact is in startling contradiction to the Malthusian situation which supposedly characterized the premodern economy of Europe.

Of course, during this period, the United States and Canada were also European colonies and, indeed, at the time of the declared independence of the United States in 1776, differences in prosperity among Mexico, Brazil, and the United States were minimal.[9] The relative gap

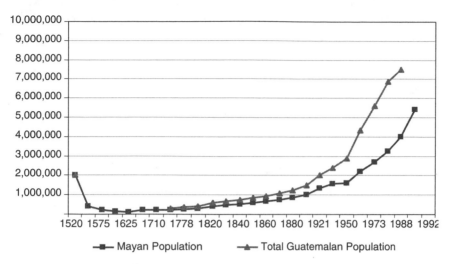

FIGURE 7.1 Historical Estimates of Population in Guatemala.
Source: W. George Lovell and Christopher Lutz, "Conquest and Population:
Maya Demography in Historical Perspective," *Latin American Research
Review* 29 (1994): 133–140.

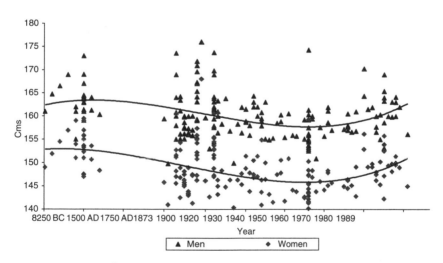

FIGURE 7.2 Height of Latin American Adult Men and Women in
Guatemala (Cubic Fit). *Source*: Barry Bogin and Ryan Keep, "Eight
Thousand Years of Economic and Political History in Latin America
Revealed by an Anthropometry," *Annals of Human Biology* 26 (1999):
333–351.

between Europe and the Americas which had existed in 1492 probably stayed about constant over the colonial period, with Europe remaining about 50 percent more prosperous, even though the level of income per capita had grown slowly everywhere.

In some sense, then, the real puzzle begins in the nineteenth century, the epoch of rapid economic divergence. By the 1820s, Latin American countries had emerged from colonialism, and though it was once believed that they remained in the grip of a British-initiated "informal empire" in the nineteenth century, the more plausible view is that rather it was Latin Americans and their governments who decided, possibly inadvertently, how their societies would evolve. As free nations, they appeared to be just as well placed as those of North America to take advantage of the full gamut of new technologies emanating from Britain, which we connect to the industrial revolution. Yet they did not. North America not only quickly adopted the new innovations, but emerged as a dynamic innovator in its own right, while Latin America stagnated. By 1900, the United States had become the most prosperous country in the world, with a level of average income about 400 percent of the Latin American level. Though Latin American countries did begin to grow after the 1880s, in the intervening years they have not narrowed this gap. Table 7.1 brings together existing historical estimates of national income per capita expressed as a percentage of the U.S. level.[10] It dramatically illustrates the divergence in the nineteenth century and the failure of Latin American countries to close the relative gap in the twentieth century.

TABLE 7.1   Gross Domestic Product (GDP) per Capita as Percentage of U.S. Level, 1700–1994

Country	1700	1800	1850	1900	1913	1950	1994
Argentina	md*	102	md	52	55	41	37
Brazil	md	36	39	10	11	15	22
Chile	md	46	md	38	40	33	34
Colombia	md	md	34	18	18	19	24
Cuba	167	112	78	md	39	md	md
Mexico	89	50	37	35	35	27	23
Peru	md	41	md	20	20	24	14
Venezuela	md	md	md	10	10	38	37
Mean	128	66	51	27	28	29	27

*md = missing data
Source: John H. Coatsworth, "Economic and Institutional Trajectories in Nineteenth Century Latin America," in *Latin America and the World Economy since 1800*, edited by John H. Coatsworth and Alan M. Taylor (Cambridge, MA: Harvard University Press, 1998), p. 26.

What Needs Explaining and Types of Explanation

This whirlwind tour of Latin American economic history suggests a number of salient puzzles which require solutions before we can reach a fuller understanding of why the economic progress of Latin American countries has been so poor historically. The first question is: why did the relative position of Latin America remain unchanged between 1492 and 1800? The second is: why did Latin American countries stagnate for most of the nineteenth century, when they experienced little or no economic growth? The third puzzle is: why, even after Latin American countries began to experience economic growth after the 1880s, did they not catch up with the rich countries of North America and the Organisation for Economic Co-operation and Development (OECD)? Why, to put it another way, has there been nothing corresponding to the so-called East Asian miracle in Latin America?

How economists explain comparative economic development and how they account for why some countries generate much higher average levels of goods and services for their citizens than do others are also pertinent issues. At a proximate level, the explanation for this is clear if you compare the United States to, say, Bolivia. An average worker in the United States produces more output than an average Bolivian worker because he works with much more sophisticated technology. Moreover, he is able to use a much wider array of complementary inputs in his production, such as capital goods and machines. In addition, a worker in the United States will be much better educated on average than a Bolivian worker, and probably healthier as well. Since the research of Solow, economists have broken down differences in per capita incomes into differences in these factors of production: physical capital, human capital (the education and skills embodied in workers), and productivity (capturing differences not only in technology, but also in the way production is organized).[11]

But explaining differences in prosperity in this way is far from satisfactory. Why is it that some societies have higher productivity and more physical capital than others, and why is it that some societies devote more resources to education and the development of human capital? To answer questions like these, it helps to formulate a more fundamental explanation of comparative prosperity. There are three main types of such theories: one emphasizes geography, another institutions, and a third culture.

The Geography Hypothesis

The idea with geographically based theories is that ultimately it is the geography, climate, and ecology of a society's location that shape both its technology and the incentives of its inhabitants. In consequence, a country's geography determines its prosperity.

There are at least three main versions of the geography hypothesis, each emphasizing a different mechanism for how geography affects prosperity. First, climate may be an important determinant of work effort, incentives, or even productivity. This idea dates back at least to the French philosopher Charles Montesquieu, who wrote in his classic book *The Spirit of the Laws*: "The heat of the climate can be so excessive that the body there will be absolutely without strength. So, prostration will pass even to the spirit; no curiosity, no noble enterprise, no generous sentiment; inclinations will all be passive there; laziness there will be happiness."[12]

Second, geography may determine the technology available to a society, especially in agriculture. Diamond espouses this view when he argues, "[P]roximate factors behind Europe's conquest of the Americas were the differences in all aspects of technology. These differences stemmed ultimately from Eurasia's much longer history of densely populated [societies dependent on food production]," which was in turn determined by geographical differences between Europe and the Americas.[13] Sachs has also argued in favor of the importance of geography in agricultural productivity, stating that, "by the start of the era of modern economic growth, if not much earlier, temperate-zone technologies were more productive than tropical-zone technologies."[14]

The third variant of the geography hypothesis, popular especially since the mid-1990s, links poverty in many areas of the world to their "disease burden." Such ideas have a long pedigree in African history, where for instance in the pre-internal-combustion-engine era, the high transportation costs in the tropical forest zone were thought to be a result of the presence of the tsetse fly, which made it impossible to use horses or mules to transport goods.[15]

The Institutions Hypothesis

Institutions can be defined as the rules and norms that determine the incentives and constraints that individuals face in society. These institutions may be economic, such as the conditions under which one can incorporate a company, or they may be political, such as the nature of the electoral system. Institutions may be formal and codified, such as a written constitution, or they may simply be informal rules that people follow. While the geography hypothesis emphasizes forces of nature as primary factors in the poverty of nations, the institutions hypothesis is about human-produced influences.

According to this view, some societies are organized in a way that upholds the rule of law; encourages investment in machinery, human capital, and better technologies; facilitates broad-based participation in economic and political life by the citizens; and supports market transactions. Others are not. The former prosper while the latter stagnate.

Crucial elements of institutions are enforcement of property rights for a broad cross-section of society, so that a variety of individuals have incentives to invest and take part in economic life; constraints on the actions of elites, politicians, and other powerful groups so that these people cannot expropriate the incomes and investments of others in the society nor create a highly uneven playing field; and finally, some degree of equal opportunity for broad segments of the society, so that they can make investments, especially in human capital, and participate in productive economic activities. Like the geography hypothesis, the institutions hypothesis has an impeccable pedigree. It goes back at least to John Locke, Adam Smith, and John Stuart Mill and features prominently in many current academic discussions and popular debates.

The Culture Hypothesis

Culture can be defined as the beliefs and values of a society. The idea that culture may influence economic performance is highly plausible to many people and formed the basis of Max Weber's argument that the Protestant Reformation played an important role in the rise of capitalism in Western Europe. In his view, the beliefs about the world that were intrinsic to Protestantism, particularly Calvinism, were crucial to the development of capitalism because they emphasized hard work, frugality, and saving, and they interpreted economic success as consistent with (if not actually signaling) being chosen by God. Weber contrasted these characteristics of Protestantism with those of other religions, such as Catholicism, which, he argued, did not promote capitalism.[16]

More recently, other cultural hypotheses have been proposed. David Landes, for example, traces Latin American economic under-performance to the imposed traditions of Iberian society where "the skills, curiosity, initiatives, and civic interests of North America were wanting. Spain itself lagged in these respects, owing to its spiritual homogeneity and docility, its wealth and pursuit of vanities; and Spain exported its weaknesses overseas."[17]

Applying the Approaches to Latin America

Armed with these different fundamental approaches, we can now evaluate some explanations for Latin America's comparative economic performance. Could geography be at the root of Latin America's economic woes? Some believe so, but even the simple evidence we have discussed so far suggests that there cannot be time-invariant implications of geography for prosperity.[18] In 1492, Bolivia was more prosperous than the United States, but now the situation is reversed. The statement of Sachs about the relative prosperity of the tropics is just wrong. Can geography explain why Bolivia suffered such a relative decline? It is possible that the types of geographical conditions that stimulate prosperity in 2005 are different from those that stimulated it in 1492. Yet anyone who has visited the Bolivian altiplano would find it hard to believe that it was a relatively favorable geographical endowment that created the complex and sophisticated organization that underlay the economic success of Tawantinsuyu.

Moreover, although relative agricultural productivity could well be sensitive to geography, as stated earlier, the great inequalities of the modern world stem from the nineteenth century and the uneven dissemination of industrialization. It is much harder to believe that geography has a large impact on the feasibility of a prosperous industrial society; indeed, Daron Acemoglu, Simon Johnson, and James Robinson tested precisely the idea that geography influenced the dissemination of the British industrial revolution and found no evidence supporting it.[19]

It is interesting to note the extent to which geography is accepted as an explanation for economic stagnation in nineteenth-century Latin America. In Colombia, for instance, this is the conventional wisdom. Colombia had a capital city located 9,000 feet up a mountain, 1,000 kilometers from the coast. The country was mountainous, fragmented, divided.[20] Yet when the liberal government of José Hilario López cut tariffs after 1850, this apparent isolation did not stop the artisans of Bogotá from being cast into unemployment and supporting a military coup. Moreover, other countries, such as neighboring Venezuela, with a capital city and large concentrations of population on the coast and with the expanding North Atlantic market beckoning invitingly, did no better than Colombia. Indeed, mountains and lack of populism aside, in the Latin American *longue durée*, Colombia's experience is entirely unremarkable. In the nineteenth century, it stagnated; and in the twentieth century, it grew steadily but remained at around 20 percent of U.S. average income.[21] When the coffee economy finally declined, and it was time to diversify into new activities, Colombian entrepreneurs chose flowers.

The notion that Latin America has a culture inimical to economic progress has received a lot of attention on the continent. As in the quote from Landes reproduced above, this is usually in the context of the inheritance of an Iberian culture, often intertwined with Catholicism. Many scholars have proposed general explanations along these lines.[22] There is some evidence that variables which capture aspects of culture are correlated with socioeconomic outcomes,[23] however, as yet, there is precious little evidence that culture has a large causal effect on economic performance. Though Spanish South America did much worse economically than British North America, in the colonial world more generally there is no relationship between the identity of the colonizing power and subsequent economic success.[24] To see this, one can note that, while the United States and Canada were British colonies, so were Guyana, Sierra Leone, and India.

Neither geographical nor cultural explanations of Latin America's comparative performance can convincingly account for its place in the world income distribution, though obviously both factors may have played some role in particular circumstances. Historical examples as well as more systematic social scientific evidence suggest that the best explanation for Latin America's economic trajectory is its institutions. That various types of institutions and prosperity are strongly associated is evident from some simple patterns in the cross-national data. Figure 7.3 shows the relationship between gross domestic product (GDP) per capita in 1995 and a broad measure of the security of property rights—protection against expropriation risk—averaged over the period 1985 to 1995.

The data on economic institutions come from Political Risk Services, a private company that assesses the risk of investments being expropriated in different countries. These data are imperfect as a measure of economic institutions, but the findings are robust when using other available measures of economic institutions. The scatter plot in figure 7.3 shows that countries with more secure property rights, i.e., better economic institutions, have higher average incomes.

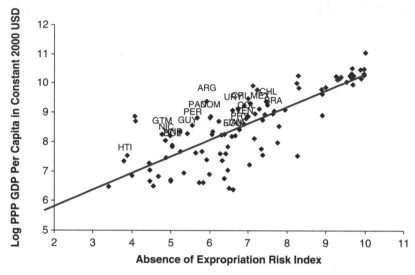

FIGURE 7.3 Log Gross Domestic Product (GDP) Per Capita (2004 Purchasing Power Parity) vs. Absence of Expropriation Risk. *Source*: Political Risk Services, www.prsgroup.com.

Figure 7.4 looks at the relationship between prosperity and one sort of political institution—constraints on the executive—from the Polity IV database. The variable of constraints on the executive captures the extent to which those who control political power are constrained or checked by others. For example, the types of checks and balances and separation of powers written into the U.S. Constitution would be a classic example of such constraints. Figure 7.4 shows that countries where political power holders are more constrained tend to be more prosperous.

Figure 7.5 looks at economic institutions another way. Apart from the stability of property rights, another key institution is the extent to which there is a level playing field in society. Good ideas and talents are widely distributed in the population, and a successful society must allow free access to profitable economic opportunities. Figure 7.5 presents data from Simeon Djankov et al., inspired by de Soto, on the number of procedures required to start a business.[25] The presence of entry costs is seen as creating monopolies and rents and indicative of a nonlevel playing field. One can see that entry barriers are negatively correlated with prosperity. As a final piece of evidence, figure 7.6 plots data on the rule of law from the World Bank's governance project. The rule of law is also associated with prosperity.

Particular types of economic and political institutions therefore tend to be strongly associated with prosperity. Of course, such

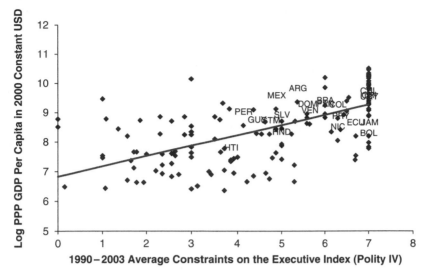

FIGURE 7.4 Log Gross Domestic Product (GDP) Per Capita (2004 Purchasing Power Parity) vs. Constraints on the Executive. *Source*: Polity IV Project on Political Regime Characteristics and Transitions, 1800–2004, Center for Global Policy, George Mason University and Center for International Development and Conflict Management, University of Maryland (dynamic dataset by subscription).

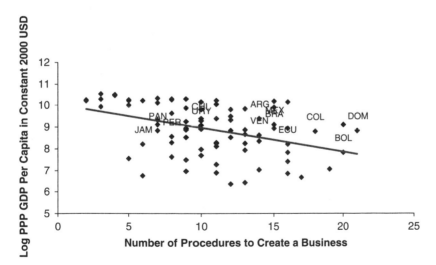

FIGURE 7.5 Log Gross Domestic Product (GDP) Per Capita (2004 Purchasing Power Parity) vs. Number of Procedures Needed to Create a Business. *Source*: Simeon Djankov, Rafael La Porta, Florencio López-de-Silanes, and Andrei Shleifer, "The Regulation of Entry," in *Quarterly Journal of Economics* 117 (2002): 1–37.

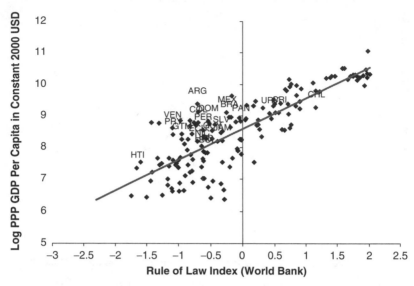

FIGURE 7.6 Log Gross Domestic Product (GDP) Per Capita (2004 Purchasing Power Parity) vs. Rule of Law. *Source*: "Rule of Law," *Worldwide Governance Indicators (WGI) Project*, World Bank, www.worldbank.org.

associations do not prove causality. For instance, there may be reverse causality running from income to institutions. More crucially, there is a potential problem of omitted variables, factors which might influence both institutions and income and whose omission may lead us to spuriously conclude there is a causal relationship between institutions and prosperity.

To understand this issue better, consider an example from the history of malaria. In the nineteenth century, doctors did not understand what caused malaria. To make progress toward protecting European troops stationed in the tropics, they developed an empirical theory of malaria by observing that people who lived or traveled close to swamps caught malaria. In other words, they turned the association between the incidence of malaria and swamps into a causal relationship—that malaria was *caused* by swamps—and elaborated on this theory by arguing that malaria was transmitted by mists, bad airs, and miasmas emitted by swamps and bogs. Of course, they were wrong, and a few decades later, other scientists proved that this statistical association was caused by an omitted factor, mosquitoes. Malaria is caused by parasites transmitted by mosquito bites, primarily by the mosquitoes of the genus *Anopheles*, which breed well in swamps, explaining the statistical association between swamps and malaria infection. In the same way, it is quite possible that an omitted factor is the root cause of the poverty of many tropical countries, and the statistical association between, for instance, insecure property rights and poverty is a mere correlation and nothing more.

In the natural sciences, causal theories are tested by conducting controlled experiments. For example, to investigate whether a proposed medication helps with headaches, we would randomly allocate a large number of otherwise similar subjects with headaches into one of two groups: the treatment group, which will receive the new medication, and a control group, which will receive a placebo, an apparently identical but actually inactive pill. We will then see whether there is an improvement in the headaches of the treatment group relative to the control group. If the answer is yes, subject to caveats related to statistical power, we can conclude that it is the medication that has the causal effect on headaches. This has to be so, since in our experiment all other conditions were kept the same between the two groups.

Controlled experiments are much harder to conduct in the social sciences. For example, it is impossible to change a country's institutions and observe what happens to the incomes and welfare of its citizens. However, even if we cannot use controlled experiments to test what determines prosperity, history offers many natural experiments where we can convincingly argue that one factor changes while other potential determinants of the outcomes of interest remain constant. This is exactly the strategy employed by Acemoglu et al. in their study of the causal effect of institutions on prosperity.[26]

The colonization of much of the world by Europeans provides a large-scale natural experiment. Beginning in the early fifteenth century and massively intensifying after 1492, Europeans conquered many nations. The colonization experience transformed the institutions in many diverse lands that were conquered or controlled by Europeans. Most important, Europeans imposed or created very different sets of institutions in different parts of their global empires. This history provides evidence that persuasively establishes the central role of economic institutions in development.

The explanation proposed by Acemoglu et al. for why figure 7.3 holds for former colonies is that Europeans created good institutions in some colonies, particularly places such as the United States, Canada, and Australia (what Alfred Crosby calls the neo-Europes), and bad ones in others (for example, Latin America and sub-Saharan Africa).[27] These institutions had a strong tendency to persist over time. Why did different institutions develop in different European colonies? The simplest answer is that the economic institutions in various colonies were shaped by Europeans to benefit themselves. Moreover, because conditions and endowments differed between colonies, Europeans consciously created different economic institutions.

There are several important empirical regularities connecting these initial conditions to current outcomes. Of particular importance are initial population density and the disease environment faced by Europeans. Figure 7.7 shows that there is a strong inverse relationship between population density in 1500 and current expropriation risk for former European colonies. Figure 7.8 shows that colonies where the disease environment was worse for Europeans also have worse economic institutions today. The data here are the mortality rates of European soldiers, sailors, and bishops stationed in the colonial world.[28]

Why did Europeans introduce better institutions in relatively unsettled and unhealthy areas than in densely settled and healthy areas? Anticipating the discussion of institutional origins in the next section, it is worth noting here that Europeans were more likely to introduce or maintain economic institutions that facilitated the extraction of resources in those areas where they would benefit from the extraction of resources. This typically meant areas controlled by a small group of Europeans and areas offering resources to be extracted. These resources

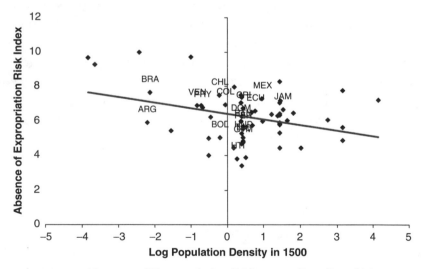

FIGURE 7.7 Absence of Expropriation Risk versus Log Population Density in 1500 in Former Colonies. *Source*: Daron Acemoglu, Simon Johnson, and James A. Robinson, "Colonial Origins of Comparative Development: An Empirical Investigation," in *American Economic Review* 91 (2001): 1369–1401.

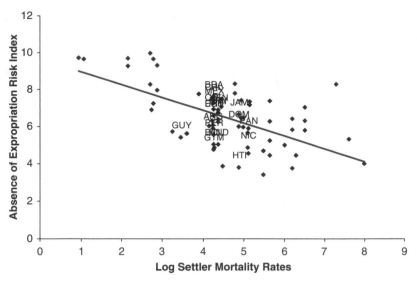

FIGURE 7.8 Absence of Expropriation Risk versus Log Settler Mortality Rates. *Source*: Daron Acemoglu, Simon Johnson, and James A. Robinson, "Colonial Origins of Comparative Development: An Empirical Investigation," in *American Economic Review* 91 (2001): 1369–1401.

included gold and silver, valuable agricultural commodities such as sugar, and, most important, people. In places with large indigenous populations, Europeans could exploit the population, in the form of taxes, tributes, or employment as forced labor in mines or plantations. This type of colonization was incompatible with institutions providing economic or civil rights to the majority of the population or with anything resembling a level playing field. Consequently, a more complex civilization and a denser population structure made it more profitable for the Europeans to introduce worse economic institutions.

In contrast, in places with little to extract and in sparsely settled places where the Europeans themselves became the majority of the population, it was in their interest to introduce economic institutions protecting their own property rights. Of course, there were often conflicts among the Europeans, and it is significant that, in the neo-Europes, these conflicts played out in ways which benefited the mass of Europeans, rather than just the elites. In addition, the disease environments differed markedly among the colonies, with obvious consequences on the attractiveness of European settlement. When Europeans settled, they established institutions with which they themselves had to live. As a result of the prevalence of yellow fever and malaria, potential

European settlers and European troops faced very different mortality rates in the colonies. For example, before 1850, the annual mortality rates for a settlement size maintained at 1,000 (through replacement) ranged from 8.55 in New Zealand, which was lower than in Europe at that time, to 49 in India, 130 in Jamaica, and around 500 in West Africa. These widely different mortality rates of potential settlers led to different settlement rates and to divergent institutional paths for various colonies.

As Acemoglu et al. noted, the historical disease environment facing Europeans influenced whether Europeans could settle or not and therefore the institutions that arose, but it is not itself a determinant of current prosperity.[29] If we hypothesize that the disease environment 200 or more years ago influences outcomes today only through its effect on institutions today, then we can use this historical disease environment as an exogenous source of variation in current institutions, which will enable us to pin down the causal effect of institutions on prosperity.

One could imagine that the relationship between the historical mortality of Europeans and current outcomes is really just capturing the effects of the current disease environment on institutional and economic outcomes. To be sure, yellow fever is largely eradicated today, but malaria is still endemic in many parts of sub-Saharan Africa, causing the deaths of millions of children every year. Nevertheless, the majority of the adult inhabitants of areas subject to malaria have either genetic or, more often, acquired immunity, ensuring that they do not die or are not incapacitated by even the most deadly strain of malaria, falciparum malaria. In contrast, especially in the nineteenth century before the causes and prevention of malaria were understood, malaria infection meant almost certain death for Europeans.

The idea that figure 7.8 captures—the effect of European settler mortality rates working via institutional development, not the direct effect of these diseases—is also supported by the mortality rates of indigenous peoples in these areas. While Europeans faced astounding death rates, the indigenous population had similar mortality rates to those of Europeans in their home countries. For example, the annual mortality rates of native troops serving in Bengal and Madras were, respectively, 11 and 13 per 1,000, similar to—in fact lower than—the annual mortality rate of British troops serving in Britain, which was approximately 15 per 1,000. In contrast, the death rates of British troops serving in these colonies were much higher because of their lack of immunity to local disease. For example, death rates in Bengal and Madras for British troops were between 70 and 170 per 1,000.

Using European mortality as a source of variation for the current enforcement of property rights, Acemoglu et al. showed that most of the gap between rich and poor countries today is due to differences in economic institutions. More precisely, they showed that, if one took two typical—in the sense that they both lie on the regression line—countries with high and low expropriation risk, like Nigeria and Chile, then almost the entire difference in incomes per capita between them could be explained by the difference in the security of property rights.[30] They also presented statistical evidence that showed that, once the effect of economic institutions on GDP per capita was properly controlled for, geographical variables, such as latitude, whether or not a country is landlocked, and the current disease environment, have no explanatory power for current prosperity. The study also showed that, to the extent that aspects of culture can be captured by such things as the identity of the colonizing power, the presence of different religions, or the proportion of people of European descent, culture has no influence on prosperity.

That the relationship in figure 7.8 does not reflect the direct effect of the disease environment is also consistent with the fact that using only information about the prevalence of yellow fever leads to similar results. Since yellow fever is largely eradicated today, this is unlikely to reflect the direct effect of yellow fever.

Demonstrating that the comparative development of Latin America can be explained by its institutions is an important first step, but we must keep exploring. We need to explain why Latin America has the institutions it has and not the institutions of North America, and how these different institutional paths have been sustained over time. The remainder of this chapter attempts to show how such an explanation can be put together through the Latin American equilibrium.

The Latin American Equilibrium

There are three pieces to an institutional explanation of Latin American development. The first part, which has already been discussed in the previous section, links current institutions to poor economic outcomes. The second and third aspects, on which this section focuses, analyze institutional origins and explain where Latin America's institutions came from; we then link these origins to current outcomes by explaining how institutions persist and evolve over time, connecting the present to the past.

The data discussed in the last section of this chapter show that the relative poverty of Latin America is related to its institutions. It is the fact that Latin America has different institutions from North America that explains why its workers have poorer technology and lower human capital and productivity. But one must now ask: where did these institutions come from?

Origins of the Latin American Equilibrium

The institutions of a society evolve over long historical periods. Historians commonly think that the institutions of modern Latin America reflect the organization of the society created after 1492 by the Spanish conquistadores.[31] The Spanish were interested in the extraction of gold and silver, and then later in taking tribute and raising taxes. The colonial societies that emerged were authoritarian and concentrated political power in the hands of a small group of Spanish elites, who created a set of economic institutions designed to extract wealth from the indigenous population and a set of political institutions designed to consolidate their power.

After Francisco Pizarro conquered the empire of Tawantinsuyu in Peru and Bolivia, and following the model developed a decade earlier in Mexico by Hernán Cortés, he imposed a series of institutions designed to extract rents from the newly conquered natives. The main institutions that eventually emerged were the *encomienda* (which gave Spanish conquistadores the right to native labor), the *mita* (a system of forced labor used in the mines and for public works), and the *repartimiento* (the forced sale of goods to the native people, typically at highly inflated prices). Pizarro created 480 *encomenderos* under whose "care" the entire indigenous population was placed; in the territory comprising modern Colombia, there were about 900 *encomenderos*, who received their charges soon after the conquest of what became New Grenada.

By the end of the sixteenth century, the Spanish Crown attempted to retract the initial grants of *encomienda* and to systematize the payment of tribute from the native population, both to the *encomenderos* and also directly to the Crown. Villamarin studied this process for the province around Bogotá in modern Colombia and showed that, when one aggregated the time which was used for forced labor in the cities and on the land with the time which was necessary to produce the crops needed to pay for the tribute, the native peoples spent 75 percent of their time working for their Spanish masters. This is an extraordinary implicit rate of taxation.[32] The feasibility of this type of economic system was determined by the relatively high population densities of indigenous peoples in many parts of the Spanish empire and also the extent to which complex societies had developed. The main factors which determined Spanish colonial activities were whether the indigenous peoples possessed "permanent intensive agriculture, stable town and village sites, strong tribute mechanisms, and dense populations."[33]

Other institutions were designed to reinforce this system. For instance, the legal system systematically discriminated against the indigenous population, and the testimony of natives in court was highly circumscribed. Although Indians certainly did use the legal system to challenge aspects of colonial rule, they could not alter the main parameters of the system. In addition to all of this, the Spanish Crown created a complex web of mercantilistic policies and monopolies in order to raise revenues for the state.

Spanish colonies that had small populations of native peoples, such as Costa Rica and Argentina, seem to have followed different paths of institutional development. The sharp contrasts along many institutional dimensions between Costa Rica, which had relatively few Native Americans, and Guatemala, where the population density was greater, have been studied extensively.[34] Interestingly, although the formal political institutions within the Spanish empire were the same everywhere, the way they functioned depended on the local conditions. For example, the lowest level of Spanish administration was the *cabildo*, a council which at least nominally had the power to levy taxes and the responsibility for administering municipal services, such as schools. The council was generally appointed by higher officials, themselves appointed by the Spanish Crown. Yet there was the possibility for a *cabildo abierto*, where all of the *vecinos*, or citizens, could meet to express their opinions and attempt to influence policy. This institution was the closest thing to a truly democratic institution in Spanish Latin America. Significantly, these meetings were seldom, if ever, held in areas such as colonial Peru, yet were active in Santiago and Buenos Aires.

The Spanish conquest around Río de la Plata during the early sixteenth century provides a telling example of how population density affected colonization.[35] Early in 1536, a large Spanish expedition arrived in the area and founded the city of Buenos Aires at the mouth of the river. The area was sparsely inhabited by nonsedentary native people, whom the Spaniards were unable to enslave. Starvation forced them to abandon Buenos Aires and move up the river to a post at Asunción. This area was more densely settled by the semi-sedentary Guaraní people, who were successfully enslaved by the Spaniards, and thus the colony of Paraguay was founded. Argentina was finally colonized later, with a higher proportion of European settlers, though with a legacy of institutions molded by the inclusion of areas closely integrated into the colonial system, such as the provinces of Tucumán, Salta, and Jujuy, along with Buenos Aires and the littoral.

The set of economic institutions that emerged in the main Spanish colonies greatly benefited the Spanish Crown and the Spanish settler elite, yet they did not promote the prosperity of Latin America. The vast majority of the population did not have secure property rights and lacked the incentives or opportunities to enter into socially desirable occupations or to invest. These economic institutions were created by and sustained in the context of specific political institutions and a particular balance of political power. Europeans maintained coercive regimes, monopolizing military and political power, while respecting few constraints on this power (unless they were imposed by the mother country in Europe). These political institutions generated the structure and incentives that ensured their own continuation and the continuation of a set of economic institutions which did not provide good economic incentives for the great mass of society.

The history of North America stands in stark contrast. Initial attempts at colonization were also based on economic motivations. British American colonies were founded by entities such as the Virginia Company and the Providence Island Company, whose aim was to make profits. The model that they had in mind was not so different from that adopted by the Spanish or Portuguese (a system that other British colonizing entities, such as the East India Company, used to great effect). Yet these colonies did not make money, and indeed both the Virginia and Providence Island companies went bankrupt. A colonial model involving the exploitation of indigenous labor and tribute systems was simply unfeasible in these places because of the lack of a large indigenous population and the absence of complex societies.

The contrast between the Spanish colonization of the Río de la Plata area discussed above and the initial attempts by the British to colonize North America is instructive. As with Spanish colonization, British colonization was undertaken by private individuals with some type of charter from the Crown. In Spanish America, when Charles V realized how profitable the colonization enterprise was, he quickly took it over. This led to serious rebellions in the colonies, for example, the one led in 1645 by Gonzalo Pizarro in Peru. In contrast, in British America, the early colonization attempts were not economically successful, and when they were taken over by the Crown, it was because they were insolvent. The Jamestown colony, founded in 1607 by the Virginia Company, struggled to survive mostly because the early colonists took Pizarro's conquest of Peru as their model. As they looked for gold, they tried to use the local indigenous population for forced labor and attempted to capture the local Algonquian chief, Powhatan, in the hope that, as with Pizarro's capture of Atahualpa, the chief would deliver all of the natives and their wealth to the colonists. However, unlike Peru, in Virginia there was no large centralized tributary empire, but rather many competing and fragmented tribes. Moreover, unlike Atahualpa, Powhatan was highly suspicious of the strangers who had arrived on his shores and sensibly refused to go to Jamestown. Furthermore, there was no gold or silver, and the Native Americans, not accustomed to paying tribute or engaging in forced labor, would not work. Thus, the Jamestown settlers were doomed to starvation.[36]

In response to these early failures, the Virginia Company tried various incentive-based schemes, including a highly punitive, almost penal, regime in an effort to make money. Such repressive efforts quickly collapsed, however, and by 1619 the company had created an unusually representative set of institutions for that era: a general assembly with adult European male suffrage.

The early experience of Virginia was replicated elsewhere in the new colony. Examples include large land grants made by Charles I and, in 1632, the granting of Maryland (approximately 10 million acres) to the second Lord Baltimore. The charter also gave Baltimore "virtually complete legal authority over his territory, with the power to establish a government in whatever form he wished."[37] His idea was to attract tenants from Britain and set up a massive manorial system. This approach to colonization was not so different from the one employed by the Portuguese in Brazil, yet things remained different in North America. As pointed out by David Galenson:

> The extreme labor shortage...allowed many early settlers to gain their economic independence from the manorial lords, and establish separate farms....Thus, just as in Virginia, in Maryland the colonial labor problem undermined the initial plans for a rigid social hierarchy, as Lord Baltimore's blueprints for a manorial society were largely swept away and early Maryland became an open and fluid society, which offered considerable economic and social opportunity.[38]

The situation in Maryland, a reflection of conditions that had made themselves felt in Jamestown, reproduced itself in Carolina, New

Jersey, and New York. Similar processes were also at work in other colonies of settlement, for example, in Canada and Australia.

In these colonies, economic institutions provided access to land to a broad cross-section of society, while the legal system became relatively impartial, ensuring secure property rights for smallholders and potential investors regardless of their political connections. These institutions created not only good incentives for investment, but also made such investment possible by generating financial development and an environment for secure contracting and business relationships. These economic institutions were supported by relatively representative political institutions. Though slaves, women, and the indigenous peoples were excluded from the benefits they provided, the proportion of slaves in the population was small in the crucial eighteenth century, never exceeding 20 percent of the population, in stark contrast to Brazil or the Caribbean sugar colonies. Moreover, as the European society expanded, it did not do so on the basis of the direct exploitation of the native population. As was the case in Latin America, there was a synergy between the economic and political institutions, but this time it was not a vicious, but rather a virtuous one: economic institutions gave and protected property rights for the great mass of people, and relatively democratic political institutions complemented them, ensuring the continuation of an environment conducive for investment and economic progress.

This picture of the early United States, supported by many other historical accounts, demonstrates the large impact of the initial conditions in the colony on the institutions that later emerged. Because there was a very low population density and no way of extracting resources using the labor of indigenous peoples nor an existing tax or tribute system, early commercial developments had to involve imported British labor. Moreover, relative to much of the colonial world, the disease environment was benign, which stimulated settlement. An interesting example of the awareness of the disease environment comes from the Pilgrim fathers, who decided to migrate to the United States rather than to Guyana because of the very high mortality rates in Guyana.[39]

Persistence of the Latin American Equilibrium

If the effects of institutions are felt today, but their origins lie in the societies that developed in the early colonial period, we need to understand how the organization of society can be so persistent over time. Such a claim seems somewhat paradoxical because, at least on the surface, there has been terrific institutional change in Latin America, particularly over the two centuries since independence. It is therefore important to clarify what we mean when we say that institutions persist. Notice that the claim here is that what persists is an *equilibrium outcome*. For example, Acemoglu et al. demonstrate that the stability of property rights today has a large causal impact on income today. They also show that the extent of the security of property rights today is linked to various historical variables. The claim is that, historically, societies were organized in particular ways, some of which did not create security of property, and this insecurity of property rights persisted.[40]

To say that Latin American countries have a history of unstable property rights, however, does not imply that the reasons for that instability have been the same over time. Nevertheless, the explanation for insecure property rights is often tied to other underlying institutions, for example, political institutions such as the extent of checks and balances or constraints on the executive, or various ways of organizing the labor market, such as slavery or other forms of forced labor. Thus, it makes sense to examine to what extent these underlying features persist, since we think of them as playing a key part in sustaining the Latin American equilibrium.

An obvious possibility is to see if particular institutions persist. For example, the U.S. Constitution, although over time amended to abolish slavery, allow women to vote, and permit the federal government to raise income taxes, has been in operation for over 200 years. In England, it is arguable, two clauses of the Magna Carta, resentfully signed at Runnymede by King John in 1215, have been in force for a continuous 800 years. Money, as a social institution, has persisted continuously since its adoption in most societies, though the Khmer Rouge did abolish it for several years in Cambodia in the 1970s.

Yet such a notion of institutional persistence will not take us far in understanding comparative development. In the case of Latin America, early colonial institutions closely associated with the control and exploitation of indigenous peoples, such as the *encomienda* and the *mita*, vanished long ago. The *encomienda* was almost dead as an institution by the end of the sixteenth century in Mexico, though it lingered longer elsewhere in the empire. The most infamous *mita*, the one for the silver mines in Potosí, was abolished when Peru and Bolivia became independent in the 1820s. Some of the specific institutions of colonial labor exploitation did continue after independence from Spain. The Indian tribute, which evolved out of the *encomienda*, was abolished gradually in the nineteenth century: in 1832 in Colombia, in 1857 in Ecuador, and in the 1870s and 1880s in Peru and Bolivia. In the late nineteenth century, other labor institutions, such as the *mandamienato* in Guatemala,[41] remarkably similar to some of those previously abolished, were reintroduced in the wake of agricultural export booms. Free labor arrived with democracy in 1945 in Guatemala. In Bolivia, some specific and highly resented aspects of unpaid labor service, such as *pongueaje*, persisted until the revolution in 1952.

If we focus instead on political institutions, the Spanish colonial empire collapsed after Napoleon's invasion of Spain in 1808. In its place, the former Spanish American countries created republican institutions with written constitutions and elected legislatures and presidents. Though nineteenth-century elections in Latin America were marred by fraud and highly restricted franchises, these were big changes relative to the eighteenth century. They were followed by more significant changes in the twentieth century: the rise of export economies, organized labor, the systematic opening of political space, and the arrival of populist parties such as the Peronists in Argentina or APRA in Peru, universal suffrage, import substitution industrialization, and a central political role for the military. These examples suggest that, although one might construct a theory of Bolivian poverty in 1952 around the endurance of *pongueaje*, a theory of the persistence of institutions cannot usefully be about the inertia of such specific institutions. Moreover, the abolition of *pongueaje* in 1952 did not lead to a dramatic improvement in Bolivian economic performance nor in the types of institutional outcomes discussed previously.

As emphasized by Acemoglu et al., institutions that fail to create incentives for investment and innovation are outcomes of a political process.[42] Though they may often be very difficult to change, one must think of a set of institutions as being held in place by a particular political equilibrium and by a particular distribution of political power. Sets of institutions have distributional consequences, and institutions that create underdevelopment may generate large returns for some groups in society. There is no presumption here that the institutions of a society will tend toward something socially efficient. This perspective indicates that the importance of *pongueaje* is that its presence was indicative of the persistence of a much wider political equilibrium and set of power relations, which had reproduced themselves historically and which can explain why Bolivia was poor in 1952. In addition, despite a revolution and the abolition of *pongueaje* in 1952, there is a fundamental sense in which the pre-1952 political equilibrium in

Bolivia persisted after the revolution, even after the neoliberal policy reforms of 1985.

How do these ideas help us to understand institutional persistence? This perspective emphasizes not the persistence of specific institutions, but rather the persistence of an underlying political equilibrium which gives rise to strategies of income redistribution and social control—and there are many possible instruments to achieve any particular goal. For example, despite losing the Civil War, antebellum political elites managed to sustain their political control of the southern United States. They successfully blocked economic reforms that might have undermined this power, such as the distribution of 40 acres and a mule to each freed slave. They also derailed political reforms they opposed, such as the enfranchisement of freed slaves. Thus, though slavery as an economic institution was abolished, southern elites were able to recreate after 1865 a labor-intensive, low-wage, low-education, and repressive economy that, in many ways, was remarkably similar to that of the antebellum South. Slavery was gone, but in its place were the Ku Klux Klan and Jim Crow.[43]

Latin America is not without examples where a clear continuity in the underlying structure of political power leads to persistence in the institutional equilibrium. Examples include the 14 families that purportedly controlled El Salvador, the persistence of colonial lineages among landowners and elites in Costa Rica, the stranglehold over political power of the landed oligarchy in the northeast of Brazil, the Creel dynasty in Mexico, and the 150-year dominance of the Liberal and Conservative parties in Colombia.[44] Even after formal democratization and surface changes in political institutions, it could be that such elites continue to wield political power and to determine economic institutions. Indeed, in all of these cases, one could document how shocks to the economic or political system led to changes in economic and even political institutions without drastically perturbing the underlying persistence of the political equilibrium or the consequences for economic development.

However, Latin American history suggests that even this notion of institutional persistence will not provide a complete explanation. Let us return again to Bolivia. In 1952, a revolution masterminded by a political party, the Movimiento Nacionalista Revolucionario (MNR), overthrew the traditional political and economic system. As in many Latin American countries, the rise of new interests and cleavages in the early twentieth century had led existing elites, often rurally based, to enter into a governing coalition with the military. This coalition was demolished in Bolivia in 1952. The tin mines were expropriated from the three great families that owned them and nationalized. All of the great haciendas were expropriated from the landed elites, and the land was distributed to the peasants. The coalition which had represented these interests in politics, known as La Rosca, was displaced, universal suffrage was introduced, the military disarmed, and *pongueaje* abolished. So why is Bolivia still poor? Why does Bolivia still have deficient institutions?

To explain this, we need to extend our notion of the persistence of institutional equilibrium. We do this by pointing out that, even though specific economic and political institutions may change, and even if existing elites are destroyed, the underlying structures and incentives which gave rise to the previous equilibrium may still remain. If this is so, then this creates an incentive for a new group in society to recreate elements of the previous institutional equilibrium from scratch. Though some changes in specific institutions did take place in Bolivia after 1952, the MNR did exactly that after 1956: it abandoned its coalition with more radical forces (like the tin miners), it rearmed the military, and it reconstituted itself as a new elite based on the patronage dispensed by a rapidly expanding state. In the countryside, social control and the extraction of rents could not be achieved by institutions such as *pongueaje*, but they could be done by different means. Indeed, Jonathan Kelley and Herbert Klein show that the dramatic fall in inequality caused by agrarian reform had been completely reversed by the early 1960s.[45]

These ideas are closely related to the "iron law of oligarchy" proposed by German sociologist Robert Michels in 1911. He predicted that radical social changes were not possible because a new elite would emerge to replace an old one with little change, except possibly in the identity of the elite.[46] In the context of this chapter, this implies that even apparently radically discontinuous change, such as a revolution, may only replace one oligarchy with another and not move a society onto a better institutional or economic path.

Seen in this perspective, one can reconcile the fact that many institutions changed in Latin America over the past 200 years with the idea of the shadow of colonial institutions. What we are trying to explain is the persistence of insecure property rights, absence of the rule of law, a nonlevel playing field, and many things which accompany these institutions, such as a lack of constraints on the exercise of political power and the concentration of that power into the hands of a relatively small subset of the population. There is little doubt that these institutions characterized colonial Latin America for the majority of the population and that these features of society persisted into the nineteenth and twentieth centuries.

Escaping the Latin American Equilibrium:
The Rise of the Chilean Gentry

There are no "iron laws" in social science, and there is no reason that the Latin American equilibrium cannot be escaped. Though institutional theories tend to emphasize the historical development of society, they are much more optimistic in this respect than geographical or cultural theories. If a set of institutions is kept in place by a structure of political power, political institutions, and incentives, then these structures and incentives can be changed. Indeed, as noted earlier, there has been a lot of change; for instance, Latin America is much more democratic than it has been historically, and many socioeconomic outcomes have consistently improved. Yet the experience with democracy has been fraught with disappointments, and the reforms of the 1980s and 1990s have failed to generate rapid economic growth.

A partial explanation for this may be drawn from the above discussion. Reforms, like the abolition of slavery in the United States after 1865 and of *pongueaje* in Bolivia after 1952, may simply reflect changes in the instruments used to redistribute income and to exercise political and social control. Introducing an independent central bank, as Argentina and Colombia did in the early 1990s, may take away one possibility, but it can be replaced by others without any net benefit for economic growth. As many political scientists have observed, neoliberal reforms in Argentina, Mexico, Peru, and elsewhere simply reflected politics as usual, as even privatization and deregulation could be molded into clientelism. Policies changed because political and economic shocks altered the composition of domestic political coalitions, but the form that these policies took did not represent a radical change of the institutional environment.[47] Even the celebrated policy reforms of the reinvented MNR in Bolivia after 1985 came at the price of a political pact with the former military dictator, Hugo Banzer, and an intensified repression of opponents and clientelism.[48] Obviously, hyperinflation is not good for the economy, but conquering it is not sufficient for a change in the underlying equilibrium.

Of course, only part of the United States was born with good institutions. The southern plantation society managed to maintain a system of low wages, low education, labor repression, and a relatively poor economy even after the abolition of slavery. As late as the 1940s, the South was still only at a level of about 50 percent of the U.S. GDP per capita. It took a series of large technological, social, economic, and political shocks to change this. These included black migration to the

North, the mechanization of cotton picking, the collective action of the civil rights movement, and the active intervention of the federal government with the Civil Rights and Voting Rights acts.

European countries also were not typically born with good institutions; they developed or created them later. An obvious example of this is Britain. Prior to the eighteenth century, Britain was ruled by absolutist dynasties like most other European countries. The Civil War and the Glorious Revolution led to a dramatic change in the balance of power and the emergence of a limited, constitutional monarchy.[49] Why?

Two key processes seem to have been at work. One, first discussed by Tawney, was the rise of the gentry. Tawney pointed out that, after the dissolution of the monasteries in 1538 by Henry VIII, a large amount of land came onto the market and was purchased by a new breed of capitalistic farmers. These upwardly mobile producers had a vested interest in secure property rights, abolishing monopolies and restrictions of trade, and reining in the powers of the king.[50] Another complementary factor, emphasized by Acemoglu et al., was the creation of a new breed of mercantile and capitalistic interests as the result of the expansion of overseas trade.[51] Their institutional interests were similar to those of the gentry, and they combined in the eighteenth century to change British institutions.

There is a remarkable parallel between the process outlined by Tawney in early modern Britain and that which has taken place in Chile over the last quarter of a century. Starting in 1967, agrarian reforms led to an expropriation of 52 percent of agricultural land by the government. After the Pinochet coup in 1973, land reform was stopped. About 30 percent of the land (still in the hands of the government at the time of the coup) was returned to the previous owners. About 10 percent was sold, 19 percent held by the government, and the rest left to the beneficiaries of reform.[52] But most of these sold out, and out of this massive destruction of the traditional agricultural system, a new breed of capitalist farmers emerged. From having the most backward agricultural sector in the 1960s, Chile's rural economy has emerged as one of the most dynamic in the world economy.[53]

Conclusions

To conclude, it would be useful to return to some of the questions posed earlier. First, why, despite the potential availability of the full gamut of European technologies, did the relative position of Latin

America never improve during the colonial period? The proposed explanation, building on the work of a large number of scholars, is that the Spanish were concerned primarily about extracting and controlling resources, and the sort of society that facilitated this was not one which created the incentives or conditions that could narrow the gap between Latin America and Europe. However, such institutions were not necessarily so costly in the early modern world. In the eighteenth century, the countries with the highest per capita income in the world were probably the sugar colonies of Cuba, Haiti, and Barbados, yet these places all had poor institutions according to the definitions proposed in this chapter. These facts can be reconciled by noting that how costly a set of institutions is for aggregate income depends on the technologies available. If the main productive activity is growing sugarcane, then the losses are small compared to what they are in an industrial society.

Of course, there were significant differences between Latin America and North America despite the fact that their income levels were similar in the eighteenth century. Average educational attainment and literacy were vastly higher in the United States, and the states also had nascent democratic assemblies.[54] These differences really mattered when the industrial revolution took off. For instance, Stephen Haber has shown the key role that political institutions played in explaining why the financial development of the United States diverged from that of Mexico in the nineteenth century.[55] Similar situations arose in premodern Europe. Britain had much better institutions than other parts of Europe in the eighteenth century, but it was only the arrival of industrial technologies that transformed this into large income gaps. So, Latin America's institutions explain why it was behind, though not that far behind, in 1800. Had sugarcane been a viable crop everywhere, it might have even been ahead.

Putting these pieces together answers the second question: why did Latin America stagnate in the nineteenth century? The institutional nexus which had not been so costly in the eighteenth century became so in the nineteenth. Hierarchical Latin American countries did not invest heavily in education, which might have destabilized the political status quo, nor develop the types of institutions required to create and sustain a vibrant industrial economy. Many other proximate reasons for poor economic performance have been discussed, for instance, the political instability that characterized much of the first 50 years of independence in Latin but not North America.[56] But political instability is a natural outcome of a society where economic institutions generate large amounts of rents for those with political power. Power is attractive, and people compete to attain it. Moreover, although sustained growth did occur in Latin America following the period when the central state consolidated—for instance, in Mexico and Argentina after the 1870s—it is the absence of catching up that is the key puzzle. The Colombian evidence is telling in this respect. After the War of a Thousand Days, which finished in 1902, the Conservatives and Liberals devised a set of political institutions to share power. Once the fighting stopped, there was peace for almost 50 years. Yet average economic growth was little different during this period and the subsequent 50 years, which saw a huge upsurge of violence and civil war. Indeed, political instability did not go away. In the twentieth century, it manifested itself in military coups, populism, and the revolutions of Mexico, Bolivia, Cuba, and Nicaragua. In the twentieth century, the Latin American equilibrium generated vast wealth for a few, but the other side of these concentrated returns is a set of institutions for society which are not consistent with rapid economic progress.

Notes

1. I would like to thank María Angélica Bautista and Camilo García for their excellent research assistance.
2. Angus Maddison, *The World Economy: A Millennial Perspective* (Paris: OECD, 2003), p. 262.
3. See Daron Acemoglu, Simon Johnson, and James A. Robinson, "Reversal of Fortune: Geography and Institutions in the Making of the Modern World Income Distribution," *Quarterly Journal of Economics* 118 (2002): 1231–1294.
4. Jared M. Diamond, *Guns, Germs and Steel: The Fate of Human Societies* (New York: Norton, 1997).
5. W. George Lovell and Christopher Lutz, "Conquest and Population: Maya Demography in Historical Perspective," *Latin American Research Review* 29 (1994): 133–140.
6. Barry Bogin and Ryan Keep, "Eight Thousand Years of Economic and Political History in Latin America Revealed by Anthropometry," *Annals of Human Biology* 26 (1999): 333–351.
7. See Robert W. Fogel, *The Escape from Hunger and Premature Death, 1700–2100* (New York: Cambridge University Press, 2004).
8. Charles Gibson, *The Aztecs under Spanish Rule* (Stanford, CA: Stanford University Press, 1964), pp. 249–252, 311–314.
9. See John H. Coatsworth, "Notes on the Comparative Economic History of Latin America and the United States," in *Development and Underdevelopment in America*, edited by Walter L. Bernecker and Hans Werner Tobler (New York: de Gruyter, 1993); Stanley L. Engerman and Kenneth L. Sokoloff, "Factor Endowments, Institutions, and Differential Growth Paths among New World Economies," in *How Latin America Fell Behind*, edited by Stephen Haber (Stanford, CA: Stanford University Press, 1997).

10. John H. Coatsworth, "Economic and Institutional Trajectories in Nineteenth Century Latin America," in *Latin America and the World Economy since 1800*, edited by John H. Coatsworth and Alan M. Taylor (Cambridge, MA: Harvard University Press, 1998), p. 26.

11. Robert M. Solow, "Technical Change and the Aggregate Production Function," *Review of Economics and Statistics* 39 (1957): 312–320.

12. Charles de Secondat Montesquieu, *The Spirit of the Laws* (New York: Cambridge University Press, 1989 [1748]).

13. Diamond, *Guns, Germs and Steel*, p. 358.

14. Jeffrey D. Sachs, *Tropical Underdevelopment*, NBER Working Paper 8119 (Cambridge, MA: National Bureau of Economic Research, 2001), p. 2.

15. Anthony G. Hopkins, *An Economic History of West Africa* (New York: Addison-Wesley and Longman, 1973).

16. Max Weber, *The Protestant Ethic and the Spirit of Capitalism* (London: Allen and Unwin, 1930).

17. David S. Landes, *The Wealth and Poverty of Nations* (New York: Norton, 1998), p. 312.

18. John L. Gallup, Alejandro Gaviria, and Eduardo Lora, *Is Geography Destiny? Lessons from Latin America* (Stanford, CA: Stanford University Press, 2003).

19. Acemoglu, Johnson, and Robinson, "Reversal of Fortune," pp. 1231–1294.

20. Frank P. Safford and Marco Palacios, *Colombia: Fragmented Land, Divided Society* (New York: Oxford University Press, 2002).

21. James A. Robinson, "A Normal Latin American Country? Colombian Economic Development in Comparative Perspective," in *An Economic History of Colombia in the 20th Century*, edited by James A. Robinson and Miguel Urrutia (Cambridge, MA: Harvard University Press, 2005).

22. See, for example, Claudio Véliz, *The New World of the Gothic Fox: Culture and Economy in English and Spanish America* (Berkeley: University of California Press, 1984); and Howard J. Wiarda, *The Soul of Latin America: The Cultural and Political Tradition* (New Haven, CT: Yale University Press, 2001).

23. See, for example, Guido Tabellini, "Culture and Institutions: Economic Development in the Regions of Europe," unpublished manuscript, Bocconi University, Milan, Italy, 2005.

24. Daron Acemoglu, Simon Johnson, and James A. Robinson, "Colonial Origins of Comparative Development: An Empirical Investigation," *American Economic Review* 91 (2001): 1369–1401.

25. Simeon Djankov, Rafael La Porta, Florencio López-de-Silanes, and Andrei Shleifer, "The Regulation of Entry," *Quarterly Journal of Economics* 117 (2001): 1–37. See also Hernando de Soto, *The Other Path* (New York: Harper & Row, 1989).

26. Acemoglu, Johnson, and Robinson, "Colonial Origins of Comparative Development."

27. Alfred W. Crosby, *Ecological Imperialism* (New York: Cambridge University Press, 1986).

28. Acemoglu, Johnson, and Robinson, "Colonial Origins of Comparative Development."

29. Ibid.

30. Ibid., p. 1387.

31. Engerman and Sokoloff, "Factor Endowments, Institutions, and Differential Growth Paths."

32. Juan A. Villamarin, "Encomenderos and Indians in the Formation of Colonial Society in the Sabana de Bogotá, Colombia, 1537–1740," Ph.D. diss., Brandeis University, 1972.

33. James Lockhart and Stuart B. Schwartz, *Early Latin America* (New York: Cambridge University Press, 1983), p. 34.
34. See, for example, Ciro F. S. Cardoso, "The Liberal Era, 1870–1930," in *Central America since Independence*, edited by Leslie Bethell (Cambridge: Cambridge University Press, 1991).
35. Lockhart and Schwartz, *Early Latin America*, pp. 259–260.
36. See Edmund S. Morgan, *American Slavery, American Freedom: The Ordeal of Colonial Virginia* (New York: Norton, 1975).
37. David W. Galenson, "The Settlement and Growth of the Colonies: Population, Labor and Economic Development," in *The Cambridge Economic History of the United States*, vol. 1: *The Colonial Era*, edited by Stanley L. Engerman and Robert E. Gallman (New York: Cambridge University Press, 1996), p. 143.
38. Ibid.
39. Crosby, *Ecological Imperialism*, pp. 143–144.
40. Acemoglu, Johnson, and Robinson, "Colonial Origins of Comparative Development."
41. David J. McCreery, *Rural Guatemala, 1760–1940* (Stanford, CA: Stanford University Press, 1994).
42. Acemoglu, Johnson, and Robinson, "Colonial Origins of Comparative Development"; and Daron Acemoglu, Simon Johnson, and James A. Robinson, "Institutions as a Fundamental Cause of Development," in *The Handbook of Economic Growth*, edited by Philippe Aghion and Steven Durlauf (Amsterdam: North-Holland, 2006).
43. Gavin Wright, *Old South, New South* (New York: Basic, 1986).
44. See Jeffery M. Paige, *Coffee and Power: Revolution and the Rise of Democracy in Central America* (Cambridge, MA: Harvard University Press, 1997); Samel Z. Stone, *The Heritage of the Conquistadores: Ruling Classes in Central America from the Conquest to the Sandinistas* (Lincoln: University of Nebraska Press, 1990); Mark Wasserman, *Capitalists, Caciques and Revolution: The Native Elite and Foreign Enterprise in Chihuahua, Mexico 1854–1911* (Chapel Hill: University of North Carolina Press, 1984); Mark Wasserman, *Persistent Oligarchs: Elites and Politics in Chihuahua, Mexico 1910–1940* (Durham, NC: Duke University Press, 1993).
45. Jonathan Kelley and Herbert S. Klein, *Revolution and the Rebirth of Inequality* (Berkeley: University of California Press, 1981).
46. Robert Michels, *Political Parties: A Sociological Study of the Oligarchical Tendencies of Modern Democracy* (New York: Free Press, 1911).
47. See Kenneth Roberts, "Neoliberalism and the Transformation of Populism in Latin America," *World Politics* 48 (1995): 82–116; Edward L. Gibson, "The Populist Road to Market Reform: Policy and Electoral Coalitions in Mexico and Argentina," *World Politics* 49 (1997): 339–370; Hector Schamis, "Distributional Coalitions and the Politics of Economic Reform in Latin America," *World Politics* 51 (1999): 236–268; and M. Victoria Murillo, "Political Bias in Policy Convergence: Privatization Choices in Latin America," *World Politics* 54 (2002): 462–493.
48. Eduardo A. Gamarra, "Hybrid Presidentialism and Democratization: The Case of Bolivia," in *Presidentialism and Democracy in Latin America*, edited by Scott Mainwaring and Matthew S. Shugart (New York: Cambridge University Press, 1997), pp. 375–376.
49. Douglass C. North and Barry Weingast, "Constitutions and Commitment: The Evolution of Institutions Governing Public Choice in Seventeenth Century England," *Journal of Economic History* 49 (1989): 803–832.

50. R. H. Tawney, "The Rise of the Gentry, 1558–1640," *Economic History Review* 11 (1941): 1–38.
51. Daron Acemoglu, Simon Johnson, and James A. Robinson, "The Rise of Europe: Atlantic Trade, Institutional Change, and Economic Growth," *American Economic Review* 95 (2005): 546–579.
52. Lovell Jarvis, *Chilean Agriculture under Military Rule* (Berkeley: Institute for International Studies, University of California, 1985).
53. Javier Martínez and Alvaro Díaz, *Chile: The Great Transformation* (Washington, DC: Brookings Institution, 1996).
54. Stanley L. Engerman and Kenneth L. Sokoloff, "The Evolution of Suffrage Institutions in the New World," *Journal of Economic History* 65, no. 4 (2005): 891–921.
55. Stephen Haber, "Political Institutions and Financial Development: Evidence from the Economic Histories of Mexico and the United States," unpublished manuscript, Department of Political Science, Stanford University, 2004.
56. See Douglass C. North, William R. Summerhill, and Barry Weingast, "Order, Disorder and Economic Change: Latin America versus North America," in *Governing for Prosperity*, edited by Bruce Bueno de Mesquita and Hilton Root (New Haven, CT: Yale University Press, 2000).

8

Do Defective Institutions Explain the Development Gap between the United States and Latin America?

FRANCIS FUKUYAMA

O NE OF THE most obvious ways that development in the United States has differed from that of Latin America concerns political institutions. The United States is the world's oldest continuously existing democracy, the country that in many respects invented modern democracy. While Latin America is, on the whole, more democratic than other parts of the world, including fast-developing Asia, no Latin American country has ever had an uninterrupted history of democratic rule, and the deviations in the region, in terms of authoritarian government, suppression of human rights, civil conflict, and violence, have frequently been severe.[1] Democracy and rule of law are ends in themselves, and they are also obviously related to a society's ability to achieve other objectives like economic growth, social equity,

---

The author would like to thank Jillian Blake for help in researching this chapter.

and political inclusion.[2] Understanding how and why political institutions differ between the United States and Latin America is, then, key to understanding the larger puzzle of the latter region's lagging development.

What is it about the political institutions of the United States that differs from those found in Latin America? Is there some clause or provision in the U.S. Constitution that does not exist in other parts of the Western Hemisphere that accounts for the difference in the quality of government? And, if so, could we fix the problem of democratic governance by fixing institutions at this level? It is not likely that the answer to these questions will be yes. Many Latin American countries deliberately modeled their political orders on that of the United States, although they differ in details; there is enough variance throughout the region, however, that if the problem lay only in the design of formal institutions, countries would have fixed whatever did not work over time and evolved toward more efficient ones.

This suggests that there is another, deeper problem in Latin America that explains the political development gap. Formal political institutions in the United States were deliberately designed to inhibit strong political action and to limit the power of government, and yet they have not prevented the United States from acting decisively at times of national crisis or need. Within America's relatively decentralized institutional structure, the society has been able to generate consensus at key junctures for reasons that have to do with a political culture that has prized consensus and compromise even as it promoted competition. This consensus broke down and could not be mediated by the political system on only one important occasion, the American Civil War, when the issue of slavery had to be settled by violence. But at all other times, social conflicts have been mediated within the constitutional framework originally laid out by the American founding fathers.

The same has not been the case in Latin America. The region's social conflicts have been more severe, and the ability of social groups to use formal political institutions to resolve, mediate, or mitigate them has been much less effective. While reform of formal institutions can ameliorate certain types of political dysfunctions (e.g., the problem of fiscal federalism in Argentina or Brazil), the root causes of political instability and weak governance are likely to exist at the deeper levels of social structure or political culture.

Indeed, I will argue in this chapter that institutions matter much less than many people think, if by "institutions" one means formal, visible macropolitical rules defined by constitutions and law: presidencies, electoral systems, federalism, and the like. While we can identify certain clearly bad or defective institutional arrangements, there is no such thing as an optimal political institution. Vastly different types of formal institutions can be made to work, while the best institutions will fail without the proper supporting structures in the surrounding society. Closing the institutional gap between the United States and Latin America will involve the much more challenging task of using politics to ameliorate some of the underlying social-structural problems and moving to a different kind of political culture that takes consensus and the rule of law more seriously.

Institutions Matter, or Do They?

In recent years, a great deal of attention has been paid to the importance of institutions for economic development, leading to a broad consensus that "institutions matter."[3] Institutions in this sense include such things as property rights, credible enforcement of contracts, the rule of law, mechanisms for conflict resolution, and so on. As a starting point for this chapter, it is assumed that this consensus on institutions is correct. There is by now a huge empirical literature supporting this case.[4]

The only systematic counterargument to the institutionalist one has been made by Jared Diamond, Jeffrey Sachs, and their followers, who all point to the importance of material factors such as resource endowments, disease burdens, climate, and geographical location as determinants of economic growth.[5] Yet the institutionalists have won this argument hands down: Easterly and Levine, as well as Acemoglu, Robinson, and Johnson, have shown, for example, that resource endowments are important only as mediated through institutions, e.g., by providing more or less favorable conditions for the emergence or survival of certain types of institutions.[6] The institutions themselves remain the proximate causes of growth and, in many cases, can be shown to be exogenous to the material conditions under which a given society develops.

If one goes further back in history, however, one finds a different kind of anti-institutional argument, which was much more popular in the years immediately following World War II, but which has not been articulated so clearly in recent years. American political science in the prewar period focused heavily on legal studies and formal political institutions. But the collapse of democracy in the 1930s in the face of the twin totalitarian challenges of communism and fascism convinced many observers that the exact specifications of formal institutions mattered much less than underlying structural conditions unconducive to democracy.

This type of anti-institutionalism was, of course, the long-standing position of most Marxists, who maintained that the state in a capitalist democracy was simply the "executive committee of the bourgeoisie," reflective of the underlying social forces and not an autonomous agent in the shaping of outcomes. In a curious way, this belief in the state as superstructure jibed with a certain American antistatist penchant that saw the state simply as a mechanical processor of societal demands, without interests or a logic of its own.[7] Much of the post–World War II research agenda focused not on the design of formal institutions, but on subjects like political culture or value systems;[8] in modernization theory, sociology and anthropology played as important a role as political science in explaining development outcomes.

Institutions and the autonomous state were reinserted into the research agenda only in the 1970s and 1980s, partly in response to recognition of the importance of state-directed development in regions like East Asia, which could not simply be accounted for by structural or cultural models.[9] In addition, the rise of Douglass North's new institutional economics gave new legitimacy to the study of institutions in economics, as well as a powerful set of new conceptual tools.[10] These converging streams led to a bursting of the dykes and the emergence of not just a large literature on the general question of state autonomy, but also a rich and contextualized literature on institutional design, which continues up to the present. The debate on presidentialism started by Juan Linz—discussed in greater depth below—was one important example of the new focus on institutions and institutional design in this tradition.[11]

However, the new institutional economics muddied the waters in one important way, leading to confusion in subsequent thinking about institutions. North defined institutions as "the humanly devised constraints that shape human interaction," whether formal or informal.[12] The eliding of formal and informal institutions made North's definition conceptually robust and useful as a means of attacking the institution-less premises of earlier neoclassical economics. But the older anti-institutionalist position had been built around the distinction between formal and informal institutions: it argued that formal legal structures, at best, depended on and, at worst, were undermined by factors like political culture, discordant value systems, or social structures that gave rise to political preferences at odds with the institutional structure.

There is also a very important practical difference between formal and informal institutions. Formal institutions can be established, abolished, or changed literally with the stroke of a pen. They are thus the typical objects of public policy to be manipulated at will. Informal institutions, by contrast, reflect embedded social practices that are often hard to perceive and measure—and even harder to manipulate through the usual levers provided by public policy. It is one thing, for example, to mandate certain terms and appointment rules for Supreme Court justices, but if politicians routinely fail to follow them because packing the Supreme Court has become a normative behavior for an entire political elite, then one has left the realm of conventional public policy. The new institutionalism of course recognized the importance of informal institutions, but often failed to separate them out clearly as a distinct conceptual category subject to very different evolutionary dynamics.

Today, there are relatively few scholars who continue to insist on the importance of the distinction between formal and informal institutions and the priority of the latter over the former.[13] One is Samuel Huntington, who has been making a larger argument in favor of the centrality of culture in shaping political outcomes; for example, in one of his works, he points to the importance of culture in the shaping of American national identity and in the success of American democracy.[14] One could not have a clearer statement of the older anti-institutionalist position than the following:

> Would America be the America it is today if in the seventeenth and eighteenth centuries it had been settled not by British Protestants but by French, Spanish, or Portuguese Catholics? The answer is no. It would not be America; it would be Quebec, Mexico, or Brazil.[15]

Although Huntington has been severely criticized for his policy prescriptions regarding Mexican immigration, his broader point that American national identity has not simply been a political one defined by institutions like the Constitution and the system of laws but also is rooted in certain religious and cultural traditions—what he labels Anglo Protestantism—would seem to be incontrovertible as a historical fact. It is an interpretation of American society that was shared by observers from Tocqueville to Bryce to Lipset, and constitutes one long-standing answer to the question of why Latin America, which upon independence from Spain or Portugal modeled many political institutions explicitly on those of the United States, has failed to achieve North American levels of either growth or political stability.

Nonetheless, this chapter does not support the argument that political culture determines political or economic outcomes. Culture changes over time and is shaped by formal institutions even as it shapes them. Formal institutions matter; they change incentives, mold preferences, and solve (or fail to resolve) collective action problems. On the other hand, the informal matrix of norms, beliefs, values, traditions, and habits that constitute a society is critical for the proper functioning of formal institutions, while a political science that pays attention only to the design of formal institutions without understanding normative and cultural factors will inevitably fail. A large cultural variable like Catholicism may not be very helpful in explaining or predicting political behavior or institutional development, but a norm that assumes that bureaucratic appointments ought to favor friends and relatives over people with formal credentials might. One must therefore look both to formal and informal institutions in explaining the difference in development outcomes between different societies, taking each side of the equation seriously, as well as the importance of their interaction.

The Perils of Presidentialism and What Comes After

This section illustrates the complexity of the problem of specifying the nature of good formal political institutions by recapping the history of the evolution of the debate over institutional design that has taken place since the mid-1980s. This debate was initiated by Linz, who argued that political instability in Latin America was due to the fact that many of the democracies there were presidential rather than parliamentary, based on a North American model that did not work well in other parts of the hemisphere.[16]

Linz pointed to four basic problems with presidential systems. First, presidential systems are inherently majoritarian, which leads to the possibility that a president may be elected by a slim plurality of the population and therefore lack legitimacy. Second, presidential systems have rigid terms and do not provide easy mechanisms for removing a president who has lost legitimacy after being elected. Parliamentary systems deal with this problem through no-confidence votes; impeachment is the messy alternative in presidential systems. Moreover, term-limited presidents often spend a great deal of time and political capital figuring out how to add terms to their tenure. The third problem has to do with dual legitimacy. In a presidential system, both the executive and the legislature are directly elected and thus have separate sources of legitimacy; since they survive separately, there is always the possibility of gridlock and political paralysis when the two branches are controlled by different parties. And finally, presidential systems tend to personalize politics, emphasizing the character and foibles of the president rather than the broad program of a political party.

Linz's critique of presidentialism was based on one prominent case, the election in 1971 of the socialist Salvador Allende as president of Chile. Allende received a mere 37 percent of the popular vote, but nonetheless proceeded to take this as a mandate to initiate a series of radical economic policies, like nationalization of the banking system, which provoked an economic crisis and then a coup by General Augusto Pinochet. Linz pointed out that, in a parliamentary system, Allende would have been forced into a coalition with the Christian Democrats, which would have constrained his ability to change economic policy as he did.

Although he did not address this issue explicitly, Linz was concerned with two separate design goals that are in some sense at crosspurposes. On the one hand, he was concerned with the effectiveness of democratic decision making and thus that the dual legitimacy of presidential systems would lead to executive-legislative deadlock. On the other hand, he was also concerned with legitimacy and the possibility that an executive would receive support from a relatively small minority of the population. One can see immediately that the mutual checking of the two branches is actually an advantage with respect to legitimacy, while the plurality election of a president may be an advantage with regard to effectiveness. What is difficult is to optimize both effectiveness and legitimacy simultaneously.

Linz's critique of presidentialism was immediately attacked by Lijphart, Horowitz, Shugart and Carey, and a variety of other authors.[17] These critics pointed out that parliamentary systems could be as weak and illegitimate as presidential ones; indeed, some, like the interwar Weimar Republic or the French Fourth Republic, became illegitimate because of their weakness. Parliamentary systems require strong political parties; while party discipline can to some extent be engineered, party fragmentation is also based on the religious, ethnic, class, and geographical structure of the underlying society. Presidentialism, by contrast, has certain advantages: voters know exactly whom they are electing, and that official remains directly accountable to voters, in contrast to parliamentary systems, where parties or coalitions of parties can remove chief executives without any change in the popular mandate. The inherent majoritarianism of presidential systems can, moreover, be tempered by requirements for second-round runoffs or, as in Nigeria or Sri Lanka, requirements that the president receive pluralities in multiple electoral districts.

	Plurality	PR
Presidential	US, Philippines	Latin America
Parliamentary	Westminster	Continental Europe

FIGURE 8.1 Presidential/PM versus Electoral Systems.
Source: Arend Lijphart, "Constitutional Choices for New Democracies," *Journal of Democracy* 2, no. 1 (1991).

Lijphart argued that a single design axis like the nature of executive power cannot be understood in isolation from other aspects of the political system;[18] electoral systems, in particular, are critical in determining the overall effectiveness of a political system. He suggested the matrix presented in figure 8.1 for characterizing combinations of executive and electoral systems.

Lijphart argued that presidential systems, coupled with single-member plurality systems like that of the United States, tend to produce two relatively strong and cohesive parties.[19] While different parties gaining control of the executive and legislative branches has been a reality for much of recent American history, this has not led necessarily to gridlock because politics is still organized around two relatively coherent competing ideological points of view. From his standpoint, the worst combination is presidentialism together with proportional representation in the legislature, which he argued characterizes many political systems in Latin America. This has led not just to gridlock, but to presidents having to bargain with disorganized and fragmented parties—the worst features of both parliamentary and presidential systems.

A More General Method for Categorizing Political Systems

It soon became clear that presidentialism interacted not just with the electoral system, but with virtually all other aspects of the political system. Gary Cox and Mathew McCubbins introduced the general concept of veto gates—that is, actors within the political system who have the power to stop or modify legislation or policy.[20] All political systems can be arrayed on a continuum from a perfect authoritarianism

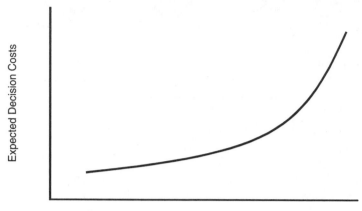

FIGURE 8.2 Participation versus Speed of Decision Making.
Source: James M. Buchanan and Gordon Tullock, *The Calculus of Consent: Logical Foundations of Constitutional Democracy* (Ann Arbor: University of Michigan Press, 1962).

that has only one veto gate (the dictator's will), to a perfect consensual democracy in which all citizens have to agree to a policy.

The concept of veto gates in a sense reprises the conceptual framework laid out by James Buchanan and Gordon Tullock to explain the principle of majority voting, where they posited a clear trade-off between legitimacy and effectiveness (see figure 8.2).[21] The more members of a society who participate in a decision, the higher are the expected decision costs; for large societies, the costs rise exponentially as one approaches consensus. Buchanan and Tullock argued that the principle of majority voting has no inherent normative logic; one can choose any point on the curve in figure 8.2 as an appropriate trade-off between effectiveness and legitimacy, and in the case of constitutional law, super-majorities are, indeed, often required. In the case of monetary policy, by contrast, many democracies delegate decision rights to an independent central bank with a very small number of decision makers.

The concept of veto gates as used by Cox and McCubbins does not refer to individual voters, but to organized institutions within the political system that, through delegation, have veto rights in political decision making. It becomes clear that legislatures and the rules under which they are elected are only one of several possible veto gates. These include:

- *The electoral system*. Proportional representation usually increases the number of veto gates over plurality systems because it leads to a more fragmented party system. Small district size (especially when combined with proportional representation) tends to increase fragmentation, as do electoral cycles not synchronized with presidential ones. Proportional representation systems with thresholds reduce fragmentation.

- *Party discipline.* Strong parties (e.g., those operating under closed-list systems) are better able to make decisions than parties with weak discipline.
- *Bicameralism.* An upper house adds another veto gate, because it is often based on territorial criteria and/or electoral rules different from those in the lower house.
- *Federalism and decentralization.* Federalism delegates important decision rights to subunits like states, which can be further delegated to even smaller subunits like municipalities and districts.
- *Independent judiciaries.* If courts are truly independent and have powers of constitutional review, as in the United States, they can constitute a major check on the powers of the other two branches. Courts can intervene in different ways as well, from merely interpreting legislative intent to initiating policies on their own.

From the above, it should be clear that political systems need to be categorized not by Lijphart's 2 × 2 matrix, but by an n-dimensional matrix that arrays all of these design axes against one another. It is possible to come up with a very large number of combinations of design features that will add or subtract veto gates from the political system, thus shifting the balance between effectiveness and legitimacy.

Because graphically portraying an n-dimensional matrix is not practical, an alternative is to substitute a continuum like that on the x axis of figure 8.2 as a means of ranking different political systems. Political systems with different types of veto gates are hard to compare in the abstract. Is a system with weak party discipline but no federalism and an independent constitutional court stronger or weaker than one with federalism, cohesive parties, and a somewhat politicized court? Is the premier-presidential system of the French Fifth Republic, whose president does not appoint the cabinet but does have clear reserved powers in foreign and defense policy and does not have to devolve powers to federal subunits, stronger or weaker than the American presidential system, whose president appoints the cabinet and shares powers in foreign affairs?

Taking these complexities into account, it is nonetheless possible to do a rough rank ordering of different political systems in terms of their aggregate number of veto gates:

1. Classical Westminster (New Zealand before 1994)
2. Parliamentary with proportional representation with cohesive parties, no federalism (Austria, Belgium, Netherlands, Thailand)
3. Premier-presidential, no federalism (French Fifth Republic, Finland)
4. Presidential with plurality voting, with federalism (United States, Philippines)
5. Parliamentary with fragmented parties (French Fourth Republic, Italy pre-1994)
6. Presidential with proportional representation and fragmented parties (Colombia, Brazil)

Of all democratic systems, the classical Westminster system has by far the fewest veto gates and is capable of the most decisive action. Such a system in its pure form is parliamentary with a plurality voting system and party discipline, leading to exaggerated majorities in the parliament; there is no federalism or decentralization, no written constitution and therefore no requirements for supermajority voting, and no judicial review.[22] A simple majority in the parliament (which, given the electoral system, can represent less than a majority of the popular vote) is sufficient to change any law in the land, which leads to what some have described as a democratic dictatorship. In the 2001 British general election, for example, the Labor Party received only 42 percent of the popular vote and yet received 62.5 percent of the seats in Parliament, while the Liberal Democrats received almost 19 percent of the popular vote and got only 8 percent of the seats.

The American system, by contrast, is deliberately designed to place many more veto gates—what Americans call checks and balances—in front of executive decision making, by adding separated powers, bicameralism, federalism, weak party discipline, and judicial review. The only important feature of the U.S. political system that increases rather than decreases decisiveness is its single-member plurality voting system. The vastly greater decisiveness of the British system can be seen in the fact that a British prime minister's budget is approved within days of its being submitted to Parliament, while an American budget takes the better part of a year to pass and never survives in the form proposed by the president.

While there are clear differences between the Westminster system and the U.S. system, and between either of them and those that prevail in Argentina or Peru, the actual behavior of political systems may not correspond to a simple quantitative tabulation of veto gates. As will be seen below, even the attempt at ranking systems above can be very misleading. Within the broad categories of veto gates given above, there are countless other rules that affect the ability of political systems to generate decisions or enforce policies. Sometimes, these rules are formal, but most outside observers (e.g., World Bank country directors or North American academic specialists) do not have the time or the patience to understand how they actually function. At other times they are informal and intrude into the realm of political culture, which will be explored further in the next section.

Legislative coherence—a pertinent example here—is the ability of legislatures to pass legislation, hopefully legislation that is public-regarding rather than patronage-based and/or clientelistic. Legislative coherence is the product of the interplay of various institutional design features, such as the electoral system (usually held to be the prime determinant), party discipline, rules concerning executive-legislative interaction (i.e., presidentialism and which branch controls the legislative agenda), and the party system, which reflects the underlying structural conditions of the society.

Political scientists associate legislative incoherence with the following factors: proportional representation systems, particularly those with open-list voting and no minimum thresholds; weak party discipline; and party systems that are not firmly anchored in important social groups or cleavages. By this account, Colombia and Brazil have traditionally been put forth as examples of weak legislative systems. The former has coherent parties but very weak party discipline: the parties are unable to control even the use of their own party labels.[23] Brazil has open-list proportional representation, a traditionally weak party system, and apparently weak party discipline.[24] Argentina, by contrast, should have much greater legislative coherence, since it has a closed-list proportional representation system and relatively coherent parties.

However, the actuality is rather different. Colombian presidents have had to work with incoherent legislatures that have demanded particularistic payoffs in return for votes, as the theory predicts. Major reforms have required Colombian presidents to resort either to emergency powers or to maneuvers of questionable legality.[25] The Brazilian Congress, on the other hand, has actually been able to pass a large volume of legislation since ratification of the 1988 Constitution; while presidents have never had legislative majorities of their own party, they have nonetheless been able to put together coalitions of parties with relatively strong party discipline in support of far-reaching reforms like the Fiscal Responsibility Law of 2000, which restricted the ability of Brazilian states to run budget deficits.[26] Argentina, on the other hand, has suffered from legislative incoherence despite the fact that presidents from both the Partido Justicialista (the PJ, or Peronist, Party) and the Alianza por el Trabajo, la Educación y la Justicia have had strong legislative majorities or pluralities in Congress.

This situation has to do with the fact that legislative coherence is the product of the interplay of many more rules than the usual ones of open- or closed-list proportional representation. Brazilian presidents, for example, through their control over fiscal policy and bureaucratic appointments, have been able to discipline legislators and enforce party-line voting. That Presidents Fernando Henrique Cardoso and Luiz Inácio "Lula" da Silva have used this power not to build clientelistic bases but to enact public-regarding reforms of fiscal federalism and the social security system may reflect changing political culture rather than formal institutions. Nonetheless, the result is contrary to the expectations of many political scientists and at odds with simple models of how formal rules correlate with policy outcomes.

In Argentina, on the other hand, legislative coherence was undermined by the way that the electoral system interacted with federalism. While the national electoral system was closed-list proportional representation, voting was done by province, making the provincial party chiefs, and not the national party, responsible for determining the voting lists. The national party was thus not a cohesive bloc, but an alliance of provincial fiefdoms. In the years leading up to the economic crisis of 2001, the Argentine government could not maintain fiscal discipline because the PJ's leader, president Carlos Menem, got into a spending duel with Eduardo Duhalde, governor of Buenos Aires province and Menem's leading rival within the Peronist party. The entrenched power of provincial party bosses is also the reason that this system will be extremely difficult to reform. The coherence of the Argentine legislature, then, was more apparent than real, which goes far in explaining why Menem continued to rule by decree even when his party possessed a majority in Congress.

Why There Is No Optimal Political System

The groundwork has already been laid for the beginning of an explanation of why there can be no such thing as optimality in the design of political systems. Political systems seek conflicting social goods between which there is often a continuous trade-off. The balance of goods that the system seeks to achieve will depend on a host of contextual factors like the society's historical traditions and political culture, the external environment, economic conditions, and the like.

Cox and McCubbins described this trade-off as one between decisiveness and resoluteness. Systems with fewer veto gates produce more decisive political decisions. On the other hand, decisions that have to be vetted by more actors within the political system generally produce more lasting results, because there are fewer players interested in overturning the initial decision—hence greater resoluteness. It should be clear that the Cox-McCubbins trade-off between decisiveness and resoluteness largely corresponds to the trade-off between effectiveness and legitimacy described earlier. That is, the more members of a society who participate in a decision, the more legitimate it is (with perfect legitimacy being perfect consensus); the reason that legitimate decisions are resolute is because there are fewer interest groups or sectors of society opposed to the decision.

To complicate matters a bit further, excessive resoluteness/legitimacy can sometimes undermine itself, while decisiveness on occasion becomes self-legitimating. That is, a democratic political system with excessive decision costs often fails to produce policies of any sort, leading to voter disillusionment not just with the current administration, but with democracy as a whole. Societies may actually express a preference for the decisiveness of authoritarian governments, which can cut through the miasma of ordinary politics and get things done.

What is the optimal political system for a developing country that seeks rapid economic growth? There was for a long time a strong bias on the part of certain academic and policy communities in favor of decisive over resolute/legitimate systems. One version of this was the "authoritarian transition," which was advocated in the 1960s by Samuel Huntington and rearticulated more recently by Huntington's student Fareed Zakaria.[27] They argued not simply that authoritarian modernizers were more decisive, but that, in many developing countries, liberal autocracy alone was capable of supplying basic public goods like physical security and public order, which are preconditions of development of any sort.

But even among those committed to development under democratic conditions, there has been a pronounced bias in favor of decisiveness.[28] The argument goes something as follows. A typical developing country needs liberalizing economic reform, usually in the form of tariff reductions, deregulation, privatization, and reductions in consumer subsidies (i.e., the famous Washington Consensus). Often, these policy reforms need to be undertaken in the context of an economic crisis, such as a current account deficit leading to currency devaluation and high interest rates. While these reforms are expected to bring stability and long-term economic growth, they also produce a great deal of transitional pain as workers are laid off or consumers lose access to subsidized goods. Technocratic experts can see the long-term logic of these policies, but ordinary voters and politicians might not; therefore, a developing country in this position needs a decisive political system that will shield technocratic experts from populist demands and push through long-term public-regarding policies. A decisive system that implemented successful reforms would then become self-legitimating as it produced long-term stability and economic growth. This was purportedly the path followed by Chile under General Pinochet.

Political systems with excessive checks and balances, by contrast, slow down decision making and impose many other decision costs as interest groups are paid off. What Barbara Geddes referred to as the "politician's dilemma" is the phenomenon that reformist governments often need to pay such a high price to implement reform that they end up undermining the goals of the reform itself.[29] This price would presumably be lower in a more decisive political system.

Mexico under the presidency of Vicente Fox illustrates this problem. The Mexican political system is roughly similar to the U.S. system: presidential and federal, though with a mixed proportional representation/plurality voting system. During the decades of dominance by the Partido Revolucionario Institucional (PRI), most observers categorized Mexico's political organization as a strong presidential system, because Mexican presidents often acted like authoritarian rulers. In retrospect, however, it is clear that this was simply the by-product of PRI dominance of the executive and legislative (and, indeed, the judicial) branches. Fox's election in 2000 produced a president of a different party, the Partido Acción Nacional (PAN), which did not command a majority in the Congress and which could not put together a coalition in favor of major reforms like modernization of utilities or reform of the judicial system. The Mexican political system, in other words, began behaving like a typical presidential system with checks and balances, biased toward resoluteness rather than decisiveness, and the result was political gridlock.

In the end, it is not clear that decisive political systems are preferable to resolute/legitimate ones from the standpoint of long-term development. Constitutional rules that amplify executive power by reducing veto gates can produce policies that come to be regarded as illegitimate; without a broader underlying social consensus, reforms are likely to be undermined over time. There have been a number of notable cases of this. The liberalizing reforms undertaken by Venezuelan president Carlos Andrés Pérez in 1989–1990 provoked opposition not just within the broader Venezuelan society, but within Pérez's own Acción Democrática (Adeco) Party.[30] Pérez used his office, supported by a small group of technocrats, to change policies, without making a broad-based effort to convince Venezuelan society of their necessity and logic. Even though the reforms produced economic growth, they were immediately undermined not just within the political system, but outside it as well (in the form of the military coups launched by Hugo Chávez).

The preference for decisive political systems, moreover, reflects a moment in history stretching from the mid-1980s through the late 1990s, during which the development problem was seen as partially caused by excessive state scope, and the posited solution was, in almost all cases, understood to be liberalizing economic reforms. In the early twenty-first century, the agenda has already begun to shift: Left-leaning or outrightly populist presidents have come to power in Brazil, Ecuador, Argentina, Uruguay, Venezuela, and Bolivia. In many cases, their agenda is the reassertion of state power, re-regulation of the economy and renationalization of certain economic sectors, and control over the media and civil society. Decisive political systems will only enhance the ability of populist presidents to enact bad economic policies and return their countries to state control and closed markets.

Institutions are only enabling devices; those that facilitate or encourage strong and decisive political decision making are only as good as the policies being pursued. What inhibits the ambitions of a liberalizing reformer also checks the power of a would-be populist dictator. If decisive government were always preferable, then we should always want Westminster-type systems with their largely unchecked executive powers. But Americans have expressed, since the founding of their republic, a strong preference for a system of checks and balances that limits government power. This relatively nondecisive political system reflects the preferences of American political culture, which has always been distrustful of state power.[31] Checks and balances make large-scale reform much more difficult, but in the long run, they also reduce the risk of the government being captured by politicians advocating policies that are not supported by the broader society. The preference for resolute/legitimate political systems over decisive ones can thus be seen as a preference for lower long-term political risk.

There is no optimal level of long-term political risk, and thus no optimal balance between decisiveness and resoluteness/legitimacy. The United States and Britain are among the world's oldest and best-established democracies, and yet they have completely different political systems arising out of very different historical experiences. The largely unchecked Westminster system is a high-risk institutional arrangement that has worked reasonably well in the English-speaking world where it has been implemented. Margaret Thatcher's reforms of the late 1970s and early 1980s could not have been carried out but for the exaggerated parliamentary majorities held by the Conservative Party. Similarly, Roger Douglas's liberalizing reforms in the mid-1980s benefited from New Zealand's even purer Westminster system.[32] Both stand in sharp contrast to the situation faced by Chancellor Angela Merkel under Germany's far less decisive institutional rules, which following the election of 2005 forced her into a coalition and sharply limited the kinds of liberalizing policies she was able to put into place.

But a Westminster system would likely produce disastrous results if transported to a country with a different social structure and political culture (e.g., an ethnically fragmented society with a dominant ethnic group). Where it has been copied, it has been heavily modified to meet local conditions, as in the case of India, the success of whose democracy would scarcely be conceivable in the absence of thoroughgoing federalism. The American presidential system, which is much less decisive than the Westminster system, has nonetheless been capable of achieving decisive action at certain critical junctures in American history. When American presidentialism was transplanted to Latin American countries, however, it worked only indifferently. How each formal set of institutional rules plays out in practice is thus highly dependent on the local social context, tradition, history, and the like.

The fact that we cannot specify an optimal set of formal institutions does not mean that we have no knowledge of the likely impact of changes to formal institutional rules. A number of institutional reforms, like a central bank or judicial independence,[33] have a clear logic and are broadly accepted as being desirable. Changes in electoral rules have broadly predictable effects. For example, there are a number of recent cases where electoral reform has produced desired results:

- Chile, which always had a coherent party system, has been operating since 1988 under an electoral system that was designed to force the country's four or five large parties into two broad Left-Right coalitions, which has in fact happened.

- Japan changed its single nontransferable vote (SNV) system to a mixture of single-member constituencies and proportional representation in 1994. The SNV system had forced parties to run multiple candidates in the same electoral district, which was blamed for the factionalism within the ruling Liberal Democratic Party. While it took over 10 years to produce the desired effect, Prime Minister Junichiro Koizumi's electoral victory in 2005 marked the demise of the faction system.
- Italy modified its low-threshold proportional representation system, which had produced notoriously weak coalition governments, into a mixed single-member proportional representation system in 1994, which had the desired effect of forcing parties into broad Left-Right coalitions. Italian politicians gamed the system, however, to ensure the survival of the smaller parties, and the system reverted back to a modified form of proportional representation in 2006.
- New Zealand, which had a classical Westminster-style single-member plurality voting system in its Parliament, changed over to a mixed-member proportional system in 1996. The result has been broader representation of smaller parties, together with relatively weak coalition governments in place of the two-and-a-half-party system that prevailed earlier.
- In Thailand's 1997 Constitution, the electoral system was changed from a multiseat, multiple vote plurality system, which had produced weak coalitions, to a mixed system of 400 single-member constituency and 100 proportional representation seats. The reform has given Prime Minister Thaksin Shinawatra an absolute legislative majority.

In addition, there is accumulating knowledge about the design of federal systems. Federalism has posed a problem for many large states in Latin America, including Argentina, Brazil, and Mexico, because the subunits were delegated too much budgetary discretion and could run fiscal deficits. This differed from the situation in the United States, where most states are constitutionally prohibited from running budget deficits and face hard budget constraints based on their own ability to raise revenues. In Argentina and Brazil, by contrast, states could run deficits that had to be covered by the federal government, a form of fiscal federalism that undermined overall budget discipline. In Argentina, the rules were particularly problematic because they were constantly being renegotiated; governors would spend a great deal of time politicking in

Buenos Aires rather than raising their own tax revenues. The solution to this problem—putting states and other subunits under hard budget constraints—is relatively straightforward conceptually, yet difficult to implement since such a reform means a de facto shift in power from the states to the federal government. Brazil, despite its supposedly weak political parties and strong federalism, moved in this direction with passage of the Fiscal Responsibility Law, while Argentina has failed to deal with this problem due to the entrenched power of state-level politicians.[34]

The fact that we can connect certain changes in institutional designs with certain behavioral outcomes does not mean that institutional change is easy to bring about; institutions are in fact very "sticky" or path dependent. The transaction costs of institutional change are often far greater than the transaction costs of weak or suboptimal institutions. Societies need to generate political will to bring about reform and to prevent new institutions from being undermined by losers in the initial struggle.

Political Culture

As noted above, most conventional analyses of the formal structure of political institutions would have come to the conclusion that Brazil would produce a weaker government than Argentina, given its open-list proportional representation system, weak political parties, and entrenched federalism. And yet, Brazil weathered the period from 1990 to 2005 better than Argentina, avoiding the latter's severe economic crisis in 2001–2002 and moving ahead with a series of structural reforms and public policies. And both countries have done much less well than neighboring Chile, not just since the 1990s, but for the preceding 15 years as well. What accounts for these differences?

One factor is clearly leadership. Economists generally do not like to talk about independent variables like leadership because it amounts to throwing a massive random-number generator into their models. They prefer modeling institutions and hierarchy endogenously, as the result of strategic interactions of individual agents who cannot achieve collective action without it. But leadership is more often than not exogenous. It was simply Argentina's bad luck that Carlos Menem chose to throw away the positive legacy of his first term as president by seeking not just a second but a third term as well, leading him into a spending competition with Eduardo Duhalde. President Cardoso, by contrast, chose not to waste his political capital seeking ways to remain in office, but used it rather to try to solve some long-standing public policy problems. Many good development outcomes are thus attributable not to the structure of formal institutions, but rather to the emergence of the right leader at the right time.

The only way in which leadership may become a more tractable variable is when a certain leadership style is not simply the outgrowth of the foibles of a particular individual, but reflective of a broader political culture. Menem was widely blamed for packing the Argentine Supreme Court with his political cronies, but he was neither the first nor the last Argentine president to do so. Argentine elites have been notorious for avoiding or manipulating rules they find inconvenient, a behavioral tendency that shows up not just in Supreme Court appointments, but in rates of tax compliance and ordinary corruption. These phenomena exist in Brazil and Chile as well, but the degree of disregard of laws and rules seems to be lower, particularly in the latter case. A well-functioning rule of law is not merely a set of visible formal institutions like courts, bar associations, police, and judges. No formal arrangement of incentives will make such a system operate properly unless the participants share a certain normative respect for laws and rules.

As already noted, there was an earlier critique of institutionalism that argued that formal institutions mattered less than variables like political culture and social structure in explaining political and development outcomes. This critique remains valid, but only if we understand political culture properly. To say that political culture is important is not necessarily to affirm the importance of certain large cultural categories like "Catholicism" or "Anglo Protestantism." Chile, Argentina, Ecuador, and Costa Rica are all predominantly Latin Catholic countries and former colonies of Spain, and yet they all have distinctive political cultures with respect to the rule of law, something that can be seen clearly in their very different rankings on various indices measuring levels of corruption and governance. Political culture varies among groups and regions within societies and over time; it is shaped not only by large symbolic forces like religion, but by shared historical experiences like war or economic crisis. And it is key to understanding why certain formal political institutions do or do not work.

The United States as an Nondecisive Form of Government

The importance of political culture can be seen clearly if we look closely at American political institutions and how they have functioned over the years. In the context of the analytical framework presented above, the United States has a relatively nondecisive set of formal institutions, meaning that the system has a large number of veto gates that bias it toward resoluteness/legitimacy. This choice was a deliberate one: the American republic was born in a revolution against centralized monarchy, and the American founders sought to create a system of checks and balances to prevent the reemergence of strong, centralized power. The dual legitimacy of its presidential system is something with which many Americans are comfortable; poll data indicate that a majority of Americans are actually happier when the presidency and Congress are controlled by different parties, and they want the two branches to serve as checks on each other's power. And yet, the American political system has been capable of decisive action as well, from mobilizing to fight a series of wars, to building a twentieth-century welfare state during the New Deal and Great Society years, to scaling back that same welfare state from the Reagan presidency to the present. The American political system has, of course, produced its share of political failure, deadlock, and missed opportunities. But over the years, it has proved adaptable to changing conditions, at least when compared to the political systems of other developed democracies in Europe and Japan.

In American history, major policy initiatives have not been achieved through the inherent powers of the executive. As noted earlier, an American president is much weaker than a British prime minister. The president has no guaranteed majority in either house of Congress, and American presidents have been stymied by Congress even when their own party controlled the legislative branch (e.g., the defeat of Bill Clinton's health care reforms in the early 1990s). Nor have American executives undertaken major initiatives through grants of special emergency powers by Congress.[35] Some of the most impressive legislative accomplishments by American presidents, like Harry Truman's passage of the Marshall Plan, or Ronald Reagan's passage of tax cuts during his first term, occurred when the other branch of government was under the control of the opposition political party.

Successful American presidents have achieved their goals not by exploiting the formal powers accorded to them, but by using their office as a "bully pulpit" to rally broad public support across party lines.[36] Indeed, some of the most effective American presidents—such as Franklin Roosevelt, Truman, and Reagan—have understood that their chief function was to communicate broad messages and build coalitions across party lines. President Lyndon Johnson, for all of his failings in foreign policy, was able to enact major legislation regarding civil rights and poverty by using his intimate knowledge of Congress gained during his days as Senate majority leader.[37] Those who took a more technocratic approach to policymaking—like Jimmy Carter or Bill Clinton (at least with regard to his health care initiative)—were far less successful.

The example of the United States shows that a political system biased toward resoluteness/legitimacy can nonetheless be capable of decisive action. Great Britain, by contrast, is a case of a political system heavily biased toward decisiveness, which nonetheless has not used its inherent executive powers to trample over the rights of minorities. While Britain entered the modern era as a relatively homogeneous country in ethnic and religious terms, it inherited a highly stratified class structure that could have been the basis for serious class conflict. Yet, despite the society's evident ideological differences, neither fascism nor communism took root there as occurred in other European countries. The Westminster system could have easily facilitated sharp oscillations in public policy between Left and Right, something that did not happen arguably until the arrival of Margaret Thatcher. Rather, Britain saw the displacement of the Liberals by the Labor Party and the steady growth of the welfare state under both Labor and Conservative governments throughout the first seven decades of the twentieth century.

Argentina began this same period with a similar degree of ethnic and religious homogeneity, and yet managed to exacerbate existing class differences through a series of violent oscillations between Left and Right. Differences in the design of the formal political system simply cannot explain this divergence in behavioral outcomes. They can, however, be readily attributed to differences in political culture.

Conclusions: Social Structure and the Limits of Institutional Design

Formal political institutions do, in the end, matter. As a result of scholarly work done over the past generation, we can relate certain institutional forms to certain outcomes, e.g., how to design an electoral system to increase or decrease the number of parties, how to improve party discipline, how to promote greater fiscal responsibility on the part of states, and how to decrease incentives for patronage and clientelism. We also know that certain types of institutions are almost always dysfunctional and should be avoided, such as an overly politicized judicial system or patronage-based public expenditures.

On the other hand, there is no such thing as an optimal political institution. Institutions are only as good as the policies they promote, and no set of procedural rules for making political decisions will by itself ensure good public policy. These rules often seek to maximize two competing social goods, like decisiveness and resoluteness/legitimacy, and societies will vary in their preference for long-term risk in policymaking. Leadership matters a great deal; with good leadership, apparently dysfunctional institutions can be made to work well, while no set of rules will fully compensate for bad leadership. And while we understand cause-and-effect relationships between certain forms of institutional design and policymaking outcomes, the institutions in question come in highly complex, interdependent packages where a change in one requires complementary changes in several others, or else it will produce unanticipated consequences.

All would-be institutional reformers face what Barbara Geddes calls the "politician's dilemma": they can either spend their political capital achieving some short-term policy change, or they can spend it reforming the underlying institution. But in pursuing the latter, they often have to pay so much to get what they want that they undermine the very policies they hoped to promote.

It is not clear that going for deeper institutional reform is always the right choice. Take the case of Mexico today. As noted above, Mexico has a presidential system and federalism that is biased toward resoluteness/legitimacy and away from decisiveness. From the standpoint of a reformer seeking to liberalize the Mexican economy, President Fox's inability to pass major reforms through the Mexican Congress was intensely frustrating. The dual legitimacy of the presidential system led to legislative-executive gridlock, while federalism allowed Fox's opponents, like Andrés Manuel López Obrador, to prosper and pursue policies at odds with those of the president. One might be tempted under these circumstances to try to change the institutional rules to increase the power of the president, by biasing the electoral system to produce more decisive majorities, by reducing the autonomy of the states, or by providing the president with emergency powers. All of these potential measures presuppose, however, that it is a liberal reformer who is president and that he is being blocked by populist or reactionary forces. Were the shoe to be on the other foot and an Hugo Chávez–type populist were to come to power, then these exact same institutions would serve as checks on a president pursuing bad policies.

The U.S. system, as noted above, is not necessarily more decisive than the Mexican one in its formal institutional rules. Presidents of the

United States who have wanted to promote ambitious reform agendas of course want as large a base for their own party as possible, but often they have sought to cross party lines to build coalitions in favor of particular policies. All of this is a function of leadership, persuasion, campaigning, compromise—in other words, traditional political skills put at the service of public-regarding policies. In the United States, building consensus has always been a slow matter, and it should not be surprising that Mexico's first president to come from a party other than the PRI should have trouble doing this. But the problem lies not in the formal institutions as much as with the skill with which they are exploited. President Cardoso's relative success in getting important legislation through a formally weak Brazilian system should be seen as an example of this.

The preceding argument that formal institutions need to be supplemented by a supportive political culture should not be taken as a form of cultural essentialism, that is, the view that societies are locked into certain outcomes due to unmanipulable cultural characteristics. Political culture reflects the shared experiences of groups of people at particular points in time and can readily evolve under the influence of leadership, education, new environments and challenges, foreign models, and the like.

Besides political culture, another factor that makes democratic politics more difficult in Latin America is social structure. Democratic institutions are designed to mitigate social conflict, but their ability to do this depends in part on how severe those social conflicts are. Latin America is full of countries with sharp class, ethnic, and racial divisions, many of which have been the fault lines that have triggered coups, insurgencies, extralegal actions, and so on. In other cases (like Argentina), new lines of social cleavage were created *de novo* where none existed previously.

Democratic politics in Latin America has often been the province of social elites. Venezuela and Colombia, considered for many decades to be the best examples of stable democracy in the region, are cases in point. The 1958 Pacto de Punto Fijo in Venezuela and the 1957 National Front accord that ended the period of *La Violencia* in Colombia were democratic transitions negotiated by two dominant elite parties that then shared power for the next four decades. This top-down approach preserved the positions of COPEI and Adeco in Venezuela and the Liberal and Conservative parties in Colombia at the expense of other political actors, leading to the progressive ossification of both political systems. Given large social stratifications and weak states in both cases, it is inevitable that the excluded parties would over time try to force their way into the system, through guerrilla insurgency in the case of Colombia and by populist military coup in Venezuela.

Countries with serious underlying social conflicts face a chicken-and-egg problem with regard to institutional development. It is hard to see how either Venezuela or Colombia can create democratic institutions that are stable in the long run without being more socially inclusive, but the very process of inclusion weakens or dismantles existing democratic institutions. Something similar is going on with regard to indigenous groups in Bolivia with the election of Evo Morales as president in 2005. Hopefully, existing democratic institutions will be used as the bridge to greater inclusion, but that depends very much on the agenda, ideas, and aims of the groups being included.

The United States began its national existence as a democracy excluding slaves, women, indigenous peoples, and propertyless whites from the political process. The system could not bring about the inclusion of the first of these groups without a bloody civil war, and the inclusion of the others was a process that stretched over 200 years and in certain respects is still incomplete. On the other hand, with the important exception of the Civil War, America's social cleavages were never so severe that they could not be managed peacefully within the system's existing rules. It helped that an open frontier, immigration, and rapid economic development reshuffled the social deck periodically in ways that weakened the positions of older entrenched elites.

The trade-off between decisiveness and resoluteness/legitimacy presumes that, at the resoluteness end of the scale, the system represents something close to the whole of the political community. The problem with elite politics in Latin America is that even those systems biased toward resoluteness/legitimacy tend to be exclusionary and are therefore not, in a full sense, legitimate. This is not due to the formal or deliberate disenfranchisement of parts of the population; rather, it is the result of social cleavages, stratification, and economic inequality. Those systems with large numbers of veto gates have the worst of both worlds: they are not capable of decisive action, nor do they buy for themselves strong social consensus. Until this larger problem is addressed through the entry of a wider range of actors into the political system, no amount of institutional engineering will ever produce stable and legitimate democracy.

Notes

1. Francis Fukuyama and Sanjay Marwah, "Comparing East Asia and Latin America: Dimensions of Development," *Journal of Democracy* 11, no. 4 (2000): 80–94.
2. Amartya K. Sen, *Development as Freedom* (New York: Knopf, 1999).

3. See World Bank, *The State in a Changing World: World Development Report 1997* (New York: Oxford University Press, 1997); World Bank, *Building Institutions for Markets: World Development Report 2002* (New York: Oxford University Press, 2002); Francis Fukuyama, *State-Building: Governance and World Order in the 21st Century* (Ithaca, NY: Cornell University Press, 2004); Ernesto Stein, Mariano Tommasi, Koldo Echebarría, Eduardo Lora, and Mark Payne, *The Politics of Policies: Economic and Social Progress in Latin America, 2006 Report* (Washington, DC: Inter-American Development Bank, 2005).

4. See, for example, Stephen Knack and Philip Keefer, "Institutions and Economic Performance: Cross-Country Tests Using Alternative Measures," *Economics and Politics* 7 (1995): 207–227; Daron Acemoglu, James A. Robinson, and Simon Johnson, "The Colonial Origins of Comparative Development: An Empirical Investigation," *American Economic Review* 91, no. 5 (2001): 1369–1401; Acemoglu, Robinson, and Johnson, "Reversal of Fortune: Geography and Institutions in the Making of the Modern World Income Distribution," *Quarterly Journal of Economics* 107 (2002): 1231–1294; Dani Rodrik and Arvind Subramanian, "The Primacy of Institutions (and What This Does and Does Not Mean)," *Finance and Development* 40, no. 2 (2003): 31–34; Daniel Kaufmann, Aart Kraay, and Massimo Mastruzzi, *Governance Matters IV: Governance Indicators for 1996–2004* (Washington, DC: World Bank Institute, 2005); and Ajay Chhibber, R. Kyle Peters, and Barbara J. Yale, eds., *Reform and Growth: Evaluating the World Bank Experience* (New Brunswick, NJ: Transaction, 2006).

5. Jared Diamond, *Guns, Germs, and Steel: The Fates of Human Societies* (New York: Norton, 1997); Jeffrey Sachs and Andrew Warner, *Natural Resource Abundance and Economic Growth*, NBER Working Paper 5398 (Cambridge, MA: National Bureau of Economic Research, 1995); Jeffrey Sachs and John W. McArthur, *Institutions and Geography: Comment on Acemoglu, Johnson, and Robinson (2000)*, NBER Working Paper 8114 (Cambridge, MA: National Bureau of Economic Research, 2001).

6. William R. Easterly and Ross Levine, *Tropics, Germs, and Crops: How Endowments Influence Economic Development*, NBER Working Paper 9106 (Cambridge, MA: National Bureau of Economic Research, 2002); Acemoglu, Robinson, and Johnson, "Reversal of Fortune."

7. J. P. Nettl, "The State as a Conceptual Variable," *World Politics* 20, no. 4 (1968): 559–592.

8. David C. McClelland, *The Achieving Society* (Princeton, NJ: Van Nostrand, 1961); Gabriel A. Almond and Sidney Verba, *The Civic Culture* (Boston: Little, Brown, 1963).

9. See Nettl, "The State as a Conceptual Variable"; Michael Mann, "The Autonomous Power of the State: Its Origins, Mechanisms, and Results," *European Journal of Sociology* 25, no. 2 (1984): 185–213; and Peter B. Evans, Dietrich Rueschemeyer, and Theda Skocpol, *Bringing the State Back In* (Cambridge: Cambridge University Press, 1985).

10. Douglass C. North, *Institutions, Institutional Change, and Economic Performance* (New York: Cambridge University Press, 1990).

11. Juan J. Linz, "The Perils of Presidentialism," *Journal of Democracy* 1, no. 1 (1990): 51–69.

12. North, *Institutions, Institutional Change, and Economic Performance*, p. 3.

13. One important source for thinking about informal institutions is the large literature on social capital.

14. Samuel P. Huntington, *Who Are We? The Challenges to America's National Identity* (New York: Simon and Schuster, 2004).

15. Ibid., p. 59.

16. Linz, "The Perils of Presidentialism." This article circulated as a mimeo for several years prior to its publication in the *Journal of Democracy*.
17. Arend Lijphart, "Constitutional Choices for New Democracies," *Journal of Democracy* 2, no. 1 (1991): 72–84; Donald Horowitz, "Debate Presidents vs. Parliaments: Comparing Democratic Systems," *Journal of Democracy* 1, no. 2 (1990): 73–83; Matthew S. Shugart and John M. Carey, *Presidents and Assemblies: Constitutional Design and Electoral Dynamics* (Cambridge: Cambridge University Press, 1992).
18. Lijphart, "Constitutional Choices for New Democracies."
19. This is Duverger's Law; see Maurice Duverger et al., *L'Influence des systemes electoraux sur la vie politique* (Paris: Colin, 1950).
20. Gary W. Cox and Mathew D. McCubbins, "The Institutional Determinants of Economic Policy Outcomes," in *Presidents, Parliaments, and Policy*, edited by Stephan Haggard and Mathew D. McCubbins (Cambridge: Cambridge University Press, 2001), pp. 21–63.
21. James M. Buchanan and Gordon Tullock, *The Calculus of Consent: Logical Foundations of Constitutional Democracy* (Ann Arbor: University of Michigan Press, 1962).
22. The British system is no longer a pure Westminster system; there is a bicameral legislature with increasing devolution of powers to different regions in Britain. In addition, the courts, including European courts, have increasingly been able to limit the discretion of the British Parliament.
23. Ron Archer and Matthew S. Shugart, "Presidential Power and Its Limits in Colombia," in *Presidentialism and Democracy in Latin America*, edited by Scott Mainwaring and Matthew S. Shugart (Cambridge: Cambridge University Press, 1997).
24. Mainwaring and Shugart, *Presidentialism and Democracy in Latin America*.
25. An example of this was President César Gaviria's bypassing of the legislature in the constitutional reform of 1991.
26. Fernando Limongi and Argelina Figueiredo, "Legislative Organization and Party Behavior in the Legislature," *Comparative Politics* 32 (2000): 151–170.
27. See Samuel P. Huntington, *Political Order in Changing Societies* (New Haven, CT: Yale University Press, 1968); and Fareed Zakaria, *The Future of Freedom: Illiberal Democracy at Home and Abroad* (New York: Norton, 2003).
28. A. See Jeffrey Sachs, "Life in the Economic Emergency Room," in *The Political Economy of Policy Reform*, edited by John Williamson (Washington, DC: Institute for International Economics, 1994), pp. 503–523.
29. Barbara Geddes, *Politician's Dilemma: Building State Capacity in Latin America* (Berkeley: University of California Press, 1996).
30. See Javier Corrales, *Presidents without Parties: The Politics of Economic Reform in Argentina and Venezuela in the 1990s* (University Park: Pennsylvania State University Press, 2002).
31. Seymour Martin Lipset, *American Exceptionalism: A Double-Edged Sword* (New York: Norton, 1995).
32. New Zealand ceased to have a pure Westminster system when its electoral system was changed from single member first-past-the-post to mixed member proportional in 1994.
33. Though even in those instances, judiciaries that are too independent of public opinion have become highly controversial in the United States and other developed democracies that take basic judicial independence for granted.
34. Stein et al., *The Politics of Policies*.

35. American presidents have taken on special powers during wartime, such as Abraham Lincoln's suspension of habeas corpus during the Civil War and Franklin D. Roosevelt's internment of Japanese American citizens during World War II. More recently, President George W. Bush claimed special powers with regard to treatment of "enemy combatants" and using wiretapping as part of the war on terrorism. But these decisions have been very controversial and unusual in American politics.
36. Richard E. Neustadt, *Presidential Power and the Modern Presidents* (New York: Free Press, 1990).
37. While the Democrats controlled both houses of Congress during his presidency, the Democratic Party itself was heavily influenced by southerners opposed to civil rights legislation and in control of many key congressional committees.

9

Why Institutions Matter

Fiscal Citizenship in Argentina and the United States

NATALIO R. BOTANA

A HISTORICAL OVERVIEW of Latin American democracies, and in particular Argentina's, reveals the weak link between each nation's political Constitution and the economy's constitution (the first is capitalized to differentiate it from the other in this play on words), which should provide the necessary framework for political institutions to function properly.[1] When considering the crucial issue of the rule of law in the case of Argentina today, the continued relevance of this perspective becomes clear: laws are either entirely unenforced or only partially enforced; promises are not kept; rights appear at times to be entirely illusory.

To think that the region's economic problems can be solved without first addressing their political underpinnings is a mistake. As events in the region have demonstrated over time, the political context in which an economy functions is not defined exclusively by the short-term decisions of those in government nor by the technicalities of a specific plan, but is more broadly framed within a set of general laws endowed with political legitimacy and designed to provide an effective mechanism to channel human activity toward endeavors to create wealth and innovation.

Argentina's economic constitution remains fragile largely because over the last half century these general laws have been undermined by a series of mandates, decrees, and resolutions that often have impacted negatively on the fiscal dimension of citizenship, which I refer to as "fiscal citizenship." With the elimination of the shared responsibility encompassed by fiscal citizenship insofar as it combines rights and obligations,[2] what has emerged in its place is a sort of partial citizenship that coexists with a hypertrophic state that is unable to effectively fulfill the functions assigned to it by the political Constitution, namely, providing security, justice, national defense, education, health services, and social security.

Since the advent of democracy in Argentina in late 1983, the traumatic distortion between the political and the economic spheres has led to a recurring cycle of economic crisis, recovery, stagnation, and crisis again, accompanied by a parallel cycle in the political arena of institutional crisis, hope in the face of brief recovery, disenchantment, and crisis once more, giving way to episodes of collective rage. It becomes apparent, then, that while the political Constitution exists to guarantee legal fairness and equal rights, a weak economic constitution opens the way for social inequality to grow. Numerous examples illustrate this point: privileged estates that are either exempt from taxation or simply get away with evading or eluding taxes are prevalent; a good portion of the population with a propensity to save tends to rely on foreign currencies or, with a mix of astuteness and distrust, to gamble on easy earnings in short-term investments; too often federal and provincial officials resort to printing more money or accruing more debt rather than streamlining spending and the size of the state (although in recent years Argentina has enjoyed a healthy fiscal situation); and an ever-growing number of individuals are being cast into marginality and poverty. It is usually an emerging or full-blown social crisis that brings such problems to the fore.

This parallelism is, thus, revealing: just as violence—understood as recurrent regressions to certain aspects of a Hobbesian state of nature—erodes and ultimately destroys public liberties (the heart of the political Constitution), so, too, fiscal disobedience or low fiscal compliance ends up debasing the currency through hyperinflation or hyperindebtedness. These two points of reference—fiscal citizenship and the currency—make up the hard core of the economic constitution.[3] Such an assessment takes on new meanings if approached comparatively as the theme of this book proposes; in fact, explaining the development gap between the United States and Latin America requires, first and foremost, a comparison. This chapter provides a comparative analysis of the political and historical problem of fiscal citizenship, focusing on the United States, Argentina, and, to some extent, Brazil.

Political Obligation

The brief preamble above highlights not only the gap that separates Latin America from the United States, but also illustrates how the prevalence of illegality in the Latin American region points to a problem inherent in the connections among the fiscal demands of the state, the objective and subjective definitions of citizenship, and the meanings, often discordant, attributed to political obligation as the essential basis for the effective enjoyment of rights. From this perspective, fiscal citizenship can be understood in its common meaning or, as this chapter proposes, it can be viewed within a historical and political framework that complements an economic and legal analysis. The common meaning of fiscal citizenship should not be set aside, however, for this level of language is an essential platform from which to explore more profound dimensions. When it is said, for example, that fiscal citizenship represents voluntary acquiescence to the fiscal laws in place or that, in its absence, the judicial branch effectively enforces those laws by imposing sanctions, reference is being made to classic political questions: the *why* and *what for* of obedience.

As explained in more detail in the next paragraph, any state requires fiscal resources to carry out its sovereign missions of ensuring a monopoly over the use of force, in keeping with arrangements involving more or less decentralization, and of instituting, over time, a hierarchy of public objectives (most important in this regard is to compare the respective preambles of the Constitutions of the United States and Argentina). This exigency presupposes both coercion and consensus. While fiscal coercion has been condemned in modern times as arbitrary and despotic (popular literature has helped a great deal in this regard), one must not forget that from the very origins of the debate on the sovereignty of the modern state, an effort was made to set some limit on the discretion of rulers engaged in extracting taxes from their subjects. As Jean Bodin affirmed in the sixteenth century: "[i]t is not in the power of any prince in the world, at his pleasure to raise taxes upon the people, no more than to take another man's goods from him."[4]

With respect to the legal and political theories of the twentieth century, the intersection between coercion and consensus brings to the fore two attributes without which the state may be seriously compromised. At play, as Norberto Bobbio postulated, is a combination of the principle of effectiveness and the principle of legitimacy:

> The principle of effectiveness is based exclusively on the finding of the (habitual) observance of the rules, considered as an external fact, and with that it is satisfied; in contrast, the principle of legitimacy requires that external compliance be in turn related to an internal fact of the observer, by one who obeys the rule because he assumes the content of the mandate [of Max Weber] as a maxim of his own conduct.[5]

This synthesis, between the thought of Hans Kelsen[6] regarding the effectiveness of a legal order and Max Weber's theory of legitimacy,[7] revolves around the meaning of legal provisions (a Constitution and the laws that derive from it) that generally meet with compliance. In summary, political obligation must be given the same attention as rights.

It is clear that political obligation has different purposes. As T. H. Green wrote in a book on the principles of political obligation published in 1895, this term encompasses "the obligation of the subject toward the sovereign, the obligation of the citizen toward the state, and the obligation of individuals to each other as enforced by a political superior."[8] In this chapter, I defend the hypothesis that political obligation, applied to the fiscal sphere, impacts these three purposes, but fundamentally it places emphasis on the relationship between the citizen and the state. As Green and Bobbio argued, that relationship refers to the external acts of legal obligation, but reaches a higher level of satisfaction, in terms of the morality of the act itself, to the extent that the subjects (in this case, the citizens) perceive that the fiscal obligation has positive consequences for them.

This value judgment is of course linked to the basic rules of the legal order, for various reasons. An individual will pay taxes, for example, because the political order is supported by an established tradition of financing the state, or because this conduct rests on an implicit calculation according to which there is a mutual exchange of benefits between the citizen and the state. In this way, the counterpart to a tax should be one or more public goods, so long as it is considered that something is a public good when, according to Philip Pettit, "everyone enjoys [them] if anyone does."[9] This definition should also encompass, in the historical formation of the concept of public goods, a process directly related to collective aspirations that become more or less institutionalized rights.

Certainly, posed in those terms, these relationships evoke a fiscal contract pursuant to which there would be an implicit pact between the citizen and the state based on a permanent flow of mutual benefits. Nonetheless, nothing could be more off the mark, from a legal point of view, than this version of a fiscal contract. In strictly normative terms, a tax is a public obligation; it is obligatory, and it is permanently established for the security and well-being of those who pay and those who don't pay taxes. This view of the effectiveness of a public order gives rise, as we already noted, to the external side of political obligation in fiscal matters whose most apparent basis is state coercion; but if to this aspect of social action we add the principle of legitimacy, which alludes to the subjective dimension of state coercion, we note that, in such relationships, citizens always seek an implicit balance between what they give and what they receive.

That evaluation has underscored, in the course of a lengthy historical debate, the value assigned by both political theory and praxis to paying taxes, directly or indirectly. Which of the two connections is more advisable for supporting the attributes particular to fiscal citizenship? It seems suggestive to imagine, in this regard, a confluence of the following hypotheses: the greater the direct relationship between the payment of taxes and the receipt of public goods provided for by the state, the less the propensity to reject the legitimacy of the provisions in this area as a structure alien to the will of citizens; inversely, the less direct the relationship between paying taxes and receiving public goods, the less the propensity of such a complex normative framework governing obligations to be perceived as a necessary effect of the tax-paying will of the citizen.

We will return to this point later in this chapter, but here it must be noted that the link between state and citizen, mediated by the payment of taxes, presupposes on the part of the subjects not only verifying what really happens, but also an implicit judgment as to what is desirable and undesirable, what is fair and unfair, what is equitable and what is not. In these relationships, there is a balance between transparency and opacity. At stake here, as shown by Juan J. Llach and María Marcela Harriague, is a "correspondence" among the citizen, the payment of taxes, and the administration and allocation of public spending.[10] That correspondence may give rise, in an extreme situation of full transparency, to a virtuous circle of fiscal citizenship or, on the flip side, to the expression, shot through with opacity, of a vicious circle of fiscal citizenship.

In the first circle, citizens pay taxes, and the state generates, administers, and guarantees the allocation of public goods; in the second, citizens evade the payment of taxes (in full or in part) because they perceive distorting elements in the fiscal laws and the scant capacity of the state to respond to that demand for public goods. Actually, each of these processes feeds back into the other, and often the state's inability to respond becomes an excuse to evade or to continue evading taxes.

Tax evasion takes on dramatic importance when viewed through the lens of the observance of rights in a constitutional democracy. Little attention is generally given, in particular in Latin American countries, to the fact that rights must be upheld. Without the enforcement of rights, and without the necessary fiscal support for that set of provisions not to appear to the governed as a scheme, societies may swing back and forth between a widespread sense of anomie, at one extreme, and at the other a diffuse awareness that those rights should operate as a sort of free gift. These processes are more complex because they put us on notice, as Stephen Holmes and Cass R. Sunstein have shown very clearly, that rights have costs:

> In practice, rights become more than mere declarations only if they confer power on bodies whose decisions are legally binding....As a general rule, unfortunate individuals who do not live under a government capable of taxing and delivering an effective remedy have no legal rights. Statelessness spells rightslessness. A legal right exists, in reality, only when and if it has budgetary costs.[11]

These words summarize the problems we mentioned above: political obligation, civic responsibility, and transparency in the path that extends from the taxpayer base to the administration in charge of public spending. Consider the circuit these authors describe with respect to property rights:

> Property rights have costs because, to protect them, the government must hire police officers. Responsibility is involved here, first, in the honest routing of taxpayers' dollars into the salaries of the police. It is involved a second time when, at considerable expense, the government trains police officers to respect the rights of suspects. And responsibility comes in a third time when the government, again at the taxpayers' expense, monitors police behavior and disciplines abuses to prevent officers from abridging civil rights and civil liberties by, for example, breaking into people's homes, manufacturing evidence, and beating up suspects.[12]

This snapshot represents the profile of what in the nineteenth century—according to the rhetoric of European and Latin American political and economic thought—was called the "gendarme state," i.e., a state devoted to protecting property, security, and defense.

Nonetheless, things are not so simple, because also from that first step in the scale of rights arise financing and organizational costs. When those fiscal costs are not addressed and are not allocated responsibly, discouragement and incredulity toward rights that are proclaimed but not enforced takes hold. One need only review a series of surveys in Argentina and elsewhere in Latin America to note that the phantom that runs through our societies is insecurity. The negative impact of that lack of state protection is not felt as heavily by the high-income sectors, which have resources to obtain private security. It is mainly the larger population of indigents, the poor, and the declining middle sectors who have lost, in their citizen life, the crucial attribute of "statehood."[13] The problem of a clear gap between written and enforced rights is at the heart of the question of the republican origins of our nations.

Fiscal Regimes: The Starting Point

According to S. E. Finer, "the more differentiated the polity, the more it needs to levy taxation."[14] The best way to understand this requirement is through a historical analysis, but one should bear in mind that there may be a point of inflection in those processes when the need to levy taxes dovetails with the design of a republican form of government and a constitutional congress. With more or less success, the procedure aimed at establishing fiscal institutions spread throughout the Americas, from north to south, beginning with the United States when it adopted its Constitution in 1787. In Argentina, the moment came in 1853 and, like the United States albeit without the same architectural originality, the undertaking had its founders and its justifiers. Alexander Hamilton, in the pages later collected in *The Federalist Papers* (1788), and Juan Bautista Alberdi, in *Sistema económico y rentístico de la Confederación Argentina según su Constitución de 1853* (1855), laid the bases of what should be, in their judgment, the most advisable fiscal regime for a newly established republic.

We can agree that the design of a Constitution for a representative republic (which echoes the cry of "no taxation without representation") has the advantage of setting the purposes of fiscal policy. For Hamilton, the main purposes that the newly established federal government (the Union) should serve were "the common defense of the members; the preservation of the public peace as well against internal convulsions as external attacks; the regulation of commerce with other nations and between the States; the superintendence of our intercourse, political and commercial, with foreign countries."[15] The two poles around which Hamilton developed his argument are typical of the tension which, theoretically, existed in the eighteenth century between the idea of a republic that cherishes civic virtues and the much more novel concept of a commercial republic. For Hamilton, the guarantees of internal and external peace went hand in hand with the development of commerce. The touchstone of the fiscal regime conceived of by Hamilton resided in the nationalization of the customs department: more commerce, more imports, more resources to the treasury. In sum, Hamilton's proposal included an unquestionable prevalence of indirect taxes over direct taxes.

Hamilton maintained his position in favor of indirect taxes without major concern, but supported it with another important element. Just as in a new republic it is "impracticable to raise any very considerable sums by direct taxation,"[16] one should also be especially careful not to fall into the mistake of drawing up rigid schemes—which are ultimately unhelpful—based on distinguishing an internal tax, entrusted to the states, from an external tax, entrusted to the federal government. Flexibility is needed to meet new demands tied to the proportionality that should always exist between the ends of the state and the fiscal means made available to them.

Could it be that Hamilton's proposal as set forth in *The Federalist Papers* had sufficient virtue to meet some criterion of fiscal justice? It does not seem that the wisdom of the legislator has advanced beyond the concepts contained in a policy of indirect taxes. Based on total tax revenues, which would come mainly from foreign commerce (although domestic commerce in principle would not be exempt from taxation), as a general rule, the consumption of the rich would always be more heavily taxed than the consumption of the poor. For Hamilton, this timid advance of the principle of proportionality constituted a felicitous convergence between the particular interests of the subjects and the public interest of the state. Hamilton's approach, above all, took account of the experience acquired in the colonial period and in the brief time between the War of Independence and the debate on the Constitution in Philadelphia in 1787.

A similar spirit was present in *Sistema económico y rentístico de la Confederación Argentina según su Constitución de 1853*, which Alberdi wrote to lay the foundation for the general rules of the economic constitution that was to support the Argentine political Constitution adopted in 1853. Inspired by an analogous rhetorical device to the one used in *The Federalist Papers*, that text was aimed at persuading those with contrary opinions. However, whereas the articles of *The Federalist Papers* were aimed at deliberations within the states so as to eventually obtain a majority consensus in support of the draft Constitution, Alberdi's book was an answer to the fact that the 1853 Constitution had been rejected by the most powerful province (Buenos Aires), which had ushered in a new chapter in an apparently never-ending civil war.

The civil war, which immediately followed the war of independence, had, according to Alberdi, a geographical and economic explanation. Argentina was a large nation in transition, largely uninhabited and isolated. In its internal structure, the country confronted the difficulty of having a single international seaport in the city of Buenos Aires, the capital of the province of the same name; thus, whoever controlled that port held the fiscal key to the country. The keystone of Alberdi's project was that it established a fiscal pact by which all of the provinces had to give up their own customs agencies (typical of a period known to Argentines as *de Confederación*) for the sake of constituting a national customs service. So long as the province of Buenos Aires would not cede that resource through a compromise or by military defeat inflicted on it by the rest of the provinces joined against it, the republic in its infancy would lack a treasury.

Alberdi clearly understood that the rentist system was dependent on several policies consistent with the Constitution. In effect, a swift transition was needed to emerge from the poverty in which the old society was vegetating: "it is wealth, capital, the population, the national well-being, [that are] the first thing[s] that should occupy [Argentina's] attention, now and for a long time." And in that endeavor, "the Government has the power to disturb or help its production, but the creation of wealth is not its role."[17] Here, one can deduce Hamilton's same imperative, shifted to the geography of South America: without wealth, in effect, there is no treasury, in the sense of this institution of the state being able to take in the tax payments of "many small ones" (*muchos pocos*) instead of "a few big ones" (*pocos muchos*).[18] In line with Alexis de Tocqueville's thinking, the most appropriate fiscal regime for carrying out this conversion from an aristocratic society to a democratic society is based on indirect taxes on foreign commerce.

While, for Alberdi, the nationalization of the customs service was the sine qua non for the existence of a public treasury, the development of wealth and indirect taxes constituted the necessary condition. The indirect contribution is thus best suited for the rentist system of the Constitution. It is the most abundant in fiscal revenues, the easiest to collect because it is imperceptible to the taxpayer, and it is the most free and voluntary contribution. The indirect contribution is also the most impersonal, the most progressive, because it makes it possible to tax consumption that is sterile when it comes to the country's progress, and, finally, the "most equal in proportion because it is paid by everyone [citizens and inhabitants, foreigners and nationals] to the extent of their enjoyments and consumption."[19] The constitutional hierarchy of indirect taxes was for Alberdi unquestionable, as can be seen both in a draft that he prepared in 1852 and in the definitive text of 1853: while the Constitution established both types of tax—indirect and direct—the express mention of the first, such as customs and the mail system, and the generic terms with which the Constitution referred to the second demonstrated the bias toward building up the treasury through an influx of indirect taxes. Indirect taxes were also important, Alberdi added to drive home his point, because Article 64.2 at the time allowed for direct federal taxes only as special contributions for a limited time.[20]

The differences between Alberdi and Hamilton are suggestive. Alberdi was more rigid in terms of leaving direct taxes in the hands of the provinces and entrusting indirect taxes to the federal government (which Hamilton ultimately left to the decision of the legislature). Alberdi's project appeared to be tied to a different intent as well: whereas for Hamilton the vesting of the power of taxation in a new republican form of government was, in itself, a valuable goal, Alberdi went about the same operation much more cautiously. Among other things, he felt that the principal virtue of the power to tax and constitute the public treasury would be in the frugality of the government and the simplicity of the laws: a small state, low indirect taxes without inquiring into the name and income of the taxpayer, and the prudent use of public credit. In Alberdi's words: *"Lowering the payment is increasing the national Treasury: a rule that does not produce that effect instantly, but that never fails to produce it in time, just as wheat does not yield the day after it is planted but rarely does it fail to produce after a certain time."*[21]

These conclusions—a faithful reflection, after a lengthy journey of ideas, of the Scottish Enlightenment in the River Plate—constituted a fundamental principle for Alberdi. Indirect taxes, at the same time, ultimately had a more pragmatic role. In a land where a free government was not favored by tradition and whose people "bereft of public spirit" survived in a state of distrust, the best thing was to cut one's losses and not apply direct taxes (moreover, according to Alberdi, the experience of direct taxes during the Rosas dictatorship had been disastrous).[22]

Hamilton's and Alberdi's recommendations contained some maxims well known to that class of legislators since Adam Smith, in 1776, had stipulated in *The Wealth of Nations* four principles common to all taxes generally. First, citizens should pay in proportion to their incomes; second, the tax that each individual is obligated to pay should be "certain, and not arbitrary"; third, every tax ought to be "levied at the time, or in the manner, in which it is most likely to be convenient for the contributor to pay it"; and, fourth, the administration for collecting taxes should not be excessive nor facilitate evasion.[23] In sum, equality, certainty, ease of payment, and restraint in what could be called the economy of tax collection were for Adam Smith the four cardinal points of sound fiscal policy. Note that they point to both the objective dimension (the legislature establishes them) and the subjective dimension (the citizen abides by them), and they do not discriminate as to the differing qualities attributed to direct or indirect taxes.

Clearly, what concerned Adam Smith were the principles of justice contained in the laws and their consequences: "[t]he law, contrary to all the ordinary principles of justice, first creates the temptation, and then punishes those who yield to it; and it commonly enhances the punishment too in proportion to the very circumstance which ought certainly to alleviate it, the temptation to commit the crime."[24] One should underscore that this vindication of justice is mainly tied to the principle of fiscal proportionality. Smith cites in this respect the six general rules of Henry Home, his colleague and friend, author of *Sketches of the History of Man*, which established that taxes were legislated "to remedy inequality of riches as much as possible, by relieving the poor and burdening the rich."[25]

To what extent can it be postulated that fiscal laws are a measure of justice in a republican regime? Immanuel Kant, for example, established the basis of this duty of justice in fiscal affairs as follows: "the government is authorized to require the wealthy to provide the means of sustenance to those who are unable to provide the most necessary needs of nature for themselves."[26] Kant did not postulate any particular taxation technique, direct or indirect, to put this into practice, but from his thinking it is clear that the responsibility imposed on the affluent to provide the means of subsistence for those who do not have the capacity to do so, reaffirms the principle of proportionality and personalizes to a much greater extent the fiscal link in relation to what arises from indirect, undifferentiated payment on a larger number of consumer goods (including luxury goods).

In the late eighteenth century, the groundwork was slowly being laid for a broader justification of direct taxes based on the concept of distributive justice, which did not keep Smith from rigorously analyzing the difficulties that, in practice, were posed by tax payments, such as those experienced in England under the rubric of the land tax. This opening to a new fiscal horizon did not come without difficulties. In the struggle of assessments and interests, the then-prevalent ideas concerning the attributes of citizenship and the disputes around the right to property and, by extension, the whole set of rights that the republican form of government should guarantee, played a key role.

From Indirect to Direct Taxation

In the nineteenth century, the exercise of citizen rights was linked to property and to being male: to be a citizen, in effect, one had to be male, of age, born in the territory (in both Argentina and the United States, *jus soli* was—and still is—the law), and have income and property.[27] The right to vote, which is at the core of political freedom, was constructed by distinguishing civil liberties (rights distributed universally) from political liberties (the right to vote distributed with restrictive criteria). Of course, there were exceptions in terms of the early adoption in some countries of universal male suffrage (very important in the U.S. states of California and New England), but for the central thrust of this chapter, the restriction on the right to vote and the exercise of political liberty was generally implemented by the registration in the census of those who had property, income, and education (hence the French expression *suffrage censitaire*). By way of this procedure, the right to vote was associated with one's status as a taxpayer. The conflicts, gains, and setbacks that occurred while in pursuit of a broader conception of suffrage that would overcome the limitations imposed by property and gender are related to this notion of incorporating in a restrictive republic the concept of the citizen taxpayer.

It took decades to resolve this issue, and perhaps its persistence as a limitation on popular demands is explained by the importance of direct taxes in relation to the concept of the citizen taxpayer. In an idyllic world typical of agrarian republicanism and in which Hamilton's thinking converged with that of his opponent Thomas Jefferson, the landowner who paid his land tax at the same time acquired the right to vote. Accordingly, the more widely property was disseminated—according to Jefferson and, in Argentina, according to Domingo F. Sarmiento, who identified with this view of the good society—the larger was the number of citizens who qualified to vote. Imbued with the virtue that emanated from small and medium agrarian holdings, these legislators distrusted the proletariat of the urban centers, whom they contemptuously called the "mob of the cities."[28]

The paradox of this first definition of fiscal citizenship lay in the fact that indirect and impersonal taxes, especially on imports, did not have a major impact on this bitter debate. Indeed, the battle was waged in a field in which mass phenomena having to do with security and war were reflected. How can one explain, in effect, restricting the vote so that police and soldiers are not able to vote, when they, inhabitants of the republic without political rights, had to offer their lives, if necessary, to defend other people's property or the territorial integrity of the country? As Holmes and Sunstein say: "The most dramatic example of such regressive taxation occurs when the poor are drafted into military service in wartime to defend, among other things, the property of the rich from foreign predators."[29] The relevance of these questions in the United States is better understood when noting that it was not until 1964 that the 24th Amendment to the Constitution did away with the last vestiges of tax-based qualifications or restrictions on the right to vote in national elections:

> The right of citizens of the United States to vote in any primary or other election for President or Vice President, for electors for President or Vice President, or for Senator or Representative in Congress, shall not be denied or abridged by the United States or any state by reason of failure to pay any poll tax or other tax.

The will to overcome these problems is condensed in one of the most attractive projects to have taken root in world consciousness during the course of the nineteenth and twentieth centuries: the universal nature of political rights, whatever the status of the citizen in terms of property and income. As Tocqueville would say, this was one of the most noticeable effects of the tendency for modern societies to move toward equality. Once this sentiment was incorporated in the repertoire of collective beliefs, societies could not turn back lest they face even more serious conflicts (the lesson derived from the Latin American experience in this regard is sufficiently enlightening). In any event, the aspirations for greater political participation strengthened the demand to support the new rights with genuine fiscal resources. How can one increase resources while answering to fairness criteria that, in general, are linked to the concept of proportional payment of taxes based on income levels? Posing this question helped to open the way to the most significant direct tax in contemporary history, the income tax. According to Kant's argument, the fiscal efforts of the wealthiest should make up for the inability of the poorest to pay.

There is no question that, at first, resistance to these direct taxes was strident. In the United States, around 1870 (without data on direct taxes in this period), the tax burden, considered as tax revenues as a percentage of gross domestic product (GDP), was 5.2 percent, with foreign commerce accounting for 2.7 percent of that figure. One year earlier, in 1869, the daily newspaper the *Tribune*, published in New York, declared that "the Income Tax is the most odious, vexatious, inquisitorial, and unequal of all our taxes...a tax on honesty....It tends to tax the quality out of existence."[30] Certainly, antecedents of taxes on rent, revenues, and income abound in the former colonies that became the United States, and the same is true in Great Britain, but even allowing for those exceptions, it was thought that such encumbrances were special measures—as in the case of the national Constitution of Argentina—and had to be dispensed with once the emergency of a war or unforeseen natural disaster had passed.

Moreover, there were contrary interpretations in the United States as to what the Constitution said in this regard, one of which was adopted by the Supreme Court to declare unconstitutional an income tax statute approved one year earlier by Congress. This debate was resolved definitively in 1913 when the 16th Amendment of the U.S. Constitution was adopted. It reads: "The Congress shall have power to lay and collect taxes on incomes, from whatever source derived, without apportionment among the several States, and without regard to any census or enumeration." This amendment, whose purpose was to accord constitutional rank to the individual income tax, was in addition to another statute of 1909, which established a federal corporate income tax. These two provisions not only defined the profile of the direct tax applied to the incomes of individuals and corporations, but also specified the jurisdictions of the two levels of a federal system of government, i.e., state and federal. While the states were limited in fiscal matters to indirect taxes (the most common was and still is the sales tax), in the federal order mostly direct taxes were levied. This possible solution, among the many that can be attempted in the federal order, insinuated what we will call a "separation of fiscal powers" regime.

In Argentina, these debates and legislative processes developed differently. The same year in which, as was noted above, the U.S. Supreme Court declared an income tax law to be unconstitutional, national legislator Emilio Berduc recognized that customs duties were the basis of the public treasury, in a proportion ranging from 25 to 60 percent, whereas the rest was covered by domestic taxes on consumption.[31] According to Berduc, this fiscal structure was regressive and had to be replaced by a scheme of direct taxes on rent and income. He focused his discourse on a decisive aspect having to do with the subjective component of fiscal citizenship: "[t]his tax is likely the only one that makes it possible to take stock of the real quota the taxpayer pays; it is the tax by which an inhabitant of the country can know for sure what he or she pays the state."[32] That proposal sought to get past the obstacles of a fiscal disorder brought about by adding up, without any logic, taxes of the most varied sort:

> What would each of its inhabitants answer if asked whether they did not prefer, instead of those many taxes—for eating, for dressing, for walking, for signing papers, and even for sleeping—if they would not prefer, I say, to contribute with a part of what they earn, instead of paying, many times even with the money they need to eat?[33]

This image has repeated itself for more than a century, to this day. It is an image that contrasts the requirement of general laws with a reality distorted by having a disjointed set of taxes. The project advocated by Berduc was rejected, before and after that date, by invoking the Alberdian scheme of the national Constitution, which reserved direct taxes to the exclusive domain of the provinces. In 1891, Senator Anacleto Gil summarized this doctrine, which was the exact opposite of what was subsequently adopted by the United States in its Constitution and legislation: "The Constitution, when establishing the authority of each government with respect to tax payments, gives to the general Government the exclusive responsibility over external taxes and gives, as a general rule, the internal taxes to the States."[34] From 1912 to 1930, at the time of the First Centennial and during the 18 years of the first transition to democracy (compulsory, male, and secret ballot), efforts to establish an income tax did not meet with much success in Argentina. It was not possible, during the presidencies of Hipólito Yrigoyen (1916–1922 and 1928–1930) or Marcelo T. de Alvear (1922–1928), to have the respective proposals passed into law by Congress.

This merits special mention because, in January 1932, shortly before the de facto government period had ended following the September 6,

1930, coup d'état, a new decree was issued establishing an emergency tax on income. What the government had not been able to institutionalize in the course of a long period of constitutional practice ended up being legislated by decree, that is, by unilateral mandate of an executive branch limited only by its polemical recognition by the Supreme Court of Justice. Absent the role of the Congress, previously dissolved, direct taxes came to be implemented in the country after a decision which, by the method adopted, turned upside down the principle of no taxation without representation. In Argentina, the expression was simpler: in terms of this type of tax, there was taxation without representation, a reversal that brought us back to the old colonial regime.

Once the powers of the Constitution were restored, months later, this situation could not be drawn out for much longer. On April 23, 1932, the executive sent to Congress a bill establishing national direct taxes on corporate income, rural and urban rental income, the net profits of commerce and industry, and wages and salaries. If there is one word capable of summarizing the parliamentary debate that ensued, that word is "emergency." According to the member reporting for the majority of the responsible committee of the Chamber of Deputies, José H. Martínez, the "national emergency tax" was determined by short-term fiscal demands and by the imperative of not violating the national Constitution. Accordingly, the income tax was in force for a set time, during which the Congress had to issue a "revenue-sharing" law that would distribute the proceeds of that tax between the federal government and the provinces. Martínez argued that this legislation "has avoided the drawbacks of other tax laws that subject the taxpayer to a real fiscal inquisition."[35] Actually, according to another legislator from the same party, Vicente Solano Lima, it was a matter of giving the nod to "bad laws...because they were adopted under the pressure of an emergency situation."[36]

The bill was finally approved, but not without first receiving a well-founded critique by the minority. Arguing in favor of this federal tax being the first step in a fruitful evolution, Silvio L. Ruggieri, a legislator from the Partido Socialista, proposed a fiscal regime "that does not go after the work or consumption of the people, and that calls for tax payment from personal fortunes to constitute the national treasury, in proportion to their volume and importance."[37] The socialists called for making the tax more progressive, proposing a rate of 35 percent for the highest incomes when the bill set it at 7 percent. No one doubted that the legislation adopted a moderate tax, though there was no lack of opinions in the subsequent debate in the national

Senate, such as that of the senator for Entre Ríos, Atanasio Eguiguren, who considered this tax "antiscientific, corrupting of the autonomy of the provinces, and violative of the Constitution."[38] In general, adverse opinions in the upper chamber agreed that it was a dangerous curtailing of the autonomy of the provinces, which is clearly provided for in the Constitution. This did not stop the bill from winning ultimate approval. Had a step forward been taken with respect to the question of equity? The senator for Catamarca, Francisco Galíndez, outlined some thoughts on this question when he recalled that whereas "taxes on consumption weigh on the middle classes and the poor classes, the income tax, in contrast, impacts on the well-to-do classes, on the rich."[39]

This being the case, the starting point of national legislation on direct taxes encompassed at least three questions not entirely resolved. There was, underlying the debate, a serious budgetary imbalance which, in the opinion of Federico Pinedo, the future minister of the treasury of that administration, was provoking "unspeakable difficulties."[40] This need to attain fiscal balance as soon as possible clashed with the interpretations of the fiscal system of federalism. Should Argentina follow the line of the United States, delimiting a separation of powers regime, thereby reserving certain types of taxes (direct or indirect) to a given jurisdiction (federal or provincial)? Or, to the contrary, should both sources of tax revenue be merged, so as to then, through a law of Congress, apportion them between the federal government and the provinces? The law on direct taxes, approved in 1932, responded to this second question by forcing Congress to issue a "law on revenue-sharing" of those resources as of January 1, 1934. That date should not be ignored, as it marks the beginning of a federal co-participation regime based much more on the merger of fiscal powers than on their separation. Since then, Argentina has not abandoned this legislative position, which gained constitutional stature with the amendments to the Constitution introduced in 1994.

This was, if you will, a practical approach that could be labeled a "constitutional bypass." This was best understood by an outstanding expert in constitutional law, the senator for Tucumán, José N. Matienzo, who hit the nail on the head in describing the differences between Argentina and the United States:

> [T]he United States does not have our *criollo* astuteness; there it was thought it was necessary to amend the Constitution....Among our kind we do not think there is a need for that: the measures are declared

on an emergency basis, and the Constitution is violated. That *criollo* astuteness, they are not familiar with it in the United States.[41]

It appears that this irony provoked laughter in the chamber. Actually, that warning was aimed at more, for it is not the same thing to reorient citizens' expectations in relation to a direct tax as important as the income tax—establishing it on a stable and continuing basis, as a permanent institution—as it is to determine that it should come into force as a sort of provisional tool, whose duration should be no longer than that of the emergency situation. In fact, it was not like that. For more than 70 years, to this day, that emergency tax has been renewed regularly, thereby obfuscating the actual situation. It poses an interesting question of what one should make of fiscal citizenship when a legal point of reference to which citizens are to attribute legitimacy is marked by the label of "provisional."

The Respective Weight of Direct and Indirect Taxes

Notwithstanding the peculiar constitutional origin of federal direct taxes, we now turn to how this type of tax has evolved in Argentina as compared to those applied in the United States. Based on the long-term perspective offered by a series that begins in 1932 and ends in 2004, what stands out most prominently on an initial reading is the weight of indirect taxes in Argentina's tax burden and the preponderance of direct taxes in the United States. As illustrated in table 9.1, never in those years did the percentage of direct taxes in Argentina overtake the percentage of indirect taxes, even including in the former the part that corresponds to land rent (various types of levies on exports that also include subsoil rents). Not only does that prevalence repeat in the five-year averages shown here, but, in addition, that ratio, though it increased during two periods in terms of favoring direct taxes (the 1946–1950 and 1956–1960 periods), tumbled sharply from 1971 to 1985.

Based on this analysis, a line of continuity imposes itself on the turbulence of changing political regimes and economic policies. During this 70-year period in Argentina, practically everything has happened, from attempts to establish democratic constitutional legitimacy—more or less consolidated as of 1983—to the worst expressions of political dictatorship: civilian and military governments, populist and conservative governments, protectionist developmentalism and openings to

TABLE 9.1 Argentina: Government Tax Revenues

Period	Federal Taxes					Provincial Taxes			Total Federal & Provincial
	Direct Taxes	Indirect Taxes	Social Security	Land Rent	Total Federal	Direct Taxes	Indirect Taxes	Total Provincial	
1932–1935	0.94%	7.31%	1.46%	0.10%	9.72%	nd	nd	n/d	9.72%
1936–1940	1.25%	6.84%	1.32%	0	9.40%	nd	nd	n/d	9.40%
1941–1945	1.97%	4.67%	1.55%	0	8.19%	nd	nd	n/d	8.19%
1946–1950	3.95%	5.33%	4.87%	0	14.15%	0.15%	0.27%	0.42%	14.58%
1951–1955	4.43%	6.15%	5.66%	0	16.24%	0.61%	1.34%	1.95%	18.19%
1956–1960	3.50%	4.79%	4.25%	0	12.54%	0.50%	1.51%	2.01%	14.55%
1961–1965	2.49%	5.28%	3.52%	0.07%	11.36%	0.59%	2.11%	2.70%	14.06%
1966–1970	2.91%	5.82%	3.85%	0.57%	13.15%	0.77%	2.54%	3.31%	16.46%
1971–1975	1.81%	4.38%	3.49%	0.71%	10.39%	0.55%	2.01%	2.57%	12.95%
1976–1980	1.74%	6.10%	3.29%	0.34%	11.47%	0.75%	2.91%	3.66%	15.14%
1981–1985	1.52%	6.36%	1.85%	0.74%	10.46%	1.00%	2.13%	3.14%	13.60%
1986–1990	2.12%	6.02%	2.37%	0.83%	11.34%	0.98%	1.95%	2.93%	14.27%
1991–1995	2.28%	9.35%	4.10%	0.07%	15.80%	1.05%	2.60%	3.65%	19.45%
1996–2000	3.58%	9.92%	3.50%	0.01%	17.02%	1.12%	3.37%	4.49%	21.50%
2001–2004	5.97%	8.59%	2.78%	1.59%	18.92%	0.84%	2.87%	3.71%	22.63%

Notes: Tax burden: ratio of tax revenues to GDP, in five-year averages.
Direct: on rent, profit, and capital gains; on property.
Indirect: internal on goods, services, and transactions; rest of taxes on international commerce and transactions; other tax resources.
nd: no data.
Nontaxable income from judicial fees and revenues earmarked for the ART (Aseguradora de Riesgos de Trabajo or Workplace Risk Insurer) and AFJP (Administradora de Fondos de Jubilaciones y Pensiones or Retirement and Pension Funds Administration) not included.
Repayments and reimbursements were not deducted from any of the categories listed.
Sources: AFIP (Administración Federal de Ingresos Públicos or Federal Administration for Public Revenue), *Estadísticas Tributarias*; and Ministry of Economy, *Dirección Nacional de Investigaciones y Análisis Fiscal*.

foreign trade with overvalued or undervalued exchange rates, inflation, mega-inflation, and hyperinflation. Nothing, however, appeared to affect the stable course of indirect taxation. In the last four-year period covered in table 9.1, this strong tendency shows signs of inflection, if one looks just at the 5.97 percent of direct taxes that does not include land rent (a polemical tax which, according to several sectors, introduces distortions).

The horizontal structure of the federal government's tax resources over the totals collected indicates the same trend. While direct taxes represented 9.7 percent on average for the period 1932–1935 (as compared to 75.3 percent indirect taxes), that percentage doubled toward the end of the period to 20.9 percent (1996–2000; see table 9.2). From 1941 to 1970, direct taxes accounted for more than 20 percent, which was not the case from 1971 to 1995, years of evident backsliding. So the recovery has occurred since 1996, which is far from constituting a trend, though even including land rent in the 2001–2004 period, direct taxes (39.5 percent) were lower than indirect taxes (45.6 percent).

Note the zigzag evolution of social security taxes. As we will see in the next paragraph, these taxes, typical of a welfare state, shot up in 1946 and then leveled off at about 30 percent through the 1976–1980 period. Afterward, they saw a sharp decline through the 2001–2004 period, when they reached levels practically identical to those of the first period, 1932–1935 (14.9 compared to 15 percent). This is a clear indication of the depth of the crisis that the weakest sectors of society, forced by the reality of the situation to move to the informal sector, had to bear in late 2001 and early 2002 (the situation was similar to the percentages during the 1981–1985 period, when hyperinflation had a devastating effect).

What is one to make, in contrast, of the comparison suggested by the tables of the fiscal development of the United States? Setting aside the immense gap in the size of the two economies and focusing instead on several salient characteristics of a series that began that same year, we find that a fiscal revolution occurred when the recently elected president, Franklin D. Roosevelt, ascended to the first office in a nation exhausted by the worst economic crisis of the twentieth century (or perhaps in its history). This fiscal revolution took place in the United States as a result of its intervention in the Second World War. This crucial transition from a republic of unquestionable international importance to one with a much more decisive role and with the achievements and obligations of an "imperial republic" (to apply Raymond Aron's concept) was reflected in the transformation away from the old, more or less balanced relationship between direct taxes

TABLE 9.2   Argentina: Government Tax Revenues

Period	Federal Taxes					Provincial Taxes		
	Direct Taxes	Indirect Taxes	Social Security	Land Rent	National Total	Direct Taxes	Indirect Taxes	Provincial Total
1932–1935	9.7%	75.3%	15.0%	0.1%	100%	nd	nd	nd
1936–1940	13.3%	72.7%	14.0%	0	100%	nd	nd	nd
1941–1945	23.8%	57.6%	18.6%	0	100%	nd	nd	nd
1946–1950	27.7%	38.4%	33.9%	0	100%	nd	nd	nd
1951–1955	27.3%	37.8%	34.9%	0	100%	31.3%	68.7%	100%
1956–1960	28.0%	38.3%	33.6%	0	100%	25.0%	75.0%	100%
1961–1965	21.8%	46.6%	31.0%	0.6%	100%	21.9%	78.1%	100%
1966–1970	22.2%	44.4%	29.2%	4.2%	100%	23.3%	76.7%	100%
1971–1975	17.1%	42.2%	33.8%	6.9%	100%	21.7%	78.3%	100%
1976–1980	15.1%	52.9%	28.8%	3.2%	100%	19.8%	80.2%	100%
1981–1985	14.5%	61.0%	17.4%	7.1%	100%	32.3%	67.7%	100%
1986–1990	18.7%	53.1%	20.9%	7.3%	100%	33.5%	66.5%	100%
1991–1995	14.5%	59.2%	25.8%	0.5%	100%	29.2%	70.8%	100%
1996–2000	20.9%	58.3%	20.7%	0	100%	24.9%	75.1%	100%
2001–2004	31.4%	45.6%	14.9%	8.1%	100%	22.7%	77.3%	100%

Notes: Each item of tax revenue is presented as a percentage of the total collected in two-week averages.

Direct: on income, profit, and capital gains; on property.

Indirect: on goods, services, and transactions; all other taxes on commerce and international transactions; other tax resources.

nd: no data.

Nontax revenues from judicial fees and revenues earmarked for the ART (Aseguradora de Riesgos de Trabajo or Workplace Risk Insurer) and AFJP (Administradora de Fondos de Jubilaciones y Pensiones or Retirement and Pension Funds Administration) are not included.

Repayments and reimbursements were not deducted from any of the categories listed.

Sources: AFIP (Administración Federal de Ingresos Públicos or Federal Administration for Public Revenue), *Estadísticas Tributarias*; and Ministry of Economy, *Dirección Nacional de Investigaciones y Análisis Fiscal*.

TABLE 9.3   United States: Government Tax Revenues

Period	Federal Taxes				State & Local Taxes	Total Federal & State/ Local
	Direct Taxes	Indirect Taxes	Social Security	Federal Total		
1932–1935	1.06%	1.41%	0.02%	4.08%	nd	4.08%
1936–1940	2.77%	2.50%	1.22%	6.51%	nd	6.51%
1941–1945	10.27%	2.65%	1.67%	14.58%	nd	14.58%
1946–1950	11.40%	3.20%	1.48%	16.08%	3.52%	19.59%
1951–1955	13.05%	2.82%	1.87%	17.75%	6.09%	23.84%
1956–1960	12.30%	2.61%	2.41%	17.33%	7.01%	24.34%
1961–1965	11.78%	2.56%	3.21%	17.55%	7.99%	25.54%
1966–1970	12.30%	2.17%	3.96%	18.43%	8.57%	27.00%
1971–1975	11.04%	1.87%	4.87%	17.78%	9.69%	27.47%
1976–1980	11.17%	1.53%	5.51%	18.21%	6.94%	25.14%
1981–1985	10.33%	1.81%	6.22%	18.36%	8.27%	26.63%
1986–1990	10.15%	1.44%	6.65%	18.23%	9.02%	27.26%
1991–1995	10.03%	1.42%	6.72%	18.17%	9.65%	27.82%
1996–2000	12.02%	1.31%	6.75%	20.07%	9.66%	29.73%
2001–2004	9.80%	1.14%	6.64%	17.59%	9.58%	27.17%

Notes: Tax burden: ratio of tax revenues to GDP.
nd: no data.
Sources: U.S. Congressional Budget Office; Organisation of Economic Co-operation and Development (OECD), Revenue Statistics 1965–2005; U.S. Department of Commerce (Bureau of Economic Analysis); U.S. Department of the Treasury; U.S. Office of Management and Budget; Executive Office of the President of the United States, *Economic Report of the President*; International Monetary Fund, Government Financial Statistics.

and indirect taxes. From 1932 to 1935—the beginning of the New Deal—indirect taxes were slightly greater than direct taxes (1.41 compared to 1.06 percent); from 1936 to 1946, there was a slight preponderance of direct over indirect taxes (2.77 percent direct, 2.5 percent indirect); from 1941 to 1945, the rise was spectacular (10.27 percent direct versus 2.65 percent indirect), and the relationship was never to turn around again.

The start of the Second World War was decisive, for it reaffirmed the importance of a direct tie between the citizens and the state thanks to which the citizens finance, proportional to their incomes, one of the great pillars in the power structure: military defense and expansion. The issue merits special attention in view of the Machiavellian dimensions involved.[42] The military might of this superpower relies, in effect, on collecting the direct taxes paid by citizens and corporations. This connection, impossible to imagine on that scale in Argentina, where direct and indirect taxes are blended in a single fiscal account, is

TABLE 9.4   United States: Government Tax Revenues

| Period | Federal Taxes | | | | State & Local Taxes | Total Federal & State/Local |
	Direct Taxes	Indirect Taxes	Social Security	National Total		
1932–1935	21.12%	28.15%	0.47%	100%	nd	100%
1936–1940	42.90%	39.40%	17.54%	100%	nd	100%
1941–1945	65.54%	20.97%	13.43%	100%	nd	100%
1946–1950	59.05%	16.57%	7.61%	83.24%	16.76%	100%
1951–1955	54.64%	11.86%	7.86%	74.40%	25.60%	100%
1956–1960	50.54%	10.74%	9.91%	71.20%	28.80%	100%
1961–1965	46.12%	10.01%	12.58%	68.72%	31.28%	100%
1966–1970	45.54%	8.04%	14.66%	68.25%	31.75%	100%
1971–1975	40.20%	6.81%	17.72%	64.73%	35.27%	100%
1976–1980	44.93%	6.16%	22.15%	73.25%	26.75%	100%
1981–1985	38.73%	6.80%	23.39%	68.92%	31.08%	100%
1986–1990	37.22%	5.29%	24.38%	66.89%	33.11%	100%
1991–1995	36.03%	5.11%	24.17%	65.31%	34.69%	100%
1996–2000	40.41%	4.41%	22.69%	67.51%	32.49%	100%
2001–2004	35.96%	4.21%	24.49%	64.66%	35.34%	100%

Notes: Each category of tax revenue is presented as a percentage of total tax revenue, in averages by five-year period.
nd: no data.
Sources: U.S. Congressional Budget Office; Organisation of Economic Co-operation and Development (OECD), Revenue Statistics 1965–2005; U.S. Department of Commerce (Bureau of Economic Analysis); U.S. Department of the Treasury; U.S. Office of Management and Budget; Executive Office of the President of the United States, *Economic Report of the President*; International Monetary Fund, Government Financial Statistics.

illustrated with greater emphasis if we review the percentage that each category represents in the total collected.

Here, the rise to which we just alluded has a much greater impact; even in periods that direct taxes were lowered, indirect taxes continued to follow a sustained downward trend. Social security taxes, on the other hand, have continued a gradual growth pattern since the 1960s. These differences are accentuated if we compare the tax revenues of the federal governments of Argentina and the United States (see, in this respect, tables 9.1, 9.2, 9.3, and 9.4). During the 1932–1935 period, the percentage of income tax, profit tax, and capital gains tax in relation to GDP reached 0.78 percent in Argentina, a figure similar to that of the United States (0.70 percent). During the 2001–2004 period, that figure climbed to 3.96 percent, the highest in the series, while in the United States it was 9.56 percent, having peaked at higher levels in 12 of the 15 five-year periods on record.

More revealing is the comparison with taxes on goods and services: in no period in the series were income taxes, profit taxes, and capital gains taxes greater in Argentina than in the United States (except for the virtual tie from 1946 to 1955, 3.66 percent compared to 3.55 percent of GDP). In contrast, domestic taxes came first only in the 1932–1935 period. Similar considerations could be offered in relation to the respective weight of foreign trade as a taxable base (important in Argentina, hardly significant in the United States). The same could be said for the horizontal structure of the tax base. The increase noted in Argentina from 1936 to 1960 in terms of income taxes, profit taxes, and capital gains taxes as a share of total tax revenues, far from increasing, fell abruptly in subsequent decades, with the result that, in the most recent five-year period, the levels were approximately the same as those for the 1941–1945 period (18.15 percent compared to 21.63 percent). In the United States, as of the 1936–1940 period, that percentage was never below 35.08 percent.

The contrasts that arise from the evolving trends of direct and indirect taxes in Argentina and the United States can also be observed in light of Brazil's experience. In this regard, Brazil is closer to the United States than Argentina in the historical series being analyzed. As of the 1981–1985 period, the burden of direct taxes began to displace indirect taxes in a steady upward trend, and, of course, so did duties on foreign trade. In relation to the tax base, whereas in Argentina in the most recent period (2001–2004), taxes on income, capital gains, and profits account for 3.96 percent, in Brazil they account for 5.8 percent, closer to the 9.56 percent (all of GDP) of the United States. These figures indicate a bifurcation—for the time being not too pronounced—that could diminish if Argentina improves its performance in the first years of the twenty-first century. Otherwise, Brazil will maintain its lead in this area. Yet, it must be noted that, to add a nuance to this hypothesis, as regards the horizontal structure of the tax base, taxes on incomes, profits, and capital gains as a percentage of total tax revenues have been similar in Brazil and Argentina in the last two five-year periods, although certainly this is not the case for social security taxes.

Government Spending and Financing

If we now analyze this historical series from the perspective of government spending and financing, distinguishing the federal government from the provincial or state governments—as happens in both

Argentina and the United States due to their federal regimes—we will see how one aspect stands out that is typical of the evolution of rights in the twentieth century and that merits special mention. On several occasions, we have mentioned the gap between the two countries, yet it should be noted that this gap may be found in a sort of snapshot provided by the current data—an image which is immobile—or it can be explored based on the relationship established between a set of values and rights sought to be institutionalized and the material support, in terms of government resources, on which implementation of the normative program depends. This link is more complicated to maintain when, due to the concurrence of several causes, the scope of the state, in the sense that Francis Fukuyama attributes to this word, begins to expand in an effort to guarantee new rights.[43]

The scope of the state began to expand precisely in the 1930s. In 1935, Roosevelt and the Congress enacted the federal law on Social Security in the United States. In Argentina, the process began in the 1940s with the rise to the presidency of Juan D. Perón, and it became consolidated over the following two or three decades. In the mid-1980s, there was an ebb in this trend that was much more dramatic in Argentina than in the United States. The dates on which this expansion of the scope of the state began coincide with the beginning of our comparative series, which allows us to better specify the relationship between spending and resources. It is clear that there are clashing tendencies that would at least put aside the principles advocated by Hamilton and Alberdi. The founding fathers thought it was necessary to strike a balance between resources and the needs of the nation; according to the new ideas (beyond exceptional moments, for example, a war), it is fully justifiable to have a policy that places the needs of the nation over and above its resources. When this tension becomes a trend, problems abound and crises ensue.

From this point of view, Argentina is a paradigmatic case. Since 1945, when Perón's leadership took off vigorously (later broadly ratified by his electoral majorities in 1946 and 1951), public spending increased substantially: from 23.6 percent, it climbed in 1948 and 1949 to 34.4 and 26.7 percent, respectively, and then stabilized around 23–25 percent. Just as it reached the highest peaks, at the time of the convention called to amend the national Constitution (January–March 1949), convention delegates Arturo Sampay and Alfredo D. Maxud each proposed including new rights that the federal government was to guarantee, providing the resources needed for that ambitious reform. These new rights included the right to protection of the family, the right to social security, the right to work backed by stable employment, the right to property based on its "social function," and the public economic right that emanated from the nationalization of the banking system, the nationalization of the subsoil, and the nationalization of the companies that provided public services. Even though in his speech on behalf of the majority there were no major allusions to the fiscal question, Sampay nonetheless recognized the need for a stable economy that would offer a stimulus to the development of social security.[44]

The fiscal issue was taken up a few days later when the proposed reforms were discussed. Convention delegate Maxud took the lead in defending them. First, there was the one corresponding to Article 4, establishing that the funds from the economic activity of the state also contribute to the national treasury; and second, the main point, were the reforms related to Article 67(2), according to which, as we have seen, the direct tax payments throughout the national territory were made for a certain time. The changes were focused on introducing the words "proportionally equal," which presupposed recognizing, according to the speaker, not only the principle of "proportionality" but also "progressivity," to "moderately tax the less well-off classes and more heavily tax the upper classes."[45] If we recall the new socioeconomic focus that came after World War II, the proposal that was stamped on the national Constitution was not very original: proportionality and progressive fiscal policies were commonly discussed, and few dared to call them into question.

What did, in contrast, leave more than one person perplexed was the curious persistence of the idea of emergency linked to direct taxes. The old principle according to which these taxes can only be applied for a limited time remained intact; it was not a subject of discussion and neither was the future course, during and after the emergency period, of income taxes. That course was very different from what at the time was being attempted in Western democracies, and, although through constitutional subterfuges the emergency became a permanent policy, what is clear is that the welfare state and the mixed economy that sought to underpin it were financed by a set of indirect policies and the transfer of resources from one state account to another, applied both to the prices of export goods and budgetary management.[46]

This set of policies had several consequences. It accelerated the growth of the state, which was already on an upward trend in the previous decade. Through policies that allowed transfers from social security funds to regular expenditures and investments by the state or by setting prices and monetary inflation, the executive exercised control over setting taxes, when, according to the Constitution (including the one amended in 1949), this should have been under the jurisdiction of the Congress. These policies also set in motion a trend that, like the preponderance of indirect over direct taxes, would continue in subsequent administrations. Another consequence was the breaking of the trust between citizens and the state, thereby negatively affecting the values of fiscal citizenship, namely, a direct relationship, transparency, and a shared perception of the public goods that are the result of individual and collective efforts. Turning these values upside down opened the way to a complicated social belief that was to become more demanding as, in response to the expanded scope of the repertoire of collective aspirations, the supply of public goods increased. As Bo Rothstein indicates, it is possible to implement a social welfare program if "(1) citizens regard the program in itself as fair; (2) they believe their fellow citizens also contribute on a solidaristic basis; and (3) they consider the program to be organized in keeping with procedural justice, and the object for evaluation is usually the government and its agents."[47]

If these conditions are held to be true, it is also important to note that ensuring the legitimacy of a correlative increase in needs and resources will depend on the actors' perceptions. If the quantitative growth of the state's share of GDP is not accompanied by a corresponding increased acceptance (here of a subjective and qualitative nature) of the belief that the extraction of taxes does not have a negative impact on individuals' juridical security, it is possible that the circuit of trust may gradually be replaced by mutual distrust. This phenomenon is directly linked to the fiscal geography of public goods. When comparing the public goods purchased with tax payments (see tables 9.5 and 9.6), it is clear that, in general, the context is not all that different in Argentina and the United States. Both states spend on general administration; defense and security; health; education and culture; economic development; and social welfare, and they set aside funds to service the public debt. If we observe the functional profile of outlays in Argentina, spending on economic development, defense and security, and social welfare is especially prominent.

In 1950, just as the first Peronist administration was drawing to a close, the leading category of spending was economic development (9.4 percent of GDP); far behind were defense and security (3.5 percent) and social welfare (3.4 percent). Contrary to what is generally argued, the salient features were not, then, just those inherent to a welfare state but those of a government that, having a preponderant participation in the economy, also accentuated the militarist bias. Ten years later,

TABLE 9.5   Argentina's Public Spending (Federal Government and Provinces): Outlays by Purpose

	1950	1960	1970	1980	1981–1985	1986–1990	1991–1995	1996–2000	2001–2003
Consolidated Public Sector	21.3%	20.9%	23.8%	30.4%	30.7%	30.5%	28.1%	29.5%	28.9%
Federal government	21.3%	15.5%	15.8%	21.2%	22.5%	20.9%	16.6%	16.8%	16.3%
Provincial governments	nd	5.4%	8.0%	9.3%	8.2%	9.6%	11.5%	12.7%	12.6%
General Administration	1.0%	1.6%	2.0%	1.7%	1.3%	1.7%	2.1%	2.2%	1.9%
Federal government	1.0%	0.7%	0.7%	0.6%	0.5%	0.7%	1.0%	1.0%	0.9%
Provincial governments	nd	0.9%	1.3%	1.1%	0.8%	0.9%	1.1%	1.2%	1.1%
Defense and Security	3.5%	3.1%	3.1%	3.5%	3.2%	2.8%	2.9%	3.0%	3.0%
Federal government	3.5%	2.5%	2.4%	2.6%	2.3%	1.7%	1.5%	1.4%	1.4%
Provincial governments	nd	0.5%	0.8%	0.9%	0.9%	1.0%	1.3%	1.5%	1.6%
Health	1.1%	1.4%	1.7%	3.4%	3.7%	3.8%	4.3%	4.5%	4.3%
Federal government	1.1%	0.7%	0.7%	2.1%	2.4%	2.4%	2.4%	2.4%	2.2%
Provincial governments	nd	0.7%	0.9%	1.3%	1.4%	1.5%	1.9%	2.0%	2.1%
Education and Culture	2.1%	2.0%	3.3%	3.2%	3.1%	3.6%	3.8%	4.4%	4.4%
Federal government	2.1%	1.2%	1.9%	1.6%	1.4%	1.4%	1.0%	1.0%	0.9%
Provincial governments	nd	0.7%	1.3%	1.6%	1.7%	2.2%	2.8%	3.4%	3.5%
Economic Development	9.4%	7.6%	6.3%	7.5%	7.5%	7.0%	2.8%	1.9%	1.7%
Federal government	9.4%	6.2%	4.2%	5.4%	6.1%	5.8%	1.7%	0.7%	0.8%
Provincial governments	nd	1.4%	2.1%	2.0%	1.4%	1.2%	1.1%	1.2%	0.9%

(continued)

TABLE 9.5 (continued)

	1950	1960	1970	1980	1981–1985	1986–1990	1991–1995	1996–2000	2001–2003
Social Welfare	3.4%	4.7%	6.3%	8.5%	7.2%	9.1%	10.3%	10.3%	10.1%
Federal government	3.4%	3.7%	4.8%	6.4%	5.2%	6.6%	7.2%	7.5%	7.3%
Provincial governments	nd	1.0%	1.5%	2.2%	2.0%	2.6%	3.1%	2.8%	2.8%
Public Debt	0.9%	0.7%	1.1%	2.5%	4.7%	2.4%	2.0%	3.1%	3.4%
Federal government	0.9%	0.6%	1.1%	2.5%	4.6%	2.3%	1.8%	2.6%	2.8%
Provincial governments	nd	0.1%	0.1%	0.1%	0.1%	0.1%	0.2%	0.5%	0.6%

Notes: As percentage of GDP, in averages per five-year period, except for 1950–1980 data, which corresponds to ten-year periods.
nd: no data.
Sources: Ministry of Economy, Secretariat of Treasury, Savings-Investment-Financing Account; Ministry of Economy, Bureau of Programming of Social Expenditure; and Alberto Porto (ed.), *Disparidades regionales y federalismo fiscal* (La Plata: Edulp, 2004).

in 1960, it maintained the imprint of an economy in which the state's role, albeit diminishing, continued to stand out (7.6 percent of GDP), but spending on social welfare had become the second leading category (4.7 percent). In the subsequent decades, the terms of the spending pyramid were inverted; since then and to this day, social welfare spending increasingly has taken the lion's share (except for 1981–1985, when a slightly larger sum was spent on economic development), with education and culture surpassing defense and security.

With respect to spending on health, education, and culture, the figures are highly revealing. Their growth, in effect, has, since the 1981–1985 period, occurred at the same time as a significant decline in defense and security spending. Moreover, the composition of the spending on health and education has been taking on federalist characteristics, due among other things to the decentralization policies in these areas for approximately 15 years (which did not automatically bring about an improvement in the quality of these public goods in the provinces). Finally, the percentage of the public debt, the third leading category of spending in the 1981–1985 period (4.7 percent of GDP) and a significant figure from 2001 to 2003 (3.4 percent), bears silent witness to the two great crises that beset Argentina since the 1980s. At first glance, as already noted, the fiscal map of the United States is not all that different from Argentina's. Yet, on closer inspection, one observes that the structure of U.S. spending compared with Argentina's accentuates the separation of fiscal powers.

In table 9.6, two horizontal lines stand out as records of undeniable continuity. From 1936 to 2004, with few exceptions, defense and security and social welfare were the leading categories of spending. Of course, there were very high peaks in the period dominated by the military effort required by World War II (from 1941 to 1945, defense spending absorbed 76.2 percent of GDP), but as of the 1971–1975 period, still in the midst of the Cold War, social welfare spending clearly overtook defense spending. And that is not all: in the years subsequent to the fall of the Berlin Wall and up until 2004, in the United States more was spent on health care than on defense. One should highlight these aspects in a republic whose military expansion, with no rival in the world, is clear. Nonetheless, outlays on defense are not the largest category. Just as the Argentina of "social justice" was more inclined to set its pace in spending on the economy and defense, the militarist republic of the United States is more geared to social welfare and health.[48]

Furthermore, if we analyze the separation of fiscal powers according to how it ties into the supply of public goods, one must bear in mind that

TABLE 9.6 United States: Federal and Subnational Public Spending:
Outlays by Purpose

	1936–1940	1941–1945	1946–1950	1951–1955	1956–1960	1961–1965
Consolidated Public Sector	100%	100%	100%	100%	100%	100%
Federal government	100%	100%	81.4%	72.9%	69.0%	67.3%
Subnational governments	0	0	18.6%	27.1%	31.0%	32.7%
General Administration	8.2%	4.8%	14.4%	5.9%	6.5%	8.3%
Federal government	8.2%	4.8%	14.4%	5.9%	6.5%	8.3%
Subnational governments	0	0	0	0	0	0
Defense and Security	17.5%	76.2%	36.2%	47.0%	38.9%	31.9%
Federal government	17.5%	76.2%	36.2%	47.0%	38.9%	31.9%
Subnational governments	0	0	0	0	0	0
Health	0.6%	0.2%	0.4%	0.4%	0.5%	0.9%
Federal government	0.6%	0.2%	0.4%	0.4%	0.5%	0.9%
Subnational governments	0	0	0	0	0	0
Education and Culture	20.8%	3.1%	0.3%	0.4%	0.6%	0.9%
Federal government	20.8%	3.1%	0.3%	0.4%	0.6%	0.9%
Subnational governments	0	0	0	0	0	0
Economic Development	24.4%	8.0%	4.3%	4.0%	4.7%	5.5%
Federal government	24.4%	8.0%	4.3%	4.0%	4.7%	5.5%
Subnational governments	0	0	0	0	0	0
Social Welfare	22.3%	6.3%	20.0%	13.3%	16.7%	18.6%
Federal government	22.3%	6.3%	20.0%	13.3%	16.7%	18.6%
Subnational governments	0	0	0	0	0	0
Public Debt	9.5%	3.5%	9.1%	5.5%	4.8%	4.6%
Federal government	9.5%	3.5%	9.1%	5.5%	4.8%	4.6%
Subnational governments	0	0	0	0	0	0
Undistributed Compensatory Resources	-3.3%	-2.2%	-3.4%	-3.6%	-3.6%	-3.3%
Federal government	-3.3%	-2.2%	-3.4%	-3.6%	-3.6%	-3.3%
Subnational governments	0	0	0	0	0	0

Notes: Data are given in percentage of GDP in averages per five-year period.
nd: no data.
Sources: U.S. Congressional Budget Office; Organisation of Economic Co-operation and
Development (OECD), Revenue Statistics 1965–2005; U.S. Department of Commerce (Bureau
of Economic Analysis); U.S. Department of the Treasury; U.S. Office of Management and

1966–1970	1971–1975	1976–1980	1981–1985	1986–1990	1991–1995	1996–2000	2001–2004
100%	100%	100%	100%	100%	100%	100%	100%
66.7%	65.5%	68.0%	70.0%	67.4%	66.1%	64.2%	63.5%
33.3%	34.5%	32.0%	30.0%	32.6%	33.9%	35.8%	36.5%
8.1%	5.7%	6.4%	9.4%	8.9%	8.2%	4.3%	3.7%
7.0%	5.7%	5.5%	4.9%	3.9%	3.5%	3.4%	3.7%
1.1%	0	0.9%	4.6%	5.0%	4.7%	0.9%	nd
29.7%	20.8%	16.0%	18.8%	19.2%	14.6%	10.9%	11.5%
29.5%	20.8%	15.9%	17.8%	18.0%	13.2%	10.6%	11.5%
0.2%	0	0.2%	0.9%	1.3%	1.4%	0.3%	nd
3.5%	4.7%	6.9%	12.0%	13.4%	18.1%	14.1%	13.7%
3.1%	4.7%	5.9%	7.1%	7.8%	10.6%	12.5%	13.7%
0.5%	0	0.9%	5.0%	5.6%	7.5%	1.6%	nd
5.1%	3.2%	6.0%	12.9%	13.0%	12.6%	4.1%	2.3%
2.7%	3.2%	3.8%	2.5%	2.0%	2.1%	2.0%	2.3%
2.5%	0	2.2%	10.4%	11.0%	10.5%	2.1%	nd
7.1%	6.0%	8.1%	8.9%	8.6%	7.2%	3.5%	3.3%
5.7%	6.0%	7.3%	5.4%	4.7%	3.7%	2.8%	3.3%
1.4%	0	0.8%	3.5%	3.9%	3.5%	0.7%	nd
18.3%	23.7%	27.7%	31.8%	29.0%	31.2%	26.7%	25.4%
17.3%	23.7%	26.6%	26.6%	23.6%	25.3%	25.5%	25.4%
1.0%	0	1.0%	5.2%	5.4%	5.9%	1.2%	nd
4.7%	4.7%	5.5%	8.8%	10.1%	10.0%	9.2%	5.3%
4.5%	4.7%	5.4%	8.3%	9.6%	9.6%	9.2%	5.3%
0.2%	0	0.1%	0.5%	0.5%	0.4%	0.1%	nd
-3.0%	-3.2%	-2.4%	-2.7%	-2.2%	-1.8%	-1.7%	-1.6%
-3.0%	-3.2%	-2.4%	-2.7%	-2.2%	-1.8%	-1.7%	-1.6%
0	0	0	0	0	0	0	nd

Budget; Executive Office of the President of the United States, *Economic Report of the President*; International Monetary Fund, Government Financial Statistics; Teresa Ter-Minassian (ed.), *Fiscal Federalism in Theory and Practice* (Washington: IMF, 1997); Vito Tanzi and Ludger Schuknecht, *Public Spending in the 20th Century* (Cambridge: Cambridge University Press, 2000); Alberto Porto (ed.), *Disparidades regionales y federalismo fiscal* (La Plata: Edulp, 2004).

the predominant outlays of the federal government in the United States (social security and defense) are financed by the payment of direct taxes. In contrast, other public goods, such as health and education, appear to answer more to a mixed formula that includes, along with federal spending, state outlays financed mainly by indirect taxes. Accordingly, and with a view to introducing a nuance to the hypotheses set forth at the outset of this chapter, fiscal citizenship does not necessarily derive from the payment of direct taxes as regards the benefit in the form of public goods that citizens and inhabitants receive for their tax payments. In effect, there may be public goods from the payment of indirect taxes.[49]

Does this mean that both types of tax, direct and indirect, play neutral roles in relation to the financing and responsible enjoyment of public goods by citizens? It does not appear to be so easy to answer this question in the affirmative if we also bear in mind the particular approach of merging fiscal powers that prevails in Argentina. When the profile of outlays by purpose depends on the predominant role of indirect taxes, this type of financing, together with the federal regime of co-participation, results in the taxpayer not knowing where taxes come from or where they go. Beyond the part that corresponds to the capture of municipal and provincial taxes, a single fiscal account, provided from below through consumption, on which indirect taxes are levied, is then distributed by a political decision of the Congress, the provincial governors, and the national executive (add to that the emergency powers that the executive obtained by delegation of Congress).[50] The situation may be different when there is a division of fiscal powers with a predominance of direct taxes.

Conclusion: Deficit, Inflation, and Debt

The political question that derives from these arguments is as obvious as it is disquieting: how is government spending being financed? A historical perspective is useful here. In the legislative debate we reviewed above on emergency taxes on profits and on wages and salaries in Argentina, deputy Manuel Fresco outlined a prediction. He then said that "there is the perception of a surplus."[51] Certainly, it is no small task to predict what is to come, but from the moment this representative of the province of Buenos Aires (and later governor of the same) made this prognosis, the fiscal performance of the state forcefully refuted it for 70 years. As illustrated in table 9.7, from 1932 to 2004 (in 2003 Argentina was just beginning to have a fiscal surplus and was

TABLE 9.7 Argentina: Resources, Expenditures, Deficit, and Financing of the Public Sector

Period	Tax Resources	Nontax Resources	Capital Resources	Other Financing	Total Resources	Current Expenditures	Capital Expenditures	Total Expenditures	Deficit	Use of Credit	Use of Monetary Issue	Sources and Financial Applications
1932–1935	nd	nd	nd	nd	nd	20.04%	3.05%	23.08%	1.70%	0.55%	nd	nd
1936–1940	nd	nd	nd	nd	nd	17.98%	4.66%	22.64%	2.67%	3.11%	nd	nd
1941–1945	nd	nd	nd	nd	nd	17.22%	4.08%	21.29%	4.75%	4.62%	nd	nd
1946–1950	nd	nd	nd	nd	nd	17.95%	8.40%	26.36%	4.14%	4.26%	nd	nd
1951–1955	nd	nd	nd	nd	nd	18.67%	6.00%	24.67%	3.90%	5.01%	nd	nd
1956–1960	nd	nd	nd	nd	nd	17.06%	4.69%	21.75%	4.78%	5.06%	nd	nd
1961–1965	15.46%	2.64%	0.50%	0	18.60%	16.72%	7.43%	24.15%	5.55%	2.38%	3.17%	0
1966–1970	18.65%	3.20%	0.44%	0	22.30%	17.19%	7.61%	24.80%	2.51%	0.46%	2.04%	0
1971–1975	15.98%	2.75%	0.27%	0	19.01%	18.64%	8.22%	26.86%	7.85%	1.65%	6.20%	0
1976–1980	16.41%	2.97%	0.24%	0	19.62%	16.40%	9.52%	25.92%	6.30%	3.45%	2.84%	0
1981–1985	14.73%	3.27%	0.22%	0.11%	18.32%	21.26%	6.40%	27.66%	9.34%	1.86%	7.47%	0
1986–1990	16.19%	2.35%	0.25%	0.24%	19.03%	19.62%	5.73%	25.35%	6.32%	1.78%	4.54%	0
1991–1995	20.19%	2.18%	1.02%	0	23.40%	22.12%	2.56%	24.69%	1.29%	1.43%	0.26%	−0.41%
1996–2000	20.70%	2.36%	0.52%	0	23.58%	24.42%	2.14%	26.56%	2.98%	3.71%	0.41%	−1.15%
2001–2004	20.90%	3.55%	0.27%	0	24.72%	25.50%	1.31%	26.80%	2.08%	1.32%	1.01%	−0.25%

Notes: Data are presented as percentage of GDP, in averages per five-year period.
There are no data on nontax resources, capital, and indebtedness before 1960.
Use of credit: includes net indebtedness (new debt net amortizations).
Monetary issue: includes debt with the Central Bank of the Argentine Republic (BCRA) and increase in net financial liabilities; as of 1993, it is indebtedness to the BCRA net returns.
Sources and financial applications: includes the net between sources and financial applications; the information is available as of 1993.
nd: no data.

Sources: Ministry of Economy, Secretariat of Treasury, Savings-Investment-Financing Account 1961–2003; A. Mann and W. Schultess, "El nivel y la composición del gasto real del sector gubernamental de la República Argentina," *Desarrollo Económico*, no. 82 (1981); Alberto Porto (ed.), *Disparidades regionales y federalismo fiscal* (La Plata: Edulp, 2004); Central Bank of the Argentine Republic (BCRA), Relevamiento Estadístico de la República Argentina 1900–1980 and 1981–1986; International Monetary Fund, Government Financial Statistics; Pablo Gerchunoff and Lucas Llach, *El ciclo de la ilusión y el desencanto* (Buenos Aires: Ariel, 1999); Carlos Díaz Alejandro, *Ensayos sobre historia económica argentina* (Buenos Aires: Amorrortu, 2002); Ministry of Economy, Secretariat of Treasury, Memorias de Hacienda; Federal Administration for Public Revenue (AFIP), Estadísticas tributarias (several issues); José García Vizcaíno, *Evolución de la deuda pública nacional* (Buenos Aires: Eudeba, 1980).

achieving results similar to those of the 1990s),[52] the fiscal deficit was an invariable rule, something like an order of normalcy upside down, depending on when it was applied.[53]

Three major problems stand out in this reading. First, there is the fact that all public sector spending from 1932 to 2004 accounted for no less than 21.29 percent and no more than 27.66 percent of GDP. Second, this picture of relative stability stands in contrast to the shortage of tax revenues since the 1961–1965 period (no information could be obtained on earlier periods). It was not until 1991 that tax revenues came to more than 20 percent of GDP. The specter of the deficit always loomed over the fiscal accounts, with the aggravating factor that, in five of the five-year periods, it was greater than 5 percent of GDP; in the early 1980s, it climbed to 9.34 percent of GDP. The remedy for such an imbalance was—and this was the third problem—printing money. According to available data, the high percentages of printing money coincide with increasingly sharp deficits, 6.20 percent against a 7.85 percent deficit from 1971 to 1975, and 7.47 percent against a 9.34 percent deficit from 1981 to 1985.

If instead of approaching this long sequence by averages, we do so by placing emphasis on certain decisive years, the situation appears more dramatic. In 1975, the deficit was approximately 40 percent of GDP and tax revenues came to 16.4 percent of GDP, whereas real salaries in the public sector were 25 percent more than those of the private sector. Toward late 1983, inflation was climbing above 400 percent annually, with a treasury that contributed barely 17.7 percent in genuine resources.[54]

What provisional conclusions can be drawn from this overview? We can see a recurrent propensity on the part of those who were in charge to conceive the state as a fiscal manipulator. Whether they were inclined toward disproportionate spending or forced to stabilize accounts, the governments always operated as though their budgets were larger than the resources actually available. The sequence is revealing because if, in an initial phase, the art of fiscal manipulation did not reach unbearable extremes, in a second stage, approximately the 1970s and 1980s, this modus operandi developed in the citizenry the perception of looting by an atrophied government. In this regard, the comparison with the United States illustrates not so much the action of a coherent government through its fiscal conduct, but how important the imperative not to cross certain basic limits may become (see table 9.8).

Total spending in the federal public sector in the United States began at a modest 9.8 percent of GDP in the 1936–1940 period (and

TABLE 9.8   United States: Revenues, Expenditures, Deficit, and Public Sector Financing

Period	Tax Revenues	Nontax Revenues	Capital Resources	Total Resources	Current Expenditures	Capital Expenditures	Total Expenditures	Deficit	Use of Credit	Monetary Issue
1936–1940	6.8%	0	0	6.8%	9.8%	0	9.8%	3.0%	5.9%	-2.9%
1941–1945	14.6%	0	0	14.6%	33.3%	0	33.3%	18.7%	21.1%	-2.3%
1946–1950	16.2%	0.1%	0	16.3%	17.4%	0	17.4%	1.2%	-2.4%	3.5%
1951–1955	17.7%	0.1%	0	17.8%	16.4%	0	16.4%	-1.4%	0.4%	-1.8%
1956–1960	17.1%	0.1%	0.1%	17.3%	16.4%	0.3%	16.7%	-0.6%	0.5%	-1.1%
1961–1965	17.3%	0.3%	0.4%	18.0%	16.9%	1.4%	18.3%	0.4%	0.4%	0
1966–1970	17.9%	0.3%	0.4%	18.6%	18.3%	0.8%	19.1%	0.5%	0.3%	0.2%
1971–1975	17.5%	0.2%	0.4%	18.1%	19.7%	0.1%	19.8%	1.7%	2.0%	-0.3%
1976–1980	17.3%	0.3%	0.3%	17.9%	19.3%	0.6%	19.9%	2.0%	1.8%	0.2%
1981–1985	18.1%	0.7%	0.2%	19.1%	22.5%	0.7%	23.3%	4.2%	4.2%	0
1986–1990	18.1%	0.8%	0.2%	19.0%	22.0%	0.9%	22.9%	3.8%	3.4%	0.4%
1991–1995	18.1%	0.7%	0.2%	19.0%	22.5%	0.5%	23.0%	3.9%	3.3%	0.6%
1996–2000	19.9%	0.5%	0.3%	20.7%	20.4%	0.2%	20.6%	-0.1%	-0.7%	0.5%
2001–2004	17.6%	0.5%	0.2%	18.3%	20.0%	0.4%	20.4%	2.2%	1.6%	0.6%

Notes: Data presented in percentage of GDP in averages per five-year period.
Includes central government spending and revenues.
Use of Credit = the year-to-year variation of indebtedness in the hands of the public, net amortizations, and Federal Reserve holdings.
Monetary Issue = calculated as the difference between the deficit and the fluctuations in the debt and includes treasury notes held by the Federal Reserve.
Sources: U.S. Congressional Budget Office; Organisation of Economic Co-operation and Development (OECD), Revenue Statistics 1965–2005; U.S. Department of Commerce (Bureau of Economic Analysis); U.S. Department of the Treasury; U.S. Office of Management and Budget; Executve Office of the President of the United States, *Economic Report of the President*; International Monetary Fund, Government Financial Statistics; Teresa Ter-Minassian (ed.), *Fiscal Federalism in Theory and Practice* (Washington: IMF, 1997); Vito Tanzi and Ludger Schuknecht, *Public Spending in the 20th Century* (Cambridge: Cambridge University Press, 2000); Alberto Porto (ed.), *Disparidades regionales y federalismo fiscal* (La Plata: Edulp, 2004).

we are not talking about a conservative government, but of the New Deal during Roosevelt's second term), then increased sharply during World War II (33.3 percent from 1941 to 1945). The impact of the collective endeavor, which generated a hitherto unseen mobilization of the society, had, as a counterpart, an 18.7 percent deficit that was financed by debt that reached 21.1 percent. Of special note here is that almost immediately, in the 1946–1950 period, the government put the brakes on, reducing the deficit to 1.2 percent, and created the conditions to reach a surplus of 1.4 percent from 1951 to 1955. The decade that propelled the United States into its status as a world power was the starting point of a trend without major fiscal fluctuations for more than 50 years: tax revenues ranged from 17.1 to 19.9 percent of GDP with total spending ranging from 16.4 to 23.3 percent.

It is true that during these times the federal government had to finance deficits of varying magnitudes (the highest was more than 4.2 percent, corresponding to the 1981–1985 period in which the policy of slashing taxes and the resulting fiscal deficit was pursued under President Ronald Reagan). It is no less true, however, that those levels of deficit, which, with a slight decline, were then drawn out over two five-year periods, are more the exception than the rule. In the seven decades covered in table 9.8, the United States has seen three five-year periods with fiscal surpluses and six five-year periods in which the deficit ranged from 0.4 to 2.2 percent. What stands out is a trend toward equilibrium that contrasts with Argentina's record.

If we speak of a gap between the two countries (this characterization could extend to other Latin American countries), we should recall that this issue has to do with the old republican debate about the limits of power. In the area of fiscal policy, those limits are very clear, and there is then no state voluntarism or manipulative skill that can get around the requirement of bringing spending into line with tax revenues. Hence, questions arise when noting that, in the last five-year period of the series, both the deficit and level of indebtedness grew in the United States. Not even the great powers are free from temptations. On the contrary: they run the risk of becoming triggers of historical processes of decline.[55]

One could continue analyzing the likely causes of the gap between the United States and Argentina, a gap that has widened over time, but it is also important to address the dilemma, rooted in republican argument, of opposing the role of the inhabitant and the role of the citizen in relation to the development of the rights and attributes of the state. This terminology, it is worth remembering, goes way back.

In the thought of the founding fathers, the sphere of public obligations was small and zealously limited in a well-developed republic. By contrast, for a large portion of contemporary thought, the republic represents a political order in which that public sphere expands as there is greater awareness, in the consciousness of persons and in the scope of the state, of a more complex array of rights. This is what in everyday usage we call democracy today. Here, reference is made to at least two basic dimensions: first, there can be no sustainable expansion in the array of rights without a consequent increase in the sense of political obligation; and second, the essential mediator between rights and obligations is a set of public institutions perceived in a positive light by the subjects in terms of their stability and accountability.

If we project the notions whose theoretical and historical genealogy we explored in the initial sections of this chapter onto the limited realm of fiscal policy, we can verify how this link among inhabitants, citizens, and governments has found expression in various moments of history. We note that a republic with a small core of rights does not necessarily suffer from a lack of cohesion resulting from a weak sense of political obligation. Alberdi, for example, did not imagine a situation of this nature. He did imagine a context in which the reduction of the sphere of obligations assured the effective application of fiscal institutions based on the predominance of indirect taxes. The problem becomes complicated when, after certain universal historical phenomena, the development of the repertoire of rights comes to pass without the necessary support of the fiscal institutions. From what we have seen, Argentina appears to represent a paradigmatic case.

This divide between the belief that we are endowed with a considerable set of rights and the belief that it is not urgent or necessary to carry out the obligations implicit in those rights generally engenders situations in which defensive attitudes—typical of an inhabitant disconnected from his or her obligations—clash with offensive attitudes typical of a government that tends to place itself above the law. Based on the perspective offered by the analysis of fiscal citizenship in Argentina, instead of establishing the principle of a government subject to the law, we have established the inverse criterion of the law depending on the government. From *rex sub lege*, the accumulation of mishaps has situated us before the unknown of *lex sub rege*.

The confusing web of offensive and defensive attitudes may be expressed through two types of conduct. First is the state playing the role of public actor—making use of its legitimate and illegitimate monopoly over the use of public force—that appropriates short-term or long-term rents. In the case of Argentina, first the government appropriated resources deposited in social security funds; then, once those resources were depleted, it resorted to printing money; and finally, when it reached bottom with hyperinflation by using such an instrument, the search for inauthentic fiscal resources was channeled through indebtedness. This offensive, which was aimed at drawing part of a certainly nonvirtuous circle, was completed, on the taxpayers' side, by the expression of two defensive attitudes. In one phase, in the early 1980s, the exponential increase in inflation provoked a rejection of the currency. In that Weimarian environment (named for events at the beginning of the Weimar Republic in Germany in the 1920s postwar period), inflation climbed from 154 percent annually in 1979 to 3,139.3 percent in 1989, and to 1,817.8 percent in 1990. Such a dislocation in the basic relations of a community shook up the social landscape, casting into it legions of persons marginalized and excluded and at the same time inducing in those with sufficient incomes to pay taxes another defensive attitude: tax evasion.

These reactions, consisting simply of not paying taxes or evading them by taking advantage of legal loopholes, have a dual component: tax evasion, insofar as it constitutes the repudiation of a political obligation, is always accompanied by a justification that holds the state accountable for failing to perform its duties. That is, because the state fails to respond with efficient public services and does not respect its social contracts, the individual decides not to pay taxes, and because those taxes are not paid, the state's capacity to offer public goods is undermined. This perspective, seen from another angle of the vicious circle that erodes fiscal citizenship, has serious effects. If, for example, we take a look at nonpayment of the value-added tax (the most important in the predominant sector of indirect taxes), we see that the percentages in recent years have been at least 25 percent of total revenues: 26.7 percent in 1997, 27.9 in 2000, 29.6 in 2001, 34.8 in 2002, 32.3 in 2003, 24.8 in 2004.[56]

Of course, these figures indicate that the nonpayment of a tax closely associated with consumption also reflects the performance of the economy (the highest percentage, 34.8 percent, in 2002 reflects the spectacular reduction—23.1 percent—in gross product that same year). Economic crises also have much to say in this respect, insofar as, like any complex social phenomenon, they do not result from a single cause. The explosion, which initially seemed uncontainable in the summer of 2001–2002, with its ominous scenes of collective rage invading streets and plazas, resulted from a plurality of causes. One of the most evident before and during the outbreak was what Pablo Gerchunoff and Lucas Llach called "exchange rate populism" (*el populismo cambiario*):[57] rigidity in managing the one-to-one relationship of the peso to the dollar, which, with the passing of the years, could not avert the lag in relative prices. Even so, in the context of that plurality of causes, the fiscal question stands out. Otherwise, it is difficult to understand the much higher debt service, in dollars, during the 1996–2000 period (3.71 percent of GDP as compared to 1.43 percent in the previous five-year period) without linking it to the fiscal woes of the state at its various levels.

With each successive crisis, sediments of memory are deposited in the consciences of a generation of citizens, which reinforce distrust and shore up defensive attitudes. Somehow, in societies of this sort, there is a geology of the memory, a juxtaposition of deposits of fear that have built up because of the repeated offenses of a state that, in one way or another, breaks its own rules. The memory of the great crises of the last century (a memory that is dying out as the generations succeed one another) is not as significant as the knotted memories in the course of a life cycle. In the United States or in Germany, that type of memory is intergenerational; in Argentina, it is intragenerational.

In the face of these disturbances, several fiscal policies are certainly possible. One of these, currently being implemented, has overlapping taxes, establishes distorting encumbrances—for example, on foreign commerce or financial transactions—and concludes by manufacturing a nominal tax burden which, ultimately, is not effective.[58] Those consequences amputate the universal and egalitarian meaning from fiscal citizenship, which should inspire its rules and conduct. When the universe of taxpayers is stratified between those who pay and those who don't, what is public is also split between, on the one hand, a group of inhabitants who do not feel politically obligated (for they ignore the threat of coercion[59] or they do not practice voluntary acquiescence) and, on the other hand, a set of citizens who, for the same motives, comply with the fiscal mandate. This image of an inclined plane, which is very close to the reality of different persons' conduct, is the one least similar to an order of justice, or of equity.

This sum of contradictions highlights a paradoxical fact. If we undertake a rapid overview, looking not at the U.S. case but at countries with an even higher tax burden of direct and progressive taxes, such as Norway, Sweden, and Denmark, we can find, based on international comparisons, that the force applied to the taxpayer does not appear to have a negative impact on the business climate nor on initiative for establishing new firms.[60] This means, then, that the better the guarantee of property rights, the greater the likelihood that taxes will not be evaded. This does not mean that the above-mentioned countries are free of serious fiscal problems. The aging of the population, the saturation in the taxpayer of the tax burden that undercuts incentives to work, the ever-higher health costs, also visible in the United States—all of these challenges present monumental unknowns for the twenty-first century. Yet, it should be noted that the plateau of development on which Latin America finds itself is not an indication that the difficulties faced in the region are those typical of mature societies with welfare states established long ago. The region is at a level more typical of countries that have not yet succeeded in establishing a fiscal system as a cornerstone of government under the rule of law (i.e., a political order in which all authority, including that of the government, is subordinate to the law).

A fiscal system, accordingly, cannot rest on the weak foundations of a complex set of rules and decisions that gives rise to uncertainty, for example, regarding property rights, state confiscation of deposits, or the imposition of releases on the debt issued by the state itself. This gives rise to an institutional countersystem not very apt to have an equity effect on income distribution. That uncertainty is not the most effective way to foster in citizens a reformist ethic aimed at modifying relationships of inequality and deprivation of justice.

Nor is it good to have a "swarm" and "maze" fiscal system that juxtaposes, in a kind of set-up provoked by short-term financial shortages, payments upon payments, emergency upon emergency. The large number of laws, decrees, and resolutions generally provokes the image of a situation made up artfully to confuse. In this process, the citizen-taxpayer becomes reliant on experts with the knowledge needed to navigate this web of rules. Following the lesson of the classical authors, modern fiscal policy—a necessary preamble to an economic constitution—should embody the characteristics of generality, simplicity, proximity, and transparency. When, instead of these attributes, there is particularism, confusion, distance, and opacity, fiscal citizenship suffers. In this way, the malformations in the state and in the subjective dimension of the citizen feed on one another, penetrating the fiscal system with interests of all sorts that are visible as much through their ties with the state as in the relationships between the federal government and the provinces.

This account suggests the need to gradually build an institutional democracy. While electoral democracy[61] is a concept that feeds into a dynamic reality (that is clearly what elections—which are fortunately abundant in Latin America—are for: to change and to define alternatives), institutional democracy delimits the playing field. Electoral democracy is, naturally, dynamic and changing—we know it all too well. Institutional democracy, on the other hand, should be more stable. Legitimately rooted institutions, beyond the personal conditions of leadership, are the only ones that can enable the representative to have reliable tools of government. It is known that institutions should have three characteristics: effectiveness in carrying out their mission, constitutional control to keep them within their proper bounds, and trust so the citizens can see in them honest support for their public and private lives. Much has been said in recent years about the twilight of the state in the age of globalization; less has been said, in contrast, on the irrefutable fact that the institutional framework of the state, as reality and as aspiration, is as relevant today as it was in the past.

In that structure, fiscal institutions are the backbone in terms of providing material support for rights, and without rights that are effectively observed, liberties are seriously compromised. For that reason, economist Jacques Rueff said, during the reconstruction period after World War II, that it is "over deficits that men lose their freedom."[62] Rueff's was a solitary voice at that time, and perhaps that judgment— something like the expression of someone crying out in the desert— might suffer from excessive emphasis. Yet, for those who have looked down into the abyss of a fiscal crisis on repeated occasions, the admonition cannot but cause mixed feelings. Fortunately, Argentina has not fallen into the terrible error, so often repeated throughout its history, of breaking with the democratic regime. Nonetheless, the country must still climb the slope that leads to a democracy capable of hosting legitimate institutions. Fiscal citizenship has an essential role in this endeavor.

Notes

1. I would like to thank my colleague Alfredo Canavese at the Universidad Torcuato Di Tella for his input and contributions to an initial version of this chapter. I would also like to thank Darío Rossignolo for his assistance in obtaining the statistical data and compiling the economic information presented in this chapter.
2. With this, perhaps it will be clear from the outset that citizenship means, in this chapter, a progressive process of the parallel acquisition of rights and obligations.
3. I initially discussed the idea of an "economic constitution" in two articles published in *La Nación* (Buenos Aires): "La constitución política y la constitución económica" (July 8, 1989) and "Las tres constituciones" (November 27, 1994).

See also Natalio R. Botana, *La república vacilante: Entre la furia y la razón* (Buenos Aires: Taurus, 2002). The concept of an economic constitution in relation to the legitimacy of currency has been taken up by Hugo Quiroga in *La Argentina en emergencia permanente* (Buenos Aires: Edhasa, 2005), chapter 8.

4. Jean Bodin, *The Six Books of the Commonwealth* [*Les six livres de la république*], translated by Robert Knolles, edited by K. D. McRae (Cambridge, MA: Harvard University Press, 1962), book 1, chapter 8, p. 97, cited by Stephen Holmes, *Passions and Constraint: On the Theory of Liberal Democracy* (Chicago: University of Chicago Press, 1995), p. 107.

5. Norberto Bobbio, "Max Weber y los clásicos," in *Norberto Bobbio: El filósofo y la política (Anthology)*, edited by José Fernández Santillán (Mexico City: Fondo de Cultura Económica, 1996), p. 99.

6. See Hans Kelsen, *General Theory of Law and State* (New York: Russell and Russell, 1961), pp. 101–119.

7. See Max Weber, *Economía y sociedad*, translated by J. Medina Echavarría, J. Roura Parella, E. García Maynez, E. Imaz, and J. Ferrater Mora (Mexico and Buenos Aires: Fondo de Cultura Económica, 1964), vol. I, part I, chapter III: *Los tipos de dominación*, and vol. II, chapter IX: *Sociología de la dominación*.

8. T. H. Green, *Lectures on the Principles of Political Obligation* (London: Longmans, Green, 1941 [1895]), p. 29.

9. Philip Pettit, "Institutional Design and Rational Choice," in *Theory of Institutional Design*, edited by Robert E. Goodin (Cambridge: Cambridge University Press, 1996), p. 64. It should also be noted that, from the point of view of economic theory, a public good is defined by two characteristics: nonrivalry in consumption, and a restriction, as a matter of principle, that no one is excluded from the enjoyment of that good. The public good of national defense exemplifies both characteristics. The fact that I enjoy a certain level of protection with respect to external threats does not mean that another individual enjoys a diminished level of defense; similarly, no individual can be excluded from the benefit of the common defense, as the preamble of the Argentine Constitution says, independent of whether he or she pays taxes.

10. Juan J. Llach and María Marcela Harriague, "Un sistema impositivo para el desarrollo y la equidad," paper presented at the Fundación Producir Conservando, Buenos Aires, June 2005, p. 45.

11. Stephen Holmes and Cass R. Sunstein, *The Cost of Rights: Why Liberty Depends on Taxes* (New York: Norton, 1999), p. 19.

12. Ibid., p. 146.

13. See ibid., p. 205.

14. S. E. Finer, *The History of Government*, vol. 1: *Ancient Monarchies and Empires* (Oxford: Oxford University Press, 1999), p. 81.

15. Alexander Hamilton, James Madison, and John Jay, *The Federalist Papers*, edited by Isaac Kramnick (New York: Penguin, 1987), article XXIII. In this quote and those that follow, the articles corresponding to Hamilton are indicated in roman numerals. See also David F. Epstein, *The Political Theory of the Federalist* (Chicago: University of Chicago Press, 1984).

16. Hamilton et al., *The Federalist Papers*, no. XII.

17. Juan Bautista Alberdi, *Sistema económico y rentístico de la Confederación Argentina según su Constitución de 1853* (Buenos Aires: La Cultura Argentina, 1921 [1855]), p. 20.

18. Ibid., p. 178.

19. Ibid., p. 199.

20. Ibid., p. 198.

21. Ibid., p. 195.

22. Ibid., p. 193.
23. Adam Smith, *The Wealth of Nations*, vol. 2, edited by Edwin Cannan (New York: Putnam's, 1904), book 5, chapter 2, part 2, pp. 310–311.
24. Ibid., p. 312.
25. Ibid., citing Henry Home, Lord Kames, *Sketches of the History of Man*, vol. 1 (1774), p. 474.
26. Immanuel Kant, *The Metaphysical Elements of Justice* (1965), pp. 92–93, cited in Stephen Holmes, *Passions and Constraint: On the Theory of Liberal Democracy* (Chicago: University of Chicago Press, 1995), pp. 249–250.
27. For Rosanvallon, the first debates in France on this issue after 1789 placed emphasis on three essential qualities of citizenship: nationality, domicile, and the payment of taxes; in other words, the citizen as a member of a state (nationality), as a member of a specific community (domicile), and as a "bon membre de la Cité" (with respect to the rule of law and contribution through payment of taxes to bearing the collective burdens). See Pierre Rosanvallon, *Le sacre du citoyen: Histoire du suffrage universel en France* (Paris: Gallimard, 1992), p. 72.
28. For more discussion, refer to Natalio R. Botana, *La tradición republicana: Alberdi, Sarmiento y las ideas políticas de su tiempo*, 3rd ed. (Buenos Aires: Sudamericana, 2005), pp. 73ff.
29. Holmes and Sunstein, *The Cost of Rights*, p. 259.
30. *Tribune*, February 5, 1869, cited by Daniel J. Boorstin, *The Americans: The Democratic Experience* (New York: Vintage, 1974), p. 207.
31. Emilio Berduc, "Discurso sobre Impuesto a la Renta," in *De la República posible a la República verdadera (1880–1910)*, edited by Natalio R. Botana and Ezequiel Gallo (Buenos Aires: Ariel Historia, 1997), p. 422.
32. Ibid., p. 420.
33. Ibid., p. 421.
34. Anacleto Gil, "Discurso sobre impuestos internos" (Senate, November 10, 1891), in Botana and Gallo, *De la República posible*, p. 411.
35. José H. Martínez, *Diario de Sesiones*, Congreso Nacional, Cámara de Diputados, (Buenos Aires, 1932), pp. 648, 650.
36. Vicente Solano Lima, in ibid., p. 694.
37. Silvio L. Ruggieri, in ibid., p. 661.
38. Atanasio Eguiguren, *Diario de Sesiones*, Congreso Nacional, Cámara de Senadores (Buenos Aires, 1932), p. 483.
39. Francisco Galíndez, in ibid., p. 489.
40. Federico Pinedo, *En tiempos de la República*, vol. 1 (Buenos Aires: Mundo Forense, 1946), p. 128.
41. José N. Matienzo, *Diario de Sesiones*, Congreso Nacional, Cámara de Senadores (Buenos Aires, 1932), p. 492.
42. The word "Machiavellian" makes reference to the republican bias in the multifaceted thinking of Nicola Machiavelli, which the reader can discern in *Discourses on the First Decade of Titus Livius* and also in his writings on the army and war. In these writings, Machiavelli insisted on the need for citizen support to assure the defense of the republic (taken to the extreme, this demand is fully expressed in the concept of the citizen in arms). It is obvious that Machiavelli did not refer in his analyses to a representative regime and a modern bureaucracy, but the connection with the taxes that directly finance the imperial role of the U.S. republic should not be ignored.
43. Francis Fukuyama, *State-Building: Governance and World Order in the 21st Century* (Ithaca, NY: Cornell University Press, 2004), p. 7. Fukuyama says in this regard:

It…makes sense to distinguish between the scope of state activities, which refers to the different functions and goals taken on by governments, and the strength of state power, or the ability of states to plan and execute policies and to enforce laws cleanly and transparently—what is now commonly referred to as state or institutional capacity.

44. See Arturo E. Sampay, "Discurso," in *La reforma de la Constitución Nacional,* vol. 2 (Buenos Aires: Presidencia de la Nación, 1950), pp. 354–363.
45. See Alfredo A. Maxud, "Discurso," in ibid., p. 503.
46. According to Roberto Cortés Conde, these fiscal instruments were as follows:

1. Undeclared taxes on work earnings. These were the funds of the social security system. On leaving in place of these funds bonds yielding interest below inflation, these ultimately lost their value. The important thing is that the workers did not feel the effects at the moment when the contributions were discounted, but much later, when they had to retire. In other words, what was assumed to be savings for the future was instead spent by the State. 2. Export duties, which arise from the difference in the exchange rate received by agricultural exports, *exchange margins.* 3. An undeclared tax on deposits. It resulted from setting a maximum interest rate, because the regime of controls on exchange prohibited the export of capital. … 4. Finally, the inflation tax, which extended to all monetary assets and which impacted especially on salaries.

Editor's translation from original: Roberto Cortés Conde, *Progreso y declinación de la economía argentina* (Buenos Aires: Fondo de Cultura Económica, 1998), pp. 62ff.

47. Bo Rothstein, *Just Institutions Matter: The Moral and Political Logic of the Universal Welfare State* (Cambridge: Cambridge University Press, 1998), p. 140.
48. Obviously, in the description of this fiscal map we did not get into the problem—which is common to practically the entire developed world—of the exponential growth in social security and health spending in relation to the demographic structure of the population. The issue, which is wide ranging and pressing, is giving rise to an abundant and polemical literature. See, for example, Paul Krugman, "America's Senior Moment," *New York Review* (March 10, 2005), a critical review of Laurence J. Kotlikoff and Scott Burns, *The Coming Generational Storm: What You Need to Know about America's Economic Future* (Cambridge, MA: MIT Press, 2004).
49. In Latin America, a relevant case in this regard is Uruguay.
50. These decisions presuppose prior negotiations that not only include the system of federal co-participation; they also include several types of special funds, transfers from the federal treasury to the provinces, industrial promotions, etc. See Alejandro Bonvecchi, "Les aspects politiques du féderalisme budgétaire argentin à l'aune des négotiations fiscales fédérales," *Problèmes politiques d'Amérique Latine,* no. 56 (2005): 159–180.
51. Manuel Fresco, *Congreso Nacional, Cámara de Diputados, Diario de Sesiones,* 1932 legislative period, p. 674.
52. These figures do not appear in the 2001–2004 period, which includes the deficit for the first two years and the surplus for the subsequent ones. A similar comment could be made on the 1991–1995 period.
53. Nonetheless, it is necessary to note that a fiscal deficit limited to financing public investment should not be alarming. In that case, it would simply be a question of not financing with current taxes—which is customary in Argentina—goods which, by definition, should also serve future generations.
54. Data taken from Cortés Conde, *Progreso y declinación de la economía argentina,* pp. 87, 88, 99.

55. See, for a long-term comparative perspective, Paul Kennedy, *The Rise and Fall of the Great Powers: Economic Change and Military Conflict from 1500 to 2000* (New York: Random House, 1987). Although the "relative decline" of the United States, which Kennedy discusses, became a thing of the past after the boisterous collapse of the Soviet Union, the point merits attention when looking at a medium- and long-term perspective.

56. Those percentages of nonpayment in relation to GDP range from 2.1 percent (2004) to 2.7 percent (1997, 2002, and 2003). The sources for these figures are *Estadísticas tributarias* (Buenos Aires: Federal Administration of Public Revenue [Administración Federal de Ingresos Públicos, AFIP],1998), and *Estimación del incumplimiento en el IVA* (Buenos Aires: AFIP, 2004).

57. Pablo Gerchunoff and Lucas Llach, *El ciclo de la ilusión y el desencanto: Un siglo de políticas económicas argentinas* (Buenos Aires: Ariel, 2005), p. 482.

58. As Juan J. Llach and María M. Harriague indicate, "If all of the taxes were collected, the tax burden in Argentina would come to 44.2 percent of GDP, thereby bringing to light that the nominal tax burden reach[es] levels similar to those of the European countries" ("Un sistema impositivo para el desarrollo y la equidad," p. 20).

59. According to a recent opinion poll, 8 percent of those surveyed in Argentina acknowledge that they comply with the law to avoid punishment, whereas 88 percent recognize themselves as disobedient and noncompliant. See Antonio María Hernández, Daniel Zovatto, and Manuel Mora y Araujo, *Argentina una sociedad anómica: Encuesta de cultura constitucional* (Mexico City: Universidad Nacional Autónoma de México, Instituto de Investigaciones Jurídicas, 2005), pp. 81ff.

60. For example, see the study by the International Finance Corporation of the World Bank, *Doing Business in 2006: Creating Jobs* (Washington, DC: World Bank, 2006). This situation also has to do with the business climate, for it is affected by the high corporate taxes imposed on companies (typical of poor countries that do not tax individuals as much as in the rich countries), which create incentives for evasion.

61. With respect to this notion, see the second section, "El desafío: De una democracia de electores a una democracia de ciudadanos," of United Nations Development Program, *La democracia en América Latina: Hacia una democracia de ciudadanos y ciudadanas* (New York: UNDP, 2004), pp. 33ff.

62. Jacques Rueff, *L'Ordre social* (Paris: Génin, 1948), pp. 631ff.

10

Conclusion

FRANCIS FUKUYAMA

A MONG THE DIFFERENT authors contributing to this volume, there is a large degree of consensus as to which factors have and have not contributed to the emergence and persistence of the development gap between the United States and Latin America. Some factors, though clearly important, do not suffice when seeking an explanation for the gap, while other causal factors can be considered critical. The key question then becomes: what to do? Although specific policy prescriptions are difficult to formulate for such a large and diverse region as Latin America, the chapters in this volume do identify several areas where improvements are necessary: economic policies, institutions, attention to politics, and what I label smart social policy.

Factors That Do *Not* Explain the Gap

We begin here with consideration of those factors that some observers have pointed to as being crucial, but which we do not see as ultimately significant. The first of these concerns geography, natural resources, disease burdens, and other characteristics of the natural environment that might explain the success or failure of development in different regions of the world. This point of view was first popularized by Jared Diamond in his book *Guns, Germs, and Steel,* in which he argued that the relative underdevelopment of Mesoamerica that left it vulnerable to Spanish conquest had to do with the fact that the region lacked domesticated animals like horses and high-yield crops like wheat— both held by Diamond to be accidents of the natural environment.[1] Jeffrey Sachs generalized this view and argued that other environmental factors, such as location in the tropics (which then increases disease burdens), access to navigable waterways, and so on explain why some countries remain stuck in "poverty traps."[2] Institutions like property rights, the rule of law, competent public administration, and the like are endogenous to economic growth, i.e., caused by growth rather than being the causes of growth.[3]

The chapter by James Robinson showed why this theory is unlikely to be true. Starting conditions in many parts of North and Latin America were not terribly different 400 years ago; indeed, important parts of Latin America were richer than lands farther north. Sachs's heavy emphasis on disease burdens and access to waterways is much more relevant in explaining Africa's relative underdevelopment than Latin America's. While tropical diseases did limit development in Central America, many parts of Latin America lie in temperate zones with access to good ports and rivers. The tropical climate of parts of Mesoamerica did not prevent the emergence and flourishing of complex pre-Columbian civilizations there. Moreover, if environmental conditions are so important, one still needs to explain growth rates that have differed over time, accelerating in some periods and slowing in others.

A second commonly cited factor explaining relative growth rates that is unlikely to be significant is culture—culture, at least, as understood as a large variable like "Catholicism" or "Iberian authoritarianism." To only a somewhat lesser degree than geography, culture in this sense remains invariant over long stretches of time, so it is hard to use it to explain slowing Latin American growth between 1820 and 1870 and accelerating growth thereafter. Moreover, unlike geography, culture does evolve over time. Catholicism, which at one time was widely regarded as an enemy both of modern democracy and of capitalist economic development, was the religion of most of the new democracies that emerged during Samuel Huntington's so-called third wave of democratization.[4] One must therefore present a theory of cultural evolution in which culture may well end up being a dependent rather than an independent variable.

As chapter 8 by Francis Fukuyama suggested, there may be a more modest type of cultural variable (usually going under the rubric of "political culture") that could be of greater value in explaining development outcomes than a large variable like religion. That is, certain societies, or groups of elites within societies, may be more inclined toward social trust and respect for law or, conversely, obligated to family and patronage, than others. All societies operate in a complex web of formal and informal rules and norms; the informal order often determines how the formal system functions. But it is very difficult to generalize about these types of fine-grained norms over as large a region as Latin America (or the United States, for that matter), even if one recognizes their importance.

The third explanatory factor that the authors of this volume by and large discount as the primary explanation for the gap concerns external influences, and particularly those coming from the United States. It is interesting to note that most of the chapters written by non–Latin Americans failed to emphasize the global economic and political system and pointed to internal factors within Latin America, whereas those authors from Latin America noted the importance of Europe and particularly the United States as explanatory factors of their own situations vis-à-vis the rest of the world. It is important, however, to explain more precisely how the external world did and did not shape the relative outcomes between north and south.

The different colonial experiences of the United States versus Latin America is of course primary in explaining the final outcomes of the regions for virtually all of the authors in this volume. James Robinson, who made a strong case that institutions are what determine the gap, also argued that the different institutional inheritances are the result of the differing colonial legacies of the respective regions. For him, the European colonial intrusion interacted with the local environment to produce different institutions; where Europeans went to settle in large numbers (as in British America), they brought with them their own institutions of property rights and self-government; where they ended up ruling over large indigenous slave populations (as in Spanish America), they left no similar enduring institutions for the great mass of citizens within the society. So, there is no question that outsiders mattered a great deal at one time.

When observers blame external actors for Latin America's lagging performance, however, they are not usually thinking about the initial colonial legacies, but about foreign influences after both the United States and Latin America had become independent. In Central America and the Caribbean, of course, U.S. influence was overwhelming and frequently took the form of military intervention. The story of the United Fruit Company in Guatemala or of Washington's involvement in the overthrow of Guatemalan president Jacobo Arbenz in 1954 is a familiar staple of regional critiques of U.S. foreign policy.

But what about the larger countries of Latin America, like Mexico, Brazil, Argentina, Chile, Colombia, Venezuela, and Peru? The United States obviously exerted tremendous influence over all of them, from serving in the nineteenth century as a model of constitutional democracy, to being a prop for oligarchic anticommunists during the Cold War. As the chapter by Tulio Halperin Donghi explained, Raúl Prebisch and the group of economists around ECLAC in the 1970s formalized a theory that explained those countries' relative lack of industrial development in terms of declining terms of trade in a global trading system and political support for "bureaucratic authoritarianism," which was held to be necessary to lock them into dependence on manufactured goods from the developed world.

It is very unlikely that American foreign policy played nearly as malign or important a role in fostering the gap as *dependencia* theory suggested for the region's large countries. *Dependencia* theory embedded an assumption that economic development required large-scale industrialization and growth of a manufacturing sector, but as Argentina proved during the early decades of the twentieth century and as Chile and Australia proved during the century's last three decades, commodity-exporting countries can grow and can raise living standards impressively. Economic openness and integration into global markets did not create situations of long-term dependence in other parts of the world, like East Asia, but rather paved the way for breakneck industrialization.

Nor was there a neat correlation among regime type, U.S. support, and economic outcomes; some bureaucratic authoritarians, like Pinochet in Chile, promoted growth, while others, like the military junta in Argentina, proved to be economically incompetent. The left-wing military regime in Peru under Velasco was a disaster; Brazil's conservative generals at first produced good results and then laid the groundwork for the debt crisis. The democratic regimes that returned to power in the 1970s and 1980s throughout the region had similarly mixed results with regard to economic outcomes. It would seem therefore that we need to look instead to policies and institutions, rather than to regime type or U.S. influence, to find the more important causes of the development gap.

Factors That *Do* Explain the Gap

The chapters in this volume have suggested a different set of causal factors that explain the development gap between Latin America and the United States. These factors fall into three large baskets: first, policies (e.g., import substitution versus openness to trade); second, institutions, including property rights, the rule of law, and political institutions meant to mitigate conflict and promote collective action; and third, social structure, meaning the underlying class, ethnic, regional, and racial divisions within each society.

Policies

As Latin America experienced the debt crisis in the 1980s and slowly tried to recover, much of the focus of development specialists centered on policies and policy reform. The period following the Great Depression and World War II saw many Latin American countries adopting autarkic economic policies that sought to protect infant industries and promote rapid industrialization behind tariff walls. This was widely seen as one of the causes of regional stagnation: domestic markets were too small to promote efficient economies; protected domestic producers turned their energies toward protecting their rents rather than increasing their global competitiveness; and governments ran growing fiscal deficits as they subsidized uncompetitive sectors or state-owned firms for political reasons. The agenda of shifting from autarky to more liberalized economies led to a set of policy prescriptions designated the Washington Consensus, which was described in the chapter by Riordan Roett and Francisco González.[5]

The Washington Consensus was designed specifically to deal with a set of pathologies that was quite prevalent in many countries in Latin America. Uncompetitive protected industries were made even more uncompetitive by overvalued exchange rates; this, combined with unconstrained fiscal spending, led to currency crises, devaluation, rising real interest rates, and a reversal of economic growth in a seemingly endless cycle. The package of liberal economic policies recommended by the International Monetary Fund and other multilateral lenders sought to break several links in this cycle by encouraging competition and openness, improving fiscal discipline, reducing opportunities for rent seeking, and eliminating the discretionary use of monetary policy to resolve fiscal problems via inflation.

This medicine by and large worked: the runaway inflation that characterized Bolivia, Peru, Argentina, Brazil, and other countries during the 1980s was tamed by the 1990s.[6] Elimination of the regressive tax represented by inflation then encouraged the return of flight capital and, indeed, increasing levels of foreign investment. The debt-relief scheme under the Brady Plan remained a burden on the region's economies during the 1990s, but sensible monetary policy, more or less independent central banks, and more responsible budgeting became the norm for the region as the twenty-first century began.

Replacing bad policies with good policies is, then, an important component of economic development. This begs the question, however, of *how* political systems generate good policies. All policies are ultimately political; any policy reform implies a shift in the distribution of resources from one group to another. Some societies find it easier to formulate and implement good policies than do others, suggesting that the real explanatory factor for superior economic performance is not the policies themselves, but rather the political institutions that lie behind the policies.

The fact that good policies are not in themselves sufficient to explain economic development may be illustrated by closer examination of the record of Latin America since the mid-twentieth century, particularly when compared to East Asia. For much of this period, and particularly for the decades from the end of World War II to the mid-1970s, neither region was following the Washington Consensus particularly closely, yet both regions were growing fairly rapidly. While import substitution fell out of favor by the 1980s, Jorge Domínguez pointed out in his chapter that Mexico and Brazil both grew rather impressively from the 1950s through the early 1970s despite their high degree of state intervention and lack of openness to the outside world. Northeast Asia (i.e., Japan, South Korea, and Taiwan) grew even more rapidly in this period despite heavy state intervention in capital markets and protection of domestic markets against foreign goods and investment. Indeed, Alice Amsden has pointed out that, by the 1970s, South Korea's average rate of tariff protection was comparable to that of Argentina.[7] Across-the-board openness to market forces and minimal state intervention were thus not the sine qua non of economic growth in either region.

Economic performance began diverging dramatically between East Asia and Latin America primarily after the oil shocks of the 1970s; the difference in long-term performance (and thus the reason for Latin America's failure to close the gap with the United States) was largely the result of Latin America's failure to adjust to the changed conditions of the external environment. As current account deficits began piling up in all non–oil producing countries, many of those in East Asia tightened their belts, cut government spending, and kept fiscal deficits under control. Latin America, by contrast, took advantage of the recycled petrodollars being offered to them by money center banks to maintain levels of consumption that proved to be unsustainable.

East Asian countries like Japan and Korea, moreover, actually implemented infant industry protection by the book: they protected young manufacturers from foreign competition only as long as was necessary to grow them to competitive scale; after that point, subsidies were removed and these industries were forced to sink or swim in global markets. Latin American governments did the opposite: they continued to protect favored sectors from the rigors of export markets and favored the interests of consumers over exporters through overvalued exchange rates.

The failure of economic adjustment was matched by a failure of the region's political institutions to manage social conflict. As Domínguez's chapter detailed, almost every country in the region saw a breakdown of its democratic institutions during the 1960s and 1970s, with the killing, torture, disappearance, and imprisonment of thousands of citizens during the period of military rule. With the partial exceptions of Chile under Pinochet and Brazil in the early years of military rule, the region's authoritarian rulers did not support prodevelopment policies nor did they lay the groundwork for long-term economic growth—again, in sharp contrast to the authoritarian governments in South Korea, Taiwan, Singapore, Malaysia, Indonesia, and other parts of East Asia. Indeed, it was military governments or authoritarian parties, as Domínguez pointed out, that presided over the debt crises of the early 1980s.

This history suggests that good policies are not, in themselves, sufficient to produce sustained economic growth. Latin America, as Dani Rodrik has pointed out, grew impressively under the sway of heterodox protectionist policies in the benign environment of the 1950s and 1960s, and its performance has been uneven during the era of liberal reform from the late 1980s onward.[8] The real problems emerged as a result of the region's failure to adjust to the oil shocks and to the sharply less benign international environment that emerged during the 1970s, something the East Asian fast developers managed much more successfully. This suggests a second critical factor that explains the development gap: institutions.

Institutions

Many of the authors in this volume, including Robinson, Roett and González, Przeworski and Curvale, and Fukuyama, identified weak or defective institutions as one of the most significant sources of the development gap. Institutions are today defined by economists as rules, formal or informal, that constrain human choice, a definition that covers a great deal of territory because it includes not just formal institutions like courts and electoral systems, but informal norms and values. There are at least three important categories of institutions that have had an important impact on economic development and the quality of political life in the region: first, institutions like property rights, legal systems that enforce contracts, and the rule of law more generally; second, macropolitical institutions like electoral systems, forms of executive authority, and federalism, which provide for representation, legitimacy, conflict resolution, and collective action; and finally, informal norms and habits that impact the way that the formal institutions operate.

James Robinson has argued here and in previous papers that, with regard to institutions, Latin America was born with a "birth defect."[9] The Spanish colonizers established vast slave empires in the New World to extract natural resources and other commodities from the land; the vast majority of the population was not initially franchised, had no property rights, and could not participate in the political system to demand greater investments in education, infrastructure, and other factors crucial to development. This initial social hierarchy perpetuated itself even after the colonial system was dismantled, formal democracies were established, and the franchise was extended to larger parts of the population. Robinson argued that the underlying unequal political equilibrium was able to perpetuate itself through a number of changes in formal political institutions, as elites found new ways of protecting their power and social positions.

The path of institutional development in British America was different. Early attempts to enslave the indigenous populations failed, while climate and geography encouraged large-scale European settlement, family farming, and a more equal initial distribution of resources. Those European settlers brought with them institutions like property rights and the common-law legal system, which they applied to themselves (but not, of course, to the institution of African slavery in the South).

As Jorge Domínguez noted in his chapter, there were violations of property rights in the United States and in several of the fast-developing

East Asian countries where land was redistributed after World War II. But, he noted, these redistributions happened infrequently, almost always after a major disruption like a war or revolution. What makes Latin America different is the ongoing insecurity of property over a prolonged period of time, which has led to low levels of investment and capital flight.

Przeworski and Curvale disagreed with Robinson and argued that the slow expansion of political participation in Latin America cannot explain its relative underdevelopment. It is not clear that the expansion was significantly slower than that of the United States, nor is it evident that expanding the franchise is necessarily good for economic growth. They argued that political systems that embed high degrees of social inequality but that are nonetheless effective in mitigating conflicts can promote economic growth. In the end, it is not clear that these authors disagree with one another substantially. Both chapters pointed to the absence of a broad class of property owners in the form of family farmers (and, later, an urban middle class), the existence of a large group of marginalized citizens, and the subsequent reproduction of social inequality over time as the elites succeeded in perpetuating themselves. Przeworski and Curvale argued that the persistence of these social cleavages over time led to political conflict and instability that was highly detrimental to growth. The periods in which the gap between Latin America and the United States widened appreciably—during the wars of independence and during the period from 1970 to 2000—were ones of political instability and social conflict. Instability is detrimental to growth for a host of fairly obvious reasons: it leads to rapid policy swings, makes for an uncertain investment climate, and diverts the attention of policymakers from development issues.

This then underlines the importance of a second aspect of institutions: their ability to resolve social conflicts peacefully and to provide for legitimate collective action. The problem is both static and dynamic. At any point in time, a society will consist of different social groups with often-conflicting interests; the purpose of a constitutional democratic political system is to represent as much of society as possible and to reconcile those conflicting interests in a rule-based rather than a violent way. They must solve what Roett and González labeled the "fight for shares." The state must deploy a monopoly of force to enforce its laws, but that force must be regarded as legitimate by its citizens. And over time, as social and economic conditions change, the state must be able to accommodate new social actors that arise within the society, like the working class, immigrants, formerly marginalized social groups, etc.

In this respect, there is a sharp contrast between Latin America and the United States. The latter experienced one breakdown of its political order since the founding of the country in 1789, when conflict over the institution of slavery led to the Civil War. Before and after, however, the American political system has been able to process conflicts and to incorporate new social actors with relative success. The franchise was expanded to include those without property, African Americans and indigenous peoples, and women. New social actors like the working class and a multitude of ethnic and/or immigrant groups found representation within the political system. While there are constant complaints about different aspects of the American political system, from corruption in campaign finance rules to overreaching by the court system to excessive ideological polarization, the system has been regarded as legitimate by an overwhelming majority of Americans, and the rule of law is treated as sacrosanct.

The same has not been true of Latin America, where not a single country has enjoyed regime continuity since independence. With the interesting exception of Mexico, rules for political succession have not been well established. Succession via military coup has unfortunately been all too common in the twentieth century (though thankfully less so at the end of the century), and nowhere more so than in the country that at one time was the region's most developed: Argentina. In recent years, political leaders in Peru, Argentina, and Colombia have spent considerable time changing constitutional rules on succession (usually by trying to give themselves extra terms). Since the 1990s, elected presidents have been repeatedly forced out of office before the end of their terms in Ecuador, Bolivia, Venezuela, and Peru.

Nor have Latin American political systems been particularly good at incorporating new social actors over time. The chapter by Roett and González detailed the variety of ways that Latin American systems have sought to incorporate the rising industrial working class in the early twentieth century, ranging from the emergence of radical, anti-oligarchic parties in Argentina and Peru to the linkage of labor movements with existing elites in Uruguay and Colombia. Where radical populist, Marxist, or communist parties emerged, social conflict became acute; countries like Peru, Bolivia, and Argentina suffered alternations of rule between conservative oligarchs and radical populists. In none of the countries where radical populist parties came to power was there a thoroughgoing redistribution of land and a subsequent security of property rights, as happened in Japan, South Korea, and Taiwan after World War II.

Latin America has seen quite a number of so-called pacted transitions, in which an elite group negotiates a set of rules for power sharing as they take over from an authoritarian ruler. This happened with the Pacto de Punto Fijo (1958) in Venezuela and the National Front Accord (1957) in Colombia. Pacted transitions have been praised by some social scientists as an effective way out of dictatorship.[10] But they carry a hidden time bomb: if the elites who crafted the pact are not flexible enough to incorporate new social actors or to change the rules in response to changed conditions, they risk losing control as new forces emerge outside of the terms of reference of the original pact. Venezuela and Colombia, both of which avoided the debt crisis and social conflicts that plagued Argentina, Mexico, and Brazil during the 1980s, saw their political systems fracture in the 1990s as new actors tried to force their way into power.

The chapters by Roett and González and by Fukuyama raise the question of whether the specific design of institutions in the region explains the poor political and economic performance of countries there. The answer is yes, but only to a limited extent. Uruguay and Colombia linked their labor movements to existing elite parties, while Venezuela and Mexico mobilized theirs into broad, inclusive parties. Those that followed either of these paths evaded the sharp political conflicts of countries like Argentina, Bolivia, and Peru.

There are other respects in which the design of political institutions makes a difference. Latin American presidentialism has been widely criticized in the academic literature; the inherently winner-take-all nature of presidential systems leads to minority presidents with weak legitimacy, as was the case in Chile in 1971 with Salvador Allende, who was elected by a little more than a third of Chilean voters. Poorly designed federalism, in which states are allowed to run budget deficits that are often covered by the federal government, has been blamed for the fiscal failures of Brazil and Argentina. On the other hand, well-designed efforts to decentralize power to a state and, even better, a municipal level have been important as a means of making government more responsive and accountable.

Perhaps the single most important institutional deficit that runs through virtually all Latin American countries has to do with a weak rule of law. This includes not just property rights, but physical security against crime and access to the legal system more generally, particularly for the poor. Hernando de Soto has documented extensively how exclusion from the formal legal system, and the enormous amounts of red tape, inefficiency, and corruption present in it, drives large numbers of Latin Americans into the informal sector.[11] There, they make use of social capital to run businesses or to squat on property, but without the protection of the state and its laws. This leads to inequalities in treatment, huge inefficiencies, and weak legitimacy for the politicians and parties that preside over the system.

The final category of institutions concerns the informal, normative rules that are needed to make formal institutions work properly. This is nowhere more important than in legal systems. The rule of law includes a host of formal, visible institutions, of course, like a country's written laws, its court and police systems, and the administrative system that stands behind rule enforcement. But no legal system can work without the support of informal norms. If politicians are willing to bend rules to get their way, if judges and lawyers routinely accept bribes in return for certain outcomes, if the police look the other way when crimes are committed or commit crimes themselves, then no formal system of rules and incentives will function properly.

The chapter by Natalio Botana, though focused narrowly on Argentina, showed how critical the proper normative structure is. Any number of observers have noted that, of all countries in Latin America, Argentina has the least excuse for being underdeveloped.[12] The country lies in a temperate zone with abundant natural resources and agricultural land and is endowed with good access to waterways and thus to international trade. It did not start out as a slave empire and has few of the ethnic conflicts that plague the Andean countries. Argentina's immigrant population was almost entirely European and not terribly different from those who settled in North America. Those who came and settled should have brought European institutions with them. And yet, Argentina has the distinction of being one of the world's formerly developed countries, having once been richer than Switzerland and today having only 7 percent of the latter's per capita GDP.

Botana's discussion of fiscal citizenship explains at least part of the reason for this outcome. Citizens are motivated to pay taxes when they believe that there is some linkage between their taxes and the public uses to which those revenues are likely to be put. Although tax evasion occurs in all countries, including the United States, its level is significantly higher in Argentina because the basic social contract legitimizing fiscal citizenship has been undermined. Argentines do not trust their currency and do not trust their government to make good use of their money. This is in many ways a perfectly rational response to a state that on repeated occasions has confiscated savings through hyperinflation and/or devaluation, misallocated fiscal revenues, and siphoned off public money for private purposes. The rule of law has been interrupted more in Argentina than in any other Latin American country from 1950 to 1990 in the form of military coups and accompanying attempts to politicize the judicial system, as the Domínguez chapter pointed out. This practice continues to the present day, with elected presidents seeking to pack the Supreme Court with their own favored candidates. Argentina simply does not have a normative order supportive of the kind of rule of law necessary to create a fully modern society.

Social Inequality

If one asks the question of why institutions are weak in Latin America, one is driven to a deeper level of explanation having to do with social inequalities and cleavages. As noted earlier, James Robinson located Latin America's defective institutions historically in the extractive and exploitative empires established by the Spanish colonialists, which left large parts of the population outside of the political system and without the ability to create strong institutions to protect their rights. Those who settled British America, by contrast, were political participants from the beginning with a self-interest in maintaining a democratic political order.

Social cleavage lies at the root of Argentina's weak rule of law. The military coup in 1930, which represented the first major break in Argentina's constitutional order, occurred because the country's landed oligarchy feared the rise of new urban middle and working classes. The undermining of the rule of law started at the top as the Supreme Court was made to retroactively endorse the legality of the coup. Suppression of popular forces then paved the way for the rise of Peronism, which, once in power, showed just as little respect for rules and laws as the oligarchs it replaced. Class differences that were mitigated by political inclusion in European countries like Britain and Sweden were exacerbated by the Argentine political system. As the chapter by Fukuyama pointed out, even the best-designed political institutions will not mitigate social conflicts if the latter are sufficiently deep.

Virtually all of the authors in this volume agreed that self-perpetuating social inequality is one of the most important deep causes of the gap between Latin America and the United States. Inequality can be measured in any number of ways: by the so-called Gini coefficient, which comprises a ratio of the incomes of the richest and poorest segments of society; by the percentage of children enrolled in school and their actual educational achievements; by the proportion of people under the poverty line; or by the percentages of the population with access to the legal system, health care, or social services. In his article, Jorge Domínguez highlighted the disparity in net enrollment in secondary education between several Latin American countries and the United States.

Social inequality affects economic development directly by leading to a shortage of educated workers who can compete in an increasingly globalized economy. Much of Latin America has now achieved "middle-income" status in World Bank rankings, meaning that they have per capita incomes in the range of $4,000–$5,000 in parity purchasing power terms. The problem they face is how to move up from that position to the next level, with per capita incomes in the $8,000–$10,000 range. Up to now, that growth has been based on commodity exports, low-skill manufacturing like textiles and *maquiladora* assembly work, and some higher-end manufacturing and services coming from increasingly competitive Latin American multinationals. While commodities will continue to be an important source of growth, it will be increasingly difficult for Latin America to compete against Asia in low-skill manufacturing. Asian countries at the same time are fast moving up the value-added chain, with China and India producing ever-larger numbers of engineers and managers every year. Greater investment in skills and education will be critical if Latin America is to stay abreast of such competition.

As Przeworski and Curvale pointed out, high levels of inequality have been compatible with high rates of growth in the past; as they and Roett and González suggested, the deeper problem engendered by inequality is an indirect political one. Inequality delegitimizes the political system, produces antisystemic social movements and political actors, and sets the stage for bitterly polarized social conflict and a zero-sum fight for shares. This is what has been happening in Andean countries like Venezuela, Ecuador, and Bolivia, where populist politicians have been busy consolidating executive power, dismantling democratic institutions, reversing liberalizing economic reforms, and engaging in social policies that are broadly favored by the poor but unsustainable in the long run.

The way that social inequality has destabilized Andean politics since the 1990s requires more careful examination, however, because its precise sources will affect the kinds of policies that will best ameliorate the problem. It is common in Latin America to talk about the "social exclusion" of the poor, and particularly of indigenous communities.

But in a sense, the region's recent instability is a result of expanding inclusiveness, which has introduced a whole new set of social actors into politics. For example, there has actually been a substantial increase in educational achievement: secondary school enrollment in Colombia has increased from 12 percent in 1960 to 67 percent in 1996; from 18 to 73 percent in Peru over the same period; and from 12 to 50 percent in Ecuador between 1960 and 1994.[13] This has been accompanied by large increases in electoral participation: in Peru, 45.3 percent of the population voted in the 2001 election, in contrast to only 14.9 percent in 1956; Bolivia went from 27.4 percent in 1960 to 35.4 percent in 2002.[14] The elections of populist leaders like Hugo Chávez in Venezuela and Evo Morales in Bolivia would scarcely have been possible if elites had retained their grip on the political system and political exclusion was a reality.

The problem that these countries face is not exclusion per se, but a classic instance of the syndrome of political decay that Huntington described in *Political Order in Changing Societies*.[15] That is, the very process of modernization has mobilized new social actors, who make demands on the political system that outstrip the latter's institutional capacity. Weak public institutions—court systems, police, schools, health care—fail to meet the demands placed on them and create tremendous cynicism and a belief that the system is controlled by elites and biased against the poor. The solution to the problem then is twofold: first, to build the capacity of the state to actually deliver basic social services more effectively to the broad mass of its citizens, and second, to incorporate these new social actors into the democratic political framework so that they do not undo the institutionalization that has already taken place.

What to Do

It is very hard to make general recommendations for initiatives that will help to close the development gap between Latin America and the United States. The persistence of this gap over 400 years suggests that it will not disappear any time soon. On the other hand, there have been periods when the gap did close, and therefore there are reasons to believe that it can do so again in the future. The chapters in this volume suggested changes in four areas: good economic policies, institutional reform, attention to politics, and finally what might be labeled smart social policy.

Good Economic Policies

For all of the criticism of the Washington Consensus that has taken place since the mid-1990s, there is little desire across Latin America to return to the bad old days of the debt crisis, with out-of-control government spending, hyperinflation, currency crises, and recession. There has been a good deal of learning in this regard; left-of-center leaders like President Luiz Inácio "Lula" da Silva in Brazil and Néstor Kirchner in Argentina have by and large pursued prudent macroeconomic policies up to now. Hugo Chávez of Venezuela is an exception, denouncing globalization, reversing integration with North America, and trying to set up an alternative economic bloc of like-minded leftist countries. He has been able to do this in the short run because high oil prices have increased state revenues, even though the state-run oil company PDVSA is starved for investment and the Venezuelan infrastructure is crumbling.

While the Washington Consensus was not a magic bullet that automatically produced sustained growth, alternatives to it are not terribly attractive. Governments in other parts of the world have intervened more actively to successfully generate economic growth, as in the case of industrial policy in Japan, South Korea, and Taiwan or in the use of undervalued exchange rates and export zones in China and some parts of Southeast Asia. But there are very specific political and institutional conditions that have made these policies successful, such as the existence of an elite, politically shielded, technocratic bureaucracy, or governments that have been ruthlessly able to control fiscal policy. Such conditions have generally not existed in Latin America. As the World Bank's 1997 *World Development Report* cautions, governments need to scale the ambitiousness of their interventions to their actual capacities to carry them out.[16]

Sustained growth remains one of the most effective ways that Latin America has of reducing poverty, and the region's growing openness to trade is a positive sign. Between 2000 and 2006, exports of goods and services as a percentage of GDP grew for the region as a whole from 20.4 to 24.4 percent, while merchandise trade as a percentage of GDP increased from 36.3 to 42.9 percent. Not only are countries like Mexico and Chile more tightly linked to the United States through the North American Free Trade Agreement (NAFTA) and the Free Trade Area of the Americas (FTAA), but China and other parts of East Asia have emerged as huge consumers of Latin American commodities. The growth rate for the region as a whole rose throughout the first years of the twenty-first century, reaching 5.5 percent in 2006.[17]

This figure represents both good and bad news. It is, of course, much better to be growing than stagnating, but virtually every part of the world was growing in this period, and Latin American growth rates remained significantly below that of other regions, like East Asia (whose overall rate of growth in 2006 was 9.4 percent). There are clearly other factors besides openness to trade holding the region back, such as the quality of institutions, education, and infrastructural investment. As the historical chapters in this book have indicated, Latin America has participated in global growth in other periods as well; the real question for the future is how it will perform when there is a downturn in the global economy and commodity prices slump. Will the fight for shares simply resume at that point, leading to a reversal of recent gains, or are there more important structural changes going on below the surface that might mitigate some of these problems? Here the glass is half full: there has been progress on institutional reform and gains in equality, but there is still a great deal of work to do.

Institutional Reform

One of the most critical sources of the development gap lies in weak Latin American institutions; closing the gap will therefore require substantial institutional reform. In this respect, there is actually more good news in the region than is often recognized. Institutional reform is incremental and often flies below the radar screen of the mainstream media.

Reforming a pension system or changing electoral rules is not a sexy issue for most people, compared to dramatic political shifts like the election of a new president. Nonetheless, a new study by the Inter-American Development Bank looked at institutional reform across the region and noted that there has been substantial progress in many areas.[18] These include central banking and fiscal policy; decentralization and federalism; and electoral reform.

Central Banking and Fiscal Policy

Perhaps the most enduring change across the region concerns institutional capacity to manage macroeconomic policy. It was noted earlier that few Latin American countries have sought to return to the poor monetary and fiscal policies of the 1970s and 1980s; this has been underpinned by greatly increased institutional capacity both on the part of central banks and on the part of finance ministries and budgeting authorities. Central bank independence has increased; the professionalism and levels of education of economic policy officials are in general substantially higher than a generation ago.

Decentralization and Federalism

Many countries, including Bolivia, Venezuela, Colombia, Peru, Argentina, and Brazil, have undertaken major reforms to shift responsibility and authority from central governments to local, municipal, and state governments. In 1980, mayors were appointed by central governments in all but six countries in Latin America; today, they are locally elected almost everywhere.[19] The logic for this is straightforward: local government is closer to the people it serves and should in principle be easier to hold accountable for performance. In many countries, this has led to considerable policy innovation and reform. In Brazil's northeastern state of Ceará, the municipal government has been widely celebrated;[20] in Colombia, many individual mayors have used their offices to launch innovative programs to combat crime and drugs.

There is also a downside to badly designed federalism. As the chapter by Fukuyama pointed out, the ability of states in Brazil and Argentina to run fiscal deficits, and the politicking this encouraged on their part with the federal government, was one of the important reasons that these countries were not able to maintain overall fiscal discipline. Changing the rules on federalism to force states to live with hard budget constraints or to raise their own revenues is thus an important means of making federal systems work properly. Decentralization to a municipal level often works better than devolving power to big units like states or provinces.

Electoral Reform

There has been a huge amount of reform of electoral systems in Latin America, not all of it for the better. Many Latin American presidents, including those in Peru, Argentina, and Colombia, have used a great deal of political capital to allow themselves to run for second or even third terms. While there are a number of principled reasons for wanting to make second terms possible (not just for presidents, but for legislators as well in countries like Colombia and Mexico), the effort to extend term limits is often simply a matter of personal ambition. Other types of electoral reforms have been more valuable, such as Mexico's elimination of a complex system designed to preserve seats for the ruling PRI's allied parties, or the greater control that Colombia's political parties will have over the use of party labels with the reform of 2005. In addition, there have been important process reforms as well, such as the strengthening of the powers of Mexico's Federal Electoral Institute to monitor and certify elections.

On the other hand, there are important areas where reforms have been attempted but have not to date produced notable results. One critical area is judicial reform, where the lack of a strong rule of law constitutes one of the greatest barriers to more rapid economic growth. There have been programs to rewrite legal codes to simplify them and efforts to increase the technical capacity of judicial systems to clear dockets and improve efficiency through better training, use of technology, and the like. Overall, however, levels of corruption remain excessively high in many countries. In a rule of law index released in a 2003 World Bank report, Argentina earned a score of –.73, Venezuela a score of –1.04, Colombia –.75, Peru –.44 and Mexico –.22 on a –2.5 to 2.5 scale. The rankings put these countries in the company of Azerbaijan, Kenya, Bangladesh, Djibouti, Ethiopia, and Lebanon. The only large Latin American country to gain a positive rating was Chile.[21]

A second area where progress has been slow is in general public administration. The 2004 *World Development Indicators* documented the length of time needed to obtain a small business license around the world, and as Jorge Domínguez's chapter indicated, Latin American countries do not score high on this scale. While it takes two to four days to obtain a license to start a small business in Australia or the United States, similar registration requires 51 days in Mexico, 68 days in Argentina, and 152 days in Brazil.[22] Public servants tend to be underpaid, and many fail to be incentivized under pay-for-performance schemes.[23]

Institutional reform is slow, painstaking, and incremental. Since attacking institutional problems often requires substantial political capital, governments have to choose their targets carefully and lay out a strategy for overcoming the obstacles they can expect to encounter. Sometimes a certain amount of chance is required: reform of Mexico's federal electoral system happened, it could be argued, because Ernesto Zedillo unexpectedly became the PRI candidate after the leading candidate was assassinated. There is a large literature on the political economy of reform, which suggests that the political will to change institutions often can be generated only in the wake of severe crises like hyperinflation, recession, or political instability. Whether on purpose or by accident or unforeseen opportunity, however, it is very important that the institutional reform agenda proceed.

Attention to Politics

Institutional reform is sometimes treated as if it were a technical issue of developing the right incentive schemes or organizational structures in a public agency. But institutions are inherently political: they serve political purposes and affect political fortunes. Without political will, they cannot be created or reformed, and in a bad political climate, they will collapse. In many ways, understanding what a good institution should look like is far easier than developing a political strategy to bring about the reform of an existing institution. Would-be reformers who disdain the dirty work of getting votes, building coalitions, cutting deals, and convincing skeptical publics seldom get very far.

A case in point is educational reform, discussed at greater length below. Implementation of serious reforms like the decentralization of school systems or the creation of pay-for-performance systems required confrontation with the powerful teachers' unions in countries like Mexico and Argentina during the early 1990s. The governments seeking reform got their way only because the ruling parties had the momentary leverage to force the unions to accept the reform package. Even so, there was considerable resistance by entrenched interests to implementing the new policies, which succeeded in vitiating a great deal of the reforms' intent.

The populist politics that has emerged since the mid-1990s is based on political entrepreneurship and the selling of a few simple ideas—like the charge that "neoliberalism" was foisted on the region by the United States and responsible for further deteriorating conditions in Latin America—in ways that appeal to voters. It does not matter that these ideas are wrong if the reasons that they are wrong cannot be communicated clearly and effectively to the public. The days are long gone when small elites could make significant policy decisions out of public sight and scrutiny. Some of the most successful U.S. presidents of the twentieth century, like Franklin Roosevelt and Ronald Reagan, were shapers of ideas and great communicators rather than masters of technical details.

Ideas do not emerge out of a vacuum. They need to be developed through public policy research, which in turn requires investments in human capital, institutions, and research. The United States is richly endowed with universities, think tanks, research organizations, and an infrastructure that generously supports the creation of new ideas on public policy issues. Latin America has made important strides in this direction in recent years, with the creation of a network of public policy institutions across the continent and a growing cadre of well-trained public policy researchers. Given the locally embedded nature of most policy problems, there is no alternative to this. While ideas may be global, actual solutions are inevitably local in nature.

Smart Social Policy

Many of the chapters in this volume have emphasized Latin America's "birth defect" of social inequality and its perpetuation in different forms across the generations. There can obviously be no simple solution to so persistent a problem, and yet a set of policy prescriptions that is to be of any use must outline at least some measures that have a chance of chipping away at the problem. These obviously lie in the realm of social policy—in issues like health, education, social security, and other policy areas where the state has an obligation not just to provide public goods but in some measure to seek some remediation of social inequalities.

The problem is that good social policy is extremely hard to implement properly. In many ways, the Reagan and Thatcher revolutions, which sought to cut back the scope of the state, occurred because the modern welfare state had become too large and dysfunctional. Europe today is facing a looming crisis of competitiveness because its labor markets are encumbered with regulations designed to protect workers but whose actual effect is to raise levels of unemployment. Transfer payments and subsidies come to be seen as entitlements; they create moral hazards and disincentives to work. What is true for wealthy countries in Western Europe is doubly so for poorer countries like Brazil and Argentina, which tried to implement European-style worker protections back in the 1940s and 1950s, when they were at a much lower level of development. Part of the overbuilt state that neoliberal reformers were trying to dismantle consisted precisely of social welfare programs that had become excessively expensive and/or counterproductive. The result was that many pro-market reformers were reluctant to address questions of social policy reform, regarding it as an excuse to reopen opportunities for rent seeking and other forms of dysfunctional behavior.

Education is a good illustration of the difficulty of improving social outcomes and making them more equal. Everyone wants better education for their children, and one of the most straightforward ways of equalizing incomes over the long term would be to improve the educational opportunities for poor children. Many of the East Asian fast developers have invested heavily in education at all levels and fostered highly competitive workforces on a par with those of the developed world. So, allocating more resources to education should address social inequality to at least some degree.

What should work in principle, however, is very difficult to achieve in practice. The problem is that, in many countries, including the United States, there is a relatively weak correlation between changes in levels of spending on education and improvement in actual educational outcomes.[24] There is a large body of social science literature, dating back to the so-called Coleman Report of the 1960s, showing that the factors that most affect educational outcomes are those like family and peers rather than average class sizes, teacher pay, libraries, and the like.[25] Michael Clemens points to a natural experiment of sorts that occurred in 1992, when the New Jersey Supreme Court ruled that the state had to equalize per capita spending on education across all school districts in the state. Over the next eight years, some $25 billion was reallocated from wealthy, high-performing school districts to poor ones; despite this massive increase in resources, there was only a marginal improvement in actual educational outcomes for New Jersey's poor.[26] Brazil's 1988 Constitution mandates that 25 percent of the federal budget be spent on education,[27] and yet the productivity of those resources is very low in terms of outcomes.

There are a number of reasons for this lack of correlation between education spending and educational outcomes. The most important have to do with what economists call agency problems, that is, the fact that the interests of the people hired to run a school system diverge from those who hire them. In many long-established education systems, resources are controlled by well-entrenched interest groups like teachers and educational administrators. Higher teacher salaries and more positions come to be regarded as something of a rent or an entitlement to benefit the adults rather than the children in the school system. Simply increasing teacher salaries or lowering teacher-student ratios may encourage more and better teachers to enter the system, but they do not necessarily incentivize teachers to do their jobs more effectively. It was this kind of experience that led many reformers to argue that teachers' unions were a particular obstacle to educational reform due to their tenacious desire to protect the status and privileges of teachers. In many Latin American countries, the teachers' union is the largest union in the country and often one of the most powerful political actors. These entrenched actors have been strongly committed to maintaining the status quo on core policies like the market share of private education, free public education, absolute job security, and preserving the nationwide scope of the union's representation.[28]

Because of this lack of correlation between spending and outcomes and the general difficulties of improving public education systems, a number of public policy specialists (many of them economists) have suggested alternative approaches for improving outcomes. Many of these incorporate market-like mechanisms to mimic the kinds of incentives that would exist in the private sector, such as vouchers that would allow parents to take their children out of poorly performing public schools or competitive bidding for the right to manage schools in the public system (charter schools).

The most common approach short of interschool competition is to try to establish pay-for-performance systems in which teachers' and administrators' pay is linked to measurable educational outcomes. Pay-for-performance schemes are fiercely resisted by teachers and school administrators, however. Such individualized incentive schemes not only threaten the group solidarity of teachers as a whole; they are also very difficult to administer. Educators rightly point out that educational outcomes are difficult to quantify; the kinds of standardized tests often used are either inaccurate or can be gamed by schools or students. There are many factors contributing to educational outcomes, of which teacher performance is only one; it is thus unfair to penalize them for results over which they have limited control. Sometimes, the best-performing schools are not ones subject to market-like discipline, but rather ones with high degrees of professionalism, idealism, and commitment.

The United States has been trying to improve the performance of its primary and secondary educational system for at least a generation now, with results that are far from decisive. Liberals have argued for more resources going into the public system, while conservatives have argued for the introduction of more market-mimicking incentive systems. Neither resources by themselves nor incentives without resources will fix the problem, but the exact mixture of the two is both difficult to determine in itself and also difficult to generate a political consensus over. The same would hold true of any concerted effort to improve educational outcomes in Latin America. This should not, however, deter people from addressing social policy.

Latin America has seen a number of innovative attempts to improve educational systems. Chile, not surprisingly, has been a leader in adopting market-based systems; it established a voucher system in which private schools compete with public ones for students and currently enroll about 40 percent of the total. The city of Bogotá has adopted a system of competitive bidding for the management of public schools. In other cases, educational reform has been approached through decentralization, devolving power over school administration to municipalities from central governments. Local authority works more or less well depending on how the system of fiscal transfers is organized; if the local government remains dependent on the central government for funding, or must constantly renegotiate the terms of its funding, its incentives for demanding better performance will be weakened. Fourteen countries in Latin America have adopted evaluation systems and have created new institutions to perform school evaluations.[29] A final approach has been to tie school attendance to cash transfer payments to the poor, a system begun in Mexico and Brazil and now extended to Argentina, Chile, Colombia, Ecuador, Honduras, Jamaica, and Nicaragua. These programs have been quite successful in raising rates of school attendance, but their ultimate impact on educational outcomes is unclear. Again, the specifics of the design of the program are critical, and the way they structure incentives will greatly affect the impact.[30]

A recent study by the Inter-American Development Bank argued that there are two kinds of education reform in Latin America, the first expanding access to education by building new schools and enrolling more students, and the second focused on improving the quality of the existing educational system. It argued that, while there is large consensus on the first goal (which accounts for the expanding school enrollments cited above), the latter is subject to a political stalemate between would-be reformers and the unions and other entrenched interests. The study concluded, "Not a single case of significant alteration in any of these core policies [i.e., those favored by the education establishment] has occurred anywhere in the region over the past decade and a half."[31]

While better quality education is clearly key to improving Latin America's global competitiveness, and also an important long-term means of tackling social inequality, other social programs have addressed the inequality problem much more directly. Conditional cash transfer programs (CCTs) were first introduced in the mid-1990s in Mexico as the Progresa program and later expanded under the title Oportunidades. These programs provide means-tested cash transfers to poor families on the condition that they either seek prenatal care (in the case of expectant mothers) or put their children in school (for families with young children). The Mexican programs were designed with built-in controls to test their effectiveness, and a growing empirical literature indicates that they have been quite effective in meeting their stated goals of increasing school attendance among children in poor families. As a result of the perceived success of CCTs, they have been widely copied all over the region and now include the Red de Protección Social program in Nicaragua, the Programa de Asignaciones Familiares in Honduras, and the Bolsa Família in Brazil. The Bolsa Família now reaches some 15 million poor Brazilians, and by itself accounts for perhaps 20 percent of the drop in Brazil's Gini coefficient between 1996 and 2005.

CCTs are only one part of an answer to the problem of poverty. Depending on how they are implemented, they are not necessarily "smart" social policies. While they improve school attendance rates, it is not clear that they actually increase educational attainment. Putting poor children in bad schools doesn't necessarily help them. Some have argued for dropping the CCTs' conditionality, on the grounds that poor families should know themselves how best to use marginal income. The long-term success of CCTs will depend on politicians avoiding the temptation to use them for patronage purposes, doling out benefits only to those who are likely to support them. There has been an effort to turn the CCTs into universal entitlements, which pose a different sort of danger of locking in high expectations for government-funded subsidies. If CCTs evolve into a negative income tax, what long-term level of funding will be sustainable through the next economic downturn?

It is not the purpose of this volume to recommend specific approaches to social policy. There are many other social sectors that need attention, including health care, pension systems, unemployment insurance, and the like. Each country—indeed, each region and city within each country—will likely have to experiment with different initiatives. As can be seen from the examples cited above, there has been a great deal of mutual observation and copying of workable programs across Latin America, which helps to generalize the results of decentralized experimentation. There are also very large parts of the region that are untouched by innovation or still under the thrall of dysfunctional social support systems from the past.

The point here is a somewhat different one: if Latin America is to ever close the gap with the United States, it must pay attention to constructing smart social policies. This must come about not by returning to the sclerosis-inducing entitlement programs of the past, but by designing systems that maximize the incentives of the poor to help themselves. The so-called first-generation reforms of the late 1980s and early 1990s focused on economic policy changes like privatization and reduction of tariffs. The second generation moved on to institutional reforms of public administration, court systems, and the like. Renewed attention to social policy constitutes a third generation of reform that is unfolding even as the agendas for the first two waves are not yet complete.

The first-generation reformers were, for understandable reasons, wary of any emphasis on new social programs, since it was social programs from the past that had created the bloated state sectors that they were trying to discipline. Some argued that rapid economic growth would by itself begin to ameliorate many social problems by creating new avenues of upward mobility for the poor. But there are a number of reasons for taking this agenda seriously, one structural and one political.

The structural reason has to do with the analysis that has been presented in this book. The development of formal democratic political institutions and the fact of long-term economic growth (although at a lower rate than that of the United States) have brought about many positive changes to Latin America. But the region's underlying social hierarchy continues to reassert itself in many ways, from the lack of a well-educated, competitive labor force, to the populist politics that threatens political stability and good policy in a number of countries. Without an effort to address this underlying problem, we can expect that the gap will replicate itself into the indefinite future.

The second reason is frankly political. Populist politicians like Hugo Chávez in Venezuela and Andrés Manuel López Obrador in Mexico are popular precisely because they are seen as caring about the poor and advocating policies geared toward helping them. The problem is that the kinds of pro-poor policies they put into place are not smart ones that create self-help incentives, but ones that increase the dependency of the poor on the state. (Indeed, that is one of the reasons that politicians like to promote such programs.) Venezuela can afford such policies because of the good fortune of rising energy prices in the early twenty-first century. Countries not similarly blessed will find themselves facing fiscal constraints in short order and hence the temptation to return to the old irresponsible macroeconomic policies of the past. The problem with populism is not that it caters to the people; the problem is that it offers short-term solutions that actually worsen the long-term prospects of the poor.

It is therefore incumbent on anyone seriously interested in closing the gap between Latin America and the United States to formulate a serious social policy agenda, one that targets substantial resources toward problems of health, education, and welfare, but does so in a way that produces real results. Finding out what works in this area will require becoming what William Easterly calls a "searcher," that is, a social policy entrepreneur willing to experiment with new approaches, to learn from others, and, more important, to abandon initiatives that are not bearing fruit.[32]

Notes

1. Jared Diamond, *Guns, Germs, and Steel: The Fates of Human Societies* (New York: Norton, 1997).
2. Jeffrey Sachs, *The End of Poverty: Economic Possibilities for Our Time* (New York: Penguin, 2005).
3. See the discussion of this theory in William R. Easterly, *The White Man's Burden: Why the West's Efforts to Aid the Rest Have Done So Much Ill and So Little Good* (New York: Penguin, 2006).
4. Samuel P. Huntington, *The Third Wave: Democratization in the Late Twentieth Century* (Oklahoma City: University of Oklahoma Press, 1991).
5. See John Williamson, *The Political Economy of Policy Reform* (Washington, DC: Institute for International Economics, 1994).
6. See John Williamson and Pedro-Pablo Kuczynski, *After the Washington Consensus: Restarting Growth and Reform in Latin America* (Washington, DC: Institute for International Economics, 2003).
7. Alice H. Amsden, *Asia's Next Giant: South Korea and Late Industrialization* (New York: Oxford University Press, 1989).
8. See Dani Rodrik, *Where Did All The Growth Go? External Shocks, Social Conflict and Growth Collapses* (London: Centre for Economic Policy Research, 1998).
9. For example, see Daron Acemoglu and James A. Robinson, "The Colonial Origins of Comparative Development: An Empirical Investigation," *American Economic Review* 91, no. 5 (2001): 1369–1401; Daron Acemoglu and James A. Robinson, *Economic Origins of Dictatorship and Democracy: Economic and Political Origins* (Cambridge: Cambridge University Press, 2005).
10. Philippe C. Schmitter and Guillermo O'Donnell, *Transitions from Authoritarian Rule: Tentative Conclusions about Uncertain Democracies* (Baltimore, MD: Johns Hopkins University Press, 1986).
11. Hernando de Soto, *The Mystery of Capital: Why Capitalism Triumphs in the West and Fails Everywhere Else* (London: Bantam, 2000).
12. See, for example, V. S. Naipaul, *The Return of Eva Peron* (New York: Vintage, 1981).
13. Scott Mainwaring, "The Crisis of Representation in the Andes," *Journal of Democracy* 17, no. 3 (2006): 13–27.
14. Ibid., p. 19.
15. Samuel P. Huntington, *Political Order in Changing Societies* (New Haven, CT: Yale University Press, 2006).
16. World Bank, *World Development Report: The State in a Changing World* (Oxford: Oxford University Press, 1997).
17. International Monetary Fund, "Latin America Sees Continued Growth," *IMF Survey Magazine: Countries and Regions*, April 23, 2007. Available at http://www.imf.org/external/pubs/ft/survey/so/2007/CAR057C.htm.

18. Eduardo Lora, ed., *The State of State Reform in Latin America* (Stanford, CA: Stanford University Press, 2006).
19. Robert Daughters and Leslie Harper, "Fiscal and Decentralization Reforms," in ibid.
20. Judith Tendler, *Good Government in the Tropics* (Baltimore, MD: Johns Hopkins University Press, 1997).
21. Daniel Kaufmann, Aart Kraay, and Massimo Mastruzzi, *Governance Matters III: Governance Indicators for 1996–2002*, World Bank Policy Research Working Paper 3106 (Washington, DC: World Bank, 2003). Available at: http://www.worldbank .org/wbi/governance/pubs/govmatters2001.htm.
22. World Bank, *World Development Indicators 2004* (Washington, DC: World Bank, 2004). See also World Bank, *Doing Business in 2006: Creating Jobs* (Washington, DC: World Bank/IFC, 2006).
23. See Koldo Echebarría and Juan Carlos Cortázar, "Las reformas de la administración y el empleo públicos en América Latina," in Lora, *The State of State Reform.*
24. See the discussion in Ernesto Stein and Mariano Tommasi, eds., *The Politics of Policies: Economic and Social Progress in Latin America, 2006 Report* (Washington, DC: Inter-American Development Bank, 2005).
25. James S. Coleman, *Equality of Educational Opportunity* (Washington, DC: U.S. Department of Health, Education, and Welfare, 1966).
26. Michael Clemens, "A Skeptic's Look at Two New Proposals to Fund the Millennium Development Goals," unpublished paper, Center for Global Development, Washington, DC, 2006, p. 5.
27. *Mandatory Funding for Early Childhood Education: A Proposal in Brazil*, Policy Brief on Early Childhood 17 (Paris: UNESCO, October 2003).
28. See Juan Carlos Navarro, "Two Kinds of Education Politics," in Stein and Tommasi, *The Politics of Policies*, pp. 221–242.
29. Juan Carlos Navarro, "Las reformas educativas como reformas del estado: América Latina en las dos últimas décadas," in Lora, *The State of State Reform.*
30. Carmelo Mesa-Lago and Gustavo Márquez, "Las reformas de los sistemas de pensiones y asistencia social," in Lora, *The State of State Reform.*
31. Stein and Tommasi, *The Politics of Policies*, p. 223.
32. Easterly, *The White Man's Burden.*

Contributors

Natalio R. Botana is professor emeritus at Torcuato Di Tella University. He is a member of two national academies in Argentina. Among his most important publications are *El orden conservador: La política argentina entre 1880 y 1916* (6th ed., 1998); *La tradición republicana: Alberdi, Sarmiento y las ideas políticas de su tiempo* (2nd ed., 1997); and *El siglo de la libertad y el miedo* (2nd ed., 2001).

Carolina Curvale is a doctoral candidate in the Political Science Department at New York University. She obtained her master's degree from the same institution and completed her undergraduate studies at San Andrés University in Argentina. Her doctoral dissertation focuses on empirical evidence of the impact of political participation on political stability in Latin America in the nineteenth and twentieth centuries.

Jorge I. Domínguez is vice provost for international affairs at Harvard University, chair of the Harvard Academy for International and Area Studies, and Antonio Madero Professor of Mexican and Latin American Politics and Economics in the Harvard Department of Government. His most recent publications include *Cuba hoy: Analizando su pasado, imaginando su futuro* (2006); and, as coeditor with B. K. Kim, *Between Compliance and Conflict: East Asia, Latin America, and the "New" Pax Americana* (2005).

Francis Fukuyama is director of the International Development Program and Bernard L. Schwartz Professor of International Political Economy at the Johns Hopkins University Paul H. Nitze School of

Advanced International Studies. Among his most salient works are *The End of History and the Last Man* (1992); *State-Building: Governance and World Order in the 21st Century* (2004); and *America at the Crossroads: Democracy, Power, and the Neoconservative Legacy* (2006).

Francisco E. González is the Riordan Roett Assistant Professor of Latin American Studies at the Johns Hopkins University Paul H. Nitze School of Advanced International Studies. His most recent publication is *Dual Transitions from Authoritarian Rule: Institutionalized Regimes in Chile and Mexico, 1970–2000* (2008); other works have appeared in academic journals such as the *British Journal of Political Science, European Review of Latin American and Caribbean Studies, Development in Practice,* and *Quorum.*

Tulio Halperin Donghi is the Muriel McKevitt Sonne Professor Emeritus of Latin American History at the University of California, Berkeley. Among his latest publications are *Argentina en el callejón* (2nd ed., 1995); *Ensayos de Historiografía* (1996); *Vida y muerte de la República verdadera* (1999); and *La Argentina y la tormenta del mundo: Ideas e ideologías entre 1930 y 1945* (2003).

Enrique Krauze is a member of the Mexican Academy of History and director of the magazine *Letras Libres.* His works on Mexico's history were collected in 1997 as *Mexico: Biography of Power.* Among his works on Mexican politics are *Por una democracia sin adjetivos* (1986); *Textos heréticos* (1992); *Tiempo contado* (1996); and *Tarea política* (2000).

Adam Przeworski is professor of politics at New York University. He received the Woodrow Wilson Award in 2001. Among his recent publications are *States and Markets: A Primer in Political Economy* (2003); "The Last Instance: Are Institutions the Primary Cause of Economic Development?" *European Archives of Sociology* (2004); and "Institutions Matter?" *Government and Opposition* (2004).

James A. Robinson is professor of government at the Institute for Quantitative Social Science, Department of Government, Harvard University. Among his most recent publications are *Economic Origins of Dictatorship and Democracy* (2006), with Daron Acemoglu; and *Economía colombiana del siglo XX: Un análisis cuantitativo,* coedited with Miguel Urrutia (2007), to be published in English as *The Colombian Economy in the 20th Century: A Quantitative Analysis.*

Riordan Roett is Sarita and Don Johnston Professor and the director of the Latin American Studies Program and Western Hemisphere Studies at the Johns Hopkins University Paul H. Nitze School of Advanced International Studies. Among his recent publications are *Brazil: Politics in a Patrimonial Society* (5th ed., 1999); *Post-Stabilization Politics in Latin America: Competition, Transition, Collapse*, coedited with Carol Wise (2003); *Mexico's Democracy at Work: Political and Economic Dynamics*, coedited with Russell Crandall and Guadalupe Paz (2005); *The Andes in Focus: Security, Democracy and Economic Reform*, coedited with Russell Crandall and Guadalupe Paz (2005); and *China's Expansion into the Western Hemisphere: Implications for Latin America and the United States*, coedited with Guadalupe Paz (2008).

Index

Page numbers followed by *f* denote figures; those followed by *t* denote tables

gentry, 187–188
income inequalities in, 74
independence effects on per capita
income in, 108t
military coups in, 89
military regime in, 144
per capita gross domestic product of,
73, 78, 164t
per capita income in, 102, 103f
political competition in, 120
secondary education statistics, 83
U.S. influences on, 271
China, 87
Citizen rights, 233
Climate, 166
Cold War, 38, 41–44
Coleman Report, 289
Colombia
economic growth in, 88, 168–169
electoral reform in, 285
independence effects on per capita
income in, 108t
legislative systems in, 205
per capita gross domestic product
growth in, 73, 85, 164t
per capita income in, 102, 103f
secondary education statistics, 83, 282
Colonialism, 164
Colonization, 180–181
Communism, 29–30, 124, 137
Comparative economic development
description of, 165, 169
institutional persistence and, 183
Competitiveness, 151–154
Conditional cash transfer programs,
291–292
Conflict theory, 119
Congress of Angostura, 13, 15
Constitution
Argentina, 236, 246
fiscal policies and, 228
Mexico, 28–29, 50
United States
description of, 183
16th Amendment, 235
24th Amendment, 234
Constructive social policy, 154
Coolidge, Calvin, 28
Corruption, 286
Cosío Villegas, Daniel, 61–62, 70
Costa Rica, 85, 108t, 179, 185
Cranial capacity, 24

Crony capitalism, 100
Cuba
description of, 55, 60–63
independence effects on per capita
income in, 108t
per capita gross domestic product of,
164t
Cuban Revolution, 37–38
Cultural hypothesis, 167–168
Culture
changes in, 199
definition of, 167
development gaps and, 269
political, 198, 212–213
Customs service, 230

Daniels, Josephus, 59
Darío, Rubén, 59–62
Darwin, Charles, 24
Debt crisis, 90, 92
Decentralization, 203, 285
Decisive political systems, 207–209, 218
Democracy
in Argentina, 223, 239
British system of, 204–205
checks and balances, 204
economic growth and, 85
electoral, 262–263
income inequality effects on, 150
in Latin America, 194
stability through, 86
third wave of, 269
in United States, 194, 204, 218
Westminster system of, 204–205,
209–210, 215
Dependencia theory, 271
Dependency theory, 38–41, 99
Destabilization, 121
Development economics
decline of, 35–36
description of, 32–33
Development gap
culture and, 269
definition of, 12
economic dimension of, 41–42
external influences as cause of, 270
factors that do not explain, 268–271
Ibero-America affected by, 12
institutions as cause of, 275–280
policies as cause of, 272–274
political institutions as example of,
194. *See also* Political institutions

Salinas de Gortari, Carlos, 62
Sampay, Arturo, 246–247
Sarmiento, Domingo Faustino
    assessment of Argentina by, 23, 234
    travel experiences of, 19–20
    United States as portrayed by,
        19, 22
    writings by, 19–23
Secondary education, 83, 282
Sierra Méndez, Justo, 54–55
Sierra O'Reilly, Justo, 52, 54
*Siete ensayos de interpretación de la realidad
    peruana*, 29
16th Amendment, 235
Slavery, 183, 185, 275
Smart state, 135, 145–149
Smith, Adam, 232
Social conflicts, 218, 274, 276
Social contract, 135, 149–155
Social inequality, 150–151, 280–282
Social policies, 288–294
Social rights, 29
Social Security, 246
Social security taxes, 241
Social structure, 217
Social welfare programs, 248
Socialism, 137
Solano Lima, Vicente, 237
Somoza, Anastasio, 60
Somoza García, Anastasio, 60, 87
South Korea
    agrarian reforms in, 86
    economic strategy, 82
    exports by, from 1950 to 1960, 79,
        81–82
    income inequalities in, 74
    per capita gross domestic product in,
        73–74, 77–78
    secondary education statistics, 83
    state-owned enterprises, 80
    tariff protections in, 273
Southeast Asia, 141
Southern Cone, 40–41, 89
Spain
    description of, 161
    Pizarro's creation of institutions,
        178–179
Spanish America
    Bolívar's writings about, 13–17
    economies in, 24, 26
    historical origin of, 17
    self-government in, 110

Spanish colonies
    collapse of, 184
    economic institutions in, 180
    Pizarro's creation of institutions in,
        178–179
"Splendid little wars," 60
Spontaneous transference, 24
Stages of Economic Growth, The, 33
State
    citizens and, relationship between, 227
    enterprises owned by, 80
    Hamilton's writings about role of,
        228–229
    role of, 79–80, 147
Suffrage
    in Latin America, 113, 114f, 123
    in United States, 111–112
Supreme Court, 198, 213

Taiwan
    exports by, from 1950 to 1960, 81
    per capita gross domestic product in,
        73–74, 77
    state-owned enterprises, 80
Tariffs, 79, 273
Tax(es)
    in Argentina. *See* Argentina, taxes in
    citizen rights and, 233–234
    direct. *See* Direct taxes
    domestic, 245
    economic performance correlated
        with nonpayment of, 260
    indirect. *See* Indirect taxes
    payment of, 225–227
    revenues from, 243t–244t
    16th Amendment provisions, 235
    Smith's principles for, 232
Tax evasion, 227, 260
Teachers
    pay-for-performance systems for, 290
    unions for, 289
TELMEX, 147
Texas, 51–52
Thailand
    education performance statistics, 84
    electoral reform in, 211
    exports by, from 1950 to 1960, 81
    secondary education statistics, 83
Thatcher, Margaret, 210, 215
Third World, 43
Tocqueville, Alexis de, 20–21
Trade liberalization programs, 93–94

UN Conference on Trade and
    Development, 34
United States
    agrarian reforms by, 82
    Argentina and, differences between,
        238–239, 258–259
    big business focus in, 61
    citizen rights in, 234
    Civil War, 53–54, 195, 277
    colonial period, 109–110
    colonization of, 180
    Constitution of, 183
    Darío's writings and poems about,
        60–61
    democracy in, 21–22, 194, 218
    economy from 1973 to 2000, 91
    education in
        performance statistics, 84
        reforms, 290
    elections in, 119
    enfranchised population in, 112f
    executive decision making in, 214
    expenditures, 257t
    government spending, 251, 252t–253t,
        254, 256, 258
    Great Depression effects on, 32
    growth of, 31–32
    Hispanics in, 70
    independence effects on per capita
        income in, 107–109, 108t
    influence on Central America,
        271–272
    institutions in, 187–188
    intellectual progress in, 20
    land ownership rates in, 82
    Latin America and, gaps between
        income inequalities, 74
        origins of, 81
        per capita gross domestic product
            growth from 1870 to 1950, 72–73
    Mexico and
        border between, 66–67
        distant reconciliation of, 62–70
        framing of relationship between,
            64–67
        future of relations between, 67
        historical and cultural roots of gap
            between, 49–70
        immigration, 48–49, 64, 68
        income inequalities, 74
        U.S. authors writing books about
            Mexico, 69

    U.S. films about Mexico, 68–69
    organized labor in, 137
    per capita gross domestic product
        growth
        from 1700 to 1870, 104
        from 1870 to 1950, 72–73
    per capita income in
        description of, 101, 102f, 164
        in early twentieth century, 164
        independence effects on, 107–109,
            108t
    political culture in, 213–215
    political institutions in, 195, 277
    political order in, 277
    political parties in, 137
    presidential system in, 210, 214,
        216–217
    property rights in, 86, 275–276
    public sector financing, 257t
    public spending in, 251, 252t–253t,
        256, 258
    recession in, 93
    Sarmiento's writings about, 19, 22
    secondary education statistics, 83
    Sierra Méndez's writings about, 54–55
    suffrage restrictions in, 111–112
    tariffs imposed by, 79
    tax revenues in, 243t–244t
    territorial expansion of, 19
    Tocqueville's writings about, 20–21
    voting rights in, 112
    Zavala's writings about, 50–51
Uruguay, 25, 89, 108t, 136–137, 144

Vargas Llosa, Mario, 87
Vasconcelos, José, 56
Véliz, Claudio, 41–42
Venezuela
    AD/COPEI elite pact system in, 140
    description of, 108t
    per capita gross domestic product of,
        164t
    Pérez administration, 209
    radical populist labor in, 139
Veto gates, 201–205, 208–209
Viajes por Europa, Africa y América, 20
Villa, Pancho, 58
Virginia Company, 181
Voting rights, 112

War of a Thousand Days, 190
War of the Reform (Mexico), 52–53